WILLIAM WYCHERLEY.

THE MERMAID SERIES.

Literal Reproductions of the Old Text, with Frontispieces.

WILLIAM WYCHERLEY

EDITED WITH INTRODUCTION AND NOTES

BY

W. C. WARD

ERNEST BENN LIMITED

LONDON

1948

" What things have we seen
Done at the Mermaid ! heard words that have been
So nimble, and so full of subtle flame,
As if that every one from whence they came
Had meant to put his whole wit in a jest,
And had resolved to live a fool the rest
Of his dull life."

Master Francis Beaumont to Ben Jonson.

" Souls of Poets dead and gone,
What Elysium have ye known,
Happy field or mossy cavern,
Choicer than the Mermaid Tavern ? "

Keats.

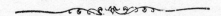

CONTENTS

As long as men are false and women vain,
Whilst gold continues to be virtue's bane,
In pointed satire WYCHERLEY shall reign.

EVELYN.

INTRODUCTION.

ILLIAM WYCHERLEY was, before Congreve arose to surpass him, the most eminent master of that artificial school of Comedy which commenced with the restoration of Charles II., and which may be said to have perished, in a blaze as of a funeral pyre, with Sheridan. Abandoning the beaten paths of English drama, the writers of this school found, in the various intrigue of the Spanish theatre, in the verbal vivacity and piquant satire of the French, a new basis for their productions. Their works, as a class, have been designated the Comedy of Manners, a title which aptly distinguishes them from the Comedy of Human Life, set forth by Shakespeare. It is a title, nevertheless, of limited applicability. The manners portrayed in these comedies, if drawn from the life, illustrate but one side of human character, and that side the most superficial. To divert by wit and ingenuity being the writer's aim, all allusion to the deeper motives of humanity was rejected as impertinent, or admitted only as an occasional contrast to the prevailing tone. Thus tne artificiality of the characters is the consequence rather of incompleteness than of untruth ; they are, as it were, but half characters ; the dialogue is no longer, as with Shakespeare, the means of their development, but the purpose of their creation.

Living in an age of loose manners and corrupt morals, the result, as has often been pointed out, of the unnatural state of repression which accompanied the Puritan supremacy, Wycherley cannot be acquitted of the vices of his time, nor can it be contended that it was altogether with the object of lashing these vices that he decked them out with all the allurements of brilliant dialogue and diverting situations. Yet I venture to assert that, in spite of their licentiousness, these comedies possess claims to recognition not lightly to be ignored. Nay, more : that their very indecency, although the most open, is certainly not the most pernicious form of immorality known to us in literature. For as the harm of licentious allusions consists in their appeal to the basest passions of human nature, so the appeal is stronger as the impression of human passion is deeper. But these *simulacra*, these puppet semblances of humanity, which Wycherley and his contemporaries summon upon the stage for our diversion, what human passion can we discover in these to which we should be in danger of unworthily responding ? As we read the plays no sense of reality disturbs us. Transfer the language they employ, the actions they perform, to the characters in a play of Shakespeare's, a novel of Richardson's, and our resentment and detestation are instantly awakened. But the *dramatis personæ* of Wycherley or of Congreve are not, as the characters of Shakespeare and Richardson, men and women whom we feel to be as real and living as those with whom we daily associate. They merely simulate humanity so far as is requisite for the proper enactment of their parts. And herein lies the test : a Cordelia, an Iago, a Clarissa, a Lovelace, are, to our feelings, real creatures of flesh and blood, whom we love or hate, as the case may be. The characters of Wycherley and Congreve, on the contrary, we neither love nor detest ; we are interested not in what they are, but only in what they say and do. They have no further existence for us than as they act and speak on the stage before our eyes ; touch them, and, like ghosts in Elysium, they turn to empty air in our grasp.

Another counter-influence to the unwholesomeness of these comedies is the current of mirth which runs through them, more or less, from end to end. For laughter may be reckoned in some sort an antidote to sensuality, at least to sensuality in its vilest and most insinuating mood. " There is no passion," as Sterne says, " so serious as lust ; " and we may safely conclude that when laughter is provoked, the wit of expression or the ludicrousness of situation is more active to our apprehension than the license of sentiment.

It is sometimes urged against the comedies of this school that Virtue, in them, is brought on the stage only to be derided. But this charge is manifestly unjust. Virtue, indeed, is an unfrequent guest in this house of mirth ; she finds a refuge in the house of mourning hard by, in the tragedies of the times. Yet if she chance to cross the unwonted threshold, it is not to be laughed out of countenance, but more often to be entertained as an honoured guest. Take, for instance, the character of Christina, in Wycherley's *Love in a Wood*, or even that of Alithea, in *The Country Wife ;* the sentiments of honour and purity that are set on their lips, or expressed in their actions, are evidently intended to excite our esteem and admiration. Nay, it may even be affirmed that if, among these shadowy creatures, there be any that affect us, beyond the others, with some sense of an approach to living reality, it is precisely the virtuous characters from whom such an impression is derived. It is true, on the other hand, that the sin of adultery, so common to the dramatic plots of this period, is treated not only without severity, but as a pleasant jest. To the husbands, in general, small mercy is shown. Yet what husbands are these—these Pinchwifes, Fondlewifes, *et hoc genus omne ?* It is less the sancity of marriage that is attacked, or held up to ridicule, in their persons, than their own vices, their jealousy, tyranny, or folly. And, after all, it is by no means in the crime itself, but in the ingenuity of intrigue, that we are expected to find diversion ; and the utter absence of genuine passion on the part of these stage criminals renders any appeal to passion in ourselves out of the question.

It is not with any intention of excusing the license which abounds in Wycherley's comedies that I have ventured to offer these few considerations in their behalf. I contend only that their laughing outrages upon decency, are infinitely less harmful, because more superficial, than the sentimental lewdness which, arising from a deeper depravity, instils a more subtle venom ; that, condemn it as we needs must, we may yet stop short of attaching to the immorality of the dramatists of the Restoration such consequence as to debar ourselves, for its sake, from enjoying to the full the admirable wit and ingenuity which constitute the chief merit of their performances.

Wycherley produced but four comedies, which, however, contain almost all of intrinsic value that remains from his pen. Besides these, he himself published but one volume, a folio of *Miscellany-Poems*, which appeared in 1704, when the author was sixty-four years of age. Of these pieces nothing favourable can be affirmed even by the friendliest critic. They form a strange *olla podrida* of so-called philosophy and obscenity ; they are dull without weight, or lewd without wit ; or if even here and there a good thought occur, the

ore is scarcely of such value as to be worth the
pains of separating from the dross. The book
suggests a curious picture of the veteran dramatist,
ever and anon laying aside his favourite Rochefoucauld or Montaigne to chuckle feebly over the
reminiscence of some smutty story of his youthful
days. The versification is, as Macaulay says,
beneath criticism ; Wycherley had no spark of
poetry in his whole composition. In fine, we may
apply to this volume, without qualification, Dryden's
remarks upon poor Elkanah Settle : " His style is
boisterous and rough-hewn ; his rhyme incorrigibly
lewd, and his numbers perpetually harsh and ill-
sounding." Yet there is one thing which redeems
the volume from utter contempt, as a testimony,
not, indeed, to the author's talent, but to the
constancy and disinterestedness of his temper. I
refer to the brave verses addressed to his friend the
Duke of Buckingham, on the occasion of that
versatile nobleman's disgrace and imprisonment in
the Tower. The key note is struck in the opening
lines :

> " Your late Disgrace is but the Court's Disgrace,
>   As its false accusation but your Praise."

These lines, it may be remarked, are intended as
a rhymed couplet, and may serve as one instance
out of many of the " incorrigible lewdness " of
Wycherley's rhyme ; but, paltry as the verses may
be, the feeling which prompted them was surely
deserving of respect.

The pieces in prose and verse, which, "having the misfortune to fall into the hands of a mercenary, were published in 1728, in 8vo, under the title of *The Posthumous Works of William Wycherley Esq.*," are on the whole superior to the *Miscellany-Poems,* yet, excepting perhaps some of the prose aphorisms which constitute the first part of the collection, little or nothing is to be found, even here, worth resuscitating. Such facility or occasional elegance as the verses possess must be wholly ascribed to the corrections of Pope ; but Pope himselı failed in the impracticable attempt to make a silk purse out of a sow's ear. Some few of the best pieces, as the lines on *Solitude,* might possibly pass muster as the worst in a better volume, while the epistle to Dryden (who had invited Wycherley's collaboration in the construction of a comedy—an honour which the younger author gratefully and modestly declined) is interesting personally, and the strain of elaborate compliment, to which, after the fashion of the day, Wycherley treated his correspondents, is here, for once, not wholly misapplied. The *Maxims,* however, contain better stuff than the verses, and fully justify Pope's repeated hints to the author that "the greater part" of his pieces "would make a much better figure as single maxims and reflections in prose, after the manner of your favourite Rochefoucauld, than in verse."[1] Although, for the

---

[1] *Correspondence between Pope and Wycherley :* Letter 26. See also Letter 15.

most part, as trite as moral aphorisms usually are, they are not without here and there a touch of wit, of terseness, or even of wisdom. Here, for instance, is a pretty simile:—"False friends, like the shadow upon a dial, are ever present to the sunshine of our fortunes, and as soon gone when we begin to be under a cloud." Here, again, is a touch of characteristic satire:—"Old men give young men good counsel, not being able longer to give them bad examples."[1] And for a specimen of his wisdom take the following:—"The silence of a wise man is more wrong to mankind than the slanderer's speech."

I have now noticed all that has appeared in print of Wycherley's authorship beyond his letters to Pope (which possess at least the merit of occasioning Pope's letters to Wycherley), and a few letters of earlier date, published by Dennis,[2] which contain, however, nothing of more consequence than a string of extravagant and affected encomiums upon his correspondent. Something remains to be said on the subject of our author's personal character, which I shall endeavour to set in a juster light than that in which it is presented by Macaulay, whose vivid scrutiny, like a strong torch-light, brings out the worse parts into sharp relief, while it leaves the better in dense obscurity.

---

[1] I ought to have remembered that this maxim is Rochefoucauld's. It may stand, however, as an instance of the untrustworthiness of Wycherley's memory. See p. xxxvi.

[2] *Letters on several Occasions:* published by John Dennis: London, 1696.

It is not to be doubted that Wycherley participated in the fashionable follies and vices of the age in which he lived. His early intrigue with the Duchess of Cleveland was notorious. The license of his own writings is a standing witness against him, and the indecency of some of the verses which he published in his old age proves that his mind reverted to the scenes of his youth with feelings other than those of a repentant sinner. Yet in accepting the evidence of Wycherley's writings we should beware of over-rating its importance. Dryden's character is well known as that of a modest and excellent man; yet Dryden occasionally produced passages abundantly obscene. Libertinism was the fashion of the age, and although the fashion had somewhat changed when Wycherley published his *Miscellany-Poems*, we can feel little surprise that the productions of an aged and infirm man should be redolent rather of the days when he was crowned with honours and sated with success, than of those later years of ill-health and obscurity. In this man's composition the clay was assuredly mingled with pure metal. Nothing in the testimony of his contemporaries is so striking as the tone of affection and esteem which they continually assume in speaking of him Dryden writes to John Dennis that he has laid aside his intention of commenting upon some friend's purpose of marriage; "for, having had the Honour to see my Dear Friend Wycherley's Letter to him on that occasion, I find nothing to be added or amended. But as well as

I love Mr. Wycherley, I confess I love myself so
well, that I will not shew how much I am inferiour
to him in Wit and Judgment, by undertaking anything after him."[1] And Dryden's regard was
gratefully and cordially reciprocated. In his first
letter to Wycherley Pope refers to the high satisfaction which he experienced in hearing the old
dramatist, at their very first meeting, " doing justice
to his dead friend, Mr. Dryden." Wycherley's own
epistle, in verse, to the great poet I have already
mentioned ; it is filled with expressions, sincere if
exaggerated, of regard and admiration ; and long
after Dryden's death, in an essay[2] which appeared
not until its author had, himself, been years in his
grave, Wycherley writes of " my once good friend,
Mr. Dryden, whose Memory will be honour'd when
I have no Remembrance."

His attachment to his friends, indeed, appears to
have been a prominent characteristic of his disposition. Major Pack, in a short memoir prefixed to
the *Posthumous Works*, declares that "he was as
impatient to hear his Friend calumniated, as some
other people would be to find themselves defamed.
I have more than once," he adds, " been a witness
of that honourable Tenderness in his Temper."

His friendship with Pope is one of the best
known incidents in his life. It commenced in 1704,
when Wycherley was sixty-four and Pope but
sixteen years of age, and, although at times inter-

---

[1] *Letters on several Occasions :* p. 57.
[2] *An Essay against Pride and Ambition,* in the Posthumous
Works.

rupted, terminated only with the death of the former in 1715. Their correspondence displays on both sides the marks of sincere regard. Wycherley's generous appreciation the young genius repaid with gratitude and affection, which, however, in the moments even of its warmest ardour, never degenerated into servility. The last published letter between them is dated May 2, 1710. It was succeeded by a period of prolonged estrangement. During the preceding year a silence of unusual duration on the part of Wycherley had aroused the anxiety of Pope, who alludes to it, in his correspondence with their common friend Cromwell, in terms of heart-felt concern. Wycherley had been dangerously ill, and Cromwell had acquainted Pope with the news of his recovery.

"You have delivered me," he replies, under date of Oct. 19, 1709, "from more anxiety than he imagines me capable of on his account, as I am convinced by his long silence. However the love of some things rewards itself, as of Virtue, and of Mr. Wycherley. I am surprised at the danger you tell me he has been in, and must agree with you that our nation would have lost in him as much wit and probity, as would have remained (for aught I know) in the rest of it. My concern for his friendship will excuse me (since I know you honour him so much, and since you know I love him above all men) if I vent a part of my uneasiness to you, and tell you that there has not been wanting one to insinuate malicious untruths of me to Mr. Wycherley, which, I fear, may have had some effect upon him."

The correspondence was renewed, with all the old kindness, in the following spring, but was soon again to be interrupted. Pope had, for some years, been engaged upon the occasional correction and emendation of Wycherley's worse than mediocre verses, and the unsparing honesty with which he discharged this delicate office, however creditable to his character, could not but be at times unpalatable to the author now seventy years of age, and rendered peevish by ill-health and loss of memory. His last published letter to Pope betrays some natural indignation at the wholesale slaughter which the young poet was making of his halting lines, although, with the politeness of an old courtier, he thanks him for his freedom, which he "shall always acknowledge with all sort of gratitude." It is probable, also, that some enemy of Pope had again possessed the old man's ear with slanders, to which his shattered memory would render him the more accessible, and Wycherley again broke off the correspondence, leaving his friend to wonder how he had displeased him, as knowing himself "guilty of no offence but of doing sincerely just what he bid me."

Pope's references to Wycherley, during this new estrangement, show him to have been deeply hurt. They indicate, however, more of sorrow than of resentment, and his delight was unfeigned when, in the autumn of 1711, his friend was once more reconciled to him, and once more wrote to him and spoke of him in terms of the warmest affection. Cromwell, from whose correspondence with Pope we derive our information regarding this second reconciliation narrates the following pleasant incident.

" Mr. Wycherley came to town on Sunday last, and, kindly surprised me with a visit on Monday morning. We dined and drank together ; and I saying, 'To our loves,' he replied, 'It is Mr. Pope's health.' " On these terms we leave them. Their correspondence of this date has not been made public, nor do we know if malice or misunderstanding again destroyed the concord thus happily re-established. Pope's letters to Cromwell, moreover, cease about this time, and those which he addressed to others contain no further mention of Wycherley, until in January 1716, he describes to Mr. Blount the closing scene of the life of " that eminent comic poet, and our friend."

In after years, speaking of Wycherley, Pope said : " We were pretty well together to the last : only his memory was so totally bad, that he did not remember a kindness done to him, even from minute to minute. He was peevish, too, latterly ; so that sometimes we were out a little, and sometimes in. He never did an unjust thing to me in his whole life ; and I went to see him on his death-bed." [1]

One more of his contemporaries I propose to bring forward as a witness to our author's character.

[1] Spence's *Anecdotes.*

George Granville, Baron Lansdowne, to the ordinary qualifications of an accomplished gentleman added some pretensions, not altogether contemptible, to the rank of a minor poet. He was the author of a vast number of elegantly written verses (usually addressed to "Mira"), of a tragedy (*Heroic Love*) commended by Dryden, and of an amusing comedy (*Once a Lover and always a Lover*) of the school of Wycherley and Congreve. In the second volume of his collected works is to be found an epistle in which he remarks, with some minuteness, upon the character and disposition of his friend Wycherley.

This letter is not dated, but, from internal evidence, must have been written about the year 1705 or 1706. Lansdowne sets out with declaring that his partiality to Wycherley as a friend might render what he says of him suspected, "if his Merit was not so well and so publickly established as to set him above Flattery. To do him barely Justice," he continues, "is an Undertaking beyond my Skill." Further he writes: "As pointed and severe as he is in his Writings, in his Temper he has all the Softness of the tenderest Disposition; gentle and inoffensive to every Man in his particular Character; he only attacks Vice as a publick Enemy, compassionating the Wound he is under a Necessity to probe." Yet, "in my Friend every Syllable, every Thought is masculine;" and it was, questionless, from this particularity that he acquired the sobriquet (alluding, at

the same time, to *The Plain Dealer*) of *Manly*
Wycherley. Of our Plain Dealer as a poet
Lansdowne candidly confesses—" It is certain he is
no Master of Numbers ; but a Diamond is not less
a Diamond for not being polish'd." And then,
addressing his correspondent : " Congreve," he
writes, " is your familiar Acquaintance, you may
judge of Wycherley by him : they have the same
manly way of Thinking and Writing, the same
Candour, Modesty, Humanity, and Integrity of
Manners : It is impossible not to love them for their
own Sakes, abstracted from the Merit of their
Works." In conclusion Lansdowne invites his
correspondent to his lodging, to meet Wycherley,
as well as " a young Poet, newly inspired," whose
" Name is Pope," who "is not above seventeen or
eighteen years of age, and promises Miracles," and
whom Wycherley and Walsh " have taken under
their Wing."

The foregoing testimonies are, I venture to think,
sufficiently explicit. Johnson, indeed, supposes
Wycherley to have been " esteemed without virtue,
and caressed without good-humour," but a statement so obviously self-contradictory deserves no
consideration. One thing is clear: that Wycherley
was both beloved and honoured by men whose
temper and capacity give irrefragable authority to
their judgment, and that judgment, based, as it was,
upon personal and intimate acquaintance, it were
presumption to dispute.

The present text is that of the first editions, which

I have carefully collated with, and occasionally corrected by, the text of the edition of 1713 (the last published during the author's life), and that of Leigh Hunt's edition of 1849. I have usually followed the punctuation of Leigh Hunt, who was the first to punctuate the plays accurately.

WM. C. WARD.

WILLIAM WYCHERLEY.

WILLIAM WYCHERLEY was born in 1640. He
was the son of a Shropshire gentleman of old
family,[2] and of what was then accounted a good
estate. The property was estimated at £600 a
year, a fortune which, among the fortunes at that
time, probably ranked as a fortune of £2,000 a
year would rank in our days.

William was an infant when the civil war broke
out; and, while he was still in his rudiments, a
Presbyterian hierarchy and a republican government were established on the ruins of the ancient
church and throne. Old Mr. Wycherley was
attached to the royal cause, and was not disposed
to intrust the education of his heir to the solemn
Puritans who now ruled the universities and the
public schools. Accordingly, the young gentleman
was sent at fifteen to France. He resided some
time in the neighbourhood of the Duke of Mon-
tausier, chief of one of the noblest families of
Touraine. The Duke's wife, a daughter of the

[1] From Macaulay's Essay on *The Comic Dramatists of the
Restoration*.
[2] Daniel Wycherley, Esq., of Clive or Cleve, in Shropshire,
about seven miles north of Shrewsbury.—ED.

house of Rambouillet, was a finished specimen of those talents and accomplishments for which her house was celebrated. The young foreigner was introduced to the splendid circle which surrounded the duchess, and there he appears to have learned some good and some evil. In a few years he returned to this country a fine gentleman and a Papist. His conversion, it may safely be affirmed, was the effect not of any strong impression on his understanding or feelings, but partly of intercourse with an agreeable society in which the Church of Rome was the fashion, and partly of that aversion to Calvinistic austerities which was then almost universal amongst young Englishmen of parts and spirit, and which, at one time, seemed likely to make one half of them Catholics and the other half Atheists.

But the Restoration came. The universities were again in loyal hands, and there was reason to hope that there would be again a national church fit for a gentleman. Wycherley became a member of Queen's College, Oxford, and abjured the errors of the Church of Rome. The somewhat equivocal glory of turning, for a short time, a good-for-nothing Papist into a very good-for-nothing Protestant is ascribed to Bishop Barlow.

Wycherley left Oxford without taking a degree, and entered at the Temple, where he lived gaily for some years, observing the humours of the town, enjoying its pleasures and picking up just as much law as was necessary to make the character of a pettifogging attorney or of a litigious client entertaining in a comedy.

From an early age, he had been in the habit of amusing himself by writing. Some wretched lines of his on the Restoration are still extant. Had he devoted himself to the making of verses, he would have been nearly as far below Tate and Blackmore as Tate and Blackmore are below Dryden. His only chance for renown would have been that he might have occupied a niche in a satire between Flecknoe and Settle. There was, however, another kind of composition in which his talents and acquirements qualified him to succeed; and to that he judiciously betook himself.

In his old age he used to say that he wrote *Love in a Wood* at nineteen, *The Gentleman Dancing-Master* at twenty-one, the *Plain Dealer* at twenty-five, and *The Country Wife* at one or two and thirty. We are incredulous, we own, as to the truth of this story. Nothing that we know of Wycherley leads us to think him incapable of sacrificing truth to vanity. And his memory in the decline of his life played him such strange tricks that we might question the correctness of his assertion without throwing any imputation on his veracity. It is certain that none of his plays was acted till 1672,[1] when he gave *Love in a Wood* to the public. It seems improbable that he should resolve, on so important an occasion as that of a first appearance before the world, to run his chance with a feeble piece, written before his talents were ripe, before his style was formed, before he

---

[1] The dates assigned by Macaulay to the first representations of Wycherley's plays are in every case incorrect. See the Introduction to each play.—ED.

had looked abroad into the world; and this when
he had actually in his desk two highly finished
plays, the fruit of his matured powers. When we
look minutely at the pieces themselves, we find in
every part of them reason to suspect the accuracy
of Wycherley's statement. In the first scene of
Love in a Wood, to go no further, we find many
passages which he could not have written when he
was nineteen. There is an allusion to gentlemen's
periwigs, which first came into fashion in 1663 ; an
allusion to guineas, which were first struck in 1663 ;
an allusion to the vests which Charles ordered to
be worn at court in 1666; an allusion to the fire
of 1666 ; and several allusions to political and
ecclesiastical affairs which must be assigned to
times later than the year of the Restoration—to
times when the government and the city were
opposed to each other, and when the Presbyterian
ministers had been driven from the parish churches
to the conventicles. But it is needless to dwell on
particular expressions. The whole air and spirit
of the piece belong to a period subsequent to that
mentioned by Wycherley. As to *The Plain Dealer*,
which is said to have been written when he was
twenty-five, it contains one scene unquestionably
written after 1675, several which are later that 1668,
and scarcely a line which can have been composed
before the end of 1666.

Whatever may have been the age at which
Wycherley composed his plays, it is certain that
he did not bring them before the public till he was
upwards of thirty. In 1672, *Love in a Wood* was
acted with more success than it deserved, and this

event produced a great change in the fortunes of
the author. The Duchess of Cleveland cast her
eyes upon him and was pleased with his appearance. This abandoned woman, not content with
her complaisant husband and her royal keeper,
lavished her fondness on a crowd of paramours of
all ranks, from dukes to rope-dancers. In the
time of the Commonwealth she commenced her
career of gallantry, and terminated it under Anne,
by marrying, when a great grandmother, that worthless fop, Beau Fielding. It is not strange that she
should have regarded Wycherley with favour. His
figure was commanding, his countenance strikingly
handsome, his look and deportment full of grace
and dignity. He had, as Pope said long after,
" the true nobleman look," the look which seems to
indicate superiority, and a not unbecoming con-
sciousness of superiority. His hair indeed, as he
says in one of his poems, was prematurely grey.
But in that age of periwigs this misfortune was of
little importance.

The Duchess admired him, and proceeded to
make love to him after the fashion of the coarse-
minded and shameless circle to which she belonged. In the Ring, when the crowd of beauties
and fine gentlemen was thickest, she put her
head out of her coach-window and bawled to
him—" Sir, you are a rascal ; you are a villain ; "
and, if she is not belied, she added another phrase
of abuse which we will not quote, but of which we
may say that it might most justly have been
applied to her own children. Wycherley called
on her Grace the next day, and with great humility

begged to know in what way he had been so unfortunate as to disoblige her.[1]   Thus began an
intimacy from which the poet probably expected
wealth and honours.   Nor were such expectations
unreasonable.   A handsome young fellow about

---

[1] Macaulay's version of the above story is derived from Spence's
Anecdotes. It differs entirely from Dennis's version, which is
evidently the correct one, as the former totally misses the point,
and makes the Duchess guilty merely of a piece of unmeaning
rudeness.   Dennis's account is as follows.—"The writing of that
Play [*Love in a Wood*] was the Occasion of his becoming acquainted
with one of King Charles's Mistresses after a very particular manner.
As Mr. Wycherley was going thro' *Pall Mall* towards *St. James's*
in his Chariot, he met the foresaid lady in hers, who, thrusting
half her Body out of the Chariot, cry'd out aloud to him, 'You,
Wycherley, you are a Son of a Whore,' at the same time laughing
aloud and heartily. . . . Mr. Wycherley was certainly very much
surpriz'd at it, yet not so much but he soon apprehended it was
spoke with Allusion to the latter End of a Song in the foremention'd
Play—

> 'Great Wits and great Braves
> Have always a Punk to their Mother.

As, during Mr. Wycherley's Surprize, the Chariots drove different
ways, they were soon at a considerable Distance from each other,
when Mr. Wycherley, recovering from his Surprize, ordered his
Coachman to drive back, and to overtake the Lady.   As soon as he
got over-against her, he said to her, 'Madam, you have been
pleased to bestow a title on me which generally belongs to the
Fortunate.   Will your Ladyship be at the Play to-night?'   'Well,'
she reply'd, 'what if I am there?'   'Why, then I will be there to
wait on your Ladyship, tho' I disappoint a very fine Woman who
has made me an Assignation.'   'So,' said she, 'you are sure to disappoint a Woman who has favour'd you for one who has not.'
'Yes,' reply'd he, 'if she who has not favour'd me is the finer
Woman of the two.   But he who will be constant to your Ladyship,
till he can find a finer Woman, is sure to die your Captive.'   The
Lady blush'd, and bade her Coachman drive away. . . . In short,
she was that Night in the first Row of the King's Box in 'Drury
Lane,' and Mr. Wycherley in the Pit under her, where he enter-
tain'd her during the whole Play."   Dennis's *Familiar Letters,*
London, 1721.—ED.

the court, known by the name of Jack Churchill was, about the same time, so lucky as to become the object of a short-lived fancy of the Duchess. She had presented him with £4,500, the price, in all probability, of some title or some pardon. The prudent youth had lent the money on high interest and on landed security; and this judicious investment was the beginning of the most splendid private fortune in Europe. Wycherley was not so lucky. The partiality with which the great lady regarded him was indeed the talk of the whole town; and, sixty years later, old men who remembered those days told Voltaire that she often stole from the court to her lover's chambers in the Temple, disguised like a country girl, with a straw hat on her head, pattens on her feet and a basket in her hand.[1]

The poet was indeed too happy and proud to be discreet. He dedicated to the Duchess the play which had led to their acquaintance, and in the dedication expressed himself in terms which could not but confirm the reports which had gone abroad. But at Whitehall such an affair was regarded in no serious light. The lady was not afraid to bring Wycherley to court and to introduce him to a splendid society, with

---

[1] This anecdote is given by Leigh Hunt on the authority of Voltaire's *Letters concerning the English Nation.* But Leigh Hunt's memory appears to have played him false. The only allusion, in Voltaire's *Letters,* to the connection between Wycherley and the Duchess, is contained in the following words :—" Mr. Wycherley, who was a long Time known publickly to be happy in the good Graces of the most celebrated Mistress of King Charles the Second."—ED.

which, as far as appears, he had never before mixed. The easy king, who allowed to his mistresses the same liberty which he claimed for himself, was pleased with the conversation and manners of his new rival. So high did Wycherley stand in the royal favour that once, when he was confined by a fever to his lodgings in Bow Street, Charles, who, with all his faults, was certainly a man of social and affable disposition, called on him, sat by his bed, advised him to try a change of air, and gave him a handsome sum of money to defray the expenses of a journey.[1] Buckingham, then Master of the Horse and one of that infamous ministry known by the name of the Cabal, had been one of the Duchess's innumerable paramours. He at first showed some symptoms of jealousy, but he soon, after his fashion, veered round from anger to fondness, and gave Wycherley a commission in his own regiment and a place in the royal household.

It would be unjust to Wycherley's memory not to mention here the only good action, as far as we know, of his whole life. He is said to have made great exertions to obtain the patronage of Buckingham for the illustrious author of *Hudibras*, who was now sinking into an obscure grave, neglected by a nation proud of his genius and by a court

---

[1] Wycherley accordingly journeyed into France, about the beginning of the winter of 1678, and returned, entirely restored, at the end of the following spring. The King received him with the utmost favour, and made choice of him as governor to his son. It was immediately after this that Wycherley went down to Tunbridge (in the summer of 1679), where he met the Countess of Drogheda. whom he soon afterwards married.—ED.

which he had served too well. His grace consented to see poor Butler ; and an appointment was made. But unhappily two pretty women passed by ; the volatile Duke ran after them ; the opportunity was lost and could never be regained.

The second Dutch war, the most disgraceful war in the whole history of England, was now raging. It was not in that age considered as by any means necessary that a naval officer should receive a professional education. Young men of rank, who were hardly able to keep their feet in a breeze, served on board the King's ships, sometimes with commissions and sometimes as volunteers. Mulgrave, Dorset, Rochester, and many others left the playhouses and the Mall for hammocks and salt pork ; and, ignorant as they were of the rudiments of naval service, showed, at least, on the day of battle, the courage which is seldom wanting in an English gentleman. All good judges of maritime affairs complained that, under this system, the ships were grossly mismanaged, and that the tarpaulins contracted the vices, without acquiring the graces, of the court. But on this subject, as on every other, the government of Charles was deaf to all remonstrances where the interests or whims of favourites were concerned. Wycherley did not choose to be out of the fashion. He embarked, was present at a battle, and celebrated it, on his return, in a copy of verses too bad for the bellman.[1]

[1] Mr. Leigh Hunt supposes that the battle at which Wycherley was present was that which the Duke of York gained over Opdam, in 1665. We believe that it was one of the battles between Rupert and De Ruyter, in 1673.

About the same time he brought on the stage his second piece, *The Gentleman Dancing-Master.* The biographers say nothing, as far as we remember, about the fate of this play. There is, however, reason to believe that, though certainly far superior to *Love in a Wood,* it was not equally successful. It was first tried at the west end of the town, and, as the poet confessed, "would scarce do there." It was then performed in Salisbury Court, but, as it should seem, with no better event. For, in the prologue to *The Country Wife,* Wycherley described himself as "the late so baffled scribbler."

In 1765, *The Country Wife* was performed with brilliant success, which, in a literary point of view, was not wholly unmerited. For, though one of the most profligate and heartless of human compositions, it is the elaborate production of a mind, not indeed rich, original or imaginative, but ingenious, observant, quick to seize hints, and patient of the toil of polishing.

The point is of no importance; and there cannot be said to be much evidence either way. We offer, however, to Mr. Leigh Hunt's consideration three arguments—of no great weight certainly—yet such as ought, we think, to prevail in the absence of better. First, it is not very likely that a young Templar, quite unknown in the world—and Wycherley was such in 1665—should have quitted his chambers to go to sea. On the other hand, it would have been in the regular course of things that, when a courtier and an equerry, he should offer his services. Secondly, his verses appear to have been written after a drawn battle, like those of 1673, and not after a complete victory, like that of 1665. Thirdly, in the epilogue to *The Gentleman Dancing-Master,* written in 1673, he says that "all gentlemen must pack to sea;" an expression which makes it probable that he did not himself mean to stay behind. [The epilogue to *The Gentleman Dancing-Master* was probably written about the end of 1671. See the Introduction to that play.—ED.

The Plain Dealer, equally immoral and equally well written, appeared in 1677. At first this piece pleased the people less than the critics ; but after a time its unquestionable merits and the zealous support of Lord Dorset, whose influence in literary and fashionable society was unbounded, established it in the public favour.

The fortune of Wycherley was now in the zenith and began to decline. A long life was still before him. But it was destined to be filled with nothing but shame and wretchedness, domestic dissensions, literary failures and pecuniary embarrassments.

The King, who was looking about for an accomplished man to conduct the education of his natural son, the young Duke of Richmond, at length fixed on Wycherley. The poet, exulting in his good luck, went down to amuse himself at Tunbridge, looked into a bookseller's shop on the Pantiles, and, to his great delight, heard a handsome woman ask for *The Plain Dealer*, which had just been published. He made acquaintance with the lady, who proved to be the Countess of Drogheda, a gay young widow with an ample jointure. She was charmed with his person and his wit, and after a short flirtation, agreed to become his wife. Wycherley seems to have been apprehensive that this connection might not suit well with the King's plans respecting the Duke of Richmond. He accordingly prevailed on the lady to consent to a private marriage. All came out. Charles thought the conduct of Wycherley both disrespectful and disingenuous. Other causes probably assisted to

alienate the sovereign from the subject who had
lately been so highly favoured. Buckingham was
now in opposition and had been committed to the
Tower ; not, as Mr. Leigh Hunt supposes, on a
charge of treason, but by an order of the House
of Lords for some expressions which he had used
in debate. Wycherley wrote some bad lines in
praise of his imprisoned patron, which, if they
came to the knowledge of the King, would certainly
have made his majesty very angry. The favour
of the court was completely withdrawn from the
poet. An amiable woman with a large fortune
might indeed have been an ample compensation
for the loss. But Lady Drogheda was ill-tempered,
imperious and extravagantly jealous. She had
herself been a maid of honour at Whitehall. She
well knew in what estimation conjugal fidelity was
held among the fine gentlemen there, and watched
her town husband as assiduously as Mr. Pinchwife
watched his country wife. The unfortunate wit was,
indeed, allowed to meet his friends at a tavern
opposite to his own house. But on such occasions
the windows were always open, in order that her
ladyship, who was posted on the other side of the
street, might be satisfied that no woman was of
the party.

The death of Lady Drogheda released the poet
from this distress ; but a series of disasters in rapid
succession broke down his health, his spirits and
his fortune. His wife meant to leave him a good
property and left him only a lawsuit. His father
could not or would not assist him. He was at
length thrown into the Fleet, and languished there

during seven years, utterly forgotten, as it should seem, by the gay and lively circle of which he had been a distinguished ornament. In the extremity of his distress, he implored the publisher who had been enriched by the sale of his works to lend him twenty pounds, and was refused. His comedies, however, still kept the stage and drew great audiences, which troubled themselves little about the situation of the author. At length, James the Second, who had now succeeded to the throne, happened to go to the theatre on an evening when *The Plain Dealer* was acted. He was pleased with the performance, and touched by the fate of the writer, whom he probably remembered as one of the gayest and handsomest of his brother's courtiers. The King determined to pay Wycherley's debts and to settle on the unfortunate poet a pension of £200 a-year. This munificence on the part of a prince who was little in the habit of rewarding literary merit, and whose whole soul was devoted to the interests of his Church, raises in us a surmise which Mr. Leigh Hunt will, we fear, pronounce very uncharitable. We cannot help suspecting that it was at this time that Wycherley returned to the communion of the Church of Rome.[1] That he did return to the communion of the Church of Rome is certain. The date of his reconversion, as far as we know, has never been mentioned by any biographer. We believe that, if we place it at this time, we do no injustice to the character either of Wycherley or James.

Not long after, old Mr. Wycherley died ; and

---

[1] There are no grounds whatever for this surmise.—ED.

his son, now past the middle of life, came to the family estate. Still, however, he was not at his ease. His embarrassments were great; his property was strictly tied up; and he was on very bad terms with the heir-at-law. He appears to have led, during a long course of years, that most wretched life, the life of an old boy about town. Expensive tastes with little money and licentious appetites with declining vigour, were the just penance for his early irregularities. A severe illness had produced a singular effect on his intellect. His memory played him pranks stranger than almost any that are to be found in the history of that strange faculty.[1] It seemed to be at once preternaturally strong and preternaturally weak. If a book was read to him before he went to bed, he would wake the next morning with his mind full of the thoughts and expressions which he had heard over night; and he would write them down, without in the least suspecting that they were not his own. In his verses the same ideas, and even the same words, came over and over again several times in a short composition. His fine person bore the marks of age, sickness and sorrow; and

---

[1] " He lost his memory (forty years before he died) by a fever, and would repeat the same thought, sometimes in the compass of ten lines, and did not dream of its being inserted but just before: when you pointed it out to him, he would say, 'Gads-so, so it is ! I thank you very much : pray blot it out.'"—POPE, in Spence's *Anecdotes*.

Elsewhere Pope states that he was forty years of age when the illness occurred. It is possible that this illness may have been the fever before mentioned, from which he sought recovery by travel, in the winter of 1678; though Dennis certainly describes him as returning " entirely restored," both in body and mind.—ED.

he mourned for his departed beauty with an effeminate regret. He could not look without a sigh at the portrait which Lely had painted of him when he was only twenty-eight, and often mur. mured, *Quantum mutatus ab illo.*

He was still nervously anxious about his literary reputation, and, not content with the fame which he still possessed as a dramatist, was determined to be renowed as a satirist and an amatory poet. In 1704, after twenty-seven years of silence, he again appeared as an author. He put forth a large folio of miscellaneous verses, which, we believe, has never been reprinted. Some of these pieces had probably circulated through the town in manuscript. For, before the volume appeared, the critics at the coffee-houses very confidently predicted that it would be utterly worthless, and were in consequence bitterly reviled by the poet in an ill-written foolish and egotistical preface. The book amply vindicated the most unfavourable prophecies that had been hazarded. The style and versification are beneath criticism ; the morals are those of Rochester. For Rochester, indeed, there was some excuse. When his offences against decorum were committed, he was a very young man, misled by a prevailing fashion. Wycherley was sixty-four. He had long outlived the times when libertinism was regarded as essential to the character of a wit and a gentleman. Most of the rising poets, Addison, for example, John Philips and Rowe, were studious of decency. We can hardly conceive anything more miserable than the figure which the ribald old man makes in the midst of so many sober and well-conducted youths.

In the very year in which this bulky volume of obscene doggerel was published, Wycherley formed an acquaintance of a very singular kind. A little, pale, crooked, sickly, bright-eyed urchin, just turned of sixteen, had written some copies of verses in which discerning judges could detect the promise of future eminence. There was, indeed, as yet nothing very striking or original in the conceptions of the young poet. But he was already skilled in the art of metrical composition. His diction and his music were not those of the great old masters ; but that which his ablest contemporaries were labouring to do he already did best. His style was not richly poetical ; but it was always neat, compact and pointed. His verse wanted variety of pause, of swell and of cadence, but never grated harshly on the ear or disappointed it by a feeble close. The youth was already free of the company of wits, and was greatly elated at being introduced to the author of *The Plain Dealer* and *The Country Wife.*

It is curious to trace the history of the intercourse which took place between Wycherley and Pope—between the representative of the age that was going out and the representative of the age that was coming in—between the friend of Rochester and Buckingham and the friend of Lyttleton and Mansfield. At first the boy was enchanted by the kindness and condescension of his new friend, haunted his door and followed him about like a spaniel from coffee-house to coffee-house. Letters full of affection, humility and fulsome flattery were interchanged between the friends. But the first ardour of affection could not last. Pope, though at no time scrupulously delicate in his writings or fastidious as to the morals of his associates, was shocked [1] by the indecency of a rake who, at seventy, was still the representative of the monstrous profligacy of the Restoration. As the youth grew older, as his mind expanded and his fame rose, he appreciated both himself and Wycherley more correctly. He felt a well-founded contempt for the old gentleman's verses, and was at no great pains to conceal his opinion. Wycherley, on the other hand, though blinded by self-love to the imperfections of what he called his poetry, could not but see that there was an immense difference between his young companion's rhymes and his own. He was divided between two feelings. He wished to have the assistance of so skilful a hand to polish his lines; and yet he shrank from the humiliation of being beholden for literary assistance to a lad who might have been his grandson.

Pope was willing to give assistance, but was by no means disposed to give assistance and flattery too. He took the trouble to retouch whole reams of feeble, stumbling verses, and inserted many vigorous lines, which the least skilful reader will distinguish in an instant. But he thought that by these services he acquired a right to express himself in terms which would not, under ordinary circumstances, become one who was

---

[1] This assertion is wholly without foundation.—ED.

addressing a man of four times his age. In one letter, he tells Wycherley that "the worst pieces are such as, to render them very good, would require almost the entire new writing of them." In another, he gives the following account of his corrections : "Though the whole be as short again as at first, there is not one thought omitted but what is a repetition of something in your first volume or in this very paper ; and the versification throughout is, I believe, such as nobody can be shocked at. The repeated permission you give me of dealing freely with you, will, I hope, excuse what I have done ; for, if I have not spared you when I thought severity would do you a kindness, I have not mangled you when I thought there was no absolute need of amputation."

Wycherley continued to return thanks for all this hacking and hewing, which was, indeed, of inestimable service to his composition. But by degrees his thanks began to sound very like reproaches. In private, he is said to have described Pope as a person who could not cut out a suit, but who had some skill in turning old coats.[1] In his letters to Pope, while he acknowledged that the versification of the poems had been greatly improved, he spoke of the whole art of versification with scorn, and sneered at those who preferred sound to sense. Pope revenged himself for this outbreak of spleen by return of post. He had in his hands a volume of

---

[1] I can find no authority for this observation. It may have been spoken in a moment of peevishness, but it is certainly very far from conveying Wycherley's real estimate of his friend's genius.—ED.

Wycherley's rhymes, and he wrote to say that this volume was so full of faults that he could not correct it without completely defacing the manuscript. "I am," he said, "equally afraid of sparing you and of offending you by too impudent a correction." This was more than flesh and blood could bear. Wycherley reclaimed his papers in a letter in which resentment shows itself plainly through the thin disguise of civility. Pope, glad to be rid of a troublesome and inglorious task, sent back the deposit, and, by way of a parting courtesy, advised the old man to turn his poetry into prose, and assured him that the public would like his thoughts much better without his versification. Thus ended this memorable correspondence.

Wycherley lived some years after the termination of the strange friendship which we have described.[1] The last scene of his life was, perhaps, the most scandalous. Ten days before his death, at seventy-five, he married a young girl, merely in order to injure his nephew, an act which proves that neither years nor adversity, nor what he called his philosophy, nor either of the religions which he had at different times professed, had taught him the rudiments of morality.[2] He died in December,

---

[1] This "strange friendship" only terminated, as has been already shown, with Wycherley's death.—ED.

[2] Our information respecting the closing scene of Wycherley's life is too scanty for the formation of a definite judgment. We are, however, under no necessity of believing the circumstances which attended it to have been in any way scandalous. Pope's letter, on this occasion, to Mr. Blount is here subjoined.

"Jan. 21, 1715—16.

"I know of nothing that will be so interesting to you at present, as some circumstances of the last act of that eminent comic

1715, and lies in the vault under the church of St. Paul in Covent Garden.

His bride soon after married a Captain

poet, and our friend, Wycherley. He had often told me, as I doubt not he did all his acquaintance, that he would marry as soon as his life was despaired of. Accordingly, a few days before his death, he underwent the ceremony : and joined together those two sacraments, which, wise men say, should be the last we receive : for, if you observe, matrimony is placed after extreme unction in our catechism, as a kind of hint of the order of time in which they are to be taken. The old man then lay down, satisfied in the conscience of having by this one act paid his just debts, obliged a woman, who, he was told, had merit, and shown an heroic resentment of the ill-usage of his next heir. Some hundred pounds, which he had with the lady, discharged those debts : a jointure of four hundred a year made her a recompense ; and the nephew he left to comfort himself as well as he could, with the miserable remains of a mortgaged estate. I saw our friend twice after this was done, less peevish in his sickness than he used to be in his health ; neither much afraid of dying, nor (which in him had been more likely) much ashamed of marrying. The evening before he expired, he called his young wife to the bedside, and earnestly entreated her not to deny him one request, the last he should make. Upon her assurances of consenting to it, he told her, 'My dear, it is only this, that you will never marry an old man again.' I cannot help remarking, that sickness, which often destroys both wit and wisdom, yet seldom has power to remove that talent which we call humour. Mr. Wycherley shewed his, even in this last compliment ; though I think his request a little hard, for why should he bar her from doubling her jointure on the same easy terms.

"So trivial as these circumstances are, I should not be displeased myself to know such trifles, when they concern or characterise any eminent person. The wisest and wittiest of men are seldom wiser or wittier than others in these sober moments. At least, our friend ended much in the character he had lived in : and Horace's rule for a play may as well be applied to him as a play-wright

'————————*Servetur ad imum*
Qualis ab incepto processerit, et sibi constet.'

"I am, &c."

It is stated that the lady's name was Jackson, and that she brought Wycherley a fortune of £1,500. The following additional particulars are given, on the authority of Pope, in Spence's *Anecdotes.*

Shrimpton, who thus became possessed of a large collection of manuscripts. These were sold to a bookseller. They were so full of erasures and interlineations that no printer could decipher them. It was necessary to call in the aid of a professed critic ; and Theobald, the editor of Shakespeare and the hero of the first *Dunciad,* was employed to ascertain the true reading. In this way, a volume of miscellanies in verse and prose was got up for the market. The collection derives all its value from the traces of Pope's hand, which are everywhere discernible.

Of the moral character of Wycherley it can hardly be necessary for us to say more. His fame as a writer rests wholly on his comedies, and chiefly on the last two. Even as a comic writer, he was neither of the best school, nor highest in his school. He was in truth a worst Congreve. His chief merit, like Congreve's, lies in the style of his dialogue. But the wit which lights up *The Plain Dealer* and *The Country Wife* is pale and flickering

"Wycherley's nephew, on whom his estate was entailed (but with power to settle a widow's jointure) would not consent to his selling any part of it ; which he wanted much to do, to pay his debts, about a thousand pounds. He had therefore long resolved to marry, in order to make a settlement from the estate, to pay off his debts with his wife's fortune, and 'to plague his damned nephew,' as he used to express it. . . . . After all, the woman he did marry proved a cheat ; was a cast mistress of the person who recommended her to him ; and was supplied by him with money for her wedding clothes." This last assertion is hardly to be reconciled with the assumption that Wycherley paid his debts with his wife's fortune. From an allusion to his nephew's "ill-carriage" to him, in a letter to Pope, dated Aug. 11, 1709, we gather that the quarrel between them was of old standing ; of its origin we are completely ignorant. —ED.

when compared with the gorgeous blaze which dazzles us almost to blindness in *Love for Love* and *The Way of the World.* Like Congreve, and, indeed, even more than Congreve, Wycherley is ready to sacrifice dramatic propriety to the liveliness of his dialogue. The poet speaks out of the mouths of all his dunces and coxcombs, and makes them describe themselves with a good sense and acuteness which puts them on a level with the wits and heroes. We will give two instances, the first which occur to us, from *The Country Wife.* There are in the world fools who find the society of old friends insipid and who are always running after new companions. Such a character is a fair subject for comedy. But nothing can be more absurd than to introduce a man of this sort saying to his comrade, " I can deny you nothing : for though I have known thee a great while, never go if I do not love thee as well as a new acquaintance." That town-wits again, have always been rather a heartless class, is true. But none of them, we will answer for it, ever said to a young lady to whom he was making love, " We wits rail and make love often but to show our parts : as we have no affections, so we have no malice." [1]

Wycherley's plays are said to have been the produce of long and patient labour. The epithet of " slow " was early given to him by Rochester,

[1] It is difficult to understand in what the impropriety of these speeches is supposed to consist. They are both placed in the mouth of Sparkish, an affected fop, whose utmost ambition is to be recorded a wit, and to whom no sacrifice would seem excessive for the sake of a smart saying. His indifference to the young lady in question occasions his loss of her in the end. — ED.

and was frequently repeated.[1] In truth, his mind, unless we are greatly mistaken, was naturally a very meagre soil, and was forced only by great labour and outlay to bear fruit which, after all, was not of the highest flavour. He has scarcely more claim to originality than Terence. It is not too much to say that there is hardly anything of the least value in his plays of which the hint is not to be found elsewhere. The best scenes in *The Gentleman Dancing-Master* were suggested by Calderon's *Maestro de Danzar*, not by any means one of the happiest comedies of the great Castilian poet. *The Country Wife* is borrowed from the *Ecole des Maris* and the *Ecole des Femmes.* The groundwork of *The Plain Dealer* is taken from the *Misanthrope* of Molière. One whole scene is almost translated from the *Critique de l'Ecole des Femmes.*[2] Fidelia is Shakespeare's Viola stolen, and marred in the stealing ; and the widow Black-

---

[1] Wycherley's "slowness" has been denied by both Pope and Lansdowne. The former declares that "he was far from being slow in general, and, in particular, wrote *The Plain Dealer* in three weeks." And Lansdowne observes, "If it had been a trouble to him to write, I am much mistaken if he would not have spared himself that trouble." It seems certain, however, that he revised and altered his plays before committing them to the public, and he by no means belonged to the class of so-called Easy Writers, with respect to whom a *bon-mot* of his is recorded in the ninth *Tatler.* "The town has for half an age been tormented with insects called Easy Writers, whose abilities Mr. Wycherley one day described excellently well in one word : 'That,' said he, 'among these fellows is called Easy Writing, which anyone may easily write.'"—ED.

[2] A remarkably free translation, one would say ; and the "whole scene" is, in fact, but a small portion of a scene. But see, for Wycherley's plagiarisms, the Introductions to the plays.—ED.

acre, beyond comparison Wycherley's best comic character, is the Countess in Racine's *Plaideurs*, talking the jargon of English instead of that of French chicane.

The only thing original about Wycherley, the only thing which he could furnish from his own mind in inexhaustible abundance, was profligacy. It is curious to observe how everything that he touched, however pure and noble, took in an instant the colour of his own mind. Compare the *Ecole des Femmes* with *The Country Wife*. Agnes is a simple and amiable girl, whose heart is indeed full of love, but of love sanctioned by honour, morality and religion. Her natural talents are great. They have been hidden and, as it might appear, destroyed by an education elaborately bad. But they are called forth into full energy by a virtuous passion. Her lover, while he adores her beauty, is too honest a man to abuse the confiding tenderness of a creature so charming and inexperienced. Wycherley takes this plot into his hands ; and forthwith this sweet and graceful courtship becomes a licentious intrigue of the lowest and least sentimental kind, between an impudent London rake and the idiot wife of a country squire. We will not go into details. In truth, Wycherley's indecency is protected against the critics as a skunk is protected against the hunters. It is safe, because it is too filthy to handle and too noisome even to approach.

It is the same with *The Plain Dealer*. How careful has Shakespeare been in *Twelfth Night* to preserve the dignity and delicacy of Viola under her disguise! Even when wearing a page's doublet and hose, she is never mixed up with any transaction which the most fastidious mind could regard as leaving a stain on her. She is employed by the Duke on an embassy of love to Olivia, but on an embassy of the most honourable kind. Wycherley borrows Viola—and Viola forthwith becomes a pandar of the basest sort. But the character of Manly is the best illustration of our meaning. Molière exhibited in his misanthrope a pure and noble mind which had been sorely vexed by the sight of perfidy and malevolence disguised under the forms of politeness. As every extreme naturally generates its contrary, Alceste adopts a standard of good and evil directly opposed to that of the society which surrounds him. Courtesy seems to him a vice; and those stern virtues which are neglected by the fops and coquettes of Paris become too exclusively the objects of his veneration. He is often to blame; he is often ridiculous: but he is always a good man; and the feeling which he inspires is regret that a person so estimable should be so unamiable. Wycherley borrowed Alceste, and turned him—we quote the words of so lenient a critic as Mr. Leigh Hunt—into "a ferocious sensualist, who believed himself as great a rascal as he thought everybody else." The surliness of Molière's hero is copied and caricatured. But the most nauseous libertinism and the most dastardly fraud are substituted for the purity and integrity of the original. And, to make the whole complete, Wycherley does not seem to have been aware that he was not drawing the portrait of an eminently honest man. So depraved was his moral taste, that, while he firmly believed that he was producing a picture of virtue too exalted for the commerce of this world, he was really delineating the greatest rascal that is to be found even in his own writings.

LOVE IN A WOOD;

OR

ST. JAMES'S PARK.

——Excludit sanos Helicone poetas
Democritus.[1]—HORAT.

[1] Democritus excludes sane poets from Helicon.—*De Art Poet.* 296—7.

YCHERLEY informed Pope that he wrote
his first comedy, *Love in a Wood*, at the
age of nineteen—*i.e.* in the year 1659-60.
If this statement be accurate, the play must
have undergone very considerable altera-
tions previous to its production on the
stage ; for not only do we discover in it occasional allusions
to events of later years, but the whole piece displays an
intimate acquaintance with life in the metropolis scarcely
commensurate with the opportunities of a youth who, from
the age of fifteen, when he was sent into France, to that of
twenty, when he became a student at Oxford, can have
passed but a few weeks, at the most, in London. From the
Biographia Britannica we learn that Wycherley returned
from France shortly before the Restoration ; from Wood's
Athenæ Oxonienses that he became a fellow commoner of
Queen's College, Oxford, also " a little before the Restoration
of Charles II., but wore not a gown, only lived in the
provost's lodgings," and "was entered in the public library
(the Bodleian) under the title of philosophiæ studiosus in
July, 1660." In the *Fasti Oxonienses*, however, the following
entry occurs under the year 1660 : "In the month of July
this year Will. Wicherley became sojourner in Oxon for the
sake of the public library." We are at liberty, therefore, to
conclude that between the date of his return to England and
the following July, part, at least, of our author's time may
have been spent in London, where he may possibly have
composed the first draught of his comedy, and where, at all
events, his quick observation would furnish him with
material sufficient for a first draught.

The year 1672 has been universally determined as that of the first performance of *Love in a Wood;* I believe, nevertheless, incorrectly. We are as certain as we can be, in the absence of direct evidence, that Wycherley's second play, *The Gentleman Dancing-Master*, was first brought upon the stage in 1671.[1] Now there is little doubt that *The Gentleman Dancing-Master* had been preceded by *Love in a Wood*, for not only do the authorities generally concur in assigning an earlier date to the production of the latter play, but Wycherley, in dedicating it to the Duchess of Cleveland, refers pointedly to himself as a " new author." Further in the dedication we find that her Grace had honoured the poet by going to see his comedy twice together, *during Lent*, and had been pleased, thereupon, to command from him a copy of the play, with which he takes occasion to offer the dedicatory epistle. These were not the days of long runs, even for the most successful dramas, nor are we likely to err in assuming that the Duchess was present at an early performance of the piece which she distinguished with her favour; or that Wycherley prefixed her title to a comedy newly brought upon the stage, rather than to one which had already been for some time the property of the public, and which had been revived, as must then have been the case, before the Duchess had seen it. Note, also, that the dedication is addressed to the Duchess of Cleveland by that title. In Lent, 1670, Barbara Palmer was Countess of Castlemaine ; she was created Duchess of Cleveland on the 3rd of August in the same year. Considering then that the piece was certainly performed during Lent, that it cannot have been produced later than 1671, and that the Duchess to whom it was inscribed enjoyed not that title until the autumn of 1670, we may conclude, with tolerable security, that the first performance of *Love in a Wood* took place some time during the spring of 1671.

Genest indeed, supposes it to have been brought out by the King's Company after their removal to the theatre in Lincoln's Inn Fields.[2] Their own house in Drury Lane having been destroyed by fire in January, 1672, they opened, on the 26th of February following, the Lincoln's Inn Fields

---

[1] See the Introduction to *The Gentleman Dancing-Master*.
[2] *Some Account of the English Stage*, vol i. p. 135.

Theatre, which had been untenanted since the migration of the Duke's Company to Dorset Gardens in the preceding November, with a representation of Beaumont and Fletcher's *Wit without Money*. This was succeeded, in order, by *Arviragus and Philicia* and Dryden's *Marriage à la Mode*, after which, Genest thinks, *Love in a Wood* was produced. But, on this supposition, the first performance of *Love in a Wood* must have taken place later than that of *The Gentleman Dancing-Master*, and in that case it seems hardly probable that Wycherley should describe himself as a *new* author in the dedication to the former play. Moreover, the prologue to Wycherley's third comedy, *The Country Wife* contains a distinct allusion to the recent ill-fortune of *The Gentleman Dancing-Master*, which we can scarcely suppose the author would have thus referred to, had a successful play of his been produced in the interval, and that by the same company which brought forward *The Country Wife*. In fact, the only argument which I can conceive it possible to adduce in support of Genest must be based upon a conjecture that not only *The Gentleman Dancing-Master*, but *Love in a Wood* also, had failed to win the favour of the public, and that it is the latter play to which allusion is intended in the prologue to *The Country Wife*. That *The Gentleman Dancing-Master* proved a failure is certain ; that *Love in a Wood* succeeded, we have no direct evidence, but of circumstantial sufficient, I think, to prove the point. The general assumption in its favour we may pass ; but the whole tone of the dedication, though it afford us no information, in so many words, as to the fate of the piece, forbids us to believe that it can have been indited by the "baffled scribbler" of a condemned comedy. Indeed, had the piece thus failed, it is quite inconceivable that Wycherley would have had the temerity to offer it to the Duchess ; he would rather have sent it into the world silently, and without the flourish of a dedication, as was actually the case with *The Gentleman Dancing-Master*. Dennis, moreover, declares expressly that *Love in a Wood* brought its author acquainted with the wits of the Court, and we may question whether the reputation of an unprosperous playwright would have proved the surest passport to their intimacy.

The reasons for rejecting the date of 1672 thus recounted, there remains but to notice one inconsiderable particular, which, could we allow it consequence, would tend to determine the production of *Love in a Wood* at a yet earlier date than that to which I have assigned it. In a conversation with the Duchess, immediately after her visit to his play, Wycherley, as reported by Dennis, continually addresses her Grace by the title of "your Ladyship." I doubt not, however, that this is a mere slip on the part of Dennis, nor can we easily imagine that Wycherley deferred, until the autumn, the presentation of his play to a lady who had "commanded" it of him, with such distinguishing marks of favour, in the preceding spring.

Love in a Wood, then, was produced by the King's company, during the spring of 1671, at the Theatre Royal, in Drury Lane. Some of the first actors of the day took part in the performances. Hart, who in tragedy yielded the palm to Betterton alone, appeared as Ranger, Mohun as Dapperwit; Lacy the comedian, soon afterwards "creator" of Bayes, as Alderman Gripe; and Kinaston, who in his youth, before women trod the boards, had been famous in female parts, now, changing sides, enacted the jealous lover, Valentine. The rôle of Lady Flippant was taken by an actress well known to us from the pages of Pepys—his favourite Mrs. Knipp, "a merry jade!"

Upon the whole this play must be owned inferior to Wycherley's other dramas. It is excelled in unity of action by *The Gentleman Dancing-Master*, in richness of humour by *The Country Wife*, in strength of satire by *The Plain Dealer*. Nevertheless, it is a highly diverting, witty comedy, and strikingly superior to most of the new plays which, since the Restoration, had preceded it upon the stage. Some critics would have us believe that Wycherley derived the suggestion of this play from Sir Charles Sedley's comedy of *The Mulberry Garden*. It is difficult to understand upon what grounds this assertion is based. In the first place, although *The Mulberry Garden* was produced on the stage in 1668, nearly three years earlier than *Love in a Wood*, it is exceedingly doubtful if it were earlier written. Indeed, if Wycherley may be credited as to the year in which his own play was composed, the question of priority is easily settled, for *The Mulberry Garden* cannot have been written until after the Restoration, as its dénouement turns upon the proclamation of the King by General Monk. Moreover, it is hardly possible that Wycherley should have known any-thing of Sedley's play before its public representation, as he seems not to have been acquainted with Sedley himself until after the production of his own drama, so that our accept-ance of the theory that he borrowed from Sedley the hint of *Love in a Wood* would involve the unwarrantable conclusion that he also, in conversation with Pope, antedated its com-position by at least eight years. But further, the only considerable point of resemblance between the two plays appears to be that while in Wycherley's part of the action takes place in St. James's Park, in Sedley's one of the scenes is laid in the Mulberry Garden, which was certainly very near to St. James's Park, being, in fact, situated at its western extremity. If the reader choose to consider this remarkable coincidence sufficient to justify a charge of plagiarism against Wycherley, I have nothing more to urge in his defence.

Love in a Wood was registered at Stationers' Hall on the 6th of October, 1671, and was published in the following year.

TO HER GRACE

THE DUCHESS OF CLEVELAND

Madam,

LL authors whatever in their dedication are poets ; but I am now to write to a lady who stands as little in need of flattery, as her beauty of art ; otherwise I should prove as ill a poet to her in my dedication, as to my reader in my play. I can do your Grace no honour, nor make you more admirers than you have already ; yet I can do myself the honour to let the world know I am the greatest you have. You will pardon me, Madam, for you know it is very hard for a new author, and poet too, to govern his ambition : for poets, let them pass in the world ever so much for modest, honest men, but begin praise to others which concludes in themselves ; and are like rooks, who lend people money but to win it back again, and so leave them in debt to 'em for nothing ; they offer laurel and incense to their heroes, but wear it themselves, and perfume themselves. This is true, Madam, upon the honest word of an author who never yet writ dedication   Yet though I cannot lie like them, I am as vain as they ; and cannot but publicly give your Grace my humble acknowledgments for the favours I have received from you :—this, I say, is the poet's gratitude, which, in plain English, is only pride and ambition ; and that the world might know your Grace did me the honour to see my play twice together.   Yet, perhaps, my enviers of your favour will suggest 'twas in Lent, and therefore for your mortification. Then, as a jealous author, I am concerned not to have your Grace's favours lessened, or rather my reputation :

and to let them know, you were pleased, after that, to command a copy from me of this play ;—the only way, without beauty and wit, to win a poor poet's heart.

'Tis a sign your Grace understands nothing better than obliging all the world after the best and most proper manner. But, Madam, to be obliging to that excess as you are (pardon me, if I tell you, out of my extreme concern and service for your Grace) is a dangerous quality, and may be very incommode to you ; for civility makes poets as troublesome, as charity makes beggars ; and your Grace will be hereafter as much pestered with such scurvy offerings as this, poems, panegyrics, and the like, as you are now with petitions : and, Madam, take it from me, no man with papers in 's hand is more dreadful than a poet ; no, not a lawyer with his declarations. Your Grace sure did not well consider what ye did, in sending for my play : you little thought I would have had the confidence to send you a dedication too. But, Madam, you find I am as unreasonable, and have as little conscience, as if I had driven the poetic trade longer than I have, and ne'er consider you had enough of the play. But (having suffered now so severely) I beseech your Grace, have a care for the future ; take my counsel, and be (if you can possible) as proud and ill-natured as other people of quality, since your quiet is so much concerned, and since you have more reason than any to value yourself :—for you have that perfection of beauty (without thinking it so) which others of your sex but think they have ; that generosity in your actions which others of your quality have only in their promises ; that spirit, wit and judgment, and all other qualifications which fit heroes to command, and would make any but your Grace proud. I begin now, elevated by my subject, to write with the emotion and fury of a poet, yet the integrity of an historian ; and I could never be weary—nay, sure this were my only way to make my readers never weary too, though they were a more impatient generation of people than they are. In fine, speaking thus of your Grace, I should please all the world but you ; therefore I must once observe and obey you against my will, and say no more, than that I am,

Madam,
Your Grace's most obliged, and most humble servant,

WILLIAM WYCHERLEY.

PROLOGUE.

CUSTOM, which bids the thief from cart harangue
All those that come to make and see him hang,
Wills the damned poet (though he knows he's gone)
To greet you ere his execution.
Not having fear of critic 'fore his eyes,
But still rejecting wholesome, good advice,
He e'en is come to suffer here to-day
For counterfeiting (as you judge) a play,
Which is against dread Phœbus highest treason ;
Damn, damning judges, therefore, you have reason :—
You he does mean who, for the selfsame fault,
That damning privilege of yours have bought.
So the huge bankers, when they needs must fail,
Send the small brothers of their trade to jail ;
Whilst they, by breaking, gentlemen are made,
Then, more than any, scorn poor men o' the trade.
You hardened renegado poets, who
Treat rhyming poets worse than Turk would do,
But vent your heathenish rage,—hang, draw, and quarter,
His Muse will die to-day a fleering martyr ;
Since for bald jest, dull libel, or lampoon,
There are who suffer persecution
With the undaunted briskness of buffoon,
And strict professors live of raillery,
Defying porter's-lodge, or pillory.
For those who yet write on our poet's fate,
Should as co-sufferers commiserate ;
But he in vain their pity now would crave,
Who for themselves, alas ! no pity have,
And their own gasping credit will not save ;
And those, much less, our criminal would spare,
Who ne'er in rhyme transgress ;—if such there are.
Well then, who nothing hopes, needs nothing fear ;
And he, before your cruel votes shall do it,
By his despair declares himself no poet.

Mr. RANGER,
Mr. VINCENT, } Young Gentlemen of the town.
Mr. VALENTINE,

Alderman GRIPE, seemingly precise, but a covetous, lecherous, old Usurer of the city.

Sir SIMON ADDLEPLOT, a Coxcomb, always in pursuit of women of great fortunes.

Mr. DAPPERWIT, a brisk, conceited, half-witted fellow of the town.

Mrs. CROSSBITE'S Landlord, and his Prentices, Servants, Waiters, and other Attendants.

CHRISTINA, VALENTINE'S Mistress.

LYDIA, RANGER'S Mistress.

Lady FLIPPANT, GRIPE'S Sister, an affected Widow in distress for a husband, though still declaiming against marriage.

Mrs. MARTHA, GRIPE'S Daughter.

Mrs. JOYNER, a Match-maker, or precise city bawd.

Mrs. CROSSBITE, an old cheating jill, and bawd to her Daughter.

Miss LUCY, Mrs. CROSSBITE'S Daughter.

ISABEL, CHRISTINA'S Woman

LEONORE, Servant to LYDIA.

SCENE—LONDON.

LOVE IN A WOOD;

OR

ST. JAMES'S PARK

ACT THE FIRST.

SCENE I.—GRIPE'S *House, in the evening.*

Enter Lady FLIPPANT *and* Mrs. JOYNER.

ADY FLIP. Not a husband to be had for money!—Come, come, I might have been a better housewife for myself, as the world goes now, if I had dealt for an heir with his guardian, uncle, or mother-in-law; and you are no better than a chouse, a cheat.

Mrs. Joyn. I a cheat, madam!

L. Flip. I am out of my money, and patience too.

Mrs. Joyn. Do not run out of your patience, whatever you do :—'tis a necessary virtue for a widow without a jointure, in truly.

L. Flip. Vile woman! though my fortune be something wasted, my person's in good repair. If I had not depended on you, I had had a husband before this time. When I gave you the last five pounds, did you not promise I should be married by Christmas?

Mrs. Joyn. And I had kept my promise if you had co-operated.

L. Flip. Co-operated! what should I have done? 'Tis well known no woman breathing could use more industry to get her a husband than I have. Has not my husband's 'scutcheon walked as much ground as the citizens' signs since the Fire?—that no quarter of the town might be ignorant of the widow Flippant.

Mrs. Joyn. 'Tis well known, madam, indeed.

L. Flip. Have I not owned myself (against my stomach) the relict of a citizen, to credit my fortune?

Mrs. Joyn. 'Tis confessed, madam.

L. Flip. Have I not constantly kept Covent-Garden church, St. Martin's, the playhouses, Hyde Park, Mulberry garden,[1] and all the other public marts where widows and maids are exposed?

Mrs. Joyn. Far be it from me to think you have an aversion to a husband. But why, madam, have you refused so many good offers?

L. Flip. Good offers, Mrs. Joyner! I'll be sworn I never had an offer since my late husband's.—If I had an offer, Mrs. Joyner!—there's the thing, Mrs. Joyner.

Mrs. Joyn. Then your frequent and public detestation of marriage is thought real; and if you have had no offer, there's the thing, madam.

L. Flip. I cannot deny but I always rail against marriage;—which is the widow's way to it certainly.

---

[1] The Mulberry Garden was situated at the further extremity of the Mall in St. James's Park, upon the site now occupied by Buckingham Palace and its grounds. Its name was derived from a plantation of mulberry trees which James I. caused to be made there. Later, the spot was converted into a public garden, with shrubberies, walks, arbours, and a house of refreshment, and was much frequented by persons of fashion as well as citizens. Pepys found it "a very silly place, worse than Spring-garden," but "a wilderness here that is somewhat pretty." The following extract from Sedley's *Mulberry Garden* gives an idea of the doings at this place. The scene is laid in the Garden:—

"*Wildish.* What, is there store of game here, gentlemen?

Modish. Troth, little or none; a few citizens that have brought their children out to air 'em, and eat cheesecakes.

Wildish. I thought this place had been so full of beauties, that like a pack of hounds in a hare warren, you could hunt one for another: what think you of an arbor and a bottle of Rhenish?"

Mrs. Joyn. 'Tis the desperate way of the desperate widows, in truly.

L. Flip. Would you have us as tractable as the wenches that eat oatmeal, and fooled like them too?

Mrs. Joyn. If nobody were wiser than I, I should think, since the widow wants the natural allurement which the virgin has, you ought to give men all other encouragements, in truly.

L. Flip. Therefore, on the contrary, because the widow's fortune (whether supposed or real) is her chiefest bait, the more chary she seems of it, and the more she withdraws it, the more eagerly the busy gaping fry will bite. With us widows, husbands are got like bishoprics, by saying "No:" and I tell you, a young heir is as shy of a widow as of a rook, to my knowledge.

Mrs. Joyn. I can allege nothing against your practice —but your ill success; and indeed you must use another method with Sir Simon Addleplot.

L. Flip. Will he be at your house at the hour?

Mrs. Joyn. He'll be there by ten :—'tis now nine. I'll warrant you he will not fail.

L. Flip. I'll warrant you then I will not fail :—for 'tis more than time I were sped.

Mrs. Joyn. Mr. Dapperwit has not been too busy with you, I hope?—Your experience has taught you to prevent a mischance.

L. Flip. No, no, my mischance (as you call it) is greater than that. I have but three months to reckon, ere I lie down with my port and equipage, and must be delivered of a woman, a footman, and a coachman :— for my coach must down, unless I can get Sir Simon to draw with me.

Mrs. Joyn. He will pair with you exactly if you knew all.   [*Aside.*

L. Flip. Ah, Mrs. Joyner, nothing grieves me like the putting down my coach! For the fine clothes, the fine lodgings,—let 'em go; for a lodging is as unnecessary a

Wycherley.   C thing to a widow that has a coach, as a hat to a man that has a good peruke. For, as you see about town, she is most properly at home in her coach :—she eats, and drinks, and sleeps in her coach ; and for her visits, she receives them in the playhouse.

Mrs. Joyn. Ay, ay, let the men keep lodgings, as you say, madam, if they will.

Enter behind, at one door, GRIPE *and* Sir SIMON ADDLE-PLOT, *the latter in the dress of a* Clerk ; *at the other,* Mrs. MARTHA.

L. Flip. Do you think if things had been with me as they have been, I would ever have housed with this counter-fashion b·other of mine, (who hates a vest as much as a surplice,) to have my patches assaulted every day at dinner, my freedom censured, and my visitants shut out of doors ?—Poor Mr. Dapperwit cannot be admitted.

Mrs. Joyn. He knows him too well to keep his acquaintance.

L. Flip. He is a censorious rigid fop, and knows nothing.

Gripe. So, so !   [*Behind.*

Mrs. Joyn. [*Aside.*] Is he here ?—[*To* Lady FLIPPANT.] Nay, with your pardon, madam, I must contradict you there. He is a prying commonwealth's-man, an implacable magistrate, a sturdy pillar of his cause, and— [*To* GRIPE] But, oh me, is your worship so near then ? if I had thought you heard me—

Gripe. Why, why, Mrs. Joyner, I have said as much of myself ere now ; and without vanity, I profess.

Mrs. Joyn. I know your virtue is proof against vain-glory ; but the truth to your face looks like flattery in your worship's servant.

Gripe. No, no ; say what you will of me in that kind, far be it from me to suspect you of flattery.

Mrs. Joyn. In truly, your worship knows yourself, and knows me, for I am none of those—

L. Flip. [*Aside.*] Now they are in—Mrs. Joyner, I'll go before to your house, you'll be sure to come after me.

Mrs. Joyn. Immediately. — [*Exit* Lady FLIPPANT.] But as I was saying, I am none of those—

Gripe. No, Mrs. Joyner, you cannot sew pillows under folks' elbows ; you cannot hold a candle to the devil ; you cannot tickle a trout to take him ; you—

Mrs. Joyn. Lord, how well you do know me indeed ! —and you shall see I know your worship as well. You cannot backslide from your principles ; you cannot be terrified by the laws ; nor bribed to allegiance by office or preferment ; you—

Gripe. Hold, hold, my praise must not interrupt yours.

Mrs. Joyn. With your worship's pardon, in truly, I must on.

Gripe. I am full of your praise, and it will run over.

Mrs. Joyn. Nay, sweet sir, you are—

Gripe. Nay, sweet Mrs. Joyner, you are—

Mrs. Joyn. Nay, good your worship, you are—

[*Stops her mouth with his handkerchief.*

Gripe. I say you are—

Mrs. Joyn. I must not be rude with your worship.

Gripe. You are a nursing mother to the saints ; through you they gather together ; through you they fructify and increase ; and through you the child cries from out of the hand-basket.

Mrs. Joyn. Through you virgins are married, or provided for as well ; through you the reprobate's wife is made a saint ; and through you the widow is not disconsolate, nor misses her husband.

Gripe. Through you—

Mrs. Joyn. Indeed you will put me to the blush.

Gripe. Blushes are badges of imperfection :—saints have no shame. You are—are the flower of matrons, Mrs. Joyner.

Mrs. Joyn. You are the pink of courteous aldermen.

Gripe. You are the muffler of secrecy.

Mrs. Joyn. You are the head-band of justice.

Gripe. Thank you, sweet Mrs. Joyner: do you think so indeed? You are—you are the bonfire of devotion.

Mrs. Joyn. You are the bellows of zeal.

Gripe. You are the cupboard of charity.

Mrs. Joyn. You are the fob of liberality.

Gripe. You are the rivet of sanctified love or wedlock.

Mrs. Joyn. You are the picklock and dark-lantern of policy; and, in a word, a conventicle of virtues.

Gripe. Your servant, your servant, sweet Mrs. Joyner! you have stopped my mouth.

Mrs. Joyn. Your servant, your servant, sweet alderman! I have nothing to say.

Sir Sim. The half pullet will be cold, sir.

Gripe. Mrs. Joyner, you shall sup with me.

Mrs. Joyn. Indeed I am engaged to supper with some of your man's friends; and I came on purpose to get leave for him too.

Gripe. I cannot deny you anything. But I have forgot to tell you what a kind of fellow my sister's Dapperwit is: before a full table of the coffee-house sages, he had the impudence to hold an argument against me in the defence of vests and protections; and therefore I forbid him my house; besides, when he came I was forced to lock up my daughter for fear of him, nay, I think the poor child herself was afraid of him.—Come hither, child, were you not afraid of Dapperwit?

Mrs. Mar. Yes indeed, sir, he is a terrible man.—Yet I durst meet with him in a piazza at midnight.   [*Aside.*

Gripe. He shall never come into my doors again.

Mrs. Mar. Shall Mr. Dapperwit never come hither again then?

Gripe. No, child.

Mrs. Mar. I am afraid he will.

Gripe. I warrant thee.

Mrs. Mar. [*Aside.*] I warrant you then I'll go to him.—
I am glad of that, for I hate him as much as a bishop.

Gripe. Thou art no child of mine, if thou dost not
hate bishops and wits.—Well, Mrs. Joyner, I'll keep you
no longer.   [*To* ADDLEPLOT.] Jonas, wait on Mrs.
Joyner.

Mrs. Joyn. Good night to your worship.

Gripe. But stay, stay, Mrs. Joyner: have you spoken
with the widow Crossbite about her little daughter, as I
desired?

Mrs. Joyn. I will to-morrow early; it shall be the first
thing I'll do after my prayers.

Gripe. If Dapperwit should contaminate her!—I cannot rest till I have redeemed her from the jaws of that
lion.—Good night.

Mrs. Joyn. Good gentleman.

[*Exeunt* GRIPE *and* Mrs. MARTHA.

Sir Sim. Ha! ha! ha! Mrs. Joyner.

Mrs. Joyn. What's the matter, Sir Simon?

Sir Sim. Ha! ha! ha!—let us make haste to your
house, or I shall burst, faith and troth, to see what fools
you and I make of these people.

Mrs. Joyn. I will not rob you of any of the credit;
I am but a feeble instrument, you are an engineer.

Sir Sim. Remember what you say now when things
succeed, and do not tell me then,—I must thank your
wit for all.

Mrs. Joyn. No, in truly, Sir Simon.

Sir Sim. Nay, I am sure Dapperwit and I have been
partners in many an intrigue, and he uses to serve
me so.

Mrs. Joyn. He is an ill man to intrigue with, as you
call it.

Sir Sim. Ay, so are all your wits; a pox! if a man's
understanding be not so public as theirs, he cannot do a
wise action but they go away with the honour of it, if he
be of their acquaintance.

Mrs. Joyn. Why do you keep such acquaintance then?

Sir Sim. There is a proverb, Mrs. Joyner, "You may know him by his company."

Mrs. Joyn. No, no, to be thought a man of parts, you must always keep company with a man of less wit than yourself.

Sir Sim. That's the hardest thing in the world for me to do, faith and troth.

Mrs. Joyn. What, to find a man of less wit than yourself? Pardon my raillery, Sir Simon.

Sir Sim. No, no, I cannot keep company with a fool: —I wonder how men of parts can do't, there's something in't.

Mrs. Joyn. If you could, all your wise actions would be your own, and your money would be your own too.

Sir Sim. Nay, faith and troth, that's true; for your wits are plaguily given to borrow. They'll borrow of their wench, coachman, or linkboy, their hire, Mrs. Joyner; Dapperwit has that trick with a vengeance.

Mrs. Joyn. Why will you keep company with him then, I say? for, to be plain with you, you have followed him so long, that you are thought but his cully;[1] for every wit has his cully, as every squire his led captain.

Sir Sim. I his cully, I his cully, Mrs. Joyner! Lord, that I should be thought a cully to any wit breathing!

Mrs. Joyn. Nay, do not take it so to heart, for the best wits of the town are but cullies themselves.

Sir Sim. To whom, to whom, to whom, Mrs. Joyner?

Mrs. Joyn. To sempstresses and bawds.

Sir Sim. To your knowledge, Mrs. Joyner.—[*Aside.*] There I was with her.

Mrs. Joyn. To tailors and vintners, but especially to the French houses.

Sir Sim. But Dapperwit is a cully to none of them; for he ticks.

---

[1] A gull; a courtesan's dupe; "one who may be easily led by the nose or put upon."—*Bailey's Dict.*

Mrs. Joyn. I care not, but I wish you were a cully to none but me ; that's all the hurt I wish you.

Sir Sim. Thank you, Mrs. Joyner. Well, I will throw off Dapperwit's acquaintance when I am married, and will only be a cully to my wife ; and that's no more than the wisest husband of 'em all is.

Mrs. Joyn. Then you think you shall carry Mrs. Martha ?

Sir Sim. Your hundred guineas are as good as in your lap.

Mrs. Joyn. But I am afraid this double plot of yours should fail : you would sooner succeed if you only designed upon Mrs. Martha, or only upon my Lady Flippant.

Sir Sim. Nay, then, you are no woman of intrigue, faith and troth : 'tis good to have two strings to one's bow. If Mrs. Martha be coy, I tell the widow I put on my disguise for her ; but if Mrs. Martha be kind to Jonas, Sir Simon Addleplot will be false to the widow : which is no more than widows are used to ; for a promise to a widow is as seldom kept as a vow made at sea, as Dapperwit says.

Mrs. Joyn. I am afraid they should discover you.

Sir Sim. You have nothing to fear ; you have your twenty guineas in your pocket for helping me into my service, and if I get into Mrs. Martha's quarters, you have a hundred more ; if into the widow's, fifty :—happy go lucky ! Will her ladyship be at your house at the hour ?

Mrs. Joyn. Yes.

Sir Sim. Then you shall see when I am Sir Simon Addleplot and myself I'll look like myself ; now I am Jonas, I look like an ass. You never thought Sir Simon Addleplot could have looked so like an ass by his ingenuity.

Mrs. Joyn. Pardon me, Sir Simon.

Sir Sim. Nay, do not flatter, faith and troth.

Mrs. Joyn. Come let us go, 'tis time.

Sir Sim. I will carry the widow to the French house.

Mrs. Joyn. If she will go.

Sir Sim. If she will go! why, did you ever know a widow refuse a treat? no more than a lawyer a fee, faith and troth: yet I know too—

No treat, sweet words, good mien, but sly intrigue
That must at length the jilting widow fegue.[1]

[*Exeunt.*

SCENE II.—*The French House. A table, wine and candles.*

Enter VINCENT, RANGER, *and* DAPPERWIT.

Dap. Pray, Mr. Ranger, let's have no drinking to night.

Vin. Pray, Mr. Ranger, let's have no Dapperwit to-night.

Ran. Nay, nay, Vincent.

Vin. A pox! I hate his impertinent chat more than he does the honest Burgundy.

Dap. But why should you force wine upon us? we are not all of your gusto.

Vin. But why should you force your chawed jests, your damned ends of your mouldy lampoons, and last year's sonnets, upon us? we are not all of your gusto.

Dap. The wine makes me sick, let me perish!

Vin. Thy rhymes make me spew.

Ran. At repartee already! Come, Vincent. I know you would rather have him pledge you: here, Dapperwit —[*Gives him the glass.*]—But why are you so eager to have him drink always?

---

[1] Fegue or feague. "To beat, to whip, to drive."—*Wright Dict. of obsolete and provincial English.* Hence our word *fag.*

Vin. Because he is so eager to talk always, and there is no other way to silence him.

Enter Waiter.

Wait. Here is a gentleman desires to speak with Mr. Vincent.

Vin. I come.   [*Exit* VINCENT *with* Waiter.

Dap. He may drink, because he is obliged to the bottle for all the wit and courage he has; 'tis not free and natural like yours.

Ran. He has more courage than wit, but wants neither.

Dap. As a pump gone dry, if you pour no water down you will get none out, so—

Ran. Nay, I bar similes too, to-night.

Dap. Why, is not the thought new? don't you apprehend it?

Ran. Yes, yes, but—

Dap. Well, well, will you comply with his sottishness too, and hate brisk things in complaisance to the ignorant dull age? I believe shortly 'twill be as hard to find a patient friend to communicate one's wit to, as a faithful friend to communicate one's secret to. Wit has as few true judges as painting, I see.

Ran. All people pretend to be judges of both.

Dap. Ay, they pretend; but set you aside, and one or two more—

Ran. But why, has Vincent neither courage nor wit?

Dap. He has no courage, because he beat his wench for giving me *les doux yeux* once; and no wit, because he does not comprehend my thoughts; and he is a son of a whore for his ignorance. I take ignorance worse from any man than the lie, because 'tis as much as to say I am no wit.

Re-enter VINCENT.

You need not take any notice, though, to him what I say.

Vin. Ranger, there is a woman below in a coach would speak with you.

Ran. With me ? [*Exit* RANGER.

Dap. This Ranger, Mr. Vincent, is as false to his friend as his wench.

Vin. You have no reason to say so, but because he is absent.

Dap. 'Tis disobliging to tell a man of his faults to his face. If he had but your grave parts and manly wit, I should adore him ; but, a pox ! he is a mere buffoon, a jack-pudding, let me perish !

Vin. You are an ungrateful fellow. I have heard him maintain you had wit, which was more than e'er you could do for yourself.—I thought you had owned him your Mæcenas.

Dap. A pox ! he cannot but esteem me, 'tis for his honour ; but I cannot but be just for all that—without favour or affection. Yet I confess I love him so well, that I wish he had but the hundredth part of your courage.

Vin. He has had courage to save you from many a beating, to my knowledge.

Dap. Come, come, I wish the man well, and, next to you, better than any man ! and, I am sorry to say it, he has not courage to snuff a candle with his fingers. When he is drunk, indeed, he dares get a clap, or so— and swear at a constable.

Vin. Detracting fop ! when did you see him desert his friend ?

Dap. You have a rough kind of a raillery, Mr. Vincent ; but since you will have it, (though I love the man heartily, I say,) he deserted me once in breaking of windows, for fear of the constables—

Re-enter RANGER.

But you need not take notice to him of what I tell you ; I hate to put a man to the blush.

Ran. I have had just now a visit from my mistress, who is as jealous of me as a wife of her husband when she lies in :—my cousin Lydia,—you have heard me speak of her.

Vin. But she is more troublesome than a wife that lies in, because she follows you to your haunts. Why do you allow her that privilege before her time?

Ran. Faith, I may allow her any privilege, and be too hard for her yet. How do you think I have cheated her to-night?—Women are poor credulous creatures, easily deceived.

Vin. We are poor credulous creatures, when we think 'em so.

Ran. Intending a ramble to St. James's Park to-night, upon some probable hopes of some fresh game I have in chase, I appointed her to stay at home; with a promise to come to her within this hour, that she might not spoil the scent and prevent my sport.

Vin. She'll be even with you when you are married, I warrant you. In the meantime here's her health, Dapperwit.

Ran. Now had he rather be at the window, writing her anagram in the glass with his diamond, or biting his nails in the corner for a fine thought to come and divert us with at the table.

Dap. No, a pox! I have no wit to-night. I am as barren and hide-bound as one of your damned scribbling poets, who are sots in company for all their wit; as a miser is poor for all his money. How do you like the thought?

Vin. Drink, drink!

Dap. Well, I can drink this, because I shall be reprieved presently.

Vin. Who will be so civil to us?

Dap. Sir Simon Addleplot :—I have bespoke him a supper here, for he treats to-night a new rich mistress.

Ran. That spark, who has his fruitless designs upon

the bed-ridden rich widow, down to the suckling heiress in her pissing-clout. He was once the sport, but now the public grievance, of all the fortunes in town ; for he watches them like a younger brother that is afraid to be mumped of his snip,[1] and they cannot steal a marriage, nor stay their stomachs, but he must know it.

Dap. He has now pitched his nets for Gripe's daughter, the rich scrivener, and serves him as a clerk to get admission to her ; which the watchful fop her father denies to all others.

Ran. I thought you had been nibbling at her once, under pretence of love to her aunt.

Dap. I confess I have the same design yet, and Addleplot is but my agent, whilst he thinks me his. He brings me letters constantly from her, and carries mine back.

Vin. Still betraying your best friends !

Dap. I cannot in honour but betray him. Let me perish! the poor young wench is taken with my person, and would scratch through four walls to come to me.

Vin. 'Tis a sign she is kept up close indeed.

Dap. Betray him ! I'll not be traitor to love for any man.

Enter Sir SIMON ADDLEPLOT *with the* Waiter.

Sir Sim. Know 'em ! you are a saucy Jack-straw to question me, faith and troth ; I know everybody, and everybody knows me.

All. Sir Simon ! Sir Simon ! Sir Simon !

Ran. And you are a welcome man to everybody.

Sir Sim. Now, son of a whore, do I know the gentlemen ?—A dog ! would have had a shilling of me before he would let me come to you !

Ran. The rogue has been bred at Court, sure.—Get you out, sirrah.   [*Exit* Waiter.

---

[1] Cheated of his portion.

Sir Sim. He has been bred at a French-house, where they are more unreasonable.

Vin. Here's to you, Sir Simon.

Sir Sim. I cannot drink, for I have a mistress within; though I would not have the people of the house to know it.

Ran. You need not be ashamed of your mistresses, for they are commonly rich.

Sir Sim. And because she is rich, I would conceal her; for I never had a rich mistress yet, but one or other got her from me presently, faith and troth.

Ran. But this is an ill place to conceal a mistress in; every waiter is an intelligencer to your rivals.

Sir Sim. I have a trick for that:—I'll let no waiters come into the room; I'll lay the cloth myself rather.

Ran. But who is your mistress?

Sir Sim. Your servant,—your servant, Mr. Ranger.

Vin. Come, will you pledge me?

Sir Sim. No, I'll spare your wine, if you will spare me Dapperwit's company; I came for that.

Vin. You do us a double favour, to take him and leave the wine.

Sir Sim. Come, come, Dapperwit.

Ran. Do not go, unless he will suffer us to see his mistress too.   [*Aside to* DAPPERWIT.

Sir Sim. Come, come, man.

Dap. Would you have me so uncivil as to leave my company?--they'll take it ill.

Sir Sim. I cannot find her talk without thee.—Pray, gentlemen, persuade Mr. Dapperwit to go with me.

Ran. We will not hinder him of better company.

Dap. Yours is too good to be left rudely.

Sir Sim. Nay, gentlemen, I would desire your company too, if you knew the lady.

Dap. They know her as well as I; you say I know her not.

Sir Sim. You are not everybody.

Ran. Perhaps we do know the lady, Sir Simon.

Sir Sim. You do not, you do not : none of you ever saw her in your lives ;—but if you could be secret, and civil—

Ran. We have drunk yet but our bottle a-piece

Sir Sim. But will you be civil, Mr. Vincent ?

Ran. He dares not look a woman in the face undei three bottles.

Sir Sim. Come along then. But can you be civil, gentlemen ? will you be civil, gentlemen ? pray be civil if you can, and you shall see her.

[*Exit, and returns with* Lady FLIPPANT *and* Mrs. JOYNER.

Dap. How, has he got his jilt here !   [*Aside.*

Ran. The widow Flippant !   [*Aside.*

Vin. Is this the woman that we never saw !   [*Aside.*

L. Flip. Does he bring us into company !—and Dapperwit one ! Though I had married the fool, I thought .o have reserved the wit as well as other ladies.   [*Aside.*

Sir Sim. Nay, look as long as you will, madam, you will find them civil gentlemen, and good company.

L. Flip. I am not in doubt of their civility, but yours.

Mrs. Joyn. You'll never leave snubbing your servants ! Did you not promise to use him kindly ?

[*Aside to* Lady FLIPPANT.

L. Flip. [*Aside to* Mrs. JOYNER.] 'Tis true.—[*Aloud.*] We wanted no good company, Sir Simon, as long as we had yours.

Sir Sim. But they wanted good company, therefore I forced 'em to accept of yours.

L. Flip. They will not think the company good they were forced into, certainly.

Sir Sim. A pox ! I must be using the words in fashion, though I never have any luck with 'em. Mrs. Joyner, help me off.

Mrs. Joyn. I suppose, madam, he means the gentlemen wanted not inclination to your company, but con-

fidence to desire so great an honour; therefore ne
forced 'em.

Dap. What makes this bawd here? Sure, mistress, you
bawds should be like the small cards, though at first you
make up a pack, yet, when the play begins, you should
be put out as useless.

Mrs. Joyn. Well, well, gibing companion: you would
have the pimps kept in only? you would so?

Vin. What, they are quarrelling!

Ran. Pimp and bawd agree now-a-days like doctor
and apothecary.

Sir Sim. Try, madam, if they are not civil gentlemen;
talk with 'em, while I go lay the cloth—no waiter comes
here.—[*Aside.*] My mother used to tell me, I should
avoid all occasions of talking before my mistress, because
silence is a sign of love as well as prudence.

[*Lays the cloth.*

L. Flip. Methinks you look a little yellow on't, Mr.
Dapperwit. I hope you do not censure me because you
find me passing away a night with this fool :—he is not a
man to be jealous of, sure.

Dap. You are not a lady to be jealous of, sure.

L. Flip. No, certainly.—But why do you look as if you
were jealous then?

Dap. If I had met you in Whetstone's park,[1] with a
drunken foot-soldier, I should not have been jealous of you.

L. Flip. Fy, fy! now you are jealous, certainly; for
people always, when they grow jealous, grow rude :—but
I can pardon it since it proceeds from love certainly.

---

[1] Whetstone's Park was the name of the district lying between
Lincoln's Inn Fields and Holborn. The character of its inhabitants
had given it at this time an ill reputation. In Crowne's comedy of
the *Country Wit* (1675) occurs the following allusion to Whetstone's
Park : "After I had gone a little way in a great broad street, I
turned into a Tavern hard by a place they call a Park ; and just as
our Park is all Trees, that Park is all Houses. I asked if they had
any Deer in it, and they told me, not half so many as they used to
have ; but that if I had a mind to a Doe, they would put a Doe
to me."

Dap. I am out of all hopes to be rid of this eternal old acquaintance : when I jeer her, she thinks herself praised ; now I call her whore in plain English she thinks I am jealous.   [*Aside.*

L. Flip. Sweet Mr. Dapperwit, be not so censorious, (I speak for your sake, not my own,) for jealousy is a great torment, but my honour cannot suffer certainly.

Dap. No, certainly ; but the greatest torment I have is—your love.

L. Flip. Alas ! sweet Mr. Dapperwit, indeed love is a torment : but 'tis a sweet torment ; but jealousy is a bitter torment.—I do not go about to cure you of the torment of my love.

Dap. 'Tis a sign so.

L. Flip. Come, come, look up, man ; is that a rival to contest with you ?

Dap. I will contest with no rival, not with my old rival your coachman ; but they have heartily my resignation ; and, to do you a favour, but myself a greater, I will help to tie the knot you are fumbling for now, betwixt your cully here and you.

L. Flip. Go, go, I take that kind of jealousy worst of all, to suspect I would be debauched to beastly matrimony.—But who are those gentlemen, pray ? are they men of fortunes, Mrs. Joyner ?

Mrs. Joyn. I believe so.

L. Flip. Do you believe so, indeed ?—Gentlemen—
                [*Advancing towards* RANGER *and* VINCENT.

Ran. If the civility we owe to ladies had not controlled our envy to Mr. Dapperwit, we had interrupted ere this your private conversation.

L. Flip. Your interruption, sir, had been most civil and obliging ;—for our discourse was of marriage.

Ran. That is a subject, madam, as grateful as common.

L. Flip. O fy, fy ! are you of that opinion too ? I cannot suffer any to talk of it in my company.

Ran. Are you married then, madam?

L. Flip. No, certainly.

Ran. I am sure so much beauty cannot despair of it.

L. Flip. Despair of it!—

Ran. Only those that are married, or cannot be married, hate to hear of marriage.

L. Flip. Yet you must know, sir, my aversion to marriage is such, that you, nor no man breathing, shall ever persuade me to it.

Ran. Cursed be the man should do so rude a thing as to persuade you to anything against your inclination! I would not do it for the world, madam.

L. Flip. Come, come, though you seem to be a civil gentleman, I think you no better than your neighbours. I do not know a man of you all that will not thrust a woman up into a corner, and then talk an hour to her impertinently of marriage.

Ran. You would find me another man in a corner, I assure you, madam; for you should not have a word of marriage from me, whatsoever you might find in my actions of it; I hate talking as much as you.

L. Flip. I hate it extremely.

Ran. I am your man then, madam; for I find just the same fault with your sex as you do with ours :—I ne'er could have to do with woman in my life, but still she would be impertinently talking of marriage to me.

L. Flip. Observe that, Mrs. Joyner.

Dap. Pray, Mr. Ranger, let's go; I had rather drink with Mr. Vincent, than stay here with you; besides 'tis Park-time.

Ran. [*To* DAPPERWIT.] I come.—[*To* Lady FLIP-PANT.] Since you are a lady that hate marriage, I'll do you the service to withdraw the company; for those that hate marriage hate loss of time.

L. Flip. Will you go then, sir? but before you go, sir, pray tell me is your aversion to marriage real?

Ran. As real as yours.

L. Flip. If it were no more real than mine—   [*Aside.*

Ran. Your servant, madam.   [*Turns to go.*

L. Flip. But do you hate marriage certainly?

[*Plucks him back.*

Ran. Certainly.

L. Flip. Come, I cannot believe it : you dissemble it only because I pretend it.

Ran. Do you but pretend it then, madam?

L. Flip. [*Aside*] I shall discover myself—[*Aloud*] I mean, because I hold against it, you do the same in complaisance :—for I have heard say, cunning men think to bring the coy and untractable women to tameness as they do some mad people—by humouring their frenzies.

Ran. I am none of those cunning men, yet have too much wit to entertain the presumption of designing upon you.

L. Flip. 'Twere no such presumption neither.

Dap. Come away; 'sdeath! don't you see your danger?

Ran. Those aims are for Sir Simon.—Good night, madam.

L. Flip. Will you needs go, then?—[*To* Sir SIMON] The gentlemen are a going, Sir Simon ; will you let 'em?

Sir Sim. Nay, madam, if you cannot keep 'em, how should I?

L. Flip. Stay, sir; because you hate marriage, I'll sing you a new song against it.   [*Sings.*

A spouse I do hate,
For either she's false or she's jealous ;
But give us a mate
Who nothing will ask us or tell us.

She stands on no terms,
Nor chaffers, by way of indenture,
Her love for your farms ;
But takes her kind man at a venture.

> If all prove not right,
> Without an act, process, or warning,
>   From wife for a night
> You may be divorced in the morning
>
> When parents are slaves,
> Their brats cannot be any other;
>   Great wits and great braves
> Have always a punk [1] to their mother.

Though it be the fashion for women of quality to sing any song whatever, because the words are not distinguished, yet I should have blushed to have done it now, but for you, sir.

Ran. The song is edifying, the voice admirable—and, once more, I am your servant, madam.

L. Flip. What, will you go too, Mr. Dapperwit?

Sir Sim. Pray, Mr. Dapperwit, do not you go too.

Dap. I am engaged.

Sir Sim. Well, if we cannot have their company, we will not have their room: ours is a private backroom; they have paid their reckoning, let's go thither again.

L. Flip. But pray, sweet Mr. Dapperwit, do not go. Keep him, Sir Simon.

Sir Sim. I cannot keep him.

      [*Exeunt* VINCENT, RANGER, *and* DAPPERWIT.
It is impossible; (the world is so;)
One cannot keep one's friend, and mistress too. [*Exeunt.*

----

[1] Strumpet.

ACT THE SECOND.

SCENE I.—*St. James's Park at night.*

Enter RANGER, VINCENT, *and* DAPPERWIT.

 Ran. Hang me, if I am not pleased extremely with this new-fashioned cater-wauling, this mid-night coursing in the park.

Vin. A man may come after supper with his three bottles in his head, reel himself sober, without reproof from his mother, aunt, or grave relation.

Ran. May bring his bashful wench, and not have her put out of countenance by the impudent honest women of the town.

Dap. And a man of wit may have the better of the dumb show of well-trimmed vest or fair peruke :—no man's now is whitest.

Ran. And now no woman's modest or proud ; for her blushes are hid, and the rubies on her lips are dyed, and all sleepy and glimmering eyes have lost their attraction.

Vin. And now a man may carry a bottle under his arm instead of his hat ;—and no observing spruce fop will miss the cravat that lies on one's shoulder, or count the pimples on one's face.

Dap. And now the brisk repartee ruins the complaisant cringe, or wise grimace.—Something 'twas, we men of virtue always loved the night.

Ran. O blessed season !

Vin. For good-fellows.

Ran. For lovers.

Dap. And for the Muses.

Ran. When I was a boy I loved the night so well, I had a strong vocation to be a bellman's apprentice.

Vin. I, a drawer.

Dap. And I, to attend the waits of Westminster, let me perish !

Ran. But why do we not do the duty of this and such other places ;—walk, censure, and speak ill of all we meet ?

Dap. 'Tis no fault of mine, let me perish !

Vin. Fy, fy ! satirical gentlemen, this is not your time ; you cannot distinguish a friend from a fop.

Dap. No matter, no matter ; they will deserve amongst 'em the worst we can say.

Ran. Who comes here, Dapperwit ?

> [*People walk slowly over the stage.*

Dap. By the toss of his head, training of his feet, and his elbows playing at bo-peep behind his back, it should be my Lord Easy.

Ran. And who the woman ?

Dap. My Lord what-d'ye-call's daughter, that had a child by—

Vin. Dapperwit, hold your tongue.

Ran. How ! are you concerned ?

Vin. Her brother's an honest fellow, and will drink his glass.

Ran. Prithee, Vincent, Dapperwit did not hinder drinking to-night, though he spake against it ; why, then, should you interrupt his sport ?—Now, let him talk of anybody.

Vin. So he will,—till you cut his throat.

Ran. Why should you on all occasions thwart him, contemn him, and maliciously look grave at his jests only ?

Vin. Why does he always rail against my friends, then, and my best friend—a beer-glass-?

Ran. Dapperwit, be your own advocate : my game, I think, is before me there.   [*Exit.*

Dap. This Ranger, I think, has all the ill qualities of all your town fops ;—leaving his company for a spruce lord or a wench.

Vin. Nay, if you must rail at your own best friends, I may forgive you railing at mine.

Enter LYDIA *and* Lady FLIPPANT.—*They walk over the stage.*

Lyd. False Ranger, shall I find thee here ?   [*Aside.*

Vin. Those are women, are they not ?   [*To* DAPPER.

Dap. The least seems to be my Lucy, sure.   [*Aside.*

Vin. Faith, I think I dare speak to a woman in the dark !—let's try.

Dap. They are persons of quality of my acquaintance ; —hold !

Vin. Nay, if they are persons of quality of your acquaintance, I may be the bolder with 'em.

[*The* Ladies *go off, they follow them.*

Re-enter LYDIA *and* Lady FLIPPANT.

Lyd. I come hither to make a discovery to-night.

L. Flip. Of my love to you, certainly ; for nobody but you could have debauched me to the Park, certainly.   I would not return another night, if it were to redeem my dear husband from his grave.

Lyd. I believe you :—but to get another, widow.

L. Flip. Another husband, another husband, foh !

Lyd. There does not pass a night here but many a match is made.

L. Flip. That a woman of honour should have the word match in her mouth !—but I hope, madam, the fellows do not make honourable love here, do they ? I abominate honourable love, upon my honour

Lyd. If they should make honourable love here, I know you would prevent 'em.

Re-enter VINCENT *and* DAPPERWIT.—*They walk slowly towards the* Ladies.

But here come two men will inform you what to do.

L. Flip. Do they come?—are they men certainly?

Lyd. Prepare for an assault, they'll put you to't.

L. Flip. Will they put us to't certainly? I was never put to't yet. If they should put us to't, I should drop down, down, certainly.

Lyd. I believe, truly, you would not have power to run away.

L. Flip. Therefore I will not stay the push.—They come! they come! oh, the fellows come!

> [Lady FLIPPANT *runs away,* LYDIA *follows, and* VINCENT *and* DAPPERWIT *after them.*

Re-enter Lady FLIPPANT *at the other side, alone.*

L. Flip. So! I am got off clear! I did not run from the men, but my companion. For all their brags, men have hardly courage to set upon us when our number is equal; now they shall see I defy 'em :—for we women have always most courage when we are alone. But, a pox! the lazy rogues come not! or they are drunk and cannot run. Oh drink! abominable drink! instead of inflaming love, it quenches it; and for one lover it encourages, it makes a thousand impotent. Curse on all wine! even Rhenish wine and sugar—

Enter Sir SIMON ADDLEPLOT, *muffled in a cloak.*

But fortune will not see me want; here comes a single bully,—I wish he may stand ;—

> For now a-nights the jostling nymph is bolder
> Than modern satyr with his cloak o'er shoulder.

Well met, sir. [*She puts on her mask.*

Sir Sim. How shall I know that, forsooth? Who are you? do you know me?

L. Flip. Who are you? don't you know me?

Sir Sim. Not I, faith and troth!

L. Flip. I am glad on't; for no man e'er liked a woman the better for having known her before.

Sir Sim. Ay, but then one can't be so free with a new acquaintance as with an old one; she may deny one the civility.

L. Flip. Not till you ask her.

Sir Sim. But I am afraid to be denied.

L. Flip. Let me tell you, sir, you cannot disoblige us women more than in distrusting us.

Sir Sim. Pish! what should one ask for, when you know one's meaning?—but shall I deal freely with you?

L. Flip. I love, of my life, men should deal freely with me; there are so few men will deal freely with one—

Sir Sim. Are you not a fireship,[1] a punk, madam?

L. Flip. Well, sir, I love raillery.

Sir Sim. Faith and troth, I do not rally, I deal freely.

L. Flip. This is the time and place for freedom, sir.

Sir Sim. Are you handsome?

L. Flip. Joan's as good as my lady in the dark, certainly: but men that deal freely never ask questions, certainly.

Sir Sim. How then! I thought to deal freely, and put a woman to the question, had been all one.

L. Flip. But, let me tell you, those that deal freely indeed, take a woman by—

Sir Sim. What, what, what, what?

L. Flip. By the hand—and lead her aside.

Sir Sim. Now I understand you; come along then.

Enter behind Musicians *with torches.*

L. Flip. What unmannerly rascals are those that bring

---

[1] A prostitute.

light into the Park? 'twill not be taken well from 'em by
the women, certainly.—[*Aside.*]   Still disappointed!

Sir Sim. Oh, the fiddles, the fiddles! I sent for them
hither to oblige the women, not to offend 'em; for I
intend to serenade the whole Park to-night.   But my
frolic is not without an intrigue, faith and troth: for I
know the fiddles will call the whole herd of vizard masks
together; and then shall I discover if a strayed mistress
of mine be not amongst 'em, whom I treated to-night at
the French-house; but as soon as the jilt had eat up my
meat and drunk her two bottles, she ran away from me,
and left me alone.

L. Flip. How! is it he? Addleplot!—that I could not
know him by his faith and troth!   [*Aside.*

Sir Sim. Now I would understand her tricks; because
I intend to marry her, and should be glad to know what
I must trust to.

L. Flip. So thou shalt;—but not yet.   [*Aside.*

Sir Sim. Though I can give a great guess already;
for if I have any intrigue or sense in me, she is as arrant
a jilt as ever pulled pillow from under husband's head,
faith and troth.   Moreover she is bow-legged, hopper-
hipped, and, betwixt pomatum and Spanish red, has a
complexion like a Holland cheese, and no more teeth left
than such as give a *haut goût* to her breath; but she is
rich, faith and troth.

L. Flip. [*Aside.*] Oh rascal! he has heard somebody
else say all this of me.   But I must not discover myself,
lest I should be disappointed of my revenge; for I will
marry him.   [*The* Musicians *approaching, exit* FLIPPANT.

Sir Sim. What, gone!—come then, strike up, my lads.

Enter Men *and* Women *in vizards—a Dance, during
which* Sir SIMON ADDLEPLOT, *for the most part,
stands still in a cloak and vizard; but sometimes goes
about peeping, and examining the* Women's *clothes—
the Dance ended, all exeunt.*

Re-enter Lady FLIPPANT *and* LYDIA, *after them* VINCENT *and* DAPPERWIT.

L. Flip. [*To* LYDIA.] Nay, if you stay any longer, I must leave you again.   [*Going off.*

Vin. We have overtaken them at last again. These are they: they separate too; and that's but a challenge to us.

Dap. Let me perish! ladies—

Lyd. Nay, good madam, let's unite, now here's the common enemy upon us.

Vin. Damn me! ladies—

Dap. Hold, a pox! you are too rough.—Let me perish! ladies—

Lyd. Not for want of breath, gentlemen :—we'll stay rather.

Dap. For want of your favour rather, sweet ladies.

L. Flip. [*Aside.*] That's Dapperwit, false villain! but he must not know I am here. If he should, I should lose his thrice agreeable company, and he would run from me as fast as from the bailiffs. [*To* LYDIA.] What! you will not talk with 'em, I hope?

Lyd. Yes, but I will.

L. Flip. Then you are a Park-woman certainly, and you will take it kindly if I leave you.

Lyd. No, you must not leave me.

L. Flip. Then you must leave them.

Lyd. I'll see if they are worse company than you, first.

L. Flip. Monstrous impudence!—will you not come?
            [*Pulls* LYDIA.

Vin. Nay, madam, I never suffer any violence to be used to a woman but what I do myself: she must stay, and you must not go.

L. Flip. Unhand me, you rude fellow!

Vin. Nay, now I am sure you will stay and be kind; for coyness in a woman is as little sign of true modesty, as huffing in a man is of true courage.

Dap. Use her gently, and speak soft things to her.

Lyd. [*Aside.*] Now do I guess I know my coxcomb.—
[*To* DAPPERWIT.] Sir, I am extremely glad I am fallen
into the hands of a gentleman that can speak soft things;
and this is so fine a night to hear soft things in;—morning, I should have said.

Dap. It will not be morning, dear madam, till you
pull off your mask.—[*Aside.*] That I think was brisk.

Lyd. Indeed, dear sir, my face would frighten back
the sun.

Dap. With glories more radiant than his own.—
[*Aside.*] I keep up with her, I think.

Lyd. But why would you put me to the trouble of
lighting the world, when I thought to have gone to
sleep?

Dap. You only can do it, dear madam, let me perish!

Lyd. But why would you (of all men) practise treason
against your friend Phœbus, and depose him for a mere
stranger?

Dap. I think she knows me.   [*Aside.*

Lyd. But he does not do you justice, I believe; and
you are so positively cock-sure of your wit, you would
refer to a mere stranger your plea to the bay-tree.

Dap. She jeers me, let me perish!   [*Aside.*

Vin. Dapperwit, a little of your aid; for my lady's in-
vincibly dumb.

Dap. Would mine had been so too!   [*Aside.*

Vin. I have used as many arguments to make her
speak, as are requisite to make other women hold their
tongues.

Dap. Well, I am ready to change sides.—Yet before
I go, madam, since the moon consents now I should see
your face, let me desire you to pull off your mask; which
to a handsome lady is a favour, I'm sure.

Lyd. Truly, sir, I must not be long in debt to you for
the obligation; pray let me hear you recite some of your
verses; which to a wit is a favour, I'm sure.

Dap. Madam, it belongs to your sex to be obliged first ; pull off your mask, and I'll pull out my paper.— [*Aside.*] Brisk again, of my side.

Lyd. 'Twould be in vain, for you would want a candle now.

Dap. [*Aside.*] I dare not make use again of the lustre of her face.—[*To* LYDIA.] I'll wait upon you home then, madam.

Lyd. Faith, no ; I believe it will not be much to our advantages to bring my face or your poetry to light : for I hope you have yet a pretty good opinion of my face, and so have I of your wit. But if you are for proving your wit, why do not you write a play ?

Dap. Because 'tis now no more reputation to write a play, than it is honour to be a knight. Your true wit despises the title of poet, as much as your true gentleman the title of knight ; for as a man may be a knight and no gentleman, so a man may be a poet and no wit, let me perish !

Lyd. Pray, sir, how are you dignified or distinguished amongst the rates of wits ? and how many rates are there ?

Dap. There are as many degrees of wits as of lawyers : as there is first your solicitor, then your attorney, then your pleading-counsel, then your chamber-counsel, and then your judge ; so there is first your court-wit, your coffee-wit, your poll-wit, or politic-wit, your chamber-wit, or scribble-wit, and last of all, your judge-wit, or critic.

Lyd. But are there as many wits as lawyers ? Lord, what will become of us !—What employment can they have ? how are they known ?

Dap. First, your court-wit is a fashionable, insinuating, flattering, cringing, grimacing fellow—and has wit enough to solicit a suit of love ; and if he fail, he has malice enough to ruin the woman with a dull lampoon :—but he rails still at the man that is absent, for you must know all wits rail ; and his wit properly lies in combing perukes,

matching ribbons, and being severe, as they call it, upon
other people's clothes.

Lyd. Now, what is the coffee-wit?

Dap. He is a lying, censorious, gossiping, quibbling
wretch, and sets people together by the ears over that sober
drink, coffee : he is a wit, as he is a commentator, upon
the Gazette ; and he rails at the pirates of Algier, the
Grand Signior of Constantinople, and the Christian
Grand Signior.

Lyd. What kind of man is your poll-wit?

Dap. He is a fidgetting, busy, dogmatical, hot-headed
fop, that speaks always in sentences and proverbs, (as
other in similitudes,) and he rails perpetually against the
present government. His wit lies in projects and mono-
polies, and penning speeches for young parliament men.

Lyd. But what is your chamber-wit, or scribble-wit?

Dap. He is a poring, melancholy, modest sot, ashamed
of the world : he searches all the records of wit, to com-
pile a breviate of them for the use of players, printers,
booksellers, and sometimes cooks, tobacco-men ; he employs his railing against the ignorance of the age, and all
that have more money than he.

Lyd. Now your last.

Dap. Your judge-wit, or critic, is all these together,
and yet has the wit to be none of them : he can think,
speak, write, as well as the rest, but scorns (himself a
judge) to be judged by posterity : he rails at all the other
classes of wits, and his wit lies in damning all but himself :—he is your true wit.

Lyd. Then, I suspect you are of his form.

Dap. I cannot deny it, madam.

Vin. Dapperwit, you have been all this time on the
wrong side ; for you love to talk all, and here's a lady
would not have hindered you.

Dap. A pox! I have been talking too long indeed
here ; for wit is lost upon a silly weak woman, as well as
courage   [*Aside.*

Vin. I have used all common means to move a woman's tongue and mask; I called her ugly, old, and old acquaintance, and yet she would not disprove me :—but here comes Ranger, let him try what he can do ; for, since my mistress is dogged, I'll go sleep alone.   [*Exit.*

Re-enter RANGER.

Lyd. [*Aside.*] Ranger! 'tis he indeed : I am sorry he is here, but glad I discovered him before I went. Yet he must not discover me, lest I should be prevented hereafter in finding him out. False Ranger !—[*To* Lady FLIPPANT.] Nay, if they bring fresh force upon us, madam, 'tis time to quit the field.

[*Exeunt* LYDIA *and* Lady FLIPPANT.

Ran. What, play with your quarry till it fly from you !

Dap. You frighten it away.

Ran. Ha ! is not one of those ladies in mourning ?

Dap. All women are so by this light.

Ran. But you might easily discern. Don't you know her ?

Dap. No.

Ran. Did you talk with her ?

Dap. Yes, she is one of your brisk silly baggages.

Ran. 'Tis she, 'tis she !—I was afraid I saw her before ; let us follow 'em : prithee make haste.—[*Aside.*] 'Tis Lydia.   [*Exeunt.*

Re-enter, on the other side, LYDIA *and* Lady FLIPPANT— DAPPERWIT *and* RANGER *following them at a distance.*

Lyd. They follow us yet, I fear.

L. Flip. You do not fear it certainly ; otherwise you would not have encouraged them.

Lyd. For Heaven's sake, madam, waive your quarrel a little, and let us pass by your coach, and so on foot to your acquaintance in the old Pall-mall [1] : for I would not be discovered by the man that came up last to us.   [*Exeunt.*

[1] The present Pall Mall, so called from the game of Pall Mall

SCENE II.—CHRISTINA'S *Lodging*.

Enter CHRISTINA *and* ISABEL.

Isa. For Heaven's sake, undress yourself, madam! They'll not return to-night : all people have left the Park an hour ago.

Chris. What is't o'clock ?

Isa. 'Tis past one.

Chris. It cannot be !

Isa. I thought that time had only stolen from happy lovers :—the disconsolate have nothing to do but to tell the clock.

Chris. I can only keep account with my misfortunes.

Isa. I am glad they are not innumerable.

Chris. And, truly, my undergoing so often your impertinency is not the least of them.

Isa. I am then more glad, madam, for then they cannot be great ; and it is in my power, it seems, to make you in part happy, if I could but hold this villainous tongue of mine : but then let the people of the town hold their tongues if they will, for I cannot but tell you what they say.

Chris. What do they say ?

Isa. Faith, madam, I am afraid to tell you, now I think on't.

Chris. Is it so ill?

Isa. O, such base, unworthy things !

Chris. Do they say I was really Clerimont's wench, as he boasted ; and that the ground of the quarrel betwixt Valentine and him was not Valentine's vindication of my honour, but Clerimont's jealousy of him ?

Isa. Worse, worse a thousand times !—such villainous things to the utter ruin of your reputation !

formerly played there with ball and mallet.   In Wycherley's time Pall Mall was already a street of houses, and the game was then played at the Mall in St. James's Park, also called Pall Mall.

Chris. What are they?

Isa. Faith, madam, you'll be angry : 'tis the old trick of lovers to hate their informers, after they have made 'em such.

Chris. I will not be angry.

Isa. They say then, since Mr. Valentine's flying into France you are grown mad, have put yourself into mourning, live in a dark room, where you'll see nobody, nor take any rest day or night, but rave and talk to yourself perpetually.

Chris. Now, what else?

Isa. But the surest sign of your madness is, they say, because you are desperately resolved (in case my Lord Clerimont should die of his wounds) to transport yourself and fortune into France to Mr. Valentine, a man that has not a groat to return you in exchange.

Chris. All this, hitherto, is true ; now to the rest.

Isa. Indeed, madam, I have no more to tell you. I was sorry, I'm sure, to hear so much of any lady of mine.

Chris. Insupportable insolence !

Isa. [*Aside.*] This is some revenge for my want of sleep to-night.—[*Knocking at the door.*] So, I hope my old second is come ; 'tis seasonable relief.   [*Exit.*

Chris. Unhappy Valentine ! couldst thou but see how soon thy absence and misfortunes have disbanded all thy friends, and turned thy slaves all renegadoes, thou sure wouldst prize my only faithful heart !

Enter Lady FLIPPANT, LYDIA, *and* ISABEL.

L. Flip. Hail, faithful shepherdess ! but, truly, I had not kept my word with you, in coming back to-night, if it had not been for this lady, who has her intrigues too with the fellows as well as you.

Lyd. Madam, under my Lady Flippant's protection, I am confident to beg yours ; being just now pursued out of the Park by a relation of mine, by whom it imports me

extremely not to be discovered :—[*Knocking at the door.*]
but I fear he is now at the door.—[*To* ISABEL, *who goes
out.*] Let me desire you to deny me to him courageously ;
—for he will hardly believe he can be mistaken in
me.

Chris. In such an occasion, where impudence is
requisite, she will serve you as faithfully as you can
wish, madam.

L. Flip. Come, come, madam, do not upbraid her with
her assurance, a qualification that only fits her for a lady's
service. A fine woman of the town can be no more without a woman that can make an excuse with assurance,
than she can be without a glass, certainly.

Chris. She needs no advocate.

L. Flip. How can any one alone manage an amorous
intrigue ? though the birds are tame, somebody must help
draw the net. If 'twere not for a woman that could make
an excuse with assurance, how should we wheedle, jilt,
trace, discover, countermine, undermine, and blow up the
stinking fellows ? which is all the pleasure I receive, or
design by them ; for I never admitted a man to my conversation, but for his punishment, certainly.

Chris. Nobody will doubt that, certainly.

Re-enter ISABEL.

Isa. Madam, the gentleman will not be mistaken : he
says you are here, he saw you come in ; he is your relation, his name's Ranger, and is come to wait upon you
home. I had much ado to keep him from coming up.

Lyd. [*To* CHRISTINA.] Madam, for Heaven's sake, help
me ! 'tis yet in your power ; if but, while I retire into
your dining-room, you will please to personate me, and
own yourself for her he pursued out of the Park : you are
in mourning too, and your stature so much mine it will
not contradict you.

Chris. I am sorry, madam, I must dispute any command of yours. I have made a resolution to see the face

of no man, till an unfortunate friend of mine, now out of the kingdom, return.

Lyd. By that friend, and by the hopes you have to see him, let me conjure you to keep me from the sight of mine now. Dear madam, let your charity prevail over your superstition.

Isa. He comes, he comes, madam !

[LYDIA *withdraws, and stands unseen at the door.*

Enter RANGER.

Ran. Ha ! this is no Lydia. [*Aside.*

Chris. What, unworthy defamer, has encouraged you to offer this insolence ?

Ran. She is liker Lydia in her style than her face. I see I am mistaken ; but to tell her I followed her for another, were an affront rather than an excuse. She's a glorious creature ! [*Aside.*

Chris. Tell me, sir, whence had you reason for this your rude pursuit of me, into my lodgings, my chamber ? why should you follow me ?

Ran. Faith, madam, because you ran away from me.

Chris. That was no sign of an acquaintance.

Ran. You'll pardon me, madam.

Chris. Then, it seems, you mistook me for another, and the night is your excuse, which blots out all distinctions. But now you are satisfied in your mistake, I hope you will seek out your woman in another place.

Ran. Madam, I allow not the excuse you make for me. If I have offended, I will rather be condemned for my love, than pardoned for my insensibility.

Lyd. How's that ? [*Aside.*

Chris. What do you say ?

Ran. Though the night had been darker, my heart would not have suffered me to follow any one but you :—he has been too long acquainted with you to mistake you.

Lyd. What means this tenderness? he mistook me for her sure.   [*Aside.*

Chris. What says the gentleman? did you know me then, sir?

Ran. [*Aside.*] Not I, the devil take me! but I must on now.—[*Aloud.*] Could you imagine, madam, by the innumerable crowd of your admirers, you had left any man free in the town, or ignorant of the power of your beauty?

Chris. I never saw your face before, that I remember.

Ran. Ah, madam! you would never regard your humblest slave; I was till now a modest lover.

Lyd. Falsest of men!   [*Aside.*

Chris. My woman said, you came to seek a relation here, not a mistress.

Ran. I must confess, madam, I thought you would sooner disprove my dissembled error, than admit my visit, and was resolved to see you.

Lyd. 'Tis clear!   [*Aside.*

Ran. Indeed, when I followed you first out of the Park, I was afraid you might have been a certain relation of mine, for your statures and habits are the same; but when you entered here, I was with joy convinced. Besides, I would not for the world have given her troublesome love so much encouragement, to have disturbed my future addresses to you; for the foolish woman does perpetually torment me to make our relation nearer; but never more in vain than since I have seen you, madam.

Lyd. How! shall I suffer this? 'tis clear he disappointed me to-night for her, and made me stay at home that I might not disappoint him of her company in the Park.   [*Aside.*

Chris. I am amazed! but let me tell you, sir, if the lady were here, I would satisfy her the sight of me should never frustrate her ambitious designs upon her cruel kinsman.

Lyd. I wish you could satisfy me.   [*Aside.*

Ran. If she were here, she would satisfy you she were
not capable of the honour to be taken for you :—though
in the dark. Faith, my cousin is but a tolerable woman
to a man that had not seen you.

Chris. Sure, to my plague, this is the first time you
ever saw me !

Ran. Sure, to the plague of my poor heart, 'tis not the
hundredth time I have seen you ! For, since the time I
saw you first, you have not been at the Park, playhouse,
Exchange,[1] or other public place, but I saw you ; for it
was my business to watch and follow.

Chris. Pray, when did you see me last at the Park,
playhouse, or Exchange ?

Ran. Some two, three days, or a week ago.

Chris. I have not been this month out of this chamber.

Lyd. That is to delude me. [*Aside.*

Chris. I knew you were mistaken.

Ran. You'll pardon a lover's memory, madam.—
[*Aside.*] A pox ! I have hanged myself in my own line.
One would think my perpetual ill-luck in lying should
break me of the quality ; but, like a losing gamester, I
am still for pushing on, till none will trust me.

Chris. Come, sir, you run out of one error into a
greater : you would excuse the rudeness of your mistake,
and intrusion at this hour into my lodgings, with your
gallantry to me,—more unseasonable and offensive.

Ran. Nay, I am in love I see, for I blush and have not
a word to say for myself.

Chris. But, sir, if you will needs play the gallant, pray
leave my house before morning, lest you should be seen

---

[1] *i.e.* The New Exchange, a long building, erected upon the
site of the stables of Durham House, on the south side of the
Strand, and nearly opposite Bedford Street. Opened in 1609, it
became a fashionable lounge after the Restoration, and was pulled
down in 1737. "It was erected partly on the plan of the Royal
Exchange, with vaults beneath, over which was an open paved
arcade ; and above were walks of shops, occupied by perfumers and
publishers, milliners and sempstresses."—*Timbs' Curiosities ¿*
London.

go hence, to the scandal of my honour. Rather than that should be, I'll call up the house and neighbours to bear witness I bid you begone.

Ran. Since you take a night visit so ill, madam, I will never wait upon you again but by day. I go, that I may hope to return ; and, for once, I wish you a good night without me.

Chris. Good night, for as long as I live.

[*Exit* RANGER.

Lyd. And good night to my love, I'm sure.   [*Aside.*

Chris. Though I have done you an inconsiderable service, I assure you, madam, you are not a little obliged to me.—[*Aside.*] Pardon me, dear Valentine !

Lyd. I know not yet whether I am more obliged than injured : when I do, I assure you, madam, I shall not be insensible of either.

Chris. I fear, madam, you are as liable to mistakes as your kinsman.

Lyd. I fear I am more subject to 'em : it may be for want of sleep, therefore I'll go home.

Chris. My Lady Flippant, good night.

L. Flip. Good night, or rather good morrow, faithful shepherdess.

Chris. I'll wait on you down.

Lyd. Your coach stays yet, I hope.

L. Flip. Certainly.   [*Exeunt.*

SCENE III.—*The Street before* CHRISTINA'S *Lodging.*

Enter RANGER *and* DAPPERWIT.

Dap. I was a faithful sentinel : nobody came out, let me perish !

Ran. No, no, I hunted upon a wrong scent ; I thought I had followed a woman, but found her an angel.

Dap. What is her name?

Ran. That you must tell me. What very fine woman is there lives hereabouts?

Dap. Faith, I know not any. She is, I warrant you, some fine woman of a term's standing or so in the town; such as seldom appear in public, but in their balconies, where they stand so constantly, one would think they had hired no other part of the house.

Ran. And look like the pictures which painters expose to draw in customers;—but I must know who she is. Vincent's lodging is hard by, I'll go and inquire of him, and lie with him to-night: but if he will not let me, I'll lie with you, for my lodging is too far off.

Dap. Then I will go before, and expect you at mine.

[*Exeunt.*

SCENE IV.—VINCENT'S *Lodging*.

Enter VINCENT *and* VALENTINE *in a riding habit, as newly from a journey.*

Vin. Your mistress, dear Valentine, will not be more glad to see you! but my wonder is no less than my joy, that you would return ere you were informed Clerimont were out of danger. His surgeons themselves have not been assured of his recovery till within these two days.

Val. I feared my mistress, not my life. My life I could trust again with my old enemy Fortune; but no longer my mistress in the hands of my greater enemies, her relations.

Vin. Your fear was in the wrong place, then: for though my Lord Clerimont live, he and his relations may put you in more danger of your life than your mistress's relations can of losing her.

Val. Would any could secure me her! I would myself secure my life, for I should value it then.

Vin. Come, come; her relations can do you no hurt. I dare swear, if her mother should but say, "Your hat did not cock handsomely," she would never ask her blessing again.

Val. Prithee leave thy fooling, and tell me if, since my departure, she has given evidences of her love, to clear those doubts I went away with :—for as absence is the bane of common and bastard love, 'tis the vindication of that which is true and generous.

Vin. Nay, if you could ever doubt her love, you deserve to doubt on; for there is no punishment great enough for jealousy—but jealousy.

Val. You may remember, I told you before my flight I had quarrelled with the defamer of my mistress, but I thought I had killed my rival.

Vin. But pray give me now the answer which the suddenness of your flight denied me ;—how could Clerimont hope to subdue her heart by the assault of her honour?

Val. Pish! it might be the stratagem of a rival to make me desist.

Vin. For shame! if 'twere not rather to vindicate her, than satisfy you, I would not tell you how like a Penelope she has behaved herself in your absence.

Val. Let me know.

Vin. Then know, the next day you went she put herself in mourning, and—

Val. That might be for Clerimont, thinking him dead, as all the world besides thought.

Vin. Still turning the dagger's point on yourself! hear me out. I say she put herself into mourning for you— locked herself in her chamber this month for you—shut out her barking relations for you—has not seen the sun or the face of man since she saw you—thinks and talks of nothing but you—sends to me daily to hear of you—

and, in short, (I think,) is mad for you. All this I can swear; for I am to her so near a neighbour, and so inquisitive a friend for you—

Enter Servant.

Serv. Mr. Ranger, sir, is coming up.

Vin. What brings him now? he comes to lie with me.

Val. Who, Ranger?

Vin. Yes. Pray retire a little, till I send him off:—unless you have a mind to have your arrival published to-morrow in the coffee-houses.

[VALENTINE *retires to the door behind.*

Enter RANGER.

Ran. What! not yet a-bed? your man is laying you to sleep with usquebaugh or brandy; is he not so?

Vin. What punk [1] will not be troubled with you to-night, therefore I am?—is it not so?

Ran. I have been turned out of doors, indeed, just now, by a woman,—but such a woman, Vincent!

Vin. Yes, yes, your women are always such women!

Ran. A neighbour of yours, and I'm sure the finest you have.

Vin. Prithee do not asperse my neighbourhood with your acquaintance; 'twould bring a scandal upon an alley.

Ran. Nay, I do not know her; therefore I come to you.

Vin. 'Twas no wonder she turned you out of doors, then; and if she had known you, 'twould have been a wonder she had let you stay. But where does she live?

Ran. Five doors off, on the right hand.

Vin. Pish! pish!—

Ran. What's the matter?

Vin. Does she live there, do you say?

---

[1] Strumpet.

Ran. Yes; I observed them exactly, that my account from you might be exact. Do you know who lives there?

Vin. Yes, so well, that I know you are mistaken.

Ran. Is she not a young lady scarce eighteen, of extraordinary beauty, her stature next to low, and in mourning?

Val. What is this? [*Aside.*

Vin. She is; but if you saw her, you broke in at window.

Ran. I chased her home from the Park, indeed, taking her for another lady who had some claim to my heart, till she showed a better title to't.

Vin. Hah! hah! hah!

Val. Was she at the Park, then? and have I a new rival? [*Aside.*

Vin. From the Park did you follow her, do you say? —I knew you were mistaken.

Ran. I tell you I am not.

Vin. If you are sure it was that house, it might be perhaps her woman stolen to the Park, unknown to her lady.

Ran. My acquaintance does usually begin with the maid first, but now 'twas with the mistress, I assure you.

Vin. The mistress!—I tell you she has not been out of her doors since Valentine's flight. She is his mistress, —the great heiress, Christina.

Ran. I tell you then again, I followed that Christina from the Park home, where I talked with her half an hour, and intend to see her to-morrow again.

Val. Would she talk with him too! [*Aside.*

Vin. It cannot be.

Ran. Christina do you call her? Faith I am sorry she is an heiress, lest it should bring the scandal of interest, and the design of lucre, upon my love.

Vin. No, no, her face and virtues will free you from that censure. But, however, 'tis not fairly done to rival your friend Valentine in his absence; and when he is

present you know 'twill be dangerous, by my Lord Clerimont's example. Faith, if you have seen her, I would
not advise you to attempt it again.

Ran. You may be merry, sir, you are not in love;
your advice I come not for, nor will I for your assistance.
—Good night.   [*Exit.*

Val. Here's your Penelope! the woman that had not
seen the sun, nor face of man, since my departure! for
it seems she goes out in the night, when the sun is absent,
and faces are not distinguished.

Vin. Why! do you believe him?

Val. Should I believe you?

Vin. 'Twere more for your interest, and you would be
less deceived. If you believe him, you must doubt the
chastity of all the fine women in town, and five miles
about.

Val. His reports of them will little invalidate his
testimony with me.

Vin. He spares not the innocents in bibs and aprons.
I'll secure you, he has made (at best) some gross mistake
concerning Christina, which to-morrow will discover; in
the meantime let us go to sleep.

Val. I will not hinder you, because I cannot enjoy it
myself :—

Hunger, Revenge, to sleep are petty foes,
But only Death the jealous eyes can close.

                                    [*Exeunt.*

ACT THE THIRD.

SCENE I.—*A Room in* Mrs. CROSSBITE'S *House.*

Enter Mrs. JOYNER *and* Mrs. CROSSBITE.

RS. JOYN. Good morrow, gossip.

Mrs. Cros. Good morrow;—but why up so early, good gossip?

Mrs. Joyn. My care and passionate concern for you and yours would not let me rest, in truly.

Mrs. Cros. For me and mine?

Mrs. Joyn. You know we have known one another long; I think it be some nine-and-thirty years since you were married.

Mrs. Cros. Nine-and-thirty years old, mistress! I'd have you to know, I am no far-born child; and if the register had not been burned in the last great fire, alas!— but my face needs no register sure: nine-and-thirty years old, said you?

Mrs. Joyn. I said you had been so long married; but, indeed, you bear your years as well as any she in Pepper-alley.

Mrs. Cros. Nine-and-thirty, mistress!

Mrs. Joyn. This it is; a woman, now-a-days, had rather you should find her faulty with a man, I warrant you, than discover her age, I warrant you.

Mrs. Cros. Marry, and 'tis the greatest secret far. Tell a miser he is rich, and a woman she is old,—you will get no money of him, nor kindness of her. To tell me I was nine-and-thirty—(I say no more) 'twas un neighbourly done of you, mistress.

Mrs. Joyn. My memory confesses my age, it seems, as much as my face; for I thought—

Mrs. Cros. Pray talk nor think no more of any one's age; but say what brought you hither so early.

Mrs. Joyn. How does my sweet god-daughter, poor wretch?

Mrs. Cros. Well, very well.

Mrs. Joyn. Ah, sweet creature! Alas! alas!—I am sorry for her.

Mrs. Cros. Why, what has she done to deserve your sorrow, or my reprehension?

Enter LUCY, *and stands unseen at the door.*

Lucy. What, are they talking of me?   [*Aside.*

Mrs. Joyn. In short, she was seen going into the meet-inghouse of the wicked, otherwise called the playhouse, hand in hand with that vile fellow Dapperwit.

Mrs. Cros. Mr. Dapperwit! let me tell you, if 'twere not for Master Dapperwit, we might have lived all this vacation upon green cheese, tripe, and ox cheek. If he had it, we should not want it; but, poor gentleman! it often goes hard with him,—for he's a wit.

Mrs. Joyn. So, then, you are the dog to be fed, while the house is broken up! I say, beware! The sweet bits you swallow will make your daughter's belly swell, mistress; and, after all your junkets, there will be a bone for you to pick, mistress.

Mrs. Cros. Sure, Master Dapperwit is no such manner of man!

Mrs. Joyn. He is a wit, you say; and what are wits, but contemners of matrons, seducers, or defamers of married women, and deflowerers of helpless virgins, even in the streets, upon the very bulks;[1] affronters of

---

[1] Bulk. "A stall before a shop."—*Bailey.*

midnight magistracy, and breakers of windows? in a word—

Mrs. Cros. But he is a little wit, a modest wit, and they do no such outrageous things as your great wits do.

Mrs. Joyn. Nay, I dare say, he will not say himself he is a little wit if you ask him.

Lucy. Nay, I cannot hear this with patience.—[*Comes forward.*] With your pardon, mother, you are as much mistaken as my godmother in Mr. Dapperwit; for he is as great a wit as any, and in what he speaks or writes as happy as any. I can assure you, he contemns all your tearing wits, in comparison of himself.

Mrs. Joyn. Alas, poor young wretch! I cannot blame thee so much as thy mother, for thou art not thyself. His bewitching madrigals have charmed thee into some heathenish imp with a hard name.

Lucy. Nymph, you mean, godmother.

Mrs. Joyn. But you, gossip, know what's what. Yesterday, as I told you, a fine old alderman of the city, seeing your daughter in so ill hands as Dapperwit's, was zealously, and in pure charity, bent upon her redemption; and has sent me to tell you, he will take her into his care and relieve your necessities, if you think good.

Mrs. Cros. Will he relieve all our necessities?

Mrs. Joyn. All.

Mrs. Cros. Mine, as well as my daughter's?

Mrs. Joyn. Yes.

Mrs. Cros. Well fare his heart!—D'ye hear, daughter, Mrs. Joyner has satisfied me clearly; Dapperwit is a vile fellow, and, in short, you must put an end to that scandalous familiarity between you.

Lucy. Leave sweet Mr. Dapperwit!—oh furious ingratitude! Was he not the man that gave me my first Farrendon[1] gown, put me out of worsted stockings and plain handkerchiefs, taught me to dress, talk, and move well?

---

[1] Or Ferrandine: a stuff made of silk and wool.

Mrs. Cros. He has taught you to talk indeed ; but, huswife, I will not have my pleasure disputed.

Mrs. Joyn. Nay, indeed, you are too tart with her, poor sweet soul.

Lucy. He taught me to rehearse, too,—would have brought me into the playhouse, where I might have had as good luck as others : I might have had good clothes, plate, jewels, and things so well about me, that my neighbours, the little gentlemen's wives of fifteen hundred or two thousand pounds a year, should have retired into the country, sick with envy of my prosperity and greatness.

Mrs. Joyn. If you follow your mother's counsel, you are like to enjoy all you talk of sooner than by Dapperwit's assistance :—a poor wretch that goes on tick for the paper he writes his lampoons on, and the very ale and coffee that inspire him, as they say.

Mrs. Cros. I am credibly informed so, indeed, Madam Joyner.

Mrs. Joyn. Well, I have discharged my conscience ; good morrow to you both.   [*Exeunt severally.*

SCENE II.—Mrs. CROSSBITE'S *Dining-room.*

Enter DAPPERWIT *and* RANGER.

Dap. This is the cabinet in which I hide my jewel ; a small house, in an obscure, little, retired street, too.

Ran. Vulgarly, an alley.

Dap. Nay, I hide my mistress with as much care as a spark of the town does his money from his dun after a good hand at play ; and nothing but you could have wrought upon me for a sight of her, let me perish.

Ran. My obligation to you is great ; do not lessen it by delays of the favour you promised.

Dap. But do not censure my honour ; for if you had not been in a desperate condition,—for as one nail must beat out another, one poison expel another, one fire draw out another, one fit of drinking cure the sickness of another,—so, the surfeit you took last night of Christina's eyes shall be cured by Lucy's this morning ; or as—

Ran. Nay, I bar more similitudes.

Dap. What, in my mistress's lodging ? that were as hard as to bar a young parson in the pulpit, the fifth of November, railing at the Church of Rome ; or as hard as to put you to bed to Lucy and defend you from touching her ; or as—

Ran. Or as hard as to make you hold your tongue.— I shall not see your mistress, I see.

Dap. Miss Lucy ! Miss Lucy !—[*Knocks at the door and returns.*]—The devil take me, if good men (I say no more) have not been upon their knees to me, to see her, and you at last must obtain it.

Ran. I do not believe you.

Dap. 'Tis such as she ; she is beautiful without affec-tation ; amorous without impertinency ; airy and brisk without impudence ; frolic without rudeness ; and, in a word, the justest creature breathing to her assignation.

Ran. You praise her as if you had a mind to part with her ; and yet you resolve, I see, to keep her to yourself.

Dap. Keep her ! poor creature, she cannot leave me ; and rather than leave her, I would leave writing lampoons or sonnets almost.

Ran. Well, I'll leave you with her then.

Dap. What, will you go without seeing her ?

Ran. Rather than stay without seeing her.

Dap. Yes, yes, you shall see her ; but let me perish if I have not been offered a hundred guineas for a sight of her ; by—I say no more.

Ran. [*Aside.*] I understand you now.—[*Aloud.*] If the favour be to be purchased, then I'll bid all I have about me for't.

Dap. Fy, fy, Mr. Ranger ! you are pleasant, i'faith. Do you think I would sell the sight of my rarity ?—like those

gentlemen who hang out flags at Charing Cross, or
like—

Ran. Nay, then I'm gone again.

Dap. What, you take it ill I refuse your money? rather
than that should be, give us it; but take notice I will
borrow it. Now I think on't, Lucy wants a gown and
some knacks.

Ran. Here.

Dap. But I must pay it you again: I will not take it
unless you engage your honour I shall pay it you again.

Ran. You must pardon me; I will not engage my
honour for such a trifle. Go, fetch her out.

Dap. Well, she's a ravishing creature: such eyes and
lips, Mr. Ranger!

Ran. Prithee go.

Dap. Such neck and breasts, Mr. Ranger!

Ran. Again, prithee go.

Dap. Such feet, legs, and thighs, Mr. Ranger!

Ran. Prithee let me see 'em.

Dap. And a mouth no bigger than your ring!—I need
say no more.

Ran. Would thou wert never to speak again!

Dap. And then so neat, so sweet a creature in bed,
that, to my knowledge, she does not change her sheets in
half a year.

Ran. I thank you for that allay to my impatience.

Dap. Miss Lucy! Miss Lucy! Miss!—

[*Knocking at the door.*

Ran. Will she not open? I am afraid my pretty miss
is not stirring, and therefore will not admit us. Is she
not gone her walk to Lamb's Conduit?[1]

Dap. Fy, fy, a quibble next your stomach in a morn-

---

[1] In 1577, William Lamb (formerly a gentleman of the chapel to
Henry VIII.) caused to be constructed, in the fields where now
stands Lamb's Conduit Street, a reservoir and a conduit by which
the water was conveyed to Snow Hill. These fields formed a place
of resort for the inhabitants of the adjoining districts. The conduit
was restored, from a design by Sir Christopher Wren, in 1667.

ing! What if she should hear us? would you lose a mistress for a quibble? that's more than I could do, let me perish!—She's within, I hear her.

Ran. But she will not hear you; she's as deaf as if you were a dun or a constable.

Dap. Pish! give her but leave to gape, rub her eyes, and put on her day pinner; the long patch under the left eye; awaken the roses on her cheeks with some Spanish wool, and warrant her breath with some lemon-peel; the doors fly off the hinges, and she into my arms. She knows there is as much artifice to keep a victory as to gain it; and 'tis a sign she values the conquest of my heart.

Ran. I thought her beauty had not stood in need of art.

Dap. Beauty's a coward still without the help of art, and may have the fortune of a conquest but cannot keep it. Beauty and art can no more be asunder than love and honour.

Ran. Or, to speak more like yourself, wit and judgment.

Dap. Don't you hear the door wag yet?

Ran. Not a whit.

Dap. Miss! miss! 'tis your slave that calls. Come, all this tricking for him!—Lend me your comb, Mr. Ranger.

Ran. No, I am to be preferred to-day, you are to set me off. You are in possession, I will not lend you arms to keep me out.

Dap. A pox! don't let me be ungrateful; if she has smugged herself up for me, let me prune and flounce my peruke a little for her. There's ne'er a young fellow in the town but will do as much for a mere stranger in the playhouse.

Ran. A wit's wig has the privilege of being uncombed in the very playhouse, or in the presence.

Dap. But not in the presence of his mistress; 'tis a greater neglect of her than himself. Pray lend me your comb.

Ran. I would not have men of wit and courage make use of every fop's mean arts to keep or gain a mistress.

Dap. But don't you see every day, though a man have never so much wit and courage, his mistress will revolt to those fops that wear and comb perukes well. I'll break off the bargain, and will not receive you my partner.

Ran. Therefore you see I am setting up for myself.

[*Combs his peruke.*

Dap. She comes, she comes !—pray, your comb.

[*Snatches* RANGER'S *comb.*

Enter Mrs. CROSSBITE.

Mrs. Cros. Bargain !—what, are you offering us to sale ?

Dap. A pox ! is't she ?—Here take your comb again then.   [*Returns the comb.*

Mrs. Cros. Would you sell us ? 'tis like you, y'fads.

Dap. Sell thee !—where should we find a chapman ? Go, prithee, mother, call out my dear Miss Lucy.

Mrs. Cros. Your Miss Lucy ! I do not wonder you have the conscience to bargain for us behind our backs, since you have the impudence to claim a propriety in us to my face.

Ran. How's this, Dapperwit?

Dap. Come, come, this gentleman will not think the worse of a woman for my acquaintance with her. He has seen me bring your daughter to the lure with a chiney-orange, from one side of the playhouse to the other.

Mrs. Cros. I would have the gentleman and you to know my daughter is a girl of reputation, though she has been seen in your company ; but is now so sensible of her past danger, that she is resolved never more to venture her pitcher to the well, as they say.

Dap. How's that, widow? I wonder at your confidence.

Mrs. Cros. I wonder at your old impudence, that where you have had so frequent repulses you should pro-

voke another, and bring your friend here to witness your
disgrace.

Dap. Hark you, widow, a little.

Mrs. Cros. What, have you mortgaged my daughter to
that gentleman ; and now would offer me a snip to join
in the security !

Dap. [*Aside.*] She overheard me talk of a bargain ;—
'twas unlucky.—[*Aloud.*] Your wrath is grounded upon a
mistake : Miss Lucy herself shall be judge ; call her out,
pray.

Mrs. Cros. She shall not ; she will not come to you.

Dap. Till I hear it from her own mouth, I cannot
believe it.

Mrs. Cros. You shall hear her say 't through the door.

Dap. I shall doubt it unless she say it to my face.

Mrs. Cros. Shall we be troubled with you no more
then ?

Dap. If she command my death, I cannot disobey her.

Mrs. Cros. Come out, child.

Enter LUCY, *holding down her head.*

Dap. Your servant, dearest miss : can you have—

Mrs. Cros. Let me ask her.

Dap. No, I'll ask her.

Ran. I'll throw up cross or pile [1] who shall ask her.

Dap. Can you have the heart to say you will never
more break a cheese-cake with me at New Spring Garden, [2]
the Neat-house, or Chelsea ? never more sit in my lap at

---

[1] "Cross or pile" : equivalent to our "heads or tails." A cross
was usually on the reverse of old English coins ; the obverse was
called the "pile," from the pile or punch with which the impression
was struck.

[2] The New Spring Garden, at Vauxhall ; afterwards under the
name of Vauxhall, the most famous place of resort of that kind in
the metropolis. It was first opened about 1661, when Evelyn describes it as "a pretty-contriv'd plantation," and was closed in
1859. Pepys has an interesting entry concerning it, under date
of May 28, 1667 : "I by water to Fox-hall, and there walked in
Spring-garden. A great deal of company, and the weather and
garden pleasant : and it is very pleasant and cheap going thither,

a new play? never more wear a suit of knots of my choice? and, last of all, never more pass away an afternoon with me again in the Green Garret?—do not forget the Green Garret.

Lucy. I wish I had never seen the Green Garret.— Damn the Green Garret!

Dap. Damn the Green Garret!—You are strangely altered!

Lucy. 'Tis you are altered.

Dap. You have refused Colby's Mulberry-garden, and the French houses, for the Green Garret; and a little something in the Green Garret pleased you more than the best treat the other places could yield; and can you of a sudden quit the Green Garret?

Lucy. Since you have a design to pawn me for the rent, 'tis time to remove my goods.

Dap. Thou art extremely mistaken.

Lucy. Besides, I have heard such strange things of you this morning.

Dap. What things?

Lucy. I blush to speak 'em.

Dap. I know my innocence, therefore take my charge as a favour. What have I done?

Lucy. Then know, vile wit, my mother has confessed just now thou wert false to me, to her too certain knowledge; and hast forced even her to be false to me too.

Dap. Faults in drink, Lucy, when we are not ourselves, should not condemn us.

Lucy. And now to let me out to hire like a hackney! —I tell you my own dear mother shall bargain for me no more; there are as little as I can bargain for themselves now-a-days, as well as properer women.

for a man may go to spend what he will, or nothing, all as one. But to hear the nightingale and other birds, and here fiddles and there a harp, and here a Jew's trump, and here laughing, and there fine people walking, is mighty divertising."—The Neat-house was a place of entertainment at Pimlico.

Mrs. Cros. Whispering all this while !—Beware of his snares again : come away, child.

Dap. Sweet, dear miss—

Lucy. Bargain for me !—you have reckoned without your hostess, as they say. Bargain for me ! bargain for me !   [*Exit.*

Dap. I must return, then, to treat with you.

Mrs. Cros. Treat me no treatings, but take a word for all. You shall no more dishonour my daughter, nor molest my lodgings, as you have done at all hours.

Dap. Do you intend to change 'em, then, to Bridewell, or Long's powdering-tub ?[1]

Mrs. Cros. No, to a bailiff's house, and then you'll be so civil, I presume, as not to trouble us.

Ran. Here, will you have my comb again, Dapperwit ?

Dap. A pox ! I think women take inconstancy from me worse than from any man breathing.

Mrs. Cros. Pray, sir, forget me before you write your next lampoon.   [*Exit.*

Enter Sir SIMON ADDLEPLOT *in the dress of a* Clerk.— RANGER *retires to the background.*

Sir Sim. Have I found you ? have I found you in your by-walks, faith and troth ? I am almost out of breath in following you. Gentlemen when they get into an alley walk so fast, as if they had more earnest business there than in the broad streets.

Dap. [*Aside.*]—How came this sot hither ? Fortune has sent him to ease my choler.—You impudent rascal, who are you, that dare intrude thus on us ?   [*Strikes him.*

Sir Sim. Don't you know me, Dapperwit ? sure you know me.   [*Softly.*

---

[1] A powdering-tub means properly a tub in which meat is salted, to sprinkle with salt being an occasional sense of the verb "to powder." Hence the name of powdering-tub was applied to places where persons afflicted with a certain disease were cured. Compare Shakespeare, *Measure for Measure*, iii. 2 ; "Troth, sir, she hath eaten up all her beef, and she is herself in the tub." Also *King Henry V.*, ii. 1.

Dap. Wilt thou dishonour me with thy acquaintance too? thou rascally, insolent, pen-and-ink man.

[*Strikes him again.*

Sir Sim. Oh! oh! sure you know me! pray know me.

[*Softly.*

Dap. By thy saucy familiarity, thou shouldst be a marker at a tennis-court, a barber, or a slave that fills coffee.

Sir Sim. Oh! oh!

Dap. What art thou?   [*Kicks him.*

Sir Sim. Nay, I must not discover myself to Ranger for a kick or two. Oh, pray hold, sir : by that you will know me.   [*Delivers him a letter.*

Dap. How, Sir Simon!

Sir Sim. Mum, mum, make no excuses, man; I would not Ranger should have known me for five hundred—kicks.

Dap. Your disguise is so natural, I protest, it will excuse me.

Sir Sim. I know that, prithee make no excuses, I say. No ceremony between thee and I, man :—read the letter.

Dap. What, you have not opened it!

Sir Sim. Prithee, don't be angry, the seal is a little cracked : for I could not help kissing Mrs. Martha's letter. The word is, now or never. Her father she finds will be abroad all this day, and she longs to see your friend Sir Simon Addleplot :—faith 'tis a pretty jest; while I am with her, and praising myself to her at no ordinary rate. Let thee and I alone at an intrigue.

Dap. Tell her I will not fail to meet her at the place and time. Have a care of your charge; and manage your business like yourself, for yourself.

Sir Sim. I warrant you.

Dap. The gaining Gripe's daughter will make me support the loss of this young jilt here.   [*Aside.*

Ran. [*Coming forward.*] What fellow's that?

Dap. A servant to a friend of mine.

Ran. Methinks he something resembles our acquaint-

ance Sir Simon ; but it is no compliment to tell him so :
for that knight is the most egregious coxcomb that ever
played with lady's fan.

Sir Sim. So ! thanks to my disguise, I know my
enemies !   [*Aside.*

Ran. The most incorrigible ass, beyond the reproof of
a kicking rival or a frowning mistress. But, if it be
possible, thou dost use him worse than his mistress or
rival can ; thou dost make such a cully of him.

Sir Sim. Does he think so too ?   [*Aside.*

Dap. Go, friend, go about your business.—[*Exit* Sir
SIMON.] A pox ! you would spoil all, just in the critical
time of projection. He brings me here a summons from
his mistress, to meet her in the evening ; will you come
to my wedding ?

Ran. Don't speak so loud, you'll break poor Lucy's
heart. Poor creature, she cannot leave you ; and, rather
than leave her, you would 'ʒave writing of lampoons or
sonnets—almost.

Dap. Come, let her go, ungrateful baggage !—But now
you talk of sonnets, I am no living wit if her love has not
cost me two thousand couplets at least.

Ran. But what would you give, now, for a new satire
against women, ready made ?—'Twould be as convenient
to buy satires against women ready made, as it is to buy
cravats ready tied.

Dap. Or as—

Ran. Hey, come away, come away, Mr., or as—
                                             [*Exeunt.*

SCENE III.—*A Room in* Mrs. CROSSBITE'S *House.*

Enter Mrs. JOYNER *and* GRIPE.

Gripe. Peace, plenty, and pastime be within these
walls !

Mrs. Joyn. 'Tis a small house, you see, and mean furniture ; for no gallants are suffered to come hither. She might have had ere now as good lodgings as any in town ; her Mortlake [1] hangings, great glasses, cabinets, china, embroidered beds, Persia carpets, gold-plate, and the like, if she would have put herself forward. But your worship may please to make 'em remove to a place fit to receive one of your worship's quality ; for this is a little scandalous, in truly.

Gripe. No, no ; I like it well enough :—I am not dainty. Besides, privacy, privacy, Mrs. Joyner ! I love privacy in opposition to the wicked, who hate it.

[Looks about.

Mrs. Joyn. What do you look for, sir ?

Gripe. Walls have ears ; but, besides, I look for a private place to retire to, in time of need. Oh ! here's one convenient.

[Turns up a hanging, and discovers the slender provisions of the family.

Mrs. Joyn. But you see, poor innocent souls, to what use they put it ;—not to hide gallants.

Gripe. Temperance is the nurse of chastity.

Mrs. Joyn. But your worship may please to mend their fare ; and, when you come, may make them entertain you better than, you see, they do themselves.

Gripe. No, I am not dainty, as I told you. I abominate entertainments ;—no entertainments, pray, Mrs. Joyner.

Mrs. Joyn. No !   *[Aside.*

Gripe. There can be no entertainment to me more luscious and savoury than communion with that little gentlewoman.—Will you call her out ? I fast till I see her.

---

[1] The Mortlake tapestry was of some note at this time. The works had been founded under the patronage of James I., and Rubens and Vandyck subsequently lent their services to the undertaking.

Mrs. Joyn. But, in truly, your worship, we should have brought a bottle or two of Rhenish and some Naples biscuit, to have entertained the young gentlewoman. 'Tis the mode for lovers to treat their mistresses.

Gripe. Modes! I tell you, Mrs. Joyner, I hate modes and forms.

Mrs. Joyn. You must send for something to entertain her with.

Gripe. Again entertaining!—we will be to each other a feast.

Mrs. Joyn. I shall be ashamed, in truly, your worship. —Besides, the young gentlewoman will despise you.

Gripe. I shall content her, I warrant you; leave it to me.

Mrs. Joyn. [*Aside.*] I am sure you will not content me, if you will not content her; 'tis as impossible for a man to love and be a miser, as to love and be wise, as they say.

Gripe. While you talk of treats, you starve my eyes; I long to see the fair one; fetch her hither.

Mrs. Joyn. I am ashamed she should find me so abominable a liar; I have so praised you to her, and, above all your virtues, your liberality; which is so great a virtue, that it often excuses youth, beauty, courage, wit, or anything.

Gripe. Pish, pish! 'tis the virtue of fools; every fool can have it.

Mrs. Joyn. And will your worship want it, then? I told her—

Gripe. Why would you tell her anything of me? you know I am a modest man. But come, if you will have me as extravagant as the wicked, take that and fetch us a treat, as you call it.

Mrs. Joyn. Upon my life a groat! what will this purchase?

Gripe. Two black pots of ale and a cake, at the cellar. —Come, the wine has arsenic in't.

Mrs. Joyn. [*Aside.*] Well, I am mistaken, and my hopes are abused : I never knew any man so mortified a miser, that he would deny his lechery anything; I must be even with thee then another way.   [*Exit.*

Gripe. These useful old women are more exorbitant and craving in their desires than the young ones in theirs. These prodigals in white perukes spoil 'em both; and that's the reason, when the squires come under my clutches, I make 'em pay for their folly and mine, and 'tis but conscience :—oh, here comes the fair one at last !

Re-enter Mrs. JOYNER *leading in* LUCY, *who hangs back-wards as she enters.*

Lucy. Oh Lord, there's a man, godmother !

Mrs. Joyn. Come in, child, thou art so bashful—

Lucy. My mother is from home too, I dare not.

Mrs. Joyn. If she were here, she'd teach you better manners.

Lucy. I'm afraid she'd be angry.

Mrs. Joyn. To see you so much an ass.—Come along, I say.

Gripe. Nay, speak to her gently; if you won't, I will.

Lucy. Thank you, sir.

Gripe. Pretty innocent ! there is, I see, one left of her age; what hap have I ! Sweet little gentlewoman, come sit down by me.

Lucy. I am better bred, I hope, sir.

Gripe. You must sit down by me.

Lucy. I'd rather stand, if you please.

Gripe. To please me, you must sit, sweetest.

Lucy. Not before my godmother, sure.

Gripe. Wonderment of innocence !

Mrs. Joyn. A poor bashful girl, sir : I'm sorry she is not better taught.

Gripe. I am glad she is not taught; I'll teach her myself.

Lucy. Are you a dancing-master then, sir? But if I should be dull, and not move as you would have me, you would not beat me, sir, I hope?

Gripe. Beat thee, honeysuckle! I'll use thee thus, and thus, and thus. [*Kisses her.*] Ah, Mrs. Joyner, prithee go fetch our treat now.

Mrs. Joyn. A treat of a groat! I will not wag.

Gripe. Why don't you go? Here, take more money, and fetch what you will; take here, nalf-a-crown.

Mrs. Joyn. What will half-a-crown do?

Gripe. Take a crown then, an angel, a piece;[1]— begone!

Mrs. Joyn. A treat only will not serve my turn; I must buy the poor wretch there some toys.

Gripe. What toys? what? speak quickly.

Mrs. Joyn. Pendants, necklaces, fans, ribbons, points, laces, stockings, gloves—

Gripe. Hold, hold! before it comes to a gown.

Mrs. Joyn. Well remembered, sir; indeed she wants a gown, for she has but that one to her back. For your own sake you should give her a new gown, for variety of dresses rouses desire, and makes an old mistress seem every day a new one.

Gripe. For that reason she shall have no new gown; for I am naturally constant, and as I am still the same, I love she should be still the same. But here, take half a piece for the other things.

Mrs. Joyn. Half a piece!—

Gripe. Prithee, begone!—take t'other piece then—two pieces—three pieces—five! here, 'tis all I have.

Mrs. Joyn. I must have the broad-seal ring too, or I stir not.

Gripe. Insatiable woman! will you have that too! Prithee spare me that, 'twas my grandfather's.

Mrs. Joyn. That's false, he had ne'er a coat.—So! now I go; this is but a violent fit, and will not hold. [*Aside.*

[1] The angel was worth 10*s.*, and the piece 22*s.*

Lucy. Oh! whither do you go, godmother? will you leave me alone?

Mrs. Joyn. The gentleman will not hurt you; you may venture yourself with him alone.

Lucy. I think I may, godmother. — [*Exit* Mrs. JOYNER.] What! will you lock me in, sir? don't lock me in, sir.   [GRIPE, *fumbling at the door, locks it.*

Gripe. 'Tis a private lesson, I must teach you, fair.

Lucy. I don't see your fiddle, sir; where is your little kit?

Gripe. I'll show it thee presently, sweetest.—[*Sets a chair against the door*].—Necessity, mother of invention! —Come, my dearest.   [*Takes her in his arms.*

Lucy. What do you mean, sir? don't hurt me, sir, will you—Oh! oh! you will kill me! Murder! murder! —Oh! oh!—help! help! oh!

The door is broken open; enter Mrs. CROSSBITE, *and her* Landlord, *and his* 'Prentice, *in aprons.*

Mrs. Cros. What, murder my daughter, villain!

Lucy. I wish he had murdered me.—Oh! oh!

Mrs. Cros. What has he done?

Lucy. Why would you go out, and leave me alone? unfortunate woman that I am!

Gripe. How now, what will this end in?   [*Aside.*

Mrs. Cros. Who brought him in?

Lucy. That witch, that treacherous false woman, my godmother, who has betrayed me, sold me to his lust.— Oh! oh!—

Mrs. Cros. Have you ravished my daughter, then, you old goat? ravished my daughter!—ravished my daughter! speak, villain.

Gripe. By yea and by nay, no such matter.

Mrs. Cros. A canting rogue, too! Take notice, land-lord, he has ravished my daughter, you see her all in tears and distraction; and see there the wicked engine of the filthy execution.—[*Pointing to the chair.*]

—Jeremy, call up the neighbours, and the constable.—
False villain ! thou shalt die for it.

Gripe. Hold ! hold !—[*Aside.*]—Nay, I am caught.

Mrs. Cros. Go, go, make haste—

Lucy. Oh ! oh !—

Mrs. Cros. Poor wretch !—Go quickly.

Gripe. Hold ! hold !—Thou young spawn of the old
serpent ! wicked, as I thought thee innocent ! wilt thou
say I would have ravished thee ?

Lucy. I will swear you did ravish me.

Gripe. I thought so, treacherous Eve !—then I am
gone, I must shift as well as I can.

Lucy. Oh ! oh !—

Mrs. Cros. Will none of you call up the neighbours,
and the authority of the alley ?

Gripe. Hold, I'll give you twenty mark[1] among you
to let me go.

Mrs. Cros. Villain ! nothing shall buy thy life.

Land. But stay, Mrs. Crossbite, let me talk with you.

Lucy. Oh ! oh !—

Land. Come, sir, I am your friend :—in a word, I
have appeased her, and she shall be contented with a
little sum.

Gripe. What is it ? what is it ?

Land. But five hundred pounds.

Gripe. But five hundred pounds !—hang me then,
hang me rather.

Land. You will say I have been your friend.

Pren. The constable and neighbours are a-coming.

Gripe. How, how; will you not take a hundred ?
pray use conscience in your ways.

[*Kneels to* Mrs. CROSSBITE.

Mrs. Cros. I scorn your money ! I will not take a
thousand.

Gripe. [*Aside.*] My enemies are many, and I shall be
a scandal to the faithful, as a laughing-stock to the

[1] The mark was worth 13*s*. 4*d*.

wicked.—[*Aloud.*] Go, prepare your engines for my persecution; I'll give you the best security I can.

Land. The instruments are drawing in the other room, if you please to go thither.

Mrs. Cros. Indeed, now I consider, a portion will do my daughter more good than his death. That would but publish her shame; money will cover it—*probatum est*, as they say. Let me tell you, sir, 'tis a charitable thing to give a young maid a portion.   [*Exeunt.*

SCENE IV.—LYDIA's *Lodging.*

Enter LYDIA *and* Lady FLIPPANT, *attended by* LEONORE.

Lyd. 'Tis as hard for a woman to conceal her indignation from her apostate lover, as to conceal her love from her faithful servant.

L. Flip. Or almost as hard as it is for the prating fellows now-a-days to conceal the favours of obliging ladies.

Lyd. If Ranger should come up, (I saw him just now in the street,) the discovery of my anger to him now would be as mean as the discovery of my love to him before.

L. Flip. Though I did so mean a thing as to love a fellow, I would not do so mean a thing as to confess it, certainly, by my trouble to part with him. If I confessed love, it should be before they left me.

Lyd. So you would deserve to be left, before you were. But could you ever do so mean a thing as to confess love to any?

L. Flip. Yes; but I never did so mean a thing as really to love any.

Lyd. You had once a husband.

L. Flip. Fy! madam, do you think me so ill bred as to love a husband?

Lyd. You had a widow's heart, before you were a widow, I see.

L. Flip. I should rather make an adventure of my honour with a gallant for a gown, a new coach, a necklace, than clap my husband's cheeks for them, or sit in his lap. I should be as ashamed to be caught in such a posture with a husband, as a brisk well-bred spark of the town would be to be caught on his knees at prayers —unless to his mistress.

Enter RANGER *and* DAPPERWIT.

Lyd. Mr. Ranger, 'twas obligingly done of you.

Ran. Indeed, cousin, I had kept my promise with you last night, but this gentleman knows—

Lyd. You mistake me; but you shall not lessen any favour you do to me. You are going to excuse your not coming to me last night, when I take it as a particular obligation, that though you threatened me with a visit, upon consideration you were so civil as not to trouble me.

Dap. This is an unlucky morning with me! here's my eternal persecution, the widow Flippant.   [*Aside.*

L. Flip. What, Mr. Dapperwit!

  [DAPPERWIT *retires to the back of the stage,*
          followed by LADY FLIPPANT.

Ran. Indeed, cousin, besides my business, another cause I did not wait on you was, my apprehension you were gone to the Park, notwithstanding your promise to the contrary.

Lyd. Therefore, you went to the Park to visit me there, notwithstanding your promise to the contrary?

Ran. Who, I at the Park! when I had promised to wait upon you at your lodging! But were you at the Park, madam?

Lyd. Who, I at the Park! when I had promised to

wait for you at home! I was no more at the Park than
you were. Were you at the Park?

Ran. The Park had been a dismal desert to me, notwithstanding all the good company in it, if I had wanted
yours.

Lyd. [*Aside.*] Because it has been the constant endeavour of men to keep women ignorant, they think us
so; but 'tis that increases our inquisitiveness, and makes
us know them ignorant as false. He is as impudent a
dissembler as the widow Flippant, who is making her
importunate addresses in vain, for aught I see.

> [Lady FLIPPANT *comes forward, driving* DAPPER-
> WIT *from one side of the stage to the other.*

L. Flip. Dear Mr. Dapperwit! merciful Mr. Dapperwit!

Dap. Unmerciful Lady Flippant!

L. Flip. Will you be satisfied?

Dap. Won't you be satisfied?

L. Flip. That a wit should be jealous; that a wit
should be jealous! there's never a brisk young fellow in
the town, though no wit, Heaven knows, but thinks too
well of himself, to think ill of his wife or mistress. Now,
that a wit should lessen his opinion of himself;—for
shame!

Dap. I promised to bring you off, but I find it enough
to shift for myself—   [*Softly, apart to* RANGER.

Lyd. What! out of breath, madam!

L. Flip. I have been defending our cause, madam;
I have beat him out of the pit. I do so mumble these
prating, censorious fellows they call wits, when I meet
with them.

Dap. Her ladyship, indeed, is the only thing in petticoats I dread. 'Twas well for me there was company in
the room; for I dare no more venture myself with her
alone, than a cully that has been bit dares venture himself in a tavern with an old rook.

L. Flip. I am the revenger of our sex, certainly.

Dap. And the most insatiable one I ever knew, madam; I dare not stand your fury longer.—Mr. Ranger, I will go before and make a new appointment with your friends that expect you at dinner at the French-house; 'tis fit business still wait on love.

Ran. Do so—but now I think on't, Sir Thomas goes out of town this afternoon, and I shall not see him here again these three months.

Lyd. Nay, pray take him with you, sir.

L. Flip. No, sir, you shall not take the gentleman from his mistress.—[*Aside* to DAPPERWIT.] Do not go yet, sweet Mr. Dapperwit.

Lyd. Take him with you, sir; I suppose his business may be there to borrow or win money, and I ought not to be his hindrance : for when he has none, he has his desperate designs upon that little I have ;—for want of money makes as devout lovers as Christians.

Dap. I hope, madam, he offers you no less security than his liberty.

Lyd. His liberty is as poor a pawn to take up money on as honour. He is like the desperate bankrupts of this age, who, if they can get people's fortunes into their hands, care not though they spend them in jail all their lives.

L. Flip. And the poor crediting ladies, when they have parted with their money, must be contented with a pitiful composition, or starve, for all them.

Ran. But widows are commonly so wise as to be sure their men are solvable before they trust 'em.

L. Flip. Can you blame 'em ! I declare I will trust no man. Pray, do not take it ill, gentlemen : quacks in their bills, and poets in the titles of their plays, do not more disappoint us, than gallants with their promises; but I trust none.

Dap. Nay, she's a very Jew in that particular. To my knowledge, she'll know her man, over and over again, before she trust him.

Ran. Well, my dearest cousin, good-morrow. When I stay from you so long again, blame me to purpose, and be extremely angry; for nothing can make me amends for the loss of your company, but your reprehension of my absence. I'll take such a chiding as kindly as Russian wives do beating.

Lyd. If you were my husband, I could not take your absence more kindly than I do.

Ran. And if you were my wife, I would trust you as much out of my sight as I could, to show my opinion of your virtue.

L. Flip. A well-bred gentleman, I warrant.—Will you go then, cruel Mr. Dapperwit?

> [*Exeunt* RANGER *and* DAPPERWIT, *followed by* Lady FLIPPANT.

Lyd. Have I not dissembled well, Leonore?

Leo. But, madam, to what purpose? why do you not put him to his trial, and see what he can say for himself?

Lyd. I am afraid lest my proofs, and his guilt, should make him desperate, and so contemn that pardon which he could not hope for.

Leo. 'Tis unjust to condemn him before you hear him.

Lyd. I will reprieve him till I have more evidence.

Leo. How will you get it?

Lyd. I will write him a letter in Christina's name, desiring to meet him; when I shall soon discover if his love to her be of a longer standing than since last night; and if it be not, I will not longer trust him with the vanity to think she gave him the occasion to follow her home from the Park; so will at once disabuse him and myself.

Leo. What care the jealous take in making sure of ills which they, but in imagination, cannot undergo!

Lyd. Misfortunes are least dreadful when most near:
  'Tis less to undergo the ill, than fear.   [*Exeunt.*

ACT THE FOURTH.

SCENE I.—*A Room in* GRIPE'S *House.*

Enter Mrs. JOYNER *and* GRIPE, *the latter in a blue gown and nightcap.*

RS. JOYN. What, not well, your worship! This it is, you will be laying out yourself beyond your strength. You have taken a surfeit of the little gentlewoman, I find. Indeed you should not have been so immoderate in your embraces; your worship is something in years, in truly.

Gripe. Graceless, perfidious woman! what makest thou here? art thou not afraid to be used like an informer, since thou hast made me pay thee for betraying me?

Mrs. Joyn. Betray your worship! what do you mean? I an informer! I scorn your words!

Gripe. Woman, I say again, thou art as treacherous as an informer, and more unreasonable; for he lets us have something for our money before he disturb us.

Mrs. Joyn. Your money, I'm sure, was laid out faithfully; and I went away because I would not disturb you.

Gripe. I had not grudged you the money I gave you:—but the five hundred pounds! the five hundred pounds! Inconscionable, false woman, the five hundred pounds!—You cheated, trepanned, robbed me, of the five hundred pounds!

Mrs. Joyn. I cheat you ! I rob you !—well, remember what you say, you shall answer it before Mr. Doublecap and the best of—

Gripe. Oh, impudent woman, speak softly !

Mrs. Joyn. I will not speak softly ; for innocence is loud as well as barefaced. Is this your return, after you have made me a mere drudge to your filthy lusts ?

Gripe. Speak softly ; my sister, daughter, and servants, will hear.

Mrs. Joyn. I would have witnesses, to take notice that you blast my good name, which was as white as a tulip, and as sweet as the head of your cane, before you wrought me to the carrying on the work of your fleshly carnal seekings.

Gripe. Softly ! softly ! they are coming in.

Enter Lady FLIPPANT *and* Mrs. MARTHA.

L. Flip. What's the matter, brother?

Gripe. Nothing, nothing, sister, only the godly woman is fallen into a fit of zeal against the enormous transgressions of the age. Go ! go ! you do not love to hear vanity reproved ; pray begone !

Mrs. Joyn. Pray stay, madam, that you may know—

Gripe. [*Aside to* Mrs. JOYNER.] Hold ! hold ! here are five guineas for thee,—pray say nothing.—[*Aloud.*] Sister, pray begone, I say.—[*Exeunt* Lady FLIPPANT *and* Mrs. MARTHA.] Would you prejudice your own reputation to injure mine ?

Mrs. Joyn. Would you prejudice your own soul to wrong my repute, in truly ? [*Pretends to weep.*

Gripe. Pray have me in excuse. Indeed, I thought you had a share of the five hundred pounds, because you took away my seal-ring ; which they made me send, together with a note to my cash-keeper for five hundred pounds. Besides, I thought none but you knew it was my wonted token to send for money by.

Mrs. Joyn. 'Tis unlucky I should forget it. and leave

it on the table!—But oh the harlotry! did she make that use of it then? 'twas no wonder you did not stay till I came back.

Gripe. I stayed till the money released me.

Mrs. Joyn. Have they the money, then? five hundred pounds!

Gripe. Too certain.

Mrs. Joyn. They told me not a word of it; and have you no way to retrieve it?

Gripe. Not any.

Mrs. Joyn. [*Aside.*] I am glad of it.—[*Aloud.*] Is there no law but against saints?

Gripe. I will not for five hundred pounds publish my transgression myself, lest I should be thought to glory in't: though, I must confess, 'twould tempt a man to conform to public praying and sinning, since 'tis so chargeable to pray and sin in private.

Mrs. Joyn. But are you resolved to give off a loser?

Gripe. How shall I help it?

Mrs. Joyn. Nay, I'll see you shall have what the young jade has, for your money: I'll make 'em use some conscience, however.—Take a man's money for nothing!

Gripe. Thou sayest honestly, indeed. And shall I have my pennyworths out of the little gentlewoman for all this?

Mrs. Joyn. I'll be engaged body for body for her, and you shall take the forfeiture on me else.

Gripe. No, no, I'll rather take your word, Mrs. Joyner.

Mrs. Joyn. Go in and dress yourself smug, and leave the rest to me.

Gripe. No man breathing would give-off a loser, as she says.   [*Exeunt.*

SCENE II.—*Another Room in the same.*

Sir SIMON ADDLEPLOT *discovered sitting at a desk writing as a* Clerk, Lady FLIPPANT *jogging him.*

Sir Sim. 'Tis a lord's mortgage, and therefore requires the more haste :—pray do not jog me, madam.

L. Flip. Dull rascal !   [*Aside.*

Sir Sim. They cannot stay for money as other folks. If you will not let me make an end on't, I shall lose my expedition-fee.

L. Flip. There are some clerks would have understood me before this.   [*Aside.*

Sir Sim. Nay, pray be quiet, madam ; if you squeeze me so to the wall, I cannot write.

L. Flip. [*Aside.*] 'Tis much for the honour of the gentlemen of this age, that we persons of quality are forced to descend to the importuning of a clerk, a butler, coachman, or footman ; while the rogues are as dull of apprehension, too, as an unfledged country squire amongst his mother's maids !   [*Jogs him again.*

Sir Sim. Again !   Let me tell you, madam, familiarity breeds contempt : you'll never leave till you have made me saucy.

L. Flip. I would I could see that.

Sir Sim. I vow and swear then, get you gone ! or I'll add a black patch or two to those on your face.—[*Aside.*] I shall have no time to get Mrs. Martha out, for her.

L. Flip. Will you, sir, will you !   [*Jogs him again.*

Sir Sim. [*Aside.*] I must have a plot for her, she is a coy woman.—[*Aloud.*] I vow and swear if you pass this crevice,[1] I'll kiss you in plain English.

L. Flip. I would I could see that !—do you defy me !
                          [*Steps to him—he kisses her.*

Sir Sim. [*Aside.*] How's this ! I vow and swear, she

---

[1] This incident is evidently borrowed from the story of " La pro-cureuse passe la raie," in *Les Cent Nouvelles Nouvelles,* or from the more recent version in Bandello's *Novelle.*

kisses as tamely as Mrs. Ticklish, and with her mouth open too.

L. Flip. I thought you would have been ashamed to have done so to your master's own sister!

Sir Sim. I hope you'll be quiet now, madam?

L. Flip. Nay, I'll be revenged of you sure.

Sir Sim. If you come again, I shall do more to you than that.—[*Aside.*] I'll pursue my plot and try if she be honest.

L. Flip. You do more to me than that! nay, if you'll do more to me than that—

[*She throws down his ink and runs out, he following her.*

Enter Mrs. JOYNER.

Mrs. Joyn. I must visit my young clients in the meantime.

Re-enter Sir SIMON, *holding up his hands.*

What's the matter, Sir Simon?

Sir Sim. Lord! who would have thought it?

Mrs. Joyn. What ails you, Sir Simon?

Sir Sim. I have made such a discovery, Mrs. Joyner!

Mrs. Joyn. What is't?

Sir Sim. Such a one that makes me at once glad and sorry; I am sorry my Lady Flippant is naught, but I'm glad I know it:—thanks still to my disguise.

Mrs. Joyn. Fy! fy!

Sir Sim. Nay, this hand can tell—

Mrs. Joyn. But how?

Sir Sim. She threw down my ink-glass, and ran away into the next room; I followed her, and, in revenge, threw her down upon the bed:—but, in short, all that I could do to her would not make her squeak.

Mrs. Joyn. She was out of breath, man, she was out of breath.

Sir Sim. Ah, Mrs. Joyner, say no more, say no more of that!

Re-enter Lady FLIPPANT.

L. Flip. You rude, unmannerly rascal !

Mrs. Joyn. You see she complains now.

Sir Sim. I know why, Mrs. Joyner, I know why.

[*Aside to* Mrs. JOYNER.

L. Flip. I'll have you turned out of the house ; you are not fit for my brother's service.

Sir Sim. Not for yours, you mean, madam.   [*Aside.*

L. Flip. I'll go and acquaint my brother—

Mrs. Joyn. [*Aside to* Lady FLIPPANT.] Hold, hold, madam, speak not so loud :—'tis Sir Simon Addleplot, your lover, who has taken this disguise on purpose to be near you, and to watch and supplant his rival.

L. Flip. What a beast was I, I could not discover it ! you have undone me ! why would you not tell me sooner of it ?   [*Aside to* Mrs. JOYNER.

Mrs. Joyn. I thought he had been discernible enough.

L. Flip. I protest, I knew him not ; for I must confess to you, my eyes are none of the best since I have used the last new wash of mercury-water.—What will he think of me !

Mrs. Joyn. Let me alone with him.—[*To* Sir SIMON.] Come, come, did you think you could disguise yourself from my lady's knowledge ? she knew you, man, or else you had ne'er had those liberties. Alas, poor lady, she cannot resist you !

L. Flip. 'Tis my weakness.

Sir Sim. How's this !—but here comes my master.

Enter GRIPE *and Mrs.* MARTHA.

Gripe. Come, Mrs. Joyner, are you ready to go ?

Mrs. Joyn. I am ever ready when your worship commands.

L. Flip. Brother, if you go to t'other end of the town, you'll set me down near the playhouse ?

Gripe. The playhouse ! do you think I will be seen near the playhouse ?

L. Flip. You shall set me down in Lincoln's-inn-fields, then; for I have earnest business there.—[*Apart to* Sir Simon.] When I come home again, I'll laugh at you soundly, Sir Simon.

Sir Sim. Has Joyner betrayed me then! 'tis time to look to my hits. [*Aside.*

Gripe. Martha, be sure you stay within now. If you go out, you shall never come into my doors again.

Mrs. Mar. No, I will not, sir; I'll ne'er come into your doors again, if once I should go out.

Gripe. 'Tis well said, girl.

[*Exeunt* Gripe, Mrs. Joyner, *and* Lady Flippant.

Sir Sim. 'Twas prettily said: I understand you, they are dull, and have no intrigue in 'em. But dear sweet Mrs. Martha, 'tis time we were gone; you have stole away your scarfs and hood from your maid, I hope?

Mrs. Mar. Nay, I am ready, but—

Sir Sim. Come, come, Sir Simon Addleplot, poor gentleman, is an impatient man, to my knowledge.

Mrs. Mar. Well, my venture is great, I'm sure, for a man I know not. But pray, Jonas, do not deceive me; is he so fine a gentleman, as you say he is.

Sir Sim. Pish! pish! he is the—gentleman of the town, faith and troth.

Mrs. Mar. But may I take your word, Jonas?

Sir Sim. 'Tis not my word, 'tis the word of all the town.

Mrs. Mar. Excuse me, Jonas, for that :—I never heard any speak well of him but Mr. Dapperwit and you.

Sir Sim. That's because he has been a rival to all men, and a gallant to all ladies. Rivals and deserted mistresses never speak well of a man.

Mrs. Mar. Has he been so general in his amours? his kindness is not to be valued then.

Sir Sim. The more by you; because 'tis for you he deserts all the rest, faith and troth.

Mrs. Mar. You plead better for him than he could for

himself, I believe ; for, indeed, they say he is no better than an idiot.

Sir Sim. Then, believe me, madam—for nobody knows him better than I—he has as much wit, courage, and as good a mien to the full, as I have.—He an idiot !

Mrs. Mar. The common gull ; so perspicuous a fop, the women find him out :—for none of 'em will marry him.

Sir Sim. You may see, now, how he and you are abused.   For that he is not married, is a sign of his wit ; and for being perspicuous, 'tis false ; he is as mysterious as a new parliament-man, or a young statesman newly taken from a coffee-house or tennis-court.

Mrs. Mar. But is it a sign of his wit because he is not married ?

Sir Sim. Yes, yes ; your women of the town ravish your fops : there's not one about the town unmarried that has anything.

Mrs. Mar. It may be then he has spent his estate.

Sir Sim. [*Aside.*] How unluckily guessed !—[*Aloud.*] If he had, he has a head can retrieve it again.

Mrs. Mar. Besides, they say he has the modish distemper.

Sir Sim. He can cure it with the best French chirurgeon in town.

Mrs. Mar. Has his practice on himself been so much ?

Sir Sim. Come, come.—

    Fame, like deserted jilt, does still belie men ;
    Who doubts her man, must be advised by Hymen ;
    For he knows best of any how to try men. [*Exeunt.*

SCENE III.—*The old Pall Mall.*

Enter RANGER *and* DAPPERWIT.

Ran. Now the Lucys have renounced us, hey for the Christinas ! She cannot use me worse than your honourable mistress did you.

Dap. A pox! some young heir or another has promised her marriage. There are so many fools in the world, 'tis impossible for a man of wit to keep his wench from being a lady, let me perish!

Ran. But have you no other acquaintance that sticks to her vocation, in spite of temptations of honour or filthy lucre? I declare, I make honourable love merely out of necessity, as your rooks play on the square rather than not play at all.

Enter LEONORE *masked, with a letter in her hand.*

Dap. Come, the devil will not lose a gamester: here's ready money for you, push freely.

Ran. Thou art as well met as if by assignation.

[*To* LEONORE.

Leo. And you are as well met as if you were the man I looked for.

Ran. Kind rogue!

Leo. Sweet sir!

Ran. Come, I am thy prisoner, (without more words,) show but thy warrant.   [*Goes to pull off her mask.*

Leo. You mistake, sir; here is my pass.

[*Gives him the letter.*

Ran. A letter! and directed to me!

[*Reads.*] "I cannot put up the injuries and affronts you did me last night;"—a challenge, upon my life! and by such a messenger!—"therefore conjure you by your honour, at eight o'clock precisely, this evening, to send your man to St. James's gate, to wait for me with a chair, to conduct me to what place you shall think most fit, for the giving of satisfaction to the injured —Christina."

Christina! I am amazed! What is it o'clock, Dapperwit?

Dap. It wants not half an hour of eight.

Ran. [*To* LEONORE.] Go then back, my pretty herald, and tell my fair enemy the service she designs

my man is only fit for my friend here; whose faith and
honour she may be secure of. He shall immediately go
wait for her at St. James's gate, whilst I go to prepare a
place for our rencounter, and myself to die at her feet.
[*Exit* LEONORE.] Dapperwit, dear Dapperwit.

Dap. What lucky surprisal's this?

Ran. Prithee ask no questions, till I have more leisure
and less astonishment. I know you will not deny to be
an instrument in my happiness.

Dap. No, let me perish! I take as much pleasure to
bring lovers together as an old woman; or as a bankrupt
gamester loves to look on, though he has no advantage
by the play; or as a bully that fights not himself, yet
takes pleasure to set people together by the ears, or as—

Ran. 'Sdeath! is this a time for similitudes?

Dap. You have made me miscarry of a good thought
now, let me perish!

Ran. Go presently to St. James's gate, where you are
to expect the coming of a lady ('tis Christina), accompanied by that woman you saw e'en now. She will
permit you to put her into a chair, and then conduct her
to my lodging; while I go before to remove some spies,
and prepare it for her reception.

Dap. Your lodging? had you not better carry her to
Vincent's? 'tis hard by; and there a vizard mask has as
free egress and regress as at the playhouse.

Ran. Faith, though it be not very prudent, yet she
shall come thither in my vindication; for he would not
believe I had seen her last night.

Dap. To have a fine woman, and not tell on't as you
say, Mr. Ranger—

Ran. Go, and bring her to Vincent's lodging; there
I'll expect you.   [*Exeunt severally.*

SCENE IV.—*The Street before* VINCENT'S *Lodging.*

Enter CHRISTINA *and* ISABEL.

Isa. This is the door, madam; here Mr. Vincent lodges.

Chris. 'Tis no matter, we will pass it by; lest the people of our lodgings should watch us. But if he should not be here now!

Isa. Who, Mr. Valentine, madam? I warrant you my intelligencer dares not fail me.

Chris. Did he come last night, said he?

Isa. Last night late.

Chris. And not see me yet! nay, not send to me!—'tis false, he is not come,—I wish he were not. I know not which I should take more unkindly from him, exposing his life to his revengeful enemies, or being almost four-and-twenty hours so near me, and not let me know't.

Isa. A lover's dangers are the only secrets kept from his mistress; he came not to you because he would not purchase his happiness with your fear and apprehensions.

Chris. Nay, he is come, I see, since you are come about again of his side.

Isa. Will you go in, madam, and disprove me, if you can? 'tis better than standing in the street.

Chris. We'll go a little further first, and return.

[*Exeunt.*

SCENE V.—VINCENT'S *Lodging.*

Enter VINCENT *and* VALENTINE.

Vin. I told you I had sent my man to Christina's this morning, to inquire of her maid, (who seldom denies him a secret,) if her lady had been at the Park last night;

which she peremptorily answered to the contrary, and assured him she had not stirred out since your departure.

Val. Will not chambermaids lie, Vincent?

Vin. Will not Ranger lie, Valentine?

Val. The circumstances of his story proved it true.

Vin. Do you think so old a master in the faculty as he will want the varnish of probability for his lies?

Val. Do you think a woman, having the advantage of her sex, and education under such a mistress, will want impudence to disavow a truth that might be prejudicial to that mistress?

Vin. But if both testimonies are fallible, why will you needs believe his? we are apter to believe the things we would have, than those we would not.

Val. My ill luck has taught me to credit my misfortunes and doubt my happiness.

Vin. But fortune we know is inconstant.

Val. And all of her sex.

Vin. Will you judge of fortune by your experience, and not do your mistress the same justice? Go see her, and satisfy yourself and her; for if she be innocent, consider how culpable you are, not only in your censures of her, but in not seeing her since your coming

Val. If she be innocent, I should be afraid to surprise her, for her sake; if false, I should be afraid to surprise her for my own.

Vin. To be jealous and not inquisitive is as hard as to love extremely and not to be something jealous.

Val. Inquisitiveness as seldom cures jealousy, as drinking in a fever quenches the thirst.

Vin. If she were at the Park last night, 'tis probable she'll not miss this. Go watch her house, see who goes out, who in; while I, in the meantime, search out Ranger; who, I'll pawn my life, upon more discourse shall avow his mistake.—Here he is; go in:—how luckily is he come!

[VALENTINE *retires to the door behind.*

Enter RANGER.

Ranger, you have prevented me: I was going to look you out, between the scenes at the playhouse, the coffee-house, tennis-court, or Gifford's.[1]

Ran. Do you want a pretence to go to a bawdy-house?—but I have other visits to make.

Vin. I forget. I should rather have sought you in Christina's lodgings, ha! ha! ha!

Ran. Well, well, I'm just come to tell you that Christina—

Vin. Proves not, by daylight, the kind lady you followed last night out of the Park.

Ran. I have better news for you, to my thinking.

Vin. What is't?

Ran. Not that I have been in Christina's lodging this morning; but that she'll be presently here in your lodging with me.

Val. How!   [*Aside.*

Vin. [*Retiring, and speaking softly to* VALENTINE.] You see now, his report was a jest, a mere jest.—[*To* RANGER.] Well, must my lodging be your vaulting-school[2] still? thou hast appointed a wench to come hither, I find.

Ran. A wench! you seemed to have more reverence for Christina last night.

Vin. Now you talk of Christina, prithee tell me what was the meaning of thy last night's romance of Christina.

Ran. You shall know the meaning of all when Christina comes; she'll be here presently.

Vin. Who will? Christina?

Ran. Yes, Christina.

Vin. Ha! ha! ha!

---

[1] Mother Gifford was a noted procuress, who is mentioned in several comedies of the time.

[2] Brothel.

Ran. Incredulous envy! thou art as envious as an impotent lecher at a wedding.

Vin. Thou art either mad, or as vain as a Frenchman newly returned home from a campaign, or obliging England.

Ran. Thou art as envious as a rival; but if thou art mine, there's that will make you desist; [*gives him a letter*] and if you are not my rival, entrusting you with such a secret will, I know, oblige you to keep it, and assist me against all other interests.

Vin. Do you think I take your secret as an obligation? don't I know, lovers, travellers, and poets, will give money to be heard? But what's the paper? a lampoon upon Christina, hatched last night betwixt squire Dapperwit and you, because her maid used you scurvily?

Ran. No, 'tis only a letter from her, to show my company was not so disgustful to her last night, but that she desires it again to-day.

Val. A letter from her! [*Aside.*

Vin. A letter from Christina! [*Reads.*]—Ha! ha! ha!

Ran. Nay, 'tis pleasant.

Vin. You mistake, I laugh at you, not the letter.

Ran. I am like the winning gamester, so pleased with my luck, I will not quarrel with any who calls me a fool for't.

Vin. Is this the style of a woman of honour?

Ran. It may be, for ought you know; I'm sure 'tis well if your female correspondents can read.

Vin. I must confess I have none of the little letters, half name or title, like your Spanish Epistles Dedicatory; but that a man so frequent in honourable intrigues as you are, should not know the summons of an impudent common woman, from that of a person of honour!

Ran. Christina is so much a person of honour she'll own what she has writ when she comes.

Vin. But will she come hither indeed?

Ran. Immediately. You'll excuse my liberty with you :

I could not conceal such a happiness from such a friend as you, lest you should have taken it unkindly.

Vin. Faith, you have obliged me indeed ; for you and others would often have made me believe your honourable intrigues, but never did me the honour to convince me of 'em before.

Ran. You are merry, I find, yet.

Vin. When you are happy I cannot be otherwise.

Ran. [*Aside.*] But I lose time ; I should lay a little parson in ambush, that lives hard by, in case Christina should be impatient to be revenged of her friends, as it often happens with a discontented heiress. Women, like old soldiers, more nimbly execute than they resolve.

[*Going out.*

Vin. What now ! you will not disappoint a woman of Christina's quality ?

Ran. I'll be here before she comes, I warrant you.

[*Exit.*

Vin. I do believe you truly !— What think you, Valentine ?

Val. [*Coming forward.*] I think, since she has the courage to challenge him, she'll have the honour of being first in the field.

Vin. Fy, your opinion of her must be as bad, as Ranger's of himself is good, to think she would write to him. I long till his bona-roba[1] comes, that you may be both disabused.

Val. And I have not patience to stay her coming, lest you should be disabused.

Enter CHRISTINA *and* ISABEL.

Vin. Here she is, i'faith ; I'm glad she's come.

Val. And I'm sorry. But I will to my post again, lest she should say she came to me.   [*Retires as before.*

Vin. [*Aside.*] By heavens, Christina herself ! 'tis she !

[CHRISTINA *pulls off her mask.*

Val. 'Tis she :—cursed be these eyes ! more cursed

---

[1] Prostitute.

than when they first betrayed me to that false bewitching
face.   [*Aside.*

Chris. You may wonder, sir, to see me here—

Vin. I must confess I do.

Chris. But the confidence your friend has in you is the
cause of mine ; and yet some blushes it does cost me to
come to seek a man.

Val. Modest creature !   [*Aside.*

Vin. How am I deceived !   [*Aside.*

Chris. Where is he, sir ? why does he not appear, to
keep me in countenance ? pray call him, sir ; 'tis something hard if he should know I'm here.

Vin. I hardly can myself believe you are here,
madam.

Chris. If my visit be troublesome or unseasonable, 'tis
your friend's fault ; I designed it not to you, sir. Pray
call him out, that he may excuse it, and take it on himself, together with my shame.

Vin. How impatient she is !   [*Aside.*

Chris. Or do you delay the happiness I ask, to make
it more welcome ? I have stayed too long for it already,
and cannot more desire it. Dear sir, call him out.
Where is he ? above, or here within ? I'll snatch the
favour which you will not give—[*Goes to the door and discovers* VALENTINE.] What ! Do you hide yourself for
shame ?

Val. [*Coming forward.*] I must confess I do.

Chris. To see me come hither—

Val. I acknowledge it.   [VALENTINE *offers to go out.*

Chris. Before you came to me ? But whither do you
go ? come, I can forgive you.

Val. But I cannot forgive you.

Chris. Whither do you go ? you need not forge a
quarrel to prevent mine to you : nor need you try if I
would follow you, you know I will ;—I have, you see.

Val. That impudence should look so like innocence !
                                            [*Aside.*

Chris. Whither would you go ? why would you go ?

Val. To call your servant to you.

Chris. She is here ; what would you have with her ?

Val. I mean your lover,—the man you came to meet.

Chris. Oh heavens ! what lover ? what man ? I came to see no man but you, whom I had too long lost.

Val. You could not know that I was here.

Chris. Ask her ; 'twas she that told me.

[*Points to* ISABEL.

Val. How could she know?

Chris. That you shall know hereafter.

Val. No, you thought me too far out of the way to disturb your assignation ; and I assure you, madam, 'twas my ill-fortune, not my design : and that it may appear so, I do withdraw, as in all good breeding and civility I am obliged ; for sure your wished-for lover's coming.

Chris. What do you mean ? are you a-weary of that title ?

Val. I am ashamed of it, since it grows common.

[*Going out.*

Chris. Nay, you will not, shall not go.

Val. My stay might give him jealousy, and so do you injury, and him the greatest in the world : heavens forbid ! I would not make a man jealous ; for though you call a thousand vows, and oaths, and tears to witness (as you safely may), that you have not the least of love for me, yet if he ever knew how I have loved you, sure he would not, could not believe you.

Chris. I do confess, your riddle is too hard for me to solve ; therefore you are obliged to do't yourself.

Val. I wish it were capable of any other interpretation than what you know already.

Chris. Is this that generous good Valentine ? who has disguised him so ?   [*Weeps.*

Vin. Nay, I must withhold you then. [*Stops* VALEN-TINE *going out.*] Methinks she should be innocent ; her tongue, and eyes, together with that flood that swells 'em, do vindicate her heart.

Val. They show but their long practice of dissimulation.   [*Going out.*

Vin. Come back: I hear Ranger coming up : stay but
till he comes.

Val. Do you think I have the patience of an alderman ?

Vin. You may go out this way, when you will, by the
back-stairs ; but stay a little, till—Oh, here he comes.

Re-enter RANGER.   *Upon his entrance* CHRISTINA
puts on her mask.

Val. My revenge will now detain me.
                               [VALENTINE *retires again.*

Ran. [*Aside.*]—What, come already ! where is Dapperwit ?—[*Aloud.*] The blessing's double that comes quickly ;
I did not yet expect you here, otherwise I had not done
myself the injury to be absent. But I hope, madam, I
have not made you stay long for me.

Chris. I have not staid at all for you.

Ran. I am glad of it, madam.

Chris. [*To* ISABEL.] Is not this that troublesome
stranger who last night followed the lady into my
lodgings ?—[*Aside.*] 'Tis he.
                       [*Removing from him to the other side.*

Ran. [*Aside.*] Why does she remove so disdainfully
from me ?—[*Aloud.*] I find you take it ill I was not at
your coming here, madam.

Chris. Indeed I do not ; you are mistaken, sir.

Ran. Confirm me by a smile then, madam; remove
that cloud, which makes me apprehend foul weather.
[*Goes to take off her mask.*]—Mr. Vincent, pray retire ;
'tis you keep on the lady's mask, and no displeasure
which she has for me.—Yet, madam, you need not distrust his honour or his faith.—But do not keep the lady
under constraint ; pray leave us a little, Master Vincent.

Chris. You must not leave us, sir ; would you leave
me with a stranger ?

Val. How's that!   [*Aside.*

Ran. [*Aside.*] I've done amiss, I find, to bring her hither.—Madam, I understand you—

                                        [*Apart to* CHRISTINA.

Chris. Sir, I do not understand you.

Ran. You would not be known to Mr. Vincent.

Chris. 'Tis your acquaintance I would avoid.

Ran. [*Aside.*] Dull brute that I was, to bring her hither!—I have found my error, madam; give me but a new appointment, where I may meet you by and by, and straight I will withdraw as if I knew you not. [*Softly to her.*

Chris. Why, do you know me?

Ran. [*Aside.*] I must not own it.—No, madam, but—
                                        [*Offers to whisper.*

Chris. Whispering, sir, argues an old acquaintance; but I have not the vanity to be thought of yours, and resolve you shall never have the disparagement of mine.— Mr. Vincent, pray let us go in here.

Ran. How's this! I am undone, I see; but if I let her go thus, I shall be an eternal laughing-stock to Vincent.
                                        [*Aside.*

Vin. Do you not know him, madam? I thought you had come hither on purpose to meet him.

Chris. To meet him!

Vin. By your own appointment.

Chris. What strange infatuation does delude you all? you know, he said he did not know me.

Vin. You writ to him; he has your letter.

Chris. Then, you know my name sure? yet you confessed but now you knew me not.

Ran. I must confess your anger has disguised you more than your mask: for I thought to have met a kinder Christina here.

Chris. [*Aside.*] Heavens! how could he know me in this place? he watched me hither sure; or is there any other of my name.—[*Aloud.*] That you may no longer

mistake me for your Christina, I'll pull off that which
soothes your error.   [*Pulls off her mask.*

Ran. Take but t'other vizard off too, (I mean your
anger,) and I'll swear you are the same, and only Christina which I wished, and thought, to meet here.

Chris. How could you think to meet me here?

Ran. [*Gives her the letter.*] By virtue of this your commission; which now, I see, was meant a real challenge:
for you look as if you would fight with me.

Chris. The paper is a stranger to me; I never writ it.
You are abused.

Vin. Christina is a person of honour, and will own
what she has written, Ranger.

Ran. [*Aside.*] So! the comedy begins; I shall be
laughed at sufficiently if I do not justify myself; I must
set my impudence to hers. She is resolved to deny all,
I see, and I have lost all hope of her.

Vin. Come, faith, Ranger—

Ran. You will deny too, madam, that I followed you
last night from the Park to your lodging, where I staid
with you till morning? you never saw me before, I
warrant.

Chris. That you rudely intruded last night into my
lodging, I cannot deny; but I wonder you have the
confidence to brag of it: sure you will not of your
reception?

Ran. I never was so ill-bred as to brag of my reception
in a lady's chamber; not a word of that, madam.

Val. [*Aside.*] How! If he lies, I revenge her; if it
be true, I revenge myself.

> [VALENTINE *draws his sword, which* VINCENT,
> *seeing, thrusts him back, and shuts the door
> upon him before he is discovered by* RANGER.

Enter LYDIA *and* LEONORE, *stopping at the door.*

Lyd. What do I see! Christina with him! a counter-
plot to mine, to make me and it ridiculous. 'Tis true,
I find, they have been long acquainted, and I long

abused ; but since she intends a triumph, in spite, as well as shame, (not emulation,) I retire. She deserves no envy, who will be shortly in my condition ; his natural inconstancy will prove my best revenge on her—on both.

[*Exeunt* LYDIA *and* LEONORE.

Enter DAPPERWIT.

Dap. Christina's going away again ; — what's the matter ?

Ran. What do you mean ?

Dap. I scarce had paid the chairmen, and was coming up after her, but I met her on the stairs, in as much haste as if she had been frightened.

Ran. Who do you talk of ?

Dap. Christina, whom I took up in a chair just now at St. James's gate.

Ran. Thou art mad ! here she is, this is Christina.

Dap. I must confess I did not see her face ; but I am sure the lady is gone that I brought just now.

Ran. I tell you again this is she : did you bring two ?

Chris. I came in no chair, had no guide but my woman there.

Vin. When did you bring your lady, Dapperwit ?

Dap. Even now, just now.

Vin. This lady has been here half-an-hour.

Ran. He knows not what he says, he is mad : you are all so ; I am so too.

Vin. 'Tis the best excuse you can make for yourself, and by owning your mistake you'll show you are come to yourself.   I myself saw your woman at the door, who but looked in, and then immediately went down again ;—as your friend Dapperwit too affirms.

Chris. You had best follow her that looked for you ; and I'll go seek out him I came to see.—Mr. Vincent, pray let me in here.

Ran. 'Tis very fine ! wondrous fine !

[CHRISTINA *goes out a little, and returns.*

Chris. Oh! he is gone! Mr. Vincent, follow him; he were yet more severe to me in endangering his life, than in his censures against me. You know the power of his enemies is great as their malice;—just Heaven preserve him from them, and me from this ill or unlucky man!

[*Exeunt* CHRISTINA, ISABEL, *and* VINCENT.

Ran. 'Tis well—nay, certainly, I shall never be master of my senses more: but why dost thou help to distract me too?

Dap. My astonishment was as great as yours to see her go away again; I would have stayed her if I could.

Ran. Yet again talking of a woman you met going out, when I talk of Christina!

Dap. I talk of Christina too.

Ran. She went out just now; the woman you found me with was she.

Dap. That was not the Christina I brought just now.

Ran. You brought her almost half an hour ago;— 'sdeath, will you give me the lie?

Dap. A lady disappointed by her gallant, the night before her journey, could not be more touchy with her maid or husband, than you are with me now after your disappointment; but if you thank me so, I'll go serve myself hereafter. For aught I know, I have disappointed Mrs. Martha for you, and may lose thirty thousand pounds by the bargain. Farewell! a raving lover is fit for solitude.   [*Exit.*

Ran. Lydia, triumph! I now am thine again. Of intrigues, honourable or dishonourable, and all sorts of rambling, I take my leave; when we are giddy, 'tis time to stand still. Why should we be so fond of the by-paths of love, where we are still waylaid with surprises, trepans, dangers, and murdering disappointments?—

Just as at blindman's buff we run at all,
Whilst those that lead us laugh to see us fall;
And when we think we hold the lady fast,
We find it but her scarf, or veil, at last.   [*Exit.*

ACT THE FIFTH.

SCENE I.—*St. James's Park.*

Enter DAPPERWIT *and* Sir SIMON ADDLEPLOT, *the latter leading* Mrs. MARTHA.

Sir Sim. At length you see I have freed the captive lady for her longing knight, Mr. Dapperwit:—who brings off a plot cleverly now?

Dap. I wish our poets were half so good at it.—Mrs. Martha, a thousand welcomes!

[DAPPERWIT *kisses and embraces* Mrs. MARTHA.

Sir Sim. Hold, hold, sir! your joy is a little too familiar, faith and troth!

Dap. Will you not let me salute Mrs. Martha?

Mrs. Mar. What, Jonas, do you think I do not know good breeding? must I be taught by you?

Sir Sim. I would have kept the maidenhead of your lips for your sweet knight, Mrs. Martha, that's all; I dare swear you never kissed any man before but your father.

Mrs. Mar. My sweet knight, if he will be knight of mine, must be contented with what he finds, as well as other knights.

Sir Sim. So smart already, faith and troth!

Mrs. Mar. Dear Mr. Dapperwit I am overjoyed to see you; but I thank honest Jonas for't.

[*She hugs* DAPPERWIT.

Sir Sim. [*Aside.*] How she hugs him !

Mrs. Mar. Poor Mr. Dapperwit, I thought I should never have seen you again ; but I thank honest Jonas there—

Sir Sim. Do not thank me, Mrs. Martha, any more than I thank you.

Mrs. Mar. I would not be ungrateful, Jonas.

Sir Sim. Then reserve your kindness only for your worthy, noble, brave, heroic knight, who loves you only, and only deserves your kindness.

Mrs. Mar. I will show my kindness to my worthy, brave, heroic knight, in being kind to his friend, his dear friend, who helped him to me. [*Hugs* DAPPERWIT *again.*

Sir Sim. But, Mistress Martha, he is not to help him always ; though he helps him to be married, he is not to help him when he is married.

Mrs. Mar. What, Mr. Dapperwit, will you love my worthy knight less after marriage than before ? that were against the custom ; for marriage gets a man friends, instead of losing those he has.

Dap. I will ever be his servant and yours, dear madam ; do not doubt me.

Mrs. Mar. I do not, sweet dear Mr. Dapperwit ; but I should not have seen you these two days if it had not been for honest Jonas there—   [*She kisses* DAPPERWIT.

Sir Sim. [*Apart to* DAPPERWIT.] For shame ! though she be young and foolish, do not you wrong me to my face.

Dap. Would you have me so ill bred as to repulse her innocent kindness ?—what a thing it is to want wit !

Sir Sim. [*Aside.*] A pox ! I must make haste to discover myself, or I shall discover what I would not discover ; but if I should discover myself in this habit, 'twould not be to my advantage.   But I'll go, put on my own clothes, and look like a knight.—[*Aloud.*] Well, Mrs. Martha, I'll go seek out your knight : are you not impatient to see him ?

Mrs. Mar. Wives must be obedient ; let him take his own time.

Sir Sim. Can you trust yourself a turn or two with Master Dapperwit ?

Mrs. Mar. Yes, yes, Jonas—as long as you will.

Sir Sim. [*Aside.*] But I would not trust you with him, if I could help it :—

So married wight sees what he dares not blame ;
And cannot budge for fear, nor stay for shame. [*Exit.*

Dap. I am glad he is gone, that I may laugh. 'Tis such a miracle of fops, that his conversation should be pleasant to me, even when it hindered me of yours.

Mrs. Mar. Indeed, I'm glad he is gone too, as pleasant as he is.

Dap. I know why, I know why, sweet Mrs. Martha. I warrant you, you had rather have the parson's company than his ?—now you are out of your father's house, 'tis time to leave being a hypocrite.

Mrs. Mar. Well, for the jest's sake, to disappoint my knight, I would not care if I disappointed myself of a ladyship.

Dap. Come, I will not keep you on the tenters ; I know you have a mind to make sure of me : I have a little chaplain (I wish he were a bishop or one of the friars) to perfect our revenge upon that zealous Jew, your father.

Mrs. Mar. Do not speak ill of my father ; he has been your friend, I'm sure.

Dap. My friend !

Mrs. Mar. His hard usage of me conspired with your good mien and wit, and to avoid slavery unto him, I stoop to your yoke.

Dap. I will be obliged to your father for nothing but a portion ; nor to you for your love ; 'twas due to my merit.

Mrs. Mar. You show yourself Sir Simon's original ; if 'twere not for that vanity—

Dap. I should be no wit—'tis the badge of my calling; for you can no more find a man of wit without vanity than a fine woman without affectation: but let us go before the knight comes again.

Mrs. Mar. Let us go before my father comes; he soon will have the intelligence.

Dap. Stay, let me think a little.   [*Pauses.*

Mrs. Mar. What are you thinking of? you should have thought before this time, or I should have thought rather.

Dap. Peace! peace!

Mrs. Mar. What are you thinking of?

Dap. I am thinking what a wit without vanity is like. He is like—

Mrs. Mar. You do not think we are in a public place, and may be surprised and prevented by my father's scouts!

Dap. What! would you have me lose my thought?

Mrs. Mar. You would rather lose your mistress, it seems.

Dap. He is like—I think I am a sot to-night, let me perish.

Mrs. Mar. Nay, if you are so in love with your thought—   [*Offers to go.*

Dap. Are you so impatient to be my wife?—He is like —he is like—a picture without shadows, or—or—a face without patches—or a diamond without a foil. These are new thoughts now, these are new!

Mrs. Mar. You are wedded already to your thoughts, I see;—good night.

Dap. Madam, do not take it ill:—

For loss of happy thought there's no amends;
For his new jest true wit will lose old friends.

That's new again,—the thought's new.   [*Exeunt.*

SCENE II.—*Another part of the same.*

Enter GRIPE, *leading* LUCY ; MRS. JOYNER *and* MRS.
CROSSBITE *following.*

Gripe. Mrs. Joyner, I can conform to this mode of
public walking by moonlight, because one is not known.

Lucy. Why, are you ashamed of your company?

Gripe. No, pretty one ; because in the dark, or as it
were in the dark, there is no envy nor scandal.   I would
neither lose you nor my reputation.

Mrs. Joyn. Your reputation ! indeed, your worship,
'tis well known there are as grave men as your worship ;
nay, men in office too, that adjourn their cares and
businesses, to come and unbend themselves at night
here, with a little vizard-mask.

Gripe. I do believe it, Mrs. Joyner.

Lucy. Ay, godmother, and carries and treats her at
Mulberry-garden.

Mrs. Cros. Nay, does not only treat her, but gives her
his whole gleaning of that day.

Gripe. They may, they may, Mrs. Crossbite ; they
take above six in the hundred.

Mrs. Cros. Nay, there are those of so much worth and
honour and love, that they'll take it from their wives and
children to give it to their misses ; now your worship has
no wife, and but one child.

Gripe. Still for my edification !   [*Aside.*

Mrs. Joyn. That's true, indeed ; for I know a great
lady that cannot follow her husband abroad to his haunts,
because her Ferrandine is so ragged and greasy, whilst
his mistress is as fine as fi'pence, in embroidered satins.

Gripe. Politicly done of him indeed ! If the truth
were known, he is a statesman by that, umph—

Mrs. Cros. Truly, your women of quality are very
troublesome to their husbands ; I have heard 'em complain, they will allow them no separate maintenance,

though the honourable jilts themselves will not marry without it.

Mrs. Joyn. Come, come, mistress; sometimes 'tis the craft of those gentlemen to complain of their wives' expenses to excuse their own narrowness to their misses; but your daughter has a gallant that can make no excuse.

Gripe. So, Mrs. Joyner!—my friend, Mrs. Joyner—

Mrs. Cros. I hope, indeed, he'll give my daughter no cause to dun him; for, poor wretch! she is as modest as her mother.

Gripe. I profess, I believe it.

Lucy. But I have the boldness to ask him for a treat.— Come, gallant, we must walk towards the Mulberry-garden.

Gripe. So!—I am afraid, little mistress, the rooms are all taken up by this time.

Mrs. Joyn. Will you shame yourself again?

[*Aside to* GRIPE.

Lucy. If the rooms be full we'll have an arbour.

Gripe. At this time of night!—besides, the waiters will ne'er come near you.

Lucy. They will be observant of good customers, as we shall be. Come along.

Gripe. Indeed, and verily, little mistress, I would go, but that I should be forsworn if I did.

Mrs. Joyn. That's so pitiful an excuse!—

Gripe. In truth, I have forsworn the place ever since I was pawned there for a reckoning.

Lucy. You have broken many an oath for the good old cause, and will you boggle at one for your poor little miss? Come along.

Enter Lady FLIPPANT *behind.*

L. Flip. Unfortunate lady that I am! I have left the herd on purpose to be chased, and have wandered this hour here; but the Park affords not so much as a satyr for me, and (that's strange!) no Burgundy man or drunken scourer will reel my way. The rag-women, and cinder-women, have better luck than I.—But who are these? if this mongrel light does not deceive me, 'tis my brother,—'tis he:—there's Joyner, too, and two other women. I'll follow 'em. It must be he, for this world hath nothing like him;—I know not what the devil may be in the other. [*Exeunt.*

SCENE III.—*Another part of the same.*

Enter Sir SIMON ADDLEPLOT, *in fine clothes,* DAPPERWIT *and* Mrs. MARTHA, *unseen by him at the door.*

Sir Sim. Well, after all my seeking, I can find those I would not find; I'm sure 'twas old Gripe, and Joyner with him, and the widow followed. He would not have been here, but to have sought his daughter, sure; but vigilant Dapperwit has spied them too, and has, no doubt, secured her from him.

Dap. And you.   [*Aside.*

Sir Sim. The rogue is as good at hiding, as I am at stealing, a mistress. 'Tis a vain, conceited fellow, yet I think 'tis an honest fellow:—but, again, he is a damnable whoring fellow; and what opportunity this air and darkness may incline 'em to, Heaven knows; for I have heard the rogue say himself, a lady will no more show her modesty in the dark than a Spaniard his courage.

Dap. Ha! ha! ha!—

Sir Sim. Nay, if you are there, my true friend, I'll forgive your hearkening, if you'll forgive my censures.— I speak to you, dear Madam Martha; dear, dear— behold your worthy knight—

Mrs. Mar. That's far from neighbours.

Sir Sim. Is come to reap the fruit of his labours.

Mrs. Mar. I cannot see the knight; well, but I'm sure I hear Jonas.

Sir Sim. I am no Jonas, Mrs. Martha.

Mrs. Mar. The night is not so dark, nor the peruke so big, but I can discern Jonas.

Sir Sim. Faith and troth, I am the very Sir Simon Addleplot that is to marry you; the same Dapperwit solicited you for; ask him else, my name is not Jonas.

Mrs. Mar. You think my youth and simplicity capable of this cheat; but let me tell you, Jonas, 'tis not your borrowed clothes and titles shall make me marry my father's man.

Sir Sim. Borrowed title! I'll be sworn I bought it of my laundress, who was a court-laundress; but, indeed, my clothes I have not paid for; therefore, in that sense, they are borrowed.

Mrs. Mar. Prithee, Jonas, let the jest end, or I shall be presently in earnest.

Sir Sim. Pray, be in earnest, and let us go; the parson and supper stay for us, and I am a knight in earnest.

Mrs. Mar. You a knight! insolent, saucy fool.

Sir Sim. The devil take me, Mrs. Martha, if I am not a knight now! a knight-baronet too! A man ought, I see, to carry his patent in his pocket when he goes to be married; 'tis more necessary than a licence. I am a knight indeed and indeed now, Mrs. Martha.

Mrs. Mar. Indeed and indeed, the trick will not pass, Jonas.

Sir Sim. Poor wretch! she's afraid she shall not be a lady.—Come, come, discover the intrigue, Dapperwit.

Mrs. Mar. You need not discover the intrigue, 'tis apparent already. Unworthy Mr. Dapperwit, after my confidence reposed in you, could you be so little generous as to betray me to my father's man? but I'll be even with you.

Sir Sim. Do not accuse him, poor man! before you hear him.—Tell her the intrigue, man.

Dap. A pox! she will not believe us.

Sir Sim. Will you not excuse yourself? but I must not let it rest so.—Know, then, Mrs. Martha—

Mrs. Mar. Come, I forgive thee before thy confession, Jonas; you never had had the confidence to have designed this cheat upon me but from Mr. Dapperwit's encouragement—'twas his plot.

Sir Sim. Nay, do not do me that wrong, madam.

Mrs. Mar. But since he has trepanned me out of my father's house, he is like to keep me as long as I live; and so good night, Jonas.

Sir Sim. Hold, hold, what d'ye mean both? prithee tell her I am Sir Simon, and no Jonas.

Dap. A pox! she will not believe us, I tell you.

Sir Sim. I have provided a supper and parson at Mulberry-garden, and invited all my friends I could meet in the Park.

Dap. Nay, rather than they shall be disappointed, there shall be a bride and bridegroom to entertain 'em; Mrs. Martha and I will go thither presently.

Sir Sim. Why, shall she be your bride?

Dap. You see she will have it so.

Sir Sim. Will you make Dapperwit your husband?

Mrs. Mar. Rather than my father's man.

Sir Sim. Oh, the devil!

Mrs. Mar. Nay, come along, Jonas, you shall make one at the wedding, since you helped to contrive it.

Sir Sim. Will you cheat yourself, for fear of being cheated?

Mrs. Mar. I am desperate now.

Sir Sim. Wilt thou let her do so ill a thing, Dapperwit, as to marry thee? open her eyes, prithee, and tell her I am a true knight.

Dap. 'Twould be in vain, by my life! you have carried yourself so like a natural clerk—and so adieu, good Jonas. [*Exeunt* Mrs. MARTHA *and* DAPPERWIT.

Sir Sim. What! ruined by my own plot, like an old cavalier! yet like him, too, I will plot on still, a plot of prevention. So! I have it—her father was here even now, I'm sure; well—I'll go tell her father of her, that I will!

And punish so her folly and his treachery:
Revenge is sweet, and makes amends for lechery.

[*Exit.*

SCENE IV.—*Another part of the same.*

Enter LYDIA *and* LEONORE.

Lyd. I wish I had not come hither to-night, Leonore.

Leo. Why did you, madam, if the place be so disagreeable to you?

Lyd. We cannot help visiting the place often where we have lost anything we value: I lost Ranger here last night.

Leo. You thought you had lost him before, a great while ago; and therefore you ought to be the less troubled.

Lyd. But 'twas here I missed him first, I'm sure.

Leo. Come, madam, let not the loss vex you; he is not worth the looking after.

Lyd. It cannot but vex me yet, if I lost him by my own fault.

Leo. You had but too much care to keep him.

Lyd. It often happens, indeed, that too much care is as bad as negligence; but I had rather be robbed than lose what I have carelessly.

Leo. But, I believe you would hang the thief if you could.

Lyd. Not if I could have my own again.

Leo. I see you would be too merciful.

Lyd. I wish I were tried.

Leo. But, madam, if you please, we will waive the discourse; for people seldom (I suppose) talk with pleasure of their real losses.

Lyd. 'Tis better than to ruminate on them ; mine, I'm sure, will not out of head nor heart.

Leo. Grief is so far from retrieving a loss, that it makes it greater; but the way to lessen it is by a comparison with others' losses.   Here are ladies in the Park of your acquaintance, I doubt not, can compare with you ; pray, madam, let us walk and find 'em out.

Lyd. 'Tis the resentment, you say, makes the loss great or little; and then, I'm sure, there is none like mine : however, go on.   [*Exeunt.*

SCENE V.—*Another part of the same.*

Enter VINCENT *and* VALENTINE.

Vin. I am glad I have found you, for now I am prepared to lead you out of the dark and all your trouble : I have good news.

Val. You are as unmerciful as the physician who with new arts keeps his miserable patient alive and in hopes, when he knows the disease is incurable.

Vin. And you, like the melancholy patient, mistrust and hate your physician, because he will not comply with your despair : but I'll cure your jealousy now.

Val. You know, all diseases grow worse by relapses.

Vin. Trust me once more.

Val. Well, you may try your experiments upon me.

Vin. Just as I shut the door upon you, the woman Ranger expected came up stairs ; but finding another woman in discourse with him, went down again ; I suppose, as jealous of him, as you of Christina.

Val. How does it appear she came to Ranger ?

Vin. Thus : Dapperwit came up after he had brought her, just then, in a chair from St. James's by Ranger's appointment ; and it is certain your Christina came to you.

Val. How can that be? for she knew not I was in the kingdom.

Vin. My man confesses, when I sent him to inquire of her woman about her lady's being here in the Park last night, he told her you were come; and she, it seems, told her mistress.

Val. [*Aside.*] That might be.—[*Aloud.*] But did not Christina confess, Ranger was in her lodging last night?

Vin. By intrusion, which she had more particularly informed me of, if her apprehensions of your danger had not posted me after you; she not having yet (as I suppose) heard of Clerimont's recovery. I left her, poor creature! at home, distracted with a thousand fears for your life and love.

Val. Her love, I'm sure, has cost me more fears than my life; yet that little danger is not past (as you think) till the great one be over.

Vin. Open but your eyes, and the fantastic goblin's vanished, and all your idle fears will turn to shame; for jealousy is the basest cowardice.

Val. I had rather, indeed, blush for myself than her.

Vin. I'm sure you will have more reason. But is not that Ranger there?

Enter RANGER, *followed by* CHRISTINA *and* ISABEL; *after them* LYDIA *and* LEONORE.

Val. I think it is.

Vin. I suppose his friend Dapperwit is not far off; I will examine them both before you, and not leave you so much as the shadow of doubt: Ranger's astonishment at my lodging confessed his mistake.

Val. His astonishment might proceed from Christina's unexpected strangeness to him.

Vin. He shall satisfy you now himself to the contrary, I warrant you; have but patience.

Val. I had rather, indeed, he should satisfy my doubts than my revenge; therefore I can have patience.

Vin. But what women are those that follow him?

Val. Stay a little—

Ran. Lydia, Lydia—poor Lydia!

Lyd. If she be my rival, 'tis some comfort yet to see her follow him, rather than he her.   [*To* LEONORE.

Leo. But if you follow them a little longer, for your comfort you shall see them go hand in hand.

Chris. Sir! sir!—   [*To* RANGER.

Leo. She calls to him already.

Lyd. But he does not hear, you see; let us go a little nearer.

Vin. Sure it is Ranger!

Val. As sure as the woman that follows him closest is Christina.

Vin. For shame! talk not of Christina; I left her just now at home, surrounded with so many fears and griefs she could not stir.

Val. She is come, it may be, to divert them here in the Park; I'm sure 'tis she.

Vin. When the moon, at this instant, scarce affords light enough to distinguish a man from a tree, how can you know her?

Val. How can you know Ranger, then?

Vin. I heard him speak.

Val. So you may her too, I'll secure you, if you will draw but a little nearer; she came, doubtless, to no other end but to speak with him: observe—

Chris. [*To* RANGER.] Sir, I have followed you hitherto; but now, I must desire you to follow me out of the company; for I would not be overheard nor disturbed.

Ran. Ha! is not this Christina's voice? it is, I am sure; I cannot be deceived now.—Dear madam—

Vin. It is she indeed.   [*Apart to* VALENTINE.

Val. Is it so?

Chris. Come, sir—   [*To* RANGER.

Val. Nay, I'll follow you too, though not invited.

     [*Aside.*

Lyd. I must not, cannot stay behind.   [*Aside.*
          [*They all go off together hastily.*

Re-enter CHRISTINA, ISABEL, *and* VALENTINE *on the other side.*

Chris. Come along, sir.

Val. So! I must stick to her when all is done; her new servant has lost her in the crowd, she has gone too fast for him; so much my revenge is swifter than his love. Now shall I not only have the deserted lover's revenge, of disappointing her of her new man, but an opportunity infallibly at once to discover her falseness, and confront her impudence.   [*Aside.*

Chris. Pray come along, sir, I am in haste.

Val. So eager, indeed!—I wish that cloud may yet withhold the moon, that this false woman may not discover me before I do her.   [*Aside.*

Chris. Here no one can hear us, and I'm sure we can not see one another.

Val. 'Sdeath! what have I giddily run myself upon? 'Tis rather a trial of myself than her;—I cannot undergo it.   [*Aside.*

Chris. Come nearer, sir.

Val. Hell and vengeance! I cannot suffer it—I cannot.   [*Aside.*

Chris. Come, come; yet nearer, — pray come nearer.

Val. It is impossible! I cannot hold! I must discover myself, rather than her infamy.   [*Aside.*

Chris. You are conscious, it seems, of the wrong you have done me, and are ashamed, though in the dark.
          [*Speaks, walking slowly.*

Val. How's this!   [*Aside.*

Chris. I'm glad to find it so; for all my business with you is to show you your late mistakes, and force a confession from you of those unmannerly injuries you have done me.

Val. What! I think she's honest; or does she know me?—sure she cannot. [*Aside.*

Chris. First, your intrusion, last night, into my lodging; which, I suppose, has begot your other gross mistakes.

Val. No, she takes me for Ranger, I see again. [*Aside.*

Chris. You are to know, then, (since needs you must,) it was not me you followed last night to my lodging from the Park, but some kinswoman of yours, it seems, whose fear of being discovered by you prevailed with me to personate her, while she withdrew, our habits and our statures being much alike; which I did with as much difficulty, as she used importunity to make me; and all this my Lady Flippant can witness, who was then with your cousin.

Val. I am glad to hear this. [*Aside.*

Chris. Now, what your claim to me, at Mr. Vincent's lodging, meant; the letter and promises you unworthily, or erroneously, laid to my charge, you must explain to me and others, or—

Val. How's this! I hope I shall discover no guilt but my own:—she would not speak in threats to a lover. [*Aside.*

Chris. Was it because you found me in Mr. Vincent's lodgings you took a liberty to use me like one of your common visitants? but know, I came no more to Mr. Vincent than you. Yet, I confess, my visit was intended to a man—a brave man, till you made him use a woman ill; worthy the love of a princess, till you made him censure mine; good as angels, till you made him unjust:—why, in the name of honour, would you do't?

Val. How happily am I disappointed!—poor injured Christina! [*Aside.*

Chris. He would have sought me out first, if you had not made him fly from me. Our mutual love, confirmed by a contract, made our hearts inseparable, till you rudely, if not maliciously, thrust in upon us, and broke the close and happy knot: I had lost him before for a month, now for ever. [*Weeps.*

Val. My joy and pity makes me as mute as my shame; yet I must discover myself.   [*Aside.*

Chris. Your silence is a confession of your guilt.

Val. I own it.   [*Aside.*

Chris. But that will not serve my turn; for straight you must go clear yourself and me to him you have injured in me! if he has not made too much haste from me to be found again. You must, I say; for he is a man that will have satisfaction; and in satisfying him, you do me.

Val. Then he is satisfied.

Chris. How! is it you? then I am not satisfied.

Val. Will you be worse than your word?

Chris. I gave it not to you.

Val. Come, dear Christina, the jealous, like the drunkard, has his punishment with his offence.

Re-enter VINCENT.

Vin. Valentine! Mr. Valentine!

Val. Vincent!—

Vin. Where have you been all this while?

[VALENTINE *holds* CHRISTINA *by the hand, who seems to struggle to get from him.*

Val. Here with my injured Christina.

Vin. She's behind with Ranger, who is forced to speak all the tender things himself; for she affords him not a word.

Val. Pish! pish! Vincent; who is blind now? who deceived now?

Vin. You are; for I'm sure Christina is with him. Come back and see.

[*They go out on one side, and return on the other.*

Re-enter LYDIA *and* LEONORE, *followed by* RANGER.

Ran. [*To* LYDIA.] Still mocked! still abused! did you not bid me follow you where we might not be disturbed or overheard?—and now not allow me a word!

Vin. Did you hear him ?   [*Apart to* VALENTINE.

Val. Yes, yes, peace.   [*Apart to* VINCENT.

Ran. Disowning your letter and me at Mr. Vincent's
lodging, declaring you came to meet another there, and
not me, with a great deal of such affronting unkindness,
might be reasonable enough, because you would not
entrust Vincent with our love ; but now, when nobody
sees us nor hears us, why this unseasonable shyness ?

Lyd. It seems she did not expect him there, but had
appointed to meet another :—I wish it were so.   [*Aside.*

Ran. I have not patience !—do you design thus to
revenge my intrusion into your lodging last night ? sure
if you had then been displeased with my company, you
would not have invited yourself to't again by a letter ? or
is this a punishment for bringing you to a house so near
your own, where, it seems, you were known too ? I do
confess it was a fault ; but make me suffer any penance
but your silence, because it is the certain mark of a
mistress's lasting displeasure.

Lyd. My—is not yet come.   [*Aside.*

Ran. Not yet a word ! you did not use me so unkindly
last night, when you chid me out of your house, and with
indignation bid me begone. Now, you bid me follow
you, and yet will have nothing to say to me ; and I am
more deceived this day and night than I was last night ;
—when, I must confess, I followed you for another—

Lyd. I'm glad to hear that.   [*Aside.*

Ran. One that would have used me better ; whose
love I have ungratefully abused for yours ; yet from no
other reason but my natural inconstancy.—[*Aside.*] Poor
Lydia ! Lydia !

Lyd. He muttered my name sure ; and with a sigh.
                                        [*Aside.*

Ran. But as last night by following (as I thought) her,
I found you, so this night, by following you in vain, I do
resolve, if I can find her again, to keep her for ever.

Lyd. Now I am obliged, and brought into debt, by his

inconstancy :—faith, now cannot I hold out any longer ;
I must discover myself.   [*Aside.*

Ran. But, madam, because I intend to see you no
more, I'll take my leave of you for good and all ; since
you will not speak, I'll try if you will squeak.

                    [*Goes to throw her down, she squeaks.*

Lyd. Mr. Ranger ! Mr. Ranger ！

Vin. Fy ! Fy ! you need not ravish Christina sure,
that loves you so.

Ran. Is it she ! Lydia all this while !—how am I
gulled ! and Vincent in the plot too !   [*Aside.*

Lyd. Now, false Ranger !

Ran. Now, false Christina too !—you thought I did
not know you now, because I offered you such an unusual
civility.

Lyd. You knew me !—I warrant you knew, too, that
I was the Christina you followed out of the Park last
night ! that I was the Christina that writ the letter
too !

Ran. Certainly, therefore I would have taken my
revenge, you see, for your tricks.

Val. Is not this the same woman that took refuge in
your house last night, madam ?   [*To* CHRISTINA.

Chris. The very same.

Val. What, Mr. Ranger, we have chopped, and
changed, and hid our Christinas so long and often, that
at last we have drawn each of us our own ?

Ran. Mr. Valentine in England !—the truth on't is,
you have juggled together, and drawn without my knowledge ; but since she will have it so, she shall wear me
for good and all now.   [*Goes to take her by the hand.*

Lyd. Come not near me.

Ran. Nay, you need not be afraid I would ravish you,
now I know you.

Lyd. And yet, Leonore, I think 'tis but justice to
pardon the fault I made him commit ?

                    [*Apart to* LEONORE, RANGER *listens.*

Ran. You consider it right, cousin; for indeed you are but merciful to yourself in it.

Lyd. Yet, if I would be rigorous, though I made a blot, your oversight has lost the game.

Ran. But 'twas rash woman's play, cousin, and ought not to be played again, let me tell you.

Enter DAPPERWIT.

Dap. Who's there? who's there?

Ran. Dapperwit.

Dap. Mr. Ranger, I am glad I have met with you, for I have left my bride just now in the house at Mulberry-garden, to come and pick up some of my friends in the Park here to sup with us.

Ran. Your bride! are you married then? where is your bride?

Dap. Here at Mulberry-garden, I say, where you, these ladies and gentlemen, shall all be welcome, if you will afford me the honour of your company.

Ran. With all our hearts:—but who have you married? Lucy?

Dap. What! do you think I would marry a wench? I have married an heiress worth thirty thousand pounds, let me perish!

Vin. An heiress worth thirty thousand pounds!

Dap. Mr. Vincent, your servant; you here too?

Ran. Nay, we are more of your acquaintance here, I think.—Go, we'll follow you, for if you have not dismissed your parson, perhaps we may make him more work.

[*Exeunt.*

SCENE VI.—*The Dining-room in Mulberry-garden House.*

Enter Sir SIMON ADDLEPLOT, GRIPE, Lady FLIPPANT, Mrs. MARTHA, Mrs. JOYNER, Mrs. CROSSBITE, *and* LUCY.

Sir Sim. 'Tis as I told you, sir, you see.

Gripe. Oh, graceless babe! married to a wit! an idle, loitering, slandering, foul-mouthed, beggarly wit! Oh that my child should ever live to marry a wit!

Mrs. Joyn. Indeed, your worship had better seen her fairly buried, as they say.

Mrs. Cros. If my daughter there should have done so, I would not have given her a groat.

Gripe. Marry a wit!

Sir Sim. Mrs. Joyner, do not let me lose the widow too :—for if you do, (betwixt friends,) I and my small annuity are both blown up : it will follow my estate.

[Aside to Mrs. JOYNER.

Mrs. Joyn. I warrant you.   [*Aside.*

L. Flip. Let us make sure of Sir Simon to-night, or—

[Aside to Mrs. JOYNER.

Mrs. Joyn. You need not fear it.—[*Aside.*] Like the lawyers, while my clients endeavour to cheat one another, I in justice cheat 'em both.

Gripe. Marry a wit!

Enter DAPPERWIT, RANGER, LYDIA, VALENTINE, CHRIS-
TINA, *and* VINCENT. DAPPERWIT *stops them, and
they stand all behind.*

Dap. What, is he here! Lucy and her mother! [*Aside.*
Gripe. Tell me how thou camest to marry a wit.

Mrs. Mar. Pray be not angry, sir, and I'll give you a good reason.

Gripe. Reason for marrying a wit!

Mrs. Mar. Indeed, I found myself six months gone with child, and saw no hopes of your getting me a husband, or else I had not married a wit, sir.

Mrs. Joyn. Then you were the wit.

Gripe. Had you that reason? nay, then——

[Holding up his hands.

Dap. How's that!   [*Aside.*
Ran. Who would have thought, Dapperwit, you would have married a wench?

Dap. [*To* RANGER.]—Well, thirty thousand pounds will make me amends; I have known my betters wink, and fall on for five or six.—[*To* GRIPE *and the rest.*] What! you are come, sir, to give me joy? you Mrs. Lucy, you and you? well, unbid guests are doubly welcome.— Sir Simon, I made bold to invite these ladies and gentle- men.—For you must know, Mr. Ranger, this worthy Sir Simon does not only give me my wedding supper, but my mistress too; and is, as it were, my father.

Sir Sim. Then I am, as it were, a grandfather to your new wife's *Hans en kelder;*[1] to which you are but, as it were, a father! there's for you again, sir—ha, ha!—

Ran. Ha! ha! ha!—   [*To* VINCENT.

Dap. Fools sometimes say unhappy things, if we would mind 'em; but—what! melancholy at your daughter's wedding, sir?

Gripe. How deplorable is my condition!

Dap. Nay, if you will rob me of my wench, sir, can you blame me for robbing you of your daughter? I cannot be without a woman.

Gripe. My daughter, my reputation, and my money gone!—but the last is dearest to me. Yet at once I may retrieve that, and be revenged for the loss of the other: and all this by marrying Lucy here: I shall get my five hundred pounds again, and get heirs to exclude my daughter and frustrate Dapperwit; besides, 'tis agreed on all hands, 'tis cheaper keeping a wife than a wench.

[*Aside.*

Dap. If you are so melancholy, sir, we will have the fiddles and a dance to divert you; come!

A Dance.

Gripe. Indeed, you have put me so upon a merry pin, that I resolve to marry too.

L. Flip. Nay, if my brother come to marrying once,

---

[1] Dutch, literally "Jack in the Cellar;" a jocular term for an unborn infant.—*Wright.*

I may too; I swore I would, when he did, little thinking—

Sir Sim. I take you at your word, madam.

L. Flip. Well, but if I had thought you would have been so quick with me—

Gripe. Where is your parson?

Dap. What! you would not revenge yourself upon the parson?

Gripe. No, I would have the parson revenge me upon you; he should marry me.

Dap. I am glad you are so frolic, sir; but who would you marry?

Gripe. That innocent lady.   [*Pointing to* LUCY.

Dap. That innocent lady!

Gripe. Nay, I am impatient, Mrs. Joyner; pray fetch him up if he be yet in the house.

Dap. We were not married here:—but you cannot be in earnest.

Gripe. You'll find it so; since you have robbed me of my housekeeper, I must get another.

Dap. Why, she was my wench!

Gripe. I'll make her honest then.

Mrs. Cros. Upon my repute he never saw her before:—but will your worship marry my daughter then?

Gripe. I promise her and you, before all this good company, to-morrow I will make her my wife.

Dap. How!

Ran. Our ladies, sir, I suppose, expect the same promise from us.   [*To* VALENTINE.

Val. They may be sure of us without a promise; but let us (if we can) obtain theirs, to be sure of them.

Dap. But will you marry her to-morrow?—[*To* GRIPE.

Gripe. I will, verily.

Dap. I am undone then! ruined, let me perish!

Sir Sim. No, you may hire a little room in Covent Garden, and set up a coffee-house:—you and your wife will be sure of the wit's custom.

Dap. Abused by him I have abused !—
  Fortune our foe we cannot overwit ;
  By none but thee our projects are cross-bit.

Val. Come, dear madam, what, yet angry ?— jealousy
sure is much more pardonable before marriage than after
it ; but to-morrow, by the help of the parson, you'll put
me out of all my fears.

Chris. I am afraid then you would give me my revenge,
and make me jealous of you ; and I had rather suspect
your faith than you should mine.

Ran. Cousin Lydia, I had rather suspect your faith
too, than you should mine ; therefore let us e'en marry
to-morrow, that I may have my turn of watching, dog-
ging, standing under the window, at the door, behind the
hanging, or—

Lyd. But if I could be desperate now and give you up
my liberty, could you find in your heart to quit all other
engagements, and voluntarily turn yourself over to one
woman, and she a wife too ? could you away with the
insupportable bondage of matrimony ?

Ran. You talk of matrimony as irreverently as my
Lady Flippant : the bondage of matrimony ! no—
  The end of marriage now is liberty.
  And two are bound—to set each other free.

EPILOGUE

Now my brisk brothers of the pit, you'll say
I'm come to speak a good word for the play;
But gallants, let me perish! if I do,
For I have wit and judgment, just like you;
Wit never partial, judgment free and bold,
For fear or friendship never bought or sold,
Nor by good-nature e'er to be cajoled.
Good-nature in a critic were a crime,
Like mercy in a judge, and renders him
Guilty of all those faults he does forgive,
Besides, if thief from gallows you reprieve,
He'll cut your throat; so poet saved from shame,
In damned lampoon will murder your good name.
Yet in true spite to him and to his play,
Good faith, you should not rail at them to-day
But to be more his foe, seem most his friend,
And so maliciously the play commend;
That he may be betrayed to writing on,
And poet let him be,—to be undone.

[1] The part of Dapperwit was originally acted by Mohun.

THE

GENTLEMAN DANCING-
MASTER.

" Non satis est risu diducere rictum
Auditorus : et est quædam tamen hic quoque virtus."[1]—Horat.

[1] 'Tis not sufficient to make the hearer laugh aloud ; although there is never-theless a certain merit even in this.—*Sat.* I. 10, 8—9.

F we may trust the author's statement to Pope, this admirable comedy was written when Wycherley was twenty-one years of age, in the year 1661-2. It is impossible to fix with certainty the date of its first performance. The Duke's Company, then under the management of the widow of Sir William Davenant, opened its new theatre in Dorset Gardens, near Salisbury Court, on the 9th of November, 1671, with a performance of Dryden's *Sir Martin Mar-all*, and Wycherley's "Prologue to the City" points to the production of his play in the new theatre shortly after its opening. Genest states, on the authority of Downes, that "*The Gentleman Dancing-Master* was the third new play acted at this theatre, and that several of the old stock plays were acted between each of the new ones." *Sir Martin Mar-all*, having been three times performed, was succeeded by Etherege's *Love in a Tub*, which, after two representations, gave place to a new piece, Crowne's tragedy of *Charles the Eighth*. This was played six times in succession, and was followed, probably after an interval devoted to stock pieces, by a second novelty, an adaptation by Ravenscroft from Molière, entitled *The Citizen turn'd Gentleman, or Mamamouchi*, which ran for nine days together. *The Gentleman Dancing-Master* was then acted, probably after another short interval, and must therefore have been produced either in December, 1671, or in January, 1672. Genest, in fact, places it first on his list of plays performed at the Dorset Gardens Theatre during the year 1672, although, in his list for the preceding year, immediately after *The Citizen turn'd Gentleman*, he mentions Lord Orrery's comedy of *Mr. Anthony* as "nearly certain" to have been brought out in the season of 1671-2. But this, again, was a new piece, making the third produced at Dorset Gardens, without including *The Gentleman Dancing-Master*, and must consequently have been brought forward later than Wycherley's play. Of *The Gentleman Dancing-Master* Genest observes that "it was not much liked, and was acted only six times."

But it is by no means clear that the first performance at Dorset Gardens was the actual first performance of our comedy. The opening verses of the prologue, indeed, seem to imply a previous and unsuccessful performance, probably by the same company, at their old theatre in Portugal Street, Lincoln's Inn Fields. This, at least, as it seems to me, is the most obvious interpretation of the following lines :

> " Our author (like us) finding 'twould scarce do
> At t'other end o' th' town, is come to you ;
> And, *since 'tis his last trial,* has that wit
> To throw himself on a substantial pit."

The presumption, therefore, is strongly in favour of 1671 as the year in which *The Gentleman Dancing-Master* was first brought upon the stage. It was published, without a dedication or the names of the actors, in 1673. The remarks about "packing to sea" in the epilogue, which, like the prologue, was written for the production, or rather, as we may suppose, the revival of the piece at the theatre in Dorset Gardens, refer, questionless, to the impending war with the Dutch, against whom the formal declaration of war was issued on the 17th of March, 1672.

The incident upon which the plot turns is borrowed from Calderon's comedy, *El Maestro de Danzar,* but a brief review of the corresponding scenes in that drama will prove how trifling was Wycherley's obligation to the great Spanish poet. Leonor, the heroine of the piece, is enjoying a stolen interview with her lover, Don Enrique, in an apartment of her father's house in Valencia. Meanwhile, lest their voices should be overheard, Ines, Leonor's maid, stations herself without the chamber, singing and accompanying herself with the guitar. She presently enters, declaring that an instrument so out of tune will attract suspicion, and Don Enrique takes up the guitar for the purpose of tuning it. At this juncture the father, Don Diego, appears suddenly upon the scene. In reply to his questioning, Leonor explains that, dancing being little in fashion at the Court, she had formerly neglected that accomplishment ; but that, finding herself, on that account, looked down upon in Valencia, where dancing was all the mode, she had engaged a master, who had but just taken up the guitar which her maid had brought him, when her father entered. This explanation proving satisfactory to

Don Diego, he seats himself, and desires that the lesson may proceed. But here a new difficulty arises, for Don Enrique owns, in an "aside" to his mistress, that he understands little or nothing of dancing. The lady, however, is equal to the occasion, and, affecting diffidence, tells her father that he must wait until she has taken a few lessons. He, nevertheless, insisting, Don Enrique takes again the guitar, and, under pretence of tuning it, screws up the string until it snaps, declaring then that the strings are worn, and that the instrument is broken. Leonor now suggests that the maestro shall carry away the guitar, to get it set in order, and shall come again on the morrow or in the evening ; and Don Diego, acquiescing, bids him neglect not to return, trusting him for the payment. Don Enrique responding that he will not fail, although he has many lessons to give, the old cavalier dismisses him with a "Vaya con Dios." In a later scene Don Enrique is again with Leonor, of whom he has conceived unjust suspicions, and is bestowing upon her the full benefit of his jealousy, when Ines announces the approach of Don Diego, and the lover, at his mistress's earnest appeal, again takes up the guitar, and pretends to be giving her a lesson. The father inquires after his daughter's improvement, and again insists on seeing her dance, a mock performance this time actually ensuing. And again, in another scene, the lovers, similarly interrupted, have recourse to a similar method of diverting Don Diego's suspicions.

In these few incidents, and in the name of Don Diego, which our author has employed as the adopted appellation of his Spain-loving Englishman, are to be found the only points of resemblance between the two plays. The merits of the one lie in a direction totally diverse from that in which the excellencies of the other are to be sought. Wycherley's play is fairly overflowing with wit and mirth, qualities in which the Spanish drama is somewhat deficient. On the other hand, the English play affords no counterpart to the high moral tone and exalted passion which are distinguishing characteristics of Calderon's comedy.

The Gentleman Dancing - Master is constructed with greater simplicity and unity of action than *Love in a Wood*, and, although less powerfully written than *The Country Wife*, it is also far less exceptionable, and more uniformly pleasing.

PROLOGUE TO THE CITY

NEWLY AFTER THE REMOVAL OF THE DUKE'S COMPANY FROM
LINCOLN'S-INN-FIELDS TO THEIR NEW THEATRE NEAR
SALISBURY-COURT.

OUR author (like us) finding 'twould scarce do
At t'other end o' th' town, is come to you ;
And, since 'tis his last trial, has that wit
To throw himself on a substantial pit ;
Where needy wit or critic dare not come,
Lest neighbour i' the cloak, with looks so grum,
Should prove a dun ;
Where punk in vizor dare not rant and tear
To put us out, since Bridewell is so near :
In short, we shall be heard, be understood,
If not, shall be admired, and that's as good.
For you to senseless plays have still been kind,
Nay, where no sense was, you a jest would find :
And never was it heard of, that the city
Did ever take occasion to be witty
Upon dull poet, or stiff player's action,
But still with claps opposed the hissing faction.
But if you hissed, 'twas at the pit, not stage ;
So, with the poet, damned the damning age,
And still, we know, are ready to engage
Against the flouting, ticking gentry, who
Citizen, player, poet, would undo :—
The poet ! no, unless by commendation,
For on the 'Change wits have no reputation :
And rather than be branded for a wit,
He with you able men would credit get.

DRAMATIS PERSONÆ.

Mr. GERRARD, } Young Gentlemen of the town, and
Mr. MARTIN, }   friends.

Mr. PARIS, or Monsieur de PARIS, a vain coxcomb, and rich city heir, newly returned from France, and mightily affected with the French language and fashions.

Mr. JAMES FORMAL, or Don DIEGO, an old rich Spanish merchant, newly returned home, much affected with the habit and customs of Spain, and Uncle to PARIS.

A little Blackamoor, Lackey to FORMAL.

A Parson.

A French Scullion.

HIPPOLITA, FORMAL'S Daughter.

Mrs. CAUTION, FORMAL'S Sister, an impertinent precise old woman.

PRUE, HIPPOLITA'S Maid.

A Lady.

Mrs. FLIRT, } Two common Women of the town.
Mrs. FLOUNCE, }

Servants, Waiter, and Attendants.

SCENE—LONDON.

THE GENTLEMAN DANCING-MASTER.

───··❧✳❧··───

ACT THE FIRST.

SCENE I.—Don DIEGO'S *House, in the evening.*

Enter HIPPOLITA *and* PRUE.

IP. To confine a woman just in her rambling age! take away her liberty at the very time she should use it! O barbarous aunt! O unnatural father! to shut up a poor girl at fourteen, and hinder her budding! All things are ripened by the sun :—to shut up a poor girl at fourteen!—

Prue. 'Tis true, miss, two poor young creatures as we are!

Hip. Not suffered to see a play in a twelve-month!—

Prue. Nor go to Punchinello,[1] nor Paradise!—

Hip. Nor to take a ramble to the Park nor Mulberry-garden![2]—

───────────

[1] Punchinello had a booth at Charing Cross in 1666; this was probably the earliest appearance of Punch in this country, under that name.

[2] See note, *ante,* p. 12.

Prue. Nor to Totnam-court, nor Islington. ![1]—

Hip. Nor to eat a syllabub in New Spring garden[2] with a cousin !—

Prue. Nor to drink a pint of wine with a friend at the Prince in the Sun !—

Hip. Nor to hear a fiddle in good company !—

Prue. Nor to hear the organs and tongs at the Gun in Moorfields !—

Hip. Nay, not suffered to go to church, because the men are sometimes there !—Little did I think I should ever have longed to go to church.

Prue. Or I either ;—but between two maids—

Hip. Nor see a man !—

Prue. Nor come near a man !—

Hip. Nor hear of a man

Prue. No, miss; but to be denied a man ! and to have no use at all of a man !—

Hip. Hold, hold !—your resentment is as much greater than mine, as your experience has been greater. But all this while, what do we make of my cousin, my husband elect, as my aunt says? We have had his company these three days ; is he no man ?

Prue. No, faith, he's but a monsieur. But you'll resolve yourself that question within these three days ; for by that time he'll be your husband, if your father come to-night—

Hip. Or if I provide not myself with another in the mean time : for fathers seldom choose well; and I will no more take my father's choice in a husband, than I would in a gown, or a suit of knots. So that if that cousin of mine were not an ill-contrived, ugly, freakish fool, in being my father's choice I should hate him. Besides, he has almost made me out of love with mirth and good-humour ; for he debases it as much as a jack-

---

[1] " Hogsdone, Islington, and Totnam Court,
    For cakes and cream had then no small resort."
        Wither's Britain's Remembrancer, 1628.

[2] See note, *ante*, p. 63.

pudding, and civility and good breeding more than a
city dancing-master.

Prue. What! won't you marry him then, madam?

Hip. Would'st thou have me marry a fool, an idiot?

Prue. Lord! 'tis a sign you have been kept up indeed,
and know little of the world, to refuse a man for a
husband only because he's a fool! Methinks he's a
pretty apish kind of a gentleman, like other gentlemen,
and handsome enough to lie with in the dark, when
husbands take their privileges; and for the day-times,
you may take the privilege of a wife.

Hip. Excellent governess! you do understand the
world, I see.

Prue. Then you should be guided by me.

Hip. Art thou in earnest then, damned jade?—would'st
thou have me marry him?—Well, there are more poor
young women undone, and married to filthy fellows by
the treachery and evil counsel of chambermaids, than by
the obstinacy and covetousness of parents.

Prue. Does not your father come on purpose out of
Spain to marry you to him? Can you release yourself
from your aunt or father any other way? Have you a
mind to be shut up as long as you live? For my part,
though you can hold out upon the lime from the walls
here, salt, old shoes, and oatmeal, I cannot live so: I
must confess my patience is worn out.

Hip. Alas, alas, poor Prue! your stomach lies another
way: I will take pity of you, and get me a husband very
suddenly, who may have a servant at your service. But
rather than marry my cousin, I will be a nun in the new
protestant nunnery they talk of; where, they say, there
will be no hopes of coming near a man.

Prue. But you can marry nobody but your cousin,
miss: your father you expect to-night; and be certain
his Spanish policy and wariness, which has kept you up
so close ever since you came from Hackney school, will
make sure of you within a day or two at farthest.

Hip. Then 'tis time to think how to prevent him—
stay—

Prue. In vain, vain, miss !

Hip. If we knew but any man, any man, though he
were but a little handsomer than the devil, so that he
were a gentleman !

Prue. What if you did know any man ? if you had an
opportunity, could you have confidence to speak to a
man first ? but if you could, how could you come to him,
or he to you ? nay, how could you send to him ? for
though you could write, which your father in his Spanish
prudence would never permit you to learn, who should
carry the letter ?—But we need not be concerned for that,
since we know not to whom to send it.

Hip. Stay—it must be so—I'll try however—

Enter Monsieur de PARIS.

Mons. Serviteur ! serviteur ! la cousine ; I come to
give the *bon soir*, as the French say.

Hip. O, cousin ! you know him ; the fine gentleman
they talk of so much in town.

Prue. What ! will you talk to him of any man else ?

Mons. I know all the *beau monde, cousine.*

Hip. Master—

Mons. Monsieur Taileur, Monsieur Esmit, Monsieur—

Hip. These are Frenchmen—

Mons. Non, non ; voud you have me say Mr. Taylor,
Mr. Smith ? Fi ! fi ! *tête non !*—

Hip. But don't you know the brave gentleman they
talk so much of in town ?

Mons. Who ? Monsieur Gerrard ?

Hip. What kind of man is that Mr. Gerrard ? and
then I'll tell you.

Mons. Why—he is truly a pretty man, a pretty man—
a pretty so so—kind of man, for an Englishman.

Hip. How a pretty man ?

Mons. Why, he is conveniently tall—but—

Hip. But what?

Mons. And not ill-shaped—but—

Hip. But what?

Mons. And handsome, as 'tis thought, but—

Hip. But! what are your exceptions to him?

Mons. I can't tell you, because they are innumerable, innumerable, *ma foi!*

Hip. Has he wit?

Mons. Ay, ay, they say, he's witty, brave, and *de bel humeur*, and well-bred, with all that—but—

Hip. But what? does he want judgment?

Mons. Non, non : they say he has good sense and judgment; but it is according to the account Englis—for—

Hip. For what?

Mons. For, *jarni!* if I think it.

Hip. Why?

Mons. Why?—why his tailor lives within Ludgate—his *valet de chambre* is no Frenchman—and he has been seen at noon-day to go into an English eating-house—

Hip. Say you so, cousin!

Mons. Then for being well-bred, you shall judge :—First, he can't dance a step, nor sing a French song, nor swear a French oate, nor use the polite French word in his conversation ; and in fine, can't play at hombre—but speaks base good Englis, with the commune home-bred pronunciation ; and in fine, to say no more, he never carries a snuff-box about with him.

Hip. Indeed!

Mons. And yet this man has been abroad as much as any man, and does not make the least show of it, but a little in his mien, not at all in his discour, *jarni!* He never talks so much as of St. Peter's church at Rome, the Escurial, or Madrid ; nay, not so much as of Henry IV., of Pont-neuf, Paris, and the new Louvre, nor of the Grand Roi.

Hip. 'Tis for his commendation, if he does not talk of his travels.

Mons. Auh! auh!—*cousine*—he is conscious to himself of his wants, because he is very envious; for he cannot endure me.

Hip. [*Aside.*] He shall be my man then for that.—Ay, ay! 'tis the same, Prue.—[*Aloud.*] No, I know he can't endure you, cousin.

Mons. How do you know it—who never stir out? *tête non!*

Hip. Well—dear cousin, — if you will promise me never to tell my aunt, I'll tell you.

Mons. I won't, I won't, *jarni!*

Hip. Nor to be concerned yourself, so as to make a quarrel of it.

Mons. Non, non—

Hip. Upon the word of a gentleman?

Mons. Foi de chevalier, I will not quarrel.

Prue. Lord, miss! I wonder you won't believe him without more ado.

Hip. Then he has the hatred of a rival for you.

Mons. Malepeste!

Hip. You know my chamber is backward, and has a door into the gallery which looks into the back yard of a tavern, whence Mr. Gerrard once spying me at the window, has often since attempted to come in at that window by the help of the leads of a low building adjoining; and, indeed, 'twas as much as my maid and I could do to keep him out.

Mons. Ah, le coquin!—

Hip. But nothing is stronger than aversion; for I hate him perfectly, even as much as I love you—

Prue. I believe so, faith!—but what design have we now on foot?   [*Aside.*

Hip. This discovery is an argument, sure, of my love to you.

Mons. Ay, ay, say no more, cousin, I doubt not your amour for me, because I doubt not your judgment. But what's to be done with this fanfaron?—I know where he eats to-night—I'll go find him out, *ventre bleu !*—

Hip. O, my dear cousin, you will not make a quarrel of it ? I thought what your promise would come to !

Mons. Would you have a man of honour—

Hip. Keep his promise?

Mons. And lose his mistress ?—That were not for my honour, *ma foi !*

Hip. Cousin, though you do me the injury to think I could be false, do not do yourself the injury to think any one could be false to you. Will you be afraid of losing your mistress ? To show such a fear to your rival, were for his honour, and not for yours, sure.

Mons. Nay, cousin, I'd have you know I was never afraid of losing my mistress in earnest.—Let me see the man can get my mistress from me, *jarni !*—But he that loves must seem a little jealous.

Hip. Not to his rival : those that have jealousy hide it from their rivals.

Mons. But there are some who say, jealousy is no more to be hid than a cough :—but it should never be discovered in me, if I had it, because it is not French at all—*ventre bleu !*

Hip. No, you should rally your rival, and rather make a jest of your quarrel to him ; and that, I suppose, is French too.

Mons. 'Tis so, 'tis so, *cousine ;* 'tis the veritable French method ; for your Englis, for want of wit, drive every thing to a serious grum quarrel, and then would make a jest on't, when 'tis too late, when they can't laugh, *jarni !*

Hip. Yes, yes, I would have you rally him soundly : do not spare him a jot.—But shall you see him to-night ?

Mons. Ay, ay.

Hip. Yes ; pray be sure to see him for the jest's sake.

Mons. I will—for I love a jest as well as any *bel esprit* of 'em all—da

Hip. Ay, and rally him soundly; be sure you rally him
soundly, and tell him just thus:—that the lady he has so
long courted, from the great window of the Ship tavern,
is to be your wife to-morrow, unless he come at his
wonted hour of six in the morning to her window to
forbid the banns; for 'tis the first and last time of asking;
and if he come not, let him for ever hereafter stay away,
and hold his tongue.

Mons. Ha! ha! ha! a ver good jest, *tête bleu!*

Hip. And if the fool should come again, I would tell
him his own, I warrant you, cousin. My gentleman
should be satisfied for good and all, I'd secure him.

Mons. Bon, bon.

Prue. Well, well, young mistress; you were not at
Hackney school for nothing, I see; nor taken away for
nothing.—A woman may soon be too old, but is never
too young to shift for herself.   [*Aside.*

Mons. Ha! ha! ha! *cousine,* dou art a merry grig, *ma
foi!*—I long to be with Gerrard; and I am the best at
improving a jest—I shall have such divertisement to-
night, *tête bleu!*

Hip. He'll deny, may be, at first, that he ever courted
any such lady.

Mons. Nay, I am sure he'll be ashamed of it, I shall
make him look so sillily, *tête non!*—I long to find him
out.—Adieu, adieu, *la cousine.*

Hip. Shall you be sure to find him?

Mons. Indubitablement, I'll search the town over, but
I'll find him: ha! ha! ha!—[*Exit* MONSIEUR, *and
returns.*]—But I'm afraid, *cousine,* if I should tell him
you are to be my wife to-morrow, he would not come:
now, I am for having him come for the jest's sake,
ventre!—

Hip. So am I, cousin, for having him come too for the
jest's sake.

Mons. Well, well, leave it to me:—ha! ha! ha!

Enter Mrs. CAUTION.

Mrs. Caut. What's all this giggling here?

Mons. Hey! do you tinke we'll tell you? no, fait, I warrant you, *tête non !*—ha! ha! ha!—

Hip. My cousin is overjoyed, I suppose, that my father is to come to-night.

Mrs. Caut. I am afraid he will not come to-night:— but you'll stay and see, nephew?

Mons. Non, non : I am to sup at t'other end of the town to-night—La, la, la—Ra, ra, ra— [*Exit, singing.*

Mrs. Caut. I wish the French levity of this young man may agree with your father's Spanish gravity.

Hip. Just as your crabbed old age and my youth agree.

Mrs. Caut. Well, malapert, I know you hate me, because I have been the guardian of your reputation: but your husband may thank me one day.

Hip. If he be not a fool, he would rather be obliged to me for my virtue than to you, since, at long run, he must, whether he will or no.

Mrs. Caut. So, so!

Hip. Nay, now I think on't, I'd have you to know, the poor man, whosoe'er he is, will have little cause to thank you.

Mrs. Caut. No!—

Hip. No; for I never lived so wicked a life as I have done this twelvemonth, since I have not seen a man.

Mrs. Caut. How, how! if you have not seen a man, how could you be wicked? how could you do any ill?

Hip. No, I have done no ill; but I have paid it with thinking.

Mrs. Caut. O that's no hurt! to think, is no hurt:— the ancient, grave, and godly, cannot help thoughts.

Hip. I warrant, you have had 'em yourself, aunt?

Mrs. Caut. Yes, yes, when I cannot sleep.

Hip. Ha! ha!—I believe it. But know, I have had

those thoughts sleeping and waking; for I have dreamt of a man.

Mrs. Caut. No matter, no matter, so that it was but a dream: I have dreamt myself. For you must know, widows are mightily given to dream; insomuch that a dream is waggishly called "the Widow's Comfort."

Hip. But I did not only dream—   [*Sighs.*

Mrs. Caut. How, how! did you more than dream? speak, young harlotry! confess; did you more than dream? How could you do more than dream in this house? speak, confess!

Hip. Well, I will then. Indeed, aunt, I did not only dream, but I was pleased with my dream when I awaked.

Mrs. Caut. Oh, is that all?—Nay, if a dream only will please you, you are a modest young woman still: but have a care of a vision.

Hip. Ay; but to be delighted when we wake with a naughty dream, is a sin, aunt; and I am so very scrupulous, that I would as soon consent to a naughty man as to a naughty dream.

Mrs. Caut. I do believe you.

Hip. I am for going into the throng of temptations.

Mrs. Caut. There I believe you again.

Hip. And making myself so familiar with them, that I would not be concerned for 'em a whit.

Mrs. Caut. There I do not believe you.

Hip. And would take all the innocent liberty of the town :—to tattle to your men under a vizard in the play-houses, and meet 'em at night in masquerade.

Mrs. Caut. There I do believe you again; I know you would be masquerading : but worse would come on't, as it has done to others who have been in a masquerade, and are now virgins but in masquerade, and will not be their own women again as long as they live. The children of this age must be wise children indeed if they know their fathers, since their mothers themselves cannot inform 'em! O, the fatal liberty of this masquerading age! when I was a young woman—

Hip. Come, come, do not blaspheme this masquerading age, like an ill-bred city-dame, whose husband is half broke by living in Covent-garden, or who has been turned out of the Temple or Lincoln's-Inn upon a masquerading night. By what I've heard, 'tis a pleasant, well-bred, complaisant, free, frolic, good-natured, pretty age: and if you do not like it, leave it to us that do.

Mrs. Caut. Lord, how impudently you talk, niece! I'm sure I remember when I was a maid—

Hip. Can you remember it, reverend aunt?

Mrs. Caut. Yes, modest niece,—that a raw young thing, though almost at woman's estate, (that was then at thirty or thirty-five years of age,) would not so much as have looked upon a man—

Hip. Above her father's butler or coachman.

Mrs. Caut. Still taking me up! Well, thou art a mad girl; and so good night. We may go to bed; for I suppose now your father will not come to-night. [*Exit.*

Hip. I'm sorry for it; for I long to see him.— [*Aside.*] But I lie: I had rather see Gerrard here; and yet I know not how I shall like him. If he has wit, he will come; and if he has none, he would not be welcome. [*Exeunt*

SCENE II.—*The French House.—A table, bottles, and candles.*

Enter Mr. GERRARD, MARTIN, *and* Monsieur de PARIS.

Mons. 'Tis ver veritable, *jarni!* what the French say of you Englis: you use the debauch so much, it cannot have with you the French operation; you are never enjoyee. But come, let us for once be *infiniment gaillard,* and sing a French sonnet.

[*Sings,—" La bouteille, la bouteille, glou, glou."*

Mar. [*To* GERRARD.] What a melodious fop it is !

Mons. Auh ! you have no complaisance.

Ger. No, we can't sing; but we'll drink to you the lady's health, whom (you say) I have so long courted at her window.

Mons. Ay, there is your complaisance : all your Englis complaisance is pledging complaisance, *ventre !*—But if I do you reason here, [*Takes the glass.*]—will you do me reason to a little French *chanson à boire* I shall begin to you ?—[*Sings.*] " *La bouteille, la bouteille—*"

Mar. [*To* GERRARD.] I had rather keep company with a set of wide-mouthed, drunken cathedral choristers.

Ger. Come, sir, drink; and he shall do you reason to your French song, since you stand upon't.—Sing him " Arthur of Bradley," or " I am the Duke of Norfolk."

Mons. Auh ! *tête bleu !*—an Englis catch ! fy ! fy ! *ventre !*—

Ger. He can sing no damned French song.

Mons. Nor can I drink the damned Englis wine.

[*Sets down the glass.*

Ger. Yes, to that lady's health, who has commanded me to wait upon her to-morrow at her window, which looks (you say) into the inward yard of the Ship tavern, near the end of what-d'ye-call't street.

Mons. Ay, ay; do you not know her ? not you ! *vert bleu !*

Ger. But, pray repeat again what she said.

Mons. Why, she said she is to be married to-morrow to a person of honour, a brave gentleman, that shall be nameless, and so, and so forth.—「*Aside.*] Little does he think who 'tis !

Ger. And what else ?

Mons. That if you make not your appearance before her window to-morrow at your wonted hour of six in the morning, to forbid the banns, you must for ever hereafter stay away and hold your tongue ; for 'tis the first and last time of asking.—Ha ! ha ! ha !

Ger. 'Tis all a riddle to me : I should be unwilling to be fooled by this coxcomb. [*Aside.*

Mons. I won't tell him all she said, lest he should not go : I would fain have him go for the jest's sake—Ha ! ha ! ha ! [*Aside.*

Ger. Her name is, you say, Hippolita, daughter to a rich Spanish merchant.

Mons. Ay, ay, you don't know her, not you ! *à d'autre, à d'autre, ma foi !*—ha ! ha ! ha !

Ger. Well, I will be an easy fool for once.

Mar. By all means go.

Mons. Ay, ay, by all means go—ha ! ha ! ha !

Ger. [*Aside.*] To be caught in a fool's trap—I'll venture it.—[*Drinks to him.*] Come, 'tis her health.

Mons. And to your good reception—*tête bleu !*—ha ! ha ! ha !

Ger. Well, monsieur, I'll say this for thee, thou hast made the best use of three months at Paris as ever English squire did.

Mons. Considering I was in a dam Englis pension too.

Mar. Yet you have conversed with some French, I see ; footmen, I suppose, at the fencing-school ? I judge it by your oaths.

Mons. French footmen ! well, well, I had rather have the conversation of a French footman than of an Englis 'squire ; there's for you, da—

Mar. I beg your pardon, monsieur ; I did not think the French footmen had been so much your friends.

Ger. Yes, yes, I warrant they have obliged him at Paris much more than any of their masters did. Well, there shall be no more said against the French footmen.

Mons. Non, de grace !—you are always turning the nation *Française* into ridicule, dat nation so accomplie, dat nation which you imitate so, dat in the conclusion, you butte turn yourself into ridicule, *ma foi !* If you are for de raillery, abuse the Dutch, why not abuse the Dutch ?

les gros villains, pendards, insolents ; but here in your England, *ma foi !*—you have more honeur, respecte, and estimation for de Dushe swabber, who come to cheat your nation, den for de Franch footman, who come to oblige your nation.

Mar. Our nation ! then you disown it for yours, it seems.

Mons. Well ! wat of dat ? are you the disobligee by dat ?

Ger. No, monsieur, far from it ; you could not oblige us, nor your country, any other way than by disowning it.

Mons. It is de brutal country, which abuse de France, and reverence de Dushe ; I will maintain, sustain, and justifie, dat one little Franch footman have more honeur, courage, and generosity, more good blood in his vaines, an mush more good manners an civility den all de State-General together, *jarni !*—Dey are only wise and valiant wen dey are drunkee.

Ger. That is, always.

Mons. But dey are never honest wen dey are drunkee ; dey are de only rogue in de varlde who are not honeste when dey are drunk—*ma foi !*

Ger. I find you are well acquainted with them, monsieur.

Mons. Ay, ay, I have made the toure of Holland, but it was *en poste,* dere was no staying for me, *tête non !*— for de gentleman can no more live dere den de toad in Ir'land, *ma foi !* for I did not see on' chevalier in de whole countree : alway, you know, de rebel hate de gens de quality. Besides, I had made sufficient observation of the *canaille barbare* de first nightee of my arrival at Amsterdamme : I did visit, you must know, one of de principal of de State-General, to whom I had recommendation from England, and did find his excellence weighing soap, *jarni !*—ha ! ha ! ha !

Ger. Weighing soap !

Mons. Weighing soap, *ma foi!* for he was a wholesale chandeleer; and his lady was taking de tale of chandels wid her own witer hands, *ma foi!* and de young lady, his excellence daughter, stringing harring, stringing harring, *jarni!*—

Ger. So!—and what were his sons doing?

Mons. Augh—his son (for he had but one) was making the tour of France, Espagne, Italy, and Germany, in a coach and six; or rader, now I tink on't, gone of an embassy hider to dere master Cromwell, whom dey did love and fear, because he was someting de greater rebel. But now I talk of de *rebelle*, none but the rebel can love the *rebelle*. And so much for you and your friend the Dushe; I'll say no more, and pray do you say no more of my friend de Franch, not so mush as of my friend de Franch footman—da—

Ger. No, no;—but, monsieur, now give me leave to admire thee, that in three months at Paris you could renounce your language, drinking, and your country, (for which we are not angry with you,) as I said, and come home so perfect a Frenchman, that the draymen of your father's own brewhouse would be ready to knock thee on the head.

Mons. Vel, vel, my father was a merchant of his own beer, as the *noblesse* of Franch of their own wine.— But I can forgive you that raillery, that bob,[1] since you say I have the eyre *Français*:—but have I the eyre *Français*?

Ger. As much as any French footman of 'em all.

Mons. And do I speak agreeable ill Englis enough?

Ger. Very ill.

Mons. Véritablement?

Ger. Véritablement.

Mons. For you must know, 'tis as ill breeding now to speak good Englis as to write good Englis, good sense, or a good hand.

---

[1] Jest; taunt.

Ger. But, indeed, methinks you are not slovenly enough for a Frenchman.

Mons. Slovenly ! you mean negligent ?

Ger. No, I mean slovenly.

Mons. Then I will be more slovenly.

Ger. You know, to be a perfect Frenchman, you must never be silent, never sit still, and never be clean.

Mar. But you have forgot one main qualification of a true Frenchman, he should never be sound, that is, be very pocky too.

Mons. Oh ! if dat be all, I am very pocky ; pocky enough, *jarni !* that is the only French qualification may be had without going to Paris, *ma foi !*

Enter Waiter.

Wait. Here are a couple of ladies coming up to you, sir.

Ger. To us !—did you appoint any to come hither, Martin ?

Mar. Not I.

Ger. Nor you, monsieur ?

Mons. Nor I.

Ger. Sirrah, tell your master, if he cannot protect us from the constable, and these midnight coursers, 'tis not a house for us.

Mar. Tell 'em you have nobody in the house, and shut the doors.

Wait. They'll not be satisfied with that, they'll break open the door. They searched last night all over the house for my Lord Fisk, and Sir Jeffery Jantee, who were fain to hide themselves in the bar under my mistress's chair and petticoats.

Mons. Wat, do the women hunt out the men so now ?

Mar. Ay, ay, things are altered since you went to Paris ; there's hardly a young man in town dares be known of his lodging for 'em.

Ger. Bailiffs, pursuivants, or a city constable, are modest people in comparison of them.

Mar. And we are not so much afraid to be taken up by the watch as by the tearing midnight ramblers, or huzza women.

Mons. Jarni! ha! ha! ha!

Ger. Where are they? I hope they are gone again.

Wait. No, sir, they are below at the stair-foot, only swearing at their coachman.

Ger. Come, you rogue, they are in fee with you waiters, and no gentleman can come hither, but they have the intelligence straight.

Wait. Intelligence from us, sir! they should never come here, if we could help it. I am sure we wish 'em choked when we see them come in; for they bring such good stomachs from St. James's Park, or rambling about in the streets, that we poor waiters have not a bit left; 'tis well if we can keep our money in our pockets for 'em. I am sure I have paid seventeen and sixpence in half-crowns for coach-hire at several times for a little damned tearing lady, and when I asked her for it again one morning in her chamber, she bid me pay myself, for she had no money; but I wanted the courage of a gentleman; besides, the lord that kept her was a good customer to our house and my friend, and I made a conscience of wronging him.

Ger. A man of honour!

Mons. Vert and *bleu!* pleasant, pleasant, *ma foi!*

Ger. Go, go, sirrah, shut the door, I hear 'em coming up.

Wait. Indeed I dare not; they'll kick me down stairs, if I should.

Ger. Go, you rascal, I say.

> [*The* Waiter *shuts the door, 'tis thrust open again.*

Enter FLOUNCE *and* FLIRT *in vizards, striking the* Waiter, *and come up to the table.*

Ger. [*Aside.*] Flounce and Flirt, upon my life!—

[*Aloud.*] Ladies, I am sorry you have no volunteers in your service ; this is mere pressing, and argues a great necessity you have for men.

Flou. You need not be afraid, sir; we will use no violence to you ; you are not fit for our service : we know you.

Flirt. The hot service you have been in formerly makes you unfit for ours now ; besides, you begin to be something too old for us ; we are for the brisk huzzas of seventeen or eighteen.

Ger. Nay, faith, I am not too old yet; but an old acquaintance will make any man old :—besides, to tell you the truth, you are come a little too early for me, for I am not drunk yet. But there are your brisk young men, who are always drunk, and, perhaps, have the happiness not to know you.

Flou. The happiness not to know us !

Flirt. The happiness not to know us !

Ger. Be not angry, ladies ; 'tis rather happiness to have pleasure to come than to have it past, and therefore these gentlemen are happy in not knowing you.

Mar. I'd have you to know, I do know the ladies too, and I will not lose the honour of the ladies' acquaintance for anything.

Flou. Not for the pleasure of beginning an acquaintance with us, as Mr. Gerrard says : but it is the general vanity of you town fops to lay claim to all good acquaintance and persons of honour ; you cannot let a woman pass in the Mall at midnight, but, damn you, you know her straight, you know her ;—but you would be damned before you would say so much for one in a mercer's shop.

Ger. He has spoken it in a French-house, where he has very good credit, and I dare swear you may make him eat his words.

Mons. She does want a gown, indeed ; she is in her *déshabillé.* This *déshabillé* is a great mode in England ;

the women love the *déshabillé* as well as the men, *ma foi !*   [*Peeping under her scarf.*

Flirt. Well, if we should stay and sup with you, I warrant you would be bragging of it to-morrow amongst your comrades, that you had the company of two women of quality at the French-house, and name us.

Mar. Pleasant jilts !   [*Aside.*

Ger. No, upon our honours, we would not brag of your company.

Flou. Upon your honours ?

Mar. No, faith.

Flou. Come, we will venture to sit down then : yet I know the vanity of you men ; you could not contain yourselves from bragging.

Ger. No, no; you women now-a-days have found out the pleasure of bragging, and will allow it the men no longer.

Mar. Therefore, indeed, we dare not stay to sup with you ; for you would be sure to tell on't.

Ger. And we are young men who stand upon our reputations.

Flou. You are very pleasant, gentlemen.

Mar. For my part I am to be married shortly, and know 'twould quickly come to my mistress's ear.

Ger. And for my part I must go visit to-morrow betimes a new city mistress ; and you know they are as inquisitive as precise in the city.

Flirt. Come, come ; pray leave this fooling ; sit down again, and let us bespeak supper.

Ger. No, faith, I dare not.

Mar. Besides, we have supped.

Flou. No matter, we only desire you should look on while we eat, and put the glass about, or so.

[GERRARD *and* MARTIN *offer to go.*

Flirt. Pray, stay.

Ger. Upon my life I dare not.

Flou. Upon our honours we will not tell, if you are in earnest.

Ger. Pshaw! pshaw!—I know the vanity of you women; you could not contain yourselves from bragging.

Mons. *Ma foi!* is it certain? ha! ha! ha!—Hark you, madam, can't you fare well but you must cry roast-meat?

You spoil your trade by bragging of your gains;
The silent sow (madam) does eat most grains.—da—

Flirt. Your servant, monsieur fop.

Flou. Nay, faith, do not go, we will no more tell—

Mons. Than you would of a clap, if you had it; dat's the only secret you can keep, *jarni!*

Mar. I am glad we are rid of these jilts.

Ger. And we have taken a very ridiculous occasion.

Mons. Wat! must we leave the lady then? dis is dam civility Englis, *ma foi!*

Flirt. Nay, sir, you have too much of the French air, to have so little honour and good breeding.

[*Pulling him back.*

Mons. Dee you tinke so then, sweet madam, I have mush of de French eyre?

Flirt. More than any Frenchman breathing.

Mons. Auh, you are the curtoise dame; *morbleu!* I shall stay then, if you think so. Monsieur Gerrard, you will be certain to see the lady to-morrow? pray not forget, ha! ha! ha!

Ger. No, no, sir.

Mar. You will go then?

Ger. I will go on a fool's errand for once.

[*Exeunt* GERRARD *and* MARTIN.

Flou. What will you eat, sir?

Mons. Wat you please, madam.

Flou. D'ye hear, waiter? then some young partridge.

Wait. What else, madam!

Flirt. Some ruffs.

Wait. What else, madam?

Flirt. Some young pheasants.

Wait. What else, madam?

Flirt. Some young rabbits ; I love rabbits.

Wait. What else, madam ?

Flou. Stay—

Mons. Dis Englis waiter wit his " Wat else, madam,"
will ruin me, *tête non !* [*Aside.*

Wait. What else, madam ?

Mons. " Wat else, madam," agen !—call up the Frencl:
waiter.

Wait. What else, madam ?

Mons. Again !—call up the French waiter or *cuisinier,*
mort ! tête ! ventre ! vite !—Auh, madam, the stupidity
of the Englis waiter ! I hate the Englis waiter, *ma foi !*

[*Exit* Waiter.

Flirt. Be not in passion, dear monsieur.

Mons. I kiss your hand, *obligeante* madam.

Enter a French Scullion.

Cher Pierrot, serviteur, serviteur.—[*Kisses the* Scullion.]—
Or-ça à manger.

Scull. En voulez-vous de cram schiquin ?

Flou. Yes.

Scull. De partrish, de faysan, de quailles ?

Mons. [*Aside.*] This *bougre* vil ruine me too ; but he
speak wit dat *bel* eyre and grace, I cannot bid him hold
his tongue, *ventre ! C'est assez, Pierrot, va-t'en.*

[*Exit* Scullion, *and returns.*

Scull. And de litel plate de—

Mons. Jarni ! va-t'en. [*Exit* Scullion, *and returns.*

Scull. And de litel plate de—

Mons. De grace, go dy way.

[*Exit* Scullion, *and returns.*

Scull. And de litel de—

Mons. De fromage de Brie, va-t'en !—go, go.

Flou. What's that ? cheese that stinks ?

Mons. Ay, ay, be sure it stinke extremente. *Pierrot,*
va-t'en ; but stay till I drink dy health :—here's to dat
pretty fellow's health, madam.

Flirt. Must we drink the scullion's health ?

Mons. Auh, you will not be *désobligeante,* madam ; he is the *cuisinier* for a king, nay, for a cardinal or French abbot.   [*Drinks. Exit* Scullion.

Flou. But how shall we divertise ourselves till supper be ready ?

Flirt. Can we have better *divertissement* than this gentleman ?

Flou. But I think we had better carry the gentleman home with us, and because it is already late, sup at home, and divertise the gentleman at cards, till it be ready.— D'ye hear, waiter ? let it be brought, when 'tis ready, to my lodging hard by, in Mustard-Alley, at the sign of the Crooked-billet.

Mons. At the Crooked-billet !

Flirt. Come, sir, come.

Mons. Morbleu ! I have take the vow (since my last clap) never to go again to the *bourdel.*

Flou. What is the *bourdel ?*

Mons. How call you the name of your house ?

Flirt. The Crooked-billet.

Mons. No, no, the—bawdy-house, *vert* and *bleu !*

Flirt. How, our lodging ! we'd have you to know—

Mons. Auh, *morbleu !* I would not know it ; de Crooked-billet, ha ! ha !

Flirt. Come, sir.

Mons. Besides, if I go wit you to the *bourdel,* you will tell, *morbleu !*

Flou. Fy ! fy ! come along.

Mons. Beside, I am to be married within these two days ; if you should tell now—

Flirt. Come, come along, we will not tell.

Mons. But you will promise then to have the care of my honour ? pray, good madam, have de care of my honour, pray have de care of my honour. Will you have care of my honour ? pray have de care of my honour, and do not tell if you can help it ; pray, dear madam, do not tell.   [*Kneels to them.*

Flirt. I would not tell for fear of losing you, my love for you will make me secret.

Mons. Why, do you love me?

Flirt. Indeed I cannot help telling you now, what my modesty ought to conceal, but my eyes would disclose it too :—I have a passion for you, sir.

Mons. A passion for me!

Flirt. An extreme passion, dear sir; you are so French, so mightily French, so agreeable French—but I'll tell you more of my heart at home : come along.

Mons. But is your pation sincere?

Flirt. The truest in the world.

Mons. Well then, I'll venture my body with thee for one night.

Flirt. For one night! don't you believe that; and so you would leave me to-morrow? but I love you so, I cannot part with you, you must keep me for good and all, if you will have me. I can't leave you for my heart.

Mons. How! keep, *jarni!* de whore Englis have notinge but keepe, keepe in dere mouths now-a-days, *tête non!*—Formerly 'twas enoughe to keep de shild, *ma foi!*

Flirt. Nay, I will be kept, else—but, come, we'll talk on't at home.

Mons. Umh—so, so, ver vel; de amour of de whore does alway end in keep, ha! keep, *ma foi!* keep, ha!—

The punk that entertains you wit her passion,

Is like kind host who makes the invitation,

At your own cost, to his *fort bonne collation.*

[*Exeunt.*

ACT THE SECOND.

SCENE I.—Don DIEGO'S *House in the morning.*

Enter Don DIEGO *in a Spanish habit, and* Mrs. CAUTION.

ON. Have you had a Spanish care of the honour of my family? that is to say, have you kept my daughter close in my absence, as I directed?

Mrs. Caut. I have sir, but it was as much as I could do.

Don. I knew that; for 'twas as much as I could do to keep up her mother;—I that have been in Spain, look you.

Mrs. Caut. Nay 'tis a hard task to keep up an Englishwoman.

Don. As hard as it is for those who are not kept up to be honest, look you, *con licencia*, sister.

Mrs. Caut. How now, brother! I am sure my husband never kept me up.

Don. I knew that, therefore I cried *con licencia*, sister, as the Spaniards have it.

Mrs. Caut. But you Spaniards are too censorious, brother.

Don. You Englishwomen, sister, give us too much cause, look you;—but you are sure my daughter has not seen a man since my departure?

Mrs. Caut. No, not so much as a churchman.

Don. As a churchman ! *voto !* I thank you for that ; not a churchman ! not a churchman !

Mrs. Caut. No, not so much as a churchman ; but of any, one would think one might trust a churchman.

Don. No, we are bold enough in trusting them with our souls, I'll never trust them with the body of my daughter, look you, *guarda !* You see what comes of trusting churchmen here in England ; and tis because the women govern the families, that chaplains are so much in fashion. Trust a churchman !—trust a coward with your honour, a fool with your secret, a gamester with your purse, as soon as a priest with your wife or daughter ; look you, *guarda !* I am no fool, look you.

Mrs. Caut. Nay, I know you are a wise man, brother.

Don. Why, sister, I have been fifteen years in Spain for it, at several times, look you : now in Spain, he is wise enough that is grave, politic enough that says little, and honourable enough that is jealous ; and though I say it, that should not say it, I am as grave, grum, and jealous, as any Spaniard breathing.

Mrs. Caut. I know you are, brother.

Don. And will be a Spaniard in everything still, and will not conform, not I, to their ill-favoured English customs, for I will wear my Spanish habit still, I will stroke my Spanish whiskers still, and I will eat my Spanish *olio* still ; and my daughter shall go a maid to her husband's bed, let the English custom be what 'twill : I would fain see any finical, cunning, insinuating monsieur of the age, debauch, or steal away my daughter. But, well, has she seen my cousin ? how long has he been in England ?

Mrs. Caut. These three days.

Don. And she has seen him, has she ? I was contented he should see her, intending him for her husband ; but she has seen nobody else upon your certain knowledge ?

Mrs. Caut. No, no, alas! how should she? 'tis impossible she should.

Don. Where is her chamber? pray let me see her.

Mrs. Caut. You'll find her, poor creature, asleep, I warrant you: or, if awake, thinking no hurt, nor of your coming this morning.

Don. Let us go to her, I long to see her, poor innocent wretch.   [*Exeunt.*

SCENE II.—*A Room in* Don DIEGO'S *House.*

Enter HIPPOLITA, GERRARD, *and* PRUE *at a distance.*

Ger. Am I not come upon your own summons, madam? and yet receive me so?

Hip. My summons, sir! no, I assure you; and if you do not like your reception, I cannot help it; for I am not used to receive men, I'd have you to know.

Ger. She is beautiful beyond all things I ever saw.

[*Aside.*

Hip. I like him extremely!   [*Aside.*

Ger. Come, fairest, why do you frown?

Hip. Because I am angry.

Ger. I am come on purpose to please you, then; do not receive me so unkindly.

Hip. I tell you, I do not use to receive men.—There has not been a man in the house before, but my cousin, this twelvemonth, I'd have you to know.

Ger. Then you ought to bid me the more welcome, I'd have you to know.

Hip. What! do you mock me too? I know I am but a home-bred simple girl! but I thought you gallants of the town had been better bred than to mock a poor girl in her father's own house. I have heard, indeed, 'tis a part of good breeding to mock people behind their backs, but not to their faces.

Ger. [*Aside.*] Pretty creature! she has not only the beauty, but the innocency of an angel.—[*To* HIPPOLITA.] Mock you, dear miss! no, I only repeated the words because they were yours, sweet miss; what we like we imitate.

Hip. "Dear miss! sweet miss!" how came you and I so well acquainted? this is one of your confident tricks, too, as I have been told; you'll be acquainted with a woman in the time you can help her over a bench in the playhouse, or to her coach. But I need not wonder at your confidence, since you could come in at the great gallery window, just now. But, pray, who shall pay for the glass you have broken?

Ger. Pretty creature! your father might have made the window bigger then, since he has so fine a daughter, and will not allow people to come in at the door to her.

Hip. A pleasant man!—well, 'tis harder playing the hypocrite with him, I see, than with my aunt or father; and if dissimulation were not very natural to a woman, I'm sure I could not use it at this time: but the mask of simplicity and innocency is as useful to an intriguing woman as the mask of religion to a statesman, they say.

[*Aside.*

Ger. Why do you look away, dearest miss?

Hip. Because you quarrelled with me just now for frowning upon you, and I cannot help it, if I look upon you.

Ger. O! let me see that face at any rate.

Hip. Would you have me frown upon you? for I shall be sure to do't.

Ger. Come, I'll stand fair: you have done your worst to my heart already.

Hip. Now I dare not look upon him, lest I should not be able to keep my word. [*Aside.*

Ger. Come, I am ready:—[*Aside.*] and yet I am afraid of her frowns.—[*To* HIPPOLITA.] Come, look, Ih—am ready, Ih—am ready.

Hip. But I am not ready.   [*Aside.*

Ger. Turn, dear miss, come, Ih—am ready.

Hip. Are you ready then? I'll look. [*Turns upon him.*]—No, faith, I cannot frown upon him, if I should be hanged.   [*Aside.*

Ger. Dear miss, I thank you, that look has no terror in't.

Hip. No, I cannot frown for my heart for blushing, I don't use to look upon men, you must know.

Ger. If it were possible anything could, those blushes would add to her beauty : well, bashfulness is the only out-of-fashioned thing that is agreeable.   [*Aside.*

Hip. Ih—h—like this man strangely, I was going to say loved him. Courage then, Hippolita! make use of the only opportunity thou canst have to enfranchise thyself. Women formerly (they say) never knew how to make use of their time till it was past ; but let it not be said so of a young woman of this age.—My damned aunt will be stirring presently :—well, then, courage, I say, Hippolita !—thou art full fourteen years old,—shift for thyself.   [*Aside.*

Ger. So! I have looked upon her so long, till I am grown bashful too. Love and modesty come together like money and covetousness, and the more we have, the less we can show it. I dare not look her in the face now, nor speak a word.   [*Aside.*

Hip. What, sir, methinks you look away now!

Ger. Because you would not look upon me, miss.

Hip. Nay, I hope you can't look me in the face, since you have done so rude a thing as to come in at the window upon me. Come, come, when once we women find the men bashful, then we take heart. Now I can look upon you as long as you will; let's see if you can frown upon me now.

Ger. Lovely innocency! no, you may swear I can't frown upon you, miss.

Hip. So! I knew you were ashamed of what you have

done. Well, since you are ashamed, and because you did not come of your own head, but were sent by my cousin, you say—

Ger. Which I wonder at.   [*Aside.*

Hip. For all these reasons, I do forgive you.

Ger. In token of your forgiveness then, dearest miss, let me have the honour to kiss your hand.

Hip. Nay, there 'tis; you men are like our little shock dogs:[1] if we don't keep you off from us, but use you a little kindly, you grow so fiddling and so troublesome, there is no enduring you.

Ger. O dear miss! if I am like your shock-dog, let it be in his privileges.

Hip. Why, I'd have you know he does not lie with me.

Ger. 'Twas well guessed, miss, for one so innocent.

Hip. No, I always kick him off from the bed, and never will let him come near it; for of late, indeed, (I do not know what's the reason,) I don't much care for my shock-dog, nor my babies.

Ger. O then, miss, I may have hopes! for after the shock-dog and the babies, 'tis the man's turn to be beloved.

Hip. Why, could you be so good-natured as to come after my shock-dog in my love? it may be, indeed, rather than after one of your brother men.

Ger Hah, ha, ha! poor creature! a wonder of innocency!   [*Aside.*

Hip. But I see you are humble, because you would kiss my hand.

Ger. No, I am ambitious therefore.

Hip. [*Aside.*] Well, all this fooling but loses time, I must make better use of it. [*To* GERRARD.] I could let you kiss my hand, but then I'm afraid you would take hold of me and carry me away.

Ger. Indeed I would not.

[1] Rough-coated.

Hip. Come, I know you would.

Ger. Truly I would not.

Hip. You would! you would! I know you would.

Ger. I'll swear I wo' not—by—

Hip. Nay, don't swear, for you'll be the apter to do it then. [*Aside.*] I would not have him forswear it neither; —he does not like me, sure, well enough to carry me away.

Ger. Dear miss, let me kiss your hand.

Hip. I am sure you would carry me away if I should.

Ger. Be not afraid of it.

Hip. [*Aside.*] Nay, I am afraid of the contrary.— Either he dislikes me, and therefore will not be troubled with me, or what is as bad, he loves me and is dull, or fearful to displease me.

Ger. Trust me, sweetest! I can use no violence to you.

Hip. Nay, I am sure you would carry me away; what should you come in at the window for, if you did not mean to steal me.

Ger. If I should endeavour it, you might cry out, and I should be prevented.

Hip. [*Aside.*] Dull, dull man of the town! are all like thee? He is as dull as a country squire at questions and commands.—[*To* GERRARD.] No, if I should cry out never so loud, this is quite at the further end of the house, and there nobody could hear me.

Ger. I will not give you the occasion, dearest.

Hip. [*Aside.*] Well, I will quicken thy sense, if it be possible.—[*To* GERRARD.] Nay, I know you come to steal me away; because I am an heiress, and have twelve hundred pounds a year, lately left me by my mother's brother, which my father cannot meddle with, and which is the chiefest reason (I suppose) why he keeps me up so close.

Ger. Ha!

Hip. So!—this has made him consider.   O money!

powerful money! how the ugly, old, crooked, straight, handsome young women are beholding to thee! [*Aside.*

Ger. Twelve hundred pounds a year!

Hip. Besides, I have been told my fortune, and the woman said I should be stolen away, because she says 'tis the fate of heiresses to be stolen away.

Ger. Twelve hundred pounds a-year!— [*Aside.*

Hip. Nay, more, she described the man to me that was to do it, and he was as like you as could be. Have you any brothers?

Ger. Not any; 'twas I, I warrant you, sweetest.

Hip. So, he understands himself now. [*Aside.*

Ger. Well, madam, since 'twas foretold you, what do you think on't? 'tis in vain, you know, to resist fate.

Hip. I do know, indeed, they say 'tis to no purpose: besides, the woman that told me my fortune, or you, have bewitched me—Ih—think. [*Sighs.*

Ger. My soul! my life! 'tis you have charms powerful as numberless, especially those of your innocency irresistible, and do surprise the wariest heart. Such mine was, while I could call it mine, but now 'tis yours for ever.

Hip. Well, well, get you gone then. I'll keep it safe for your sake.

Ger. Nay, you must go with me, sweetest.

Hip. Well, I see you will part with the jewel; but you will have the keeping of the cabinet to which you commit it.

Ger. Come, come, my dearest, let us be gone: Fortune as well as women must be taken in the humour.

As they are going out, PRUE *runs hastily to them.*

Prue. O miss, miss! your father, it seems, is just now arrived, and is here coming in upon you.

Hip. My father.

Enter Don DIEGO *and* Mrs. CAUTION.

Don. My daughter and a man !

Mrs. Caut. A man ! a man in the house !

Ger. Ha ! what mean these ?—a Spaniard !

Hip. What shall I do ? Stay—Nay, pray stir not from me ; but lead me about, as if you led me a corant.[1]

[*Leads her about.*

Don. Is this your government, sister ? and this your innocent charge, that 'hath not seen the face of a man this twelvemonth ? *en hora mala !*

Mrs. Caut. O, sure, it is not a man ! it cannot be a man !   [*Puts on her spectacles*

Don. It cannot be a man ! if he be not a man, he's a devil. He has her lovingly by the hand too, *valgame el cielo !*

Hip. Do not seem to mind them, but dance on, or lead me about still.

Ger. What d'ye mean by it ?   [*Apart to* HIPPOLITA.

Don. Hey, they are frolic, a-dancing !

Mrs. Caut. Indeed, they are dancing, I think.—Why, niece !

Don. Nay, hold a little : I'll make 'em dance in the devil's name ; but it shall not be *la gallarda.*

[*Draws his sword.*

Mrs. Caut. O niece ! why niece !

[Mrs. CAUTION *holds him.*

Ger. Do you hear her ? what do you mean ?

[*Apart to* HIPPOLITA.

Hip. Take no notice of them ; but walk about still, and sing a little, sing a corant.

Ger. I can't sing : but I'll hum, if you will.

Don. Are you so merry ? well I'll be with you : *en hora mala !*

Mrs. Caut. O niece, niece ! why niece ! oh—

---

[1] Coranto, a quick and lively dance.

Don. Why, daughter, my dainty daughter ! My shame ! my ruin ! my plague !

> [*Struggling, gets from* Mrs. CAUTION, *goes towards them with his sword drawn.*

Hip. Mind him not, but dance and sing on.

Ger. A pretty time to dance and sing, indeed, when I have a Spaniard with a naked Toledo at my tail ! No, pray excuse me, miss, from fooling any longer.

Hip. [*Turning about.*] O, my father, my father ! poor father ! you are welcome ; pray give me your blessing.

Don. My blessing, *en hora mala !*

Hip. What ! am I not your daughter, sir ?

Don. My daughter ! *mi mal ! mi muerte !*

Hip. My name's Hippolita, sir : I don't own your Spanish names. But, pray father, why do you frighten one so ? you know I don't love to see a sword : what do you mean to do with that ugly thing out ?

Don. I'll show you. *Traidor ! ladron de mi honra !* thou diest. [*Runs at* GERRARD.

Ger. Not if I can help it, good Don. But by the names you give me, I find you mistake your man : I suppose some Spaniard has affronted you. [*Draws.*

Don. None but thee, *ladron !* and thou diest for't.

> [*Fight.*

Mrs. Caut. Oh ! oh ! oh !—help ! help ! help !

Hip. O—what, will you kill my poor dancing-master ?

> [*Kneels.*

Don. A dancing-master ! he's a fencing-master rather, I think. But is he your dancing-master ? umph—

Ger. So much wit and innocency were never togeth'r before. [*Aside.*

Don. Is he a dancing-master ? [*Pausing.*

Mrs. Caut. Is he a dancing-master ? He does not look like a dancing-master.

Hip. Pish !—you don't know a dancing-master : you have not seen one these threescore years, I warrant.

Mrs. Caut. No matter: but he does not look like a dancing-master.

Don. Nay, nay, dancing-masters look like gentlemen enough, sister: but he's no dancing master, by drawing a sword so briskly. Those tripping outsides of gentlemen are like gentlemen enough in everything but in drawing a sword; and since he is a gentleman, he shall die by mine.   [*They fight again.*

Hip. Oh! hold! hold!

Mrs. Caut. Hold! hold!—Pray, brother, let's talk with him a little first; I warrant you I shall trap him; and if he confesses, you may kill him; but those that confess, they say, ought to be hanged—Let's see—

Ger. Poor Hippolita! I wish I had not had this occasion of admiring thy wit; I have increased my love, whilst I have lost my hopes; the common fate of poor lovers.   [*Aside.*

Mrs. Caut. Come, you are guilty, by that hanging down of your head. Speak: are you a dancing-master? Speak, speak; a dancing-master?

Ger. Yes, forsooth, I am a dancing-master: ay, ay—

Don. How does it appear?

Hip. Why, there is his fiddle, there upon the table, father.

Mrs. Caut. No, busybody, but it is not:—that is my nephew's fiddle.

Hip. Why, he lent it to my cousin: I tell you it is his.

Mrs. Caut. Nay, it may be, indeed; he might lend it to him for aught I know.

Don. Ay, ay: but ask him, sister, if he be a dancing-master, where.

Mrs. Caut. Pray, brother, let me alone with him, I know what to ask him, sure.

Don. What, will you be wiser than I? nay, then stand away. Come, if you are a dancing-master, where's your school? *Donde? donde?*

Mrs. Caut. Why, he'll say, may be, he has ne'er a one.

Don. Who asked you, nimble chaps? So you have put an excuse in his head.

Ger. Indeed, sir, 'tis no excuse: I have no school.

Mrs. Caut. Well; but who sent you? how came you hither?

Ger. There I am puzzled indeed. [*Aside.*

Mrs. Caut. How came you hither, I say? how—

Ger. Why, how, how should I come hither?

Don. Ay, how should he come hither? Upon his legs.

Mrs. Caut. So, so! now you have put an excuse in his head too, that you have, so you have; but stay—

Don. Nay, with your favour, mistress, I'll ask him now.

Mrs. Caut. Y'facks, but you shan't! I'll ask him, and ask you no favour, that I will.

Don. Y'fackins, but you shan't ask him! if you go there too, look you, you prattle-box you, I'll ask him.

Mrs. Caut. I will ask him, I say!—come!

Don. Where?

Mrs. Caut. What!

Don. Mine's a shrewd question.

Mrs. Caut. Mine's as shrewd as yours.

Don. Nay, then, we shall have it.—Come, answer me; where's your lodging? come, come, sir.

Mrs. Caut. A shrewd question, indeed! at the Surgeons'-arms, I warrant you; for 'tis spring-time, you know.

Don. Must you make lies for him?

Mrs. Caut. But come, sir; what's your name?—answer me to that; come.

Don. His name! why, 'tis an easy matter to tell you a false name, I hope.

Mrs. Caut. So! must you teach him to cheat us?

Don. Why did you say my questions were not shrewd questions, then?

Mrs. Caut. And why would you not let me ask him the question, then? Brother, brother, ever while you live,

for all your Spanish wisdom, let an old woman make dis-
coveries: the young fellows cannot cheat us in anything,
I'd have you to know. Set your old woman still to
grope out an intrigue, because, you know, the mother
found her daughter in the oven. A word to the wise,
brother.

Don. Come, come, leave this tattling: he has dishonoured my family, debauched my daughter; and what
if he could excuse himself? The Spanish proverb says,
excuses neither satisfy creditors nor the injured. The
wounds of honour must have blood and wounds, *St. Jago
para mi!*

[*Kisses the cross of his sword, and runs at* GERRARD.

Hip. O hold, dear father! and I'll confess all.

Ger. She will not, sure, after all.   [*Aside.*

Hip. My cousin sent him; because, as he said,
he would have me recover my dancing a little before
our wedding, having made a vow he would never marry a
wife who could not dance a corant. I am sure I was
unwilling; but he would have him come, saying I was to
be his wife as soon as you came, and therefore expected
obedience from me.

Don. Indeed, the venture is most his, and the shame
would be most his; for I know here in England, 'tis not
the custom for the father to be much concerned what the
daughter does; but I will be a Spaniard still.

Hip. Did not you hear him say last night he would
send me one this morning?

Mrs. Caut. No, not I, sure. If I had, he had never
come here.

Hip. Indeed, aunt, you grow old I see; your memory
fails you very much. Did not you hear him, Prue, say
he would send him to me?

Prue. Yes, I'll be sworn did I.

Hip. Look you there, aunt.

Mrs. Caut. I wonder I should not remember it.

Don. Come, come, you are a doting old fool.

Mrs. Caut. So ! So ! the fault will be mine now. But pray, mistress, how did he come in ? I am sure I had the keys of the doors, which, till your father came in, were not opened to-day.

Hip. He came in just after my father, I suppose.

Mrs. Caut. It might be, indeed, while the porters brought in the things, and I was talking with you.

Don. O, might he so, forsooth ! you are a brave governante ! Look you, you a duenna, *voto !*—and not know who comes in and out !

Mrs. Caut. So ! 'tis my fault, I know.

Don. Your maid was in the room with you ; was she not, child ?

Hip. Yes, indeed, and indeed, father, all the while.

Don. Well, child, I am satisfied then.—But I hope he does not use the dancing-master's tricks, of squeezing your hands, setting your legs and feet, by handling your thighs and seeing your legs.

Hip. No, indeed, father : I'd give him a box on the ear if he should.

Don. Poor innocent !—Well, I am contented you should learn to dance, since, for aught I know, you shall be married to-morrow, or the next day at farthest : by that time you may recover a corant—a saraband I would say.[1] And since your cousin, too, will have a dancing wife, it shall be so ; and I'll see you dance myself. You shall be my charge these two days, and then I dare venture you in the hand of any dancing-master, even a saucy French dancing-master, look you.

Mrs. Caut. Well, have a care, though ; for this man is not dressed like a dancing-master.

Don. Go, go, you dote ; are they not (for the most part) better dressed and prouder than many a good gentleman ? you would be wiser than I, would you. *cuerno ?*

Mrs. Caut. Well, I say only, look to't, look to't.

---

[1] The saraband was a slow and stately dance.

Don. Hey, hey! Come, friend, to your business; teach her her lesson over again; let's see.

Hip. Come, master.

Don. Come, come, let's see your English method; I understand something of dancing myself—come.

Hip. Come, master.

Ger. I shall betray you yet, dearest miss; for I know not a step: I could never dance. [*Apart to* HIPPOLITA.

Hip. No!

Don. Come, come, child.

Hip. Indeed I'm ashamed, father.

Don. You must not be ashamed, child; you'll never dance well if you are ashamed.

Hip. Indeed, I can't help it, father.

Don. Come, come, I say, go to't.

Hip. Indeed I can't, father, before you: 'tis my first lesson, and I shall do it so ill.—Pray, good father, go into the next room for this once; and the next time my master comes, you shall see I shall be confident enough.

Don. Poor, foolish, innocent creature!—Well, well, I will, child. Who but a Spanish kind of a father could have so innocent a daughter in England?—Well, I would fain see any one steal or debauch my daughter from me.

Hip. Nay, won't you go, father?

Don. Yes, yes, I go, child: we will all go but your maid.— You can dance before your maid?

Hip. Yes, yes, father: a maid at most times with her mistress is nobody. [*Exeunt* DIEGO *and* Mrs. CAUTION.

Ger. He peeps yet at the door.

Hip. Nay, father, you peep; indeed you must not see me. When we have done, you shall come in.

[*She pulls the door to.*

Prue. Indeed, little mistress, like the young kitten, you see you played with your prey till you had almost lost it.

Hip. 'Tis true, a good old mouser like you had taken it up, and run away with it presently.

Ger. Let me adore you, dearest miss, and give you—
[*Going to embrace her.*

Hip. No, no embracing, good master! that ought to be the last lesson you are to teach me, I have heard.

Ger. Though an aftergame be the more tedious and dangerous, 'tis won, miss, with the more honour and pleasure: for all that, I repent we were put to't. The coming in of your father, as he did, was the most unlucky thing that ever befel me.

Hip. What then, you think I would have gone with you?

Ger. Yes; and you will go with me yet, I hope.— Courage, miss! we have yet an opportunity; and the gallery-window is yet open.

Hip. No, no; if I went, I would go for good and all: but now my father will soon come in again, and may quickly overtake us. Besides, now I think on't, you are a stranger to me; I know not where you live, nor whither you might carry me. For aught I know, you might be a spirit, and carry me to Barbadoes.

Ger. No, dear miss, I would carry you to court, the playhouses, and Hyde-park—

Hip. Nay, I know 'tis the trick of all you that spirit women away, to speak 'em mighty fair at first: but when you have got 'em in your clutches, you carry 'em into Yorkshire, Wales, or Cornwall, which is as bad as to Barbadoes; and rather than be served so, I would be a prisoner in London still as I am.

Ger. I see the air of this town, without the pleasures of it, is enough to infect women with an aversion for the country. Well, miss, since it seems you have some diffidence in me, give me leave to visit you as your dancing-master, now you have honoured me with the character; and under that I may have your father's permission to see you, till you may better know me

and my heart, and have a better opportunity to reward it.

Hip. I am afraid to know your heart would require a
great deal of time ; and my father intends to marry me
very suddenly to my cousin, who sent you hither.

Ger. Pray, sweet miss, let us make the better use of
our time if it be short. But how shall we do with that
cousin of yours in the mean time? we must needs charm
him.

Hip. Leave that to me.

Ger. But (what's worse) how shall I be able to act
a dancing-master, who ever wanted inclination and
patience to learn myself?

Hip. A dancing-school in half an hour will furnish
you with terms of the art. Besides, Love (as I have
heard say) supplies his scholars with all sorts of capacities
they have need of, in spite of nature :—but what has love
to do with you?

Ger. Love, indeed, has made a grave gouty statesmen
fight duels, the soldier fly from his colours, a pedant a
fine gentlemen, nay, and the very lawyer a poet ; and,
therefore, may make me a dancing-master.

Hip. If he were your master.

Ger. I'm sure, dearest miss, there is nothing else
which I cannot do for you already ; and, therefore, may
hope to succeed in that.

Re-enter Don DIEGO.

Don. Come, have you done?

Hip. O, my father again !

Don. Come, now let us see you dance.

Hip. Indeed I am not perfect yet : pray excuse me
till the next time my master comes. But when must he
come again, father?

Don. Let me see—friend, you must needs come after
dinner again, and then at night again, and so three times
to-morrow too. If she be not married to-morrow, (which

I am to consider of,) she will dance a corant in twice or thrice teaching more ; will she not ? for 'tis but a twelve-month since she came from Hackney-school.

Ger. We will lose no time, I warrant you, sir, if she be to be married to-morrow.

Don. True, I think she may be married to-morrow ; therefore, I would not have you lose any time, look you.

Ger. You need not caution me, I warrant you, sir.— Sweet scholar, your humble servant : I will not fail you immediately after dinner.

Don. No, no, pray do not ; and I will not fail to satisfy you very well, look you.

Hip. He does not doubt his reward, father, for his pains. If you should not, I would make that good to him.

Don. Come, let us go in to your aunt : I must talk with you both together, child.

Hip. I follow you, sir.

[*Exeunt* GERRARD *and* Don DIEGO.

Prue. Here's the gentlewoman o' th' next house come to see you, mistress.

Hip. [*Aside.*] She's come, as if she came expressly to sing the new song she sung last night. I must hear it ; for 'tis to my purpose now.—

Enter Lady.

Madam, your servant : I dreamt all night of the song you sung last ; the new song against delays in love. Pray, let's hear it again.

Lady. (*Sings.*)

    Since we poor slavish women know
        Our men we cannot pick and choose,
    To him we like why say we no,
        And both our time and lover lose ?
    With feigned repulses and delays
        A lover's appetite we pall ;
    And if too long the gallant stays,
        His stomach's gone for good and all.

Or our impatient amorous guest
 Unknown to us away may steal,
And rather than stay for a feast,
 Take up with some coarse ready meal.
When opportunity is kind,
 Let prudent women be so too ;
And if the man be to your mind,
 Till needs you must, ne'er let him go.

The match soon made is happy still,
 For only love has there to do.
Let no one marry 'gainst her will,
 But stand off when her parents woo,
And only to their suits be coy :
 For she whom jointure can obtain,
To let a fop her bed enjoy,
 Is but a lawful wench for gain.

Prue. Your father calls for you, miss.

[Steps to the door.

Hip. I come, I come ; I must be obedient as long as
I am with him. [*Pausing.*

Our parents who restrain our liberty,
 But take the course to make us sooner free,
 Though all we gain be but new slavery ;
 We leave our fathers, and to husbands flee.

[Exeunt

ACT THE THIRD.

SCENE I.—Don Diego's *House.*

Enter Monsieur de Paris, Hippolita, *and* Prue.

ONS. *Serviteur, serviteur, la cousine.* Your maid told me she watched at the stair-foot for my coming ; because you had a mind to speak wit me before I saw your fader, it seem.

Hip. I would so, indeed, cousin.

Mons. Or-ça ! or-ça ! I know your affair. It is to tell me wat recreation you ade with Monsieur Gerrard. But did he come ? I was afrait he would not come.

Hip. Yes, yes, he did come.

Mons. Ha ! ha ! ha !—and were you not infiniment divertisee and please ? Confess.

Hip. I was indeed, cousin, I was very well pleased.

Mons. I do tinke so. I did tinke to come and be divertisee myself this morning with the sight of his reception : but I did rancounter last night wit dam company dat keep me up so late, I could not rise in de morning, *malepeste de putains !*—

Hip. Indeed, we wanted you here mightily, cousin.

Mons. To elpe you to laugh : for if I adde been here, I had made such recreation wit dat coxcomb Gerrard !

Hip. Indeed, cousin, you need not have any subject or property to make one laugh, you are so pleasant your-

self; and when you are but alone, you would make one
burst.

Mons. Am I so happy, cousin, then, in the *bon* quality
of making people laugh?

Hip. Mighty happy, cousin.

Mons. De grace?

Hip. Indeed.

Mons. Nay, *sans vanité*, I observe, wheresoe'er I
come, I make everybody merry; *sans vanité*—da—

Hip. I do believe you do.

Mons. Nay, as I marche in de street, I can make de
dull apprenty laugh and sneer.

Hip. This fool, I see, is as apt as an ill poet to mistake the contempt and scorn of people for applause and
admiration.   [*Aside.*

Mons. Ah, cousin, you see what it is to have been in
France! Before I went into France, I could get nobody
to laugh at me, *ma foi!*

Hip. No? truly, cousin, I think you deserved it before; but you are improved, indeed, by going into
France.

Mons. Ay, ay, the French education make us *propre
à tout.* Beside, cousin, you must know, to play the
fool is the science in France, and I didde go to the
Italian academy at Paris thrice a-week to learn to play
de fool of Signior Scaramouche,[1] who is the most
excellent personage in the world for dat noble science.
Angel is a dam English fool to him.

Hip. Methinks, now, Angel is a very good fool.

Mons. Naugh, naugh, Nokes is a better fool; but
indeed the Englis are not fit to be fools: here are ver

[1] A farcical personage of the Italian stage, in the character of a
military braggart. Tiberio Fiurelli, the creator of this part, was
acting in Wycherley's time at the Italian Theatre in Paris. Angel
and Nokes were eminent comic actors of the day, and this scene
must have been sufficiently diverting if, as Genest supposes, the part
of Monsieur de Paris was actually played by Nokes, and that of Don
Diego by Angel.

few good fools. 'Tis true, you have many a young
cavalier who go over into France to learn to be de
buffoon ; but for all dat, dey return but *mauvais* buffoon,
jarni!

Hip. I'm sure, cousin, you have lost no time there.

Mons. Auh, *le brave* Scaramouche !

Hip. But is it a science in France, cousin ? and is
there an academy for fooling ? sure none go to it but
players.

Mons. Dey are comedians dat are de *maîtres*; but all
the *beau monde* go to learn, as they do here of Angel and
Nokes. For if you did go abroad into company, you
would find the best almost of de nation conning in all
places the lessons which dey have learned of the fools
dere *maîtres*, Nokes and Angel.

Hip. Indeed !

Mons. Yes, yes, dey are de *gens de qualité* that practise
dat science most, and the most *ambitieux ;* for fools and
buffoons have been always most welcome to courts, and
desired in all companies. Auh, to be de fool, de buffoon,
is to be de great personage.

Hip. Fools have fortune, they say, indeed.

Mons. So say old Senèque.

Hip. Well, cousin, not to make you proud, you are
the greatest fool in England, I am sure.

Mons, Non, non, *de grace; non :* Nokes de comedian
is a pretty man, a pretty man for a comedian, da—

Hip. You are modest, cousin.—But lest my father
should come in presently, which he will do as soon as he
knows you are here, I must give you a caution, which 'tis
fit you should have before you see him.

Mons. Vell, vell, cousin, vat is dat ?

Hip. You must know, then (as commonly the conclusion of all mirth is sad), after I had a good while
pleased myself in jesting, and leading the poor gentleman
you sent into a fool's paradise, and almost made him
believe I would go away with him, my father, coming

home this morning, came in upon us, and caught him
with me.

Mons. *Malepeste!*

Hip. And drew his sword upon him, and would have
killed him; for you know my father's Spanish fierceness
and jealousy.

Mons. But how did he come off then, *tête non?*

Hip. In short, I was fain to bring him off by saying he
was my dancing-master.

Mons. Ha! ha! ha! ver good jeste.

Hip. I was unwilling to have the poor man killed, you
know, for our foolish frolic with him: but then, upon my
aunt's and father's inquiry, how he came in, and who sent
him, I was forced to say you did, desiring I should be
able to dance a corant before our wedding.

Mons. A ver good jest—da—still better as better.

Hip. Now, all that I am to desire of you is, to own
you sent him, that I may not be caught in a lie.

Mons. Yes, yes, a ver good iest: Gerrard a *maître de
danse!* ha! ha! ha!

Hip. Nay, the jest is like to be better yet; for my
father himself has obliged him now to come and teach
me: so that now he must take the dancing-master upon
him, and come three or four times to me before our
wedding, lest my father, if he should come no more,
should be suspicious I had told him a lie. And, for
aught I know, if he should know, or but guess he were
not a dancing-master, in his Spanish strictness and
punctilios of honour, he might kill me as the shame and
stain of his honour and family, which he talks of so
much. Now, you know the jealous cruel fathers in
Spain serve their poor innocent daughters often so; and
he is more than a Spaniard.

Mons. *Non, non,* fear noting; I warrant you, he shall
come as often as you will to de house; and your father
shall never know who he is till we are married. But
then I'll tell him all for the jest's sake.

Hip. But will you keep my counsel, dear cousin, till we are married?

Mons. Poor dear fool! I warrant thee, *ma foi!*

Hip. Nay, what a fool am I indeed! for you would not have me killed. You love me too well, sure, to be an instrument of my death.

Enter Don DIEGO, *walking gravely,* a Black boy *behind him; and* Mrs. CAUTION.

But here comes my father, remember.

Mons. I would no more tell him of it than I would tell you if I had been with a wench, *jarni!* [*Aside.*]—She's afraid to be killed, poor wretch, and he's a capricious, jealous fop enough to do't:—but here he comes.—[*To* HIPPOLITA.] I'll keep thy counsel, I warrant thee, my dear soul, *mon petit cœur.*

Hip. Peace! peace! my father's coming this way.

Mons. Ay, but by his march he won't be near enough to hear us this half hour, ha! ha! ha!

[Don DIEGO *walks leisurely round* Monsieur, *surveying him, and shrugging up his shoulders, whilst* Monsieur *makes legs and faces aside.*

Don. Is that thing my cousin, sister?

Mrs. Caut. 'Tis he, sir.

Don. Cousin, I am sorry to see you—

Mons. Is that a Spanish compliment?

Don. So much disguised, cousin.

Mons. [*Aside.*] Oh! is it out at last, *ventre?*—[*To* Don DIEGO.] — *Serviteur, serviteur, à monsieur mon oncle;* and I am glad to see you here within doors, most Spanish *oncle,* ha! ha! ha! but I should be sorry to see you in the streets, *tête non!*

Don. Why so?—would you be ashamed of me, hah—*voto á St. Jago!* would you? hauh—

Mons. Ay; it may be you would be ashamed yourself, *monsieur mon oncle,* of the great train you would get to wait upon your Spanish hose, puh—the boys would

follow you, and hoot at you—*vert* and *bleu !* pardon my
Franch *franchise, monsieur mon oncle.*

Hip. We shall have sport anon, betwixt these two
contraries.   [*Apart to* PRUE.

Don. Dost thou call me " monsieur ?" *voto á St. Jago !*

Mons. No, I did not call you Monsieur Voto á St.
Jago ! Sir, I know you are my uncle, Mr. James Formal
—da—

Don. But I can hardly know you are my cousin, Mr.
Nathaniel Paris.—But call me, sir, Don Diego henceforward, look you, and no monsieur. Call me monsieur !
guarda !

Mons. I confess my error, sir ; for none but a blind
man would call you monsieur, ha ! ha !—But, pray, do
not call me neder Paris, but de Paris, de Paris, (*s'il vous
plait,*) Monsieur de Paris. Call me monsieur, and
welcome, da—

Don. Monsieur de Pantaloons then, *voto*—

Mons. Monsieur de Pantaloons ! a pretty name, a
pretty name, *ma foi !* da—*bien trouvé* de Pantaloons !
how much better den your de la Fountaines, de la
Rivieres, de la Roches, and all the *de's* in France—da
—well ; but have you not the admiration for my
pantaloon, Don Diego, *mon oncle ?*

Don. I am astonished at them, *verdaderamente,* they
are wonderfully ridiculous.

Mons. Redicule ! redicule ! ah—'tis well you are my
uncle, da—redicule ! ha—is dere any ting in the universe
so *gentil* as de pantaloons ? any ting so *ravissant* as de
pantaloons ? Auh—I could kneel down and varship
a pair of *gentil* pantaloons. Vat, vat, you would have me
have de admiration for dis outward skin of your thigh,
which you call Spanish hose, fi ! fi ! fi !—ha ! ha ! ha !

Don. Dost thou deride my Spanish hose, young man,
hauh ?

Mons. In comparison of pantaloon, I do undervalue
em indeed, Don Diego, *mon oncle,* ha ! ha ! ha !

Don. Thou art then a *gabacho*[1] *de mal gusto*, look you.

Mons. You may call me vat you vill, *oncle* Don Diego; but I must needs say, your Spanish hose are scurvy hose, ugly hose, lousy hose, and stinking hose.

Don. Do not provoke me, *borracho !*

[*Puts his hand to his sword.*

Mons. Indeed, as for lousy, I recant dat epithete, for dere is scarce room in 'em for dat little animal, ha ! ha ! ha ! but for stinking hose, dat epithete may stand; for how can they choose but stink, since they are so *furieusement* close to your Spanish tail, da ?

Hip. Ha ! ha ! ridiculous ! [*Aside.*

Don. Do not provoke me, I say, *en hora mala !*

[*Seems to draw.*

Mons. Nay, *oncle*, I am sorry you are in de pation; but I must live and die for de pantaloon against de Spanish hose, da.

Don. You are a rash young man; and while you wear pantaloons, you are beneath my passion, *voto*—auh—they make thee look and waddle (with all those gewgaw ribbons) like a great, old, fat, slovenly water-dog.

Mons. And your Spanish hose, and your nose in the air, make you look like a great, grizzled, long Irish greyhound reaching a crust off from a high shelf, ha ! ha ! ha !

Don. Bueno ! bueno !

Mrs. Caut. What, have you a mind to ruin yourself and break off the match?

Mons. Pshaw—wat do you tell me of the matche ! d'ye tinke I will not vindicate pantaloons, *morbleu !*

Don. [*Aside.*] Well, he is a lost young man, I see, and desperately far gone in the epidemic malady of our nation, the affectation of the worst of French vanities; but I must be wiser than him, as I am a Spaniard. Look you, Don Diego, and endeavour to reclaim him by

---

[1] *Gavanho* in former editions, but there is no such word in the Spanish language. I venture to substitute *gabach*, a term of contempt applied to a Frenchman.

art and fair means, look you, Don Diego; if not, he
shall never marry my daughter, look you, Don
Diego, though he be my own sister's son, and has two
thousand five hundred seventy-three pounds sterling,
twelve shillings and twopence a year pennyrent, *segura-
mente !*—[*To* Monsieur.] Come, young man, since you
are so obstinate, we will refer our difference to arbitration ;
your mistress, my daughter, shall be umpire betwixt us,
concerning Spanish hose and pantaloons.

Mons. Pantaloons and Spanish hose, *s'il vous plait.*

Don. Your mistress is the fittest judge of your dress, sure.

Mons. I know ver vel dat most of the *jeunesse* of
England will not change de ribband upon de crevat
without de consultation of dere *maîtresse ;* but I am no
Anglais, da—nor shall I make de reference of my dress
to any in the universe, da—I judge by any in England !
tête non ! I would not be judge by any English looking-
glass, *jarni !*

Don. Be not *positivo,* young man.

Mrs. Caut. Nay, pray refer it, cousin, pray do.

Mons. Non, non, your servant, your servant, aunt.

Don. But, pray, be not so positive. Come hither
daughter, tell me which is best.

Hip. Indeed, father, you have kept me in universal
ignorance, I know nothing.

Mons. And do you tink I shall refer an affair of that
consequence to a poor young ting who have not seen the
vorld, da ? I am wiser than so, *voto !*

Don. Well, in short, if you will not be wiser, and leave
off your French dress, stammering, and tricks, look you
you shall be a fool, and go without my daughter, *voto !*

Mons. How ! must I leave off my jantee French
accoutrements, and speak base Englis too, or not marry
my cousin, *mon oncle* Don Diego ? Do not break
off the match, do not ; for know, I will not leave off my
pantaloon and French pronuntiation for ne'er a cousin in
England't, da

Don. I tell you again, he that marries my daughter shall at least look like a wise man, for he shall wear the Spanish habit; I am a Spanish *positivo.*

Mons. Ver vel! ver vel! and I am a French *positivo.*

Don. Then I am *definitivo;* and if you do not go immediately into your chamber, and put on a Spanish habit, I have brought over on purpose for your wedding-clothes, and put off all these French fopperies and *vanidades,* with all your grimaces, agreeables, adorables, *ma fois,* and *jarnis;* I swear you shall never marry my daughter (and by an oath by Spaniard never broken) by my whiskers and snuff-box!

Mons. O hold! do not swear, uncle, for I love your daughter *furieusement.*

Don. If you love her, you'll obey me.

Mons. Auh, wat will become of me! but have the consideration. Must I leave off all the Franch *beautés,* graces, and embellisments, bote of my person, and language?

> [*Exeunt* HIPPOLITA, Mrs. CAUTION, *and* PRUE,
>   *laughing.*

Don. I will have it so.

Mons. I am ruinne den, undonne. Have some consideration for me, for dere is not de least ribbon of my *garniture* but is as dear to me as your daughter, *jarni!*

Don. Then, you do not deserve her; and for that reason I will be satisfied you love her better, or you shall not have her, for I am *positivo.*

Mons. Vill you break mine arte? Pray have de consideration for me.

Don. I say again, you shall be dressed before night from top to toe in the Spanish habit, or you shall never marry my daughter, look you.

Mons. If you will not have de consideration for me, have de consideration for your daughter; for she have de passionate *amour* for me, and like me in dis habite bettre den in yours, da.

Don. What I have said I have said, and I am *un positivo.*

Mons. Will you not so mush as allow me one little French oate?

Don. No, you shall look like a Spaniard, but speak and swear like an Englishman, look you.

Mons. Hélas! hélas! den I shall take my leave, *mort! tête! ventre! jarni! tête bleu! ventre bleu! ma foi!* certes!

Don. [*Calls at the door.*] Pedro, Sanchez, wait upon this *cavaliero* into his chamber with those things I ordered you to take out of the trunks.—I would have you a little accustomed to your clothes before your wedding; for, if you comply with me, you shall marry my daughter to-morrow, look you.

Mons. Adieu then, dear pantaloon! dear belte! dear sword! dear peruke! and dear *chapeau retroussé*, and dear shoe, *jarni!* adieu! adieu! adieu! *Hélas! hélas! hélas!* will you have yet no pity?

Don. I am a Spanish *positivo*, look you.

Mons. And more cruel than de Spanish inquisitiono, to compel a man to a habit against his conscience; *hélas! hélas! hélas!*   [*Exit.*

Re-enter PRUE *with* GERRARD.

Prue. Here's the dancing-master, shall I call my mistress, sir?

Don. Yes.—[*Exit* PRUE.]   O, you are as punctual as a Spaniard: I love your punctual men; nay, I think 'tis before your time something.

Ger. Nay, I am resolved your daughter, sir, shall lose no time by my fault.

Don. So, so, 'tis well.

Ger. I were a very unworthy man, if I should not be punctual with her, sir.

Don. You speak honestly, very honestly, friend; and I believe a very honest man, though a dancing-master.

Ger. I am very glad you think me so, sir.

Don. What, you are but a young man, are you married yet?

Ger. No, sir; but I hope I shall, sir, very suddenly, if things hit right.

Don. What, the old folks her friends are wary, and cannot agree with you so soon as the daughter can?

Ger. Yes, sir, the father hinders it a little at present; but the daughter, I hope, is resolved, and then we shall do well enough.

Don. What! you do not steal her, according to the laudable custom of some of your brother dancing-masters?

Ger. No, no, sir; steal her, sir! steal her! you are pleased to be merry, sir, ha! ha! ha!—[*Aside.*] I cannot but laugh at that question.

Don. No, sir, methinks you are pleased to be merry, but you say the father does not consent?

Ger Not yet, sir; but 'twill be no matter whether he does or no.

Don. Was she one of your scholars? if she were, 'tis a hundred to ten but you steal her.

Ger. [*Aside.*] I shall not be able to hold laughing.
[*Laughs.*

Don. Nay, nay, I find by your laughing you steal her: she was your scholar; was she not?

Ger. Yes, sir, she was the first I ever had, and may be the last too; for she has a fortune (if I can get her) will keep me from teaching to dance any more.

Don. So, so, then she is your scholar still it seems, and she has a good portion; I'm glad on't; nay, I knew you stole her.

Ger. [*Aside.*] My laughing may give him suspicions, yet I cannot hold.   [*Laughs.*

Don. What! you laugh, I warrant, to think how the young baggage and you will mump the poor old father! but if all her dependence for a fortune be upon the father, he may chance to mump you both and spoil the jest.

Ger. I hope it will not be in his power, sir, ha! ha! ha!—[*Aside.*] I shall laugh too much anon.—[*To* Don DIEGO.] Pray, sir, be pleased to call for your daughter, I am impatient till she comes, for time was never more precious with me, and with her too; it ought to be so, sure, since you say she is to be married to-morrow.

Don. She ought to bestir her, as you say, indeed. Wuh, daughter! daughter! Prue! Hippolita! come away, child, why do you stay so long   [*Calls at the door.*

Re-enter HIPPOLITA, PRUE, *and* Mrs. CAUTION.

Hip. Your servant, master; indeed I am ashamed you have stayed for me.

Ger. O, good madam, 'tis my duty; I know you came as soon as you could.

Hip. I knew my father was with you, therefore I did not make altogether so much haste as I might; but if you had been alone, nothing should have kept me from you. I would not have been so rude as to have made you stay a minute for me, I warrant you.

Don. Come, fiddle faddle, what a deal of ceremony there is betwixt your dancing-master and you, *cuerno!*—

Hip. Lord, sir! I hope you'll allow me to show my respect to my master, for I have a great respect for my master.

Ger. And I am very proud of my scholar, and am a very great honourer of my scholar.

Don. Come, come, friend, about your business, and honour the king.—[*To* Mrs. CAUTION.] Your dancing-masters and barbers are such finical, smooth-tongued, tattling fellows; and if you set 'em once a-talking, they'll ne'er a-done, no more than when you set 'em a-fiddling: indeed, all that deal with fiddles are given to impertinency.

Mrs. Caut. Well, well, this is an impertinent fellow, without being a dancing-master. He is no more a dancing-master than I am a maid.

Don. What! will you still be wiser than I? *voto!*—Come, come, about with my daughter, man.

Prue. So he would, I warrant you, if your worship would let him alone.

Don. How now, Mrs. Nimblechaps!

Ger. Well, though I have got a little canting at the dancing-school since I was here, yet I do all so bunglingly, he'll discover me.   [*Aside to* HIPPOLITA.

Hip. [*Aside.*] Try.—[*Aloud.*] Come take my hand, master.

Mrs. Caut. Look you, brother, the impudent harlotry gives him her hand.

Don. Can he dance with her without holding her by the hand?

Hip. Here, take my hand, master.

Ger. I wish it were for good and all.   [*Aside to her.*

Hip. You dancing-masters are always so hasty, so nimble.

Don. *Voto à St. Jago!* not that I see; about with her, man.

Ger. Indeed, sir, I cannot about with her as I would do, unless you will please to go out a little, sir; for I see she is bashful still before you, sir.

Don. Hey, hey, more fooling yet! come, come, about, about with her.

Hip. Nay, indeed, father, I am ashamed, and cannot help it.

Don. But you shall help it, for I will not stir.   Move her, I say.—Begin, hussy, move when he'll have you.

Prue. I cannot but laugh at that, ha! ha! ha! [*Aside.*

Ger. [*Apart to* HIPPOLITA.] Come, then, madam, since it must be so, let us try; but I shall discover all.—One, two, and coupee.

Mrs. Caut. Nay, d'ye see how he squeezes her hand, brother! O the lewd villain!

Don. Come, move, I say, and mind her not.

Ger. One, two, three, four, and turn round.

Mrs. Caut. D'ye see again ? he took her by the bare arm.

Don. Come, move on, she's mad.

Ger. One, two, and a coupee.

Don. Come, one, two, and turn out your toes.

Mrs. Caut. There, there, he pinched her by the thigh : will you suffer it ?

Ger. One, two, three, and fall back.

Don. Fall back, fall back, back; some of you are forward enough to back.

Ger. Back, madam.

Don. Fall back, when he bids you, hussy.

Mrs. Caut. How ! how ! fall back, fall back ! marry, but she shall not fall back when he bids her.

Don. I say she shall.—Huswife, come.

Ger. She will, she will, I warrant you, sir, if you won't be angry with her.

Mrs. Caut. Do you know what he means by that now? You a Spaniard !

Don. How's that ? I not a Spaniard ! say such a word again—

Ger. Come forward, madam, three steps again.

Mrs. Caut. See, see, she squeezes his hand now : O the debauched harlotry !

Don. So, so, mind her not ; she moves forward pretty well ; but you must move as well backward as forward, or you'll never do anything to purpose.

Mrs. Caut. Do you know what you say, brother, yourself, now ? are you at your beastliness before your young daughter ?

Prue. Ha ! ha ! ha !

Don. How now, mistress, are you so merry ?—Is this your staid maid as you call her, sister Impertinent ?

Ger. I have not much to say to you, miss ; but I shall not have an opportunity to do it, unless we can get your father out.   [*Aside to* Hippolita.

Don. Come, about again with her.

Mrs. Caut. Look you there, she squeezes his hand hard again.

Hip. Indeed, and indeed, father, my aunt puts me quite out; I cannot dance while she looks on for my heart, she makes me ashamed and afraid together.

Ger. Indeed, if you would please to take her out, sir, I am sure I should make my scholar do better, than when you are present, sir. Pray, sir, be pleased for this time to take her away; for the next time, I hope I shall order it so, we shall trouble neither of you.

Mrs. Caut. No, no, brother, stir not, they have a mind to be left alone. Come, there's a beastly trick in't; he's no dancing-master, I tell you.

Ger. Damned jade! she'll discover us.

[*Aside to* HIPPOLITA.

Don. What, will you teach me? nay, then I will go out, and you shall go out too, look you.

Mrs. Caut. I will not go out, look you.

Don. Come, come, thou art a censorious wicked woman, and you shall disturb them no longer.

Mrs. Caut. What! will you bawd for your daughter?

Don. Ay, ay; come go out, out, out.

Mrs. Caut. I will not go out, I will not go out; my conscience will not suffer me, for I know by experience what will follow.

Ger. I warrant you, sir, we'll make good use of our time when you are gone.

Mrs. Caut. Do you hear him again? don't you know what he means?

[*Exit* Don DIEGO *thrusting* Mrs. CAUTION *out.*

Hip. 'Tis very well!—you are a fine gentleman to abuse my poor father so.

Ger. 'Tis but by your example, miss.

Hip. Well, I am his daughter, and may make the bolder with him, I hope.

Ger. And I am his son-in-law, that shall be; and

therefore may claim my privilege too of making bold
with him, I hope.

Hip. Methinks you should be contented in making
bold with his daughter (for you have made very bold
with her) sure.

Ger. I hope I shall make bolder with her yet.

Hip. I do not doubt your confidence, for you are a
dancing-master.

Ger. Why, miss, I hope you would not have me a fine,
senseless, whining, modest lover ; for modesty in a man
is as ill as the want of it in a woman.

Hip. I thank you for that, sir, now you have made
bold with me indeed ; but if I am such a confident piece,
I am sure you made me so : if you had not had the
confidence to come in at the window, I had not had the
confidence to look upon a man : I am sure I could not
look upon a man before.

Ger. But that I humbly conceive, sweet miss, was
your father's fault, because you had not a man to look
upon. But, dearest miss, I do not think you confident,
you are only innocent ; for that which would be called
confidence, nay impudence, in a woman of years, is called
innocency in one of your age ; and the more impudent you
appear, the more innocent you are thought.

Hip. Say you so ? has youth such privileges ? I do not
wonder then, most women seem impudent, since it is to
be thought younger than they are, it seems. But indeed,
master, you are as great an encourager of impudence, I
see, as if you were a dancing-master in good earnest.

Ger. Yes, yes, a young thing may do anything ; may
leap out of the window and go away with her dancing
master, if she please.

Hip. So, so, the use follows the doctrine very suddenly.

Ger. Well, dearest, pray let us make the use we should
of it ; lest your father should make too bold with us, and
come in before we would have him.

Hip. Indeed, old relations are apt to take that ill-bred

freedom of pressing into young company at unseasonable
hours.

Ger. Come, dear miss, let me tell you how I have designed matters ; for in talking of anything else we lose
time and opportunity. People abroad indeed say, the
English women are the worst in the world in using an
opportunity, they love tittle-tattle and ceremony.

Hip. 'Tis because, I warrant, opportunities are not so
scarce here as abroad, they have more here than they
can use ; but let people abroad say what they will of
English women, because they do not know 'em, but what
say people at home?

Ger. Pretty innocent ! ha ! ha ! ha !—Well, I say you
will not make use of your opportunity.

Hip. I say, you have no reason to say so yet.

Ger. Well then, anon at nine of the clock at night I'll
try you : for I have already bespoke a parson, and have
taken up the three back-rooms of the tavern, which front
upon the gallery-window, that nobody may see us escape ;
and I have appointed (precisely betwixt eight and nine of
the clock when it is dark) a coach and six to wait at the
tavern-door for us.

Hip. A coach and six ! a coach and six, do you say?
nay, then I see you are resolved to carry me away ; for a
coach and six, though there were not a man but the
coachman with it, would carry away any young girl of my
age in England :—a coach and six !

Ger. Then you will be sure to be ready to go with me ?

Hip. What young woman of the town could ever say
no to a coach and six, unless it were going into the
country?—A coach and six ! 'tis not in the power of
fourteen years old to resist it.

Ger. You will be sure to be ready?

Hip. You are sure 'tis a coach and six?

Ger. I warrant you, miss.

Hip. I warrant you then they'll carry us merrily away :
—a coach and six !

Ger. But have you charmed your cousin the monsieur (as you said you would) that he in the mean time say nothing to prevent us?

Hip. I warrant you.

Re-enter Don DIEGO; Mrs. CAUTION *pressing in after him.*

Mrs. Caut. I will come in.

Don. Well, I hope by this time you have given her full instructions; you have told her what and how to do, you have done all.

Ger. We have just done indeed, sir.

Hip. Ay, sir, we have just done, sir.

Mrs. Caut. And I fear just undone, sir.

Ger. D'ye hear that damned witch?

[*Aside to* HIPPOLITA.

Don. Come, leave your censorious prating; thou hast been a false, right woman thyself in thy youth, I warrant you.

Mrs. Caut. I right! I right! I scorn your words, I'd have you to know, and 'tis well known. I right! no, 'tis your dainty minx, that Jillflirt, your daughter here, that is right; do you see how her handkerchief is ruffled, and what a heat she's in?

Don. She has been dancing.

Mrs. Caut. Ay, ay, Adam and Eve's dance, or the beginning of the world; d'ye see how she pants?

Don. She has not been used to motion.

Mrs. Caut. Motion! motion! motion d'ye call it? no indeed, I kept her from motion till now :—motion with a vengeance!

Don. You put the poor bashful girl to the blush, you see, hold your peace.

Mrs. Caut. 'Tis her guilt, not her modesty, marry!

Don. Come, come, mind her not, child.—Come, master, let me see her dance now the whole dance roundly together; come, sing to her.

Ger. Faith, we shall be discovered after all ; you know I cannot sing a note, miss. [*Aside to* HIPPOLITA.

Don. Come, come, man.

Hip. Indeed, father, my master's in haste now ; pray let it alone till anon at night, when, you say, he is to come again, and then you shall see me dance it to the violin ; pray stay till then, father.

Don. I will not be put off so ; come, begin.

Hip. Pray, father.

Don. Come, sing to her ; come, begin.

Ger. Pray, sir, excuse me till anon, I am in some haste.

Don. I say, begin, I will not excuse you : come, take her by the hand, and about with her.

Mrs. Caut. I say, he shall not take her by the hand, he shall touch her no more ; while I am here, there shall be no more squeezing and tickling her palm. Good Mr. Dancing-master, stand off. [*Thrusts* GERRARD *away.*

Don. Get you out, Mrs. Impertinence. — [*To* GERRARD.] Take her by the hand, I say.

Mrs. Caut. Stand off, I say. He shall not touch her, he has touched her too much already.

Don. If patience were not a Spanish virtue, I would lay it aside now : I say, let 'em dance.

Mrs. Caut. I say, they shall not dance.

Hip. Pray, father, since you see my aunt's obstinacy, let us alone till anon, when you may keep her out.

Don. Well then, friend, do not fail to come.

Hip. Nay, if he fail me at last—

Don. Be sure you come, for she's to be married to-morrow :—do you know it?

Ger. Yes, yes, sir. — Sweet scholar, your humble servant, till night ; and think in the mean time of the instructions I have given you, that you may be the readier when I come.

Don. Ay, girl, be sure you do,—and do you be sure to come.

Mrs. Caut. You need not be so concerned, he'll be sure to come I warrant you; but if I could help it, he should never set foot again in the house.

Don. You would frighten the poor dancing-master from the house,—but be sure you come for all her.

Ger. Yes, sir.—[*Aside.*] But this jade will pay me when I am gone.

Mrs. Caut. Hold, hold, sir, I must let you out, and I wish I could keep you out. He a dancing-master! he's a chouse, a cheat, a mere cheat, and that you'll find.

Don. I find any man a cheat! I cheated by any man! I scorn your words.—I that have so much Spanish care, circumspection, and prudence, cheated by a man! Do you think I, who have been in Spain, look you, and have kept up my daughter a twelve-month, for fear of being cheated of her, look you? I cheated of her!

Mrs. Caut. Well, say no more.

[*Exeunt* Don Diego, Hippolita, Mrs. Caution, *and* Prue.

Ger. Well, old Formality, if you had not kept up your daughter, I am sure I had never cheated you of her.

The wary fool is by his care betrayed,
As cuckolds by their jealousy are made.   [*Exit.*

ACT THE FOURTH.

SCENE I.—*A Room in* Don DIEGO'S *House.*

Enter Monsieur de PARIS *without a peruke, with a Spanish hat, a Spanish doublet, stockings, and shoes, but in pantaloons, a waist-belt, and a Spanish dagger in it, and a cravat about his neck.*—HIPPOLITA *and* PRUE *behind laughing.*

MONS. To see wat a fool love do make of one, *jarni!* It do metamorphose de brave man in de beast, de sot, de animal.

Hip. Ha! ha! ha!

Mons. Nay, you may laugh, 'tis ver vell, I am become as ridicule for you as can be, *morbleu!* I have deform myself into a ugly Spaniard.

Hip. Why, do you call this disguising yourself like a Spaniard, while you wear pantaloons still, and the cravat?

Mons. But is here not the double doublet, and the Spanish dagger *aussi?*

Hip. But 'tis as long as the French sword, and worn like it. But where's your Spanish beard, the thing of most consequence?

Mons. Jarni! do you tink beards are as easy to be had as in the playhouses? non; but if here be no the ugly long Spanish beard, here are, I am certain, the ugly long Spanish ear.

Hip. That's very true, ha! ha! ha!

Mons. Auh de ingrate, dat de woman is! wen we

poor men are your gallants, you laugh at us yourselves, and wen we are your husband, you make all the world laugh at us, *jarni !*—Love, dam love, it makes the man more ridicule, than poverty, poetry, or a new title of honour, *jarni !*

Enter Don DIEGO *and* Mrs. CAUTION.

Don. What ! at your *jarnis* still ? *voto !*

Mons. Why, *oncle*, you are at your *votos* still.

Don. Nay, I'll allow you to be at your *votos* too, but not to make the incongruous match of Spanish doublet, and French pantaloons.

[*Holding his hat before his pantaloons.*

Mons. Nay, pray, dear *oncle*, let me unite France and Spain ; 'tis the mode of France now, *jarni, voto !*

Don. Well, I see I must pronounce : I told you, if you were not dressed in the Spanish habit to-night, you should not marry my daughter to-morrow, look you.

Mons. Well ! am I not *habillé* in de Spanish habit ? my doublet, ear and hat, leg and feet, are Spanish, that dey are.

Don. I told you I was a Spanish *positivo, voto !*

Mons. Will you not spare my pantaloon ! begar, I will give you one little finger to excuse my pantaloon, da—

Don. I have said, look you.

Mons. Auh, *cher* pantaloons ! Speak for my pantaloons, cousin. My poor pantaloons are as dear to me as de scarf to de countree capitane, or de new-made officer : therefore have de compassion for my pantaloons, Don Diego, *mon oncle. Hélas ! hélas ! hélas !* [*Kneels.*

Don. I have said, look you, your dress must be Spanish, and your language English : I am *un positivo.*

Mons. And must speak base good English too ! Ah ! *la pitié ! hélas !*

Don. It must be done ; and I will see this great change ere it be dark, *voto !*—Your time is not long ; look to't, look you.

Mons. Hélas! hélas! hélas! dat *Espagne* should con-
quer *la France* in England! Hélas! hélas! hélas! [*Exit.*

Don. You see what pains I take to make him the
more agreeable to you, daughter.

Hip. But indeed, and indeed, father, you wash the
blackamoor white, in endeavouring to make a Spaniard
of a monsieur, nay, an English monsieur too; consider
that, father : for when once they have taken the French
plie (as they call it) they are never to be made so much
as Englishmen again, I have heard say.

Don. What! I warrant you are like the rest of the
young silly baggages of England, that like nothing but
what is French? You would not have him reformed,
you would have a monsieur to your husband, would you,
cuerno?

Hip. No, indeed, father, I would not have a monsieur
to my husband; not I indeed : and I am sure you'll
never make my cousin otherwise.

Don. I warrant you.

Hip. You can't, you can't indeed, father : and you
have sworn, you know, he shall never have me, if he does
not leave off his monsieurship. Now, as I told you, 'tis
as hard for him to cease being a monsieur, as 'tis for you
to break a Spanish oath; so that I am not in any great
danger of having a monsieur to my husband.

Don. Well, but you shall have him for your husband,
look you.

Hip. Then you will break your Spanish oath.

Don. No, I will break him of his French tricks; and
you shall have him for your husband, *cuerno!*

Hip. Indeed and indeed, father, I shall not have him.

Don. Indeed you shall, daughter.

Hip. Well, you shall see, father.

Mrs. Caut. No, I warrant you, she will not have him,
she'll have her dancing-master rather : I know her meaning, I understand her.

Don. Thou malicious foolish woman! you understand

her!—But I do understand her; she says, I will not break my oath, nor he his French customs ; so, through our difference, she thinks she shall not have him : but she shall.

Hip. But I shan't. [hates him.

Mrs. Caut. I know she will not have him, because she

Don. I tell you, if she does hate him, 'tis a sign she will have him for her husband ; for 'tis not one of a thousand that marries the man she loves, look you. Besides, 'tis all one whether she loves him now or not ; for as soon as she's married, she'd be sure to hate him. That's the reason we wise Spaniards are jealous, and only expect, nay, will be sure our wives shall fear us, look you.

Hip. Pray, good father and aunt, do not dispute about nothing ; for I am sure he will never be my husband to hate.

Mrs. Caut. I am of your opinion, indeed : I understand you. I can see as far as another.

Don. You ! you cannot see so much as through your spectacles !—But I understand her : 'tis her mere desire to marriage makes her say she shall not have him ; for your poor young things, when they are once in the teens, think they shall never be married.

Hip. Well, father, think you what you will ; but I know what I think.

Re-enter Monsieur de PARIS *in the Spanish habit entire, only with a cravat, and followed by the little* Blackamoor *with a golilla* [1] *in his hand.*

Don. Come, did not I tell you, you should have him? look you there, he has complied with me, and is a perfect Spaniard.

Mons. Ay ! ay ! I am ugly rogue enough now, sure, for my cousin. But 'tis your father's fault, cousin, that

---

[1] The *golilla* was a collar of pasteboard, covered with white muslin, starched and plaited. It was at this time generally worn in Spain, but later only by lawyers.

you han't the handsomest, best-dressed man in the nation;
a man *bien mis.*

Don. Yet again at your French! and a cravat on still!
voto á St. Jago! off, off, with it!

Mons. Nay, I will ever hereafter speak clownish good
English, do but spare me my cravat.

Don. I am *un positivo,* look you.

Mons. Let me not put on that Spanish yoke, but spare
me my cravat; for I love cravat *furieusement.*

Don. Again at your *furieusements!*

Mons. Indeed I have forgot myself: but have some
mercy.   [*Kneels.*

Don. Off, off, off with it, I say! Come, refuse the *orna-
mento* principal of the Spanish habit!

> [*Takes him by the cravat, pulls it off, and the*
> Black *puts on the golilla.*

Mons. Will you have no mercy, no pity? alas! alas!
alas! Oh! I had rather put on the English pillory, than
that Spanish *golilla,* for 'twill be all a case I'm sure:
for when I go abroad, I shall soon have a crowd of boys
about me, peppering me with rotten eggs and turnips.
Hélas! hélas!   [Don DIEGO *puts on the golilla.*

Don. *Hélas,* again!

Mons. Alas! alas! alas!

Hip. I shall die!   )
Prue. I shall burst! } Ha! ha! ha!

Mons. Ay! ay! you see what I am come to for your
sake, cousin: and, uncle, pray take notice how ridiculous
I am grown to my cousin, that loves me above all the
world: she can no more forbear laughing at me, I vow
and swear, than if I were as arrant a Spaniard as yourself.

Don. Be a Spaniard like me, and ne'er think people
laugh at you: there was never a Spaniard that thought
any one laughed at him. But what! do you laugh at a
golilla, baggage?—Come, sirrah black, now do you teach
him to walk with the *verdadero gesto, gracia,* and *gravidad*
of a true Castilian.

Mons. Must I have my dancing-master too?—Come, little master, then, lead on.

> [*The* Black *struts about the stage,* Monsieur
> *follows him, imitating awkwardly all he does.*

Don. Malo! malo! with your hat on your poll, as if it hung upon a pin!—the French and English wear their hats as if their horns would not suffer 'em to come over their foreheads, *voto!*

Mons. 'Tis true, there are some well-bred gentlemen have so much reverence for their peruke, that they would refuse to be grandees of your Spain for fear of putting on their hats, I vow and swear!

Don. Come, black, teach him now to make a Spanish leg.[1]

Mons. Ha! ha! ha! your Spanish leg is an English courtesy, I vow and swear, hah! hah! hah!

Don. Well, the hood does not make the monk; the ass was an ass still, though he had the lion's skin on. This will be a light French fool, in spite of the grave Spanish habit, look you.—But, black, do what you can; make the most of him; walk him about.

Prue. Here are the people, sir, you sent to speak with about provisions for the wedding; and here are your clothes brought home too, mistress.

> [*Goes to the door and returns.*

Don. Well, I come.—Black, do what you can with him; walk him about.

Mons. Indeed, uncle, if I were as you, I would not have the grave Spanish habit so travestied: I shall disgrace it, and my little black master too, I vow and swear.

Don. Learn, learn of him; improve yourself by him—and do you walk him, walk him about soundly.—Come, sister, and daughter, I must have your judgments, though I shall not need 'em, look you.—Walk him, see you walk him.

> [*Exeunt* Don DIEGO, HIPPOLITA, *and* Mrs. CAUTION.

---

[1] *i.e.,* To bow in the Spanish fashion.

Mons. Jarni! he does not only make a Spaniard of me, but a Spanish jennet, in giving me to his lackey to walk.—But come along, little master.

> [*The* Black *instructs* Monsieur *on one side of the stage,* PRUE *standing on the other.*

Prue. O the unfortunate condition of us poor chambermaids! who have all the carking and caring, the watching and sitting up, the trouble and danger of our mistresses' intrigues, whilst they go away with all the pleasure! And if they can get their man in a corner, 'tis well enough; they ne'er think of the poor watchful chambermaid, who sits knocking her heels in the cold, for want of better exercise, in some melancholy lobby or entry, when she could employ her time every whit as well as her mistress, for all her quality, if she were but put to't.   [*Aside.*

Black. Hold up your head, hold up your head sir :—a stooping Spaniard, *malo!*

Mons. True, a Spaniard scorns to look upon the ground.

Prue. We can shift for our mistresses, and not for ourselves. Mine has got a handsome proper young man, and is just going to make the most of him; whilst I must be left in the lurch here with a couple of ugly little blackamoor boys in bonnets, and an old withered Spanish eunuch; not a servant else in the house, nor have I hopes of any comfortable society at all.   [*Aside.*

Black. Now let me see you make your visit-leg, thus.

Mons. Auh, *tête non!*—ha! ha! ha!

Black. What! a Spaniard, and laugh aloud! No, if you laugh, thus only—so—Now your salutation in the street, as you pass by your acquaintance; look you, thus —if to a woman, thus—putting your hat upon your heart; if to a man, thus, with a nod—so—but frown a little more, frown :—but if to a woman you would be very ceremonious to, thus—so—your neck nearer your shoulder —so—Now, if you would speak contemptibly of any man,

or thing, do thus with your hand—so—and shrug up your
shoulders till they hide your ears.—[Monsieur *imitating
the* Black.]   Now walk again.

[*The* Black *and* Monsieur *walk off the stage.*

Prue. All my hopes are in that coxcomb there : I must
take up with my mistress's leavings, though we chambermaids are wont to be beforehand with them.   But he is
the dullest, modestest fool, for a frenchified fool, as ever I
saw ; for nobody could be more coming to him than I
have been, though I say it, and yet I am ne'er the
nearer.   I have stolen away his handkerchief, and told
him of it ; and yet he would never so much as struggle
with me to get it again : I have pulled off his peruke,
untied his ribbons, and have been very bold with him :
yet he would never be so with me : nay, I have pinched
him, punched him and tickled him ; and yet he would
never do the like for me.

Re-enter the Black *and* Monsieur.

Black. Nay, thus, thus, sir.

Prue. And to make my person more acceptable to
him, I have used art, as they say ; for every night since
he came, I have worn the forehead-piece of bees-wax and
hog's-grease, and every morning washed with butter-milk
and wild tansy ; and have put on every day for his only
sake my Sunday's bowdy[1] stockings, and have new-
chalked my shoes, as constantly as the morning came: nay,
I have taken occasion to garter my stockings before him,
as if unawares of him ; for a good leg and foot, with good
shoes and stockings, are very provoking, as they say ;
but the devil a bit would he be provoked.—But I must
think of a way.   [*Aside.*

Black. Thus, thus.

---

[1] Scarlet.   A new method of dyeing scarlet was brought to
England in 1643 by a German, who established his dye-house at
Bow ; hence Bow-dye came to signify scarlet.   It is also used as a
verb : " Now a cup of nappy ale will bow-dye a man's face."

Mons. What, so! Well, well, I have lessons enough for this time, little master; I will have no more, lest the multiplicity of them make me forget them, da.—Prue, art thou there and so pensive? what art thou thinking of?

Prue. Indeed, I am ashamed to tell your worship.

Mons. What, ashamed! wert thou thinking then of my beastliness? ha! ha! ha!

Prue. Nay, then I am forced to tell your worship in my own vindication.

Mons. Come then.

Prue. But indeed, your worship—I'm ashamed, that I am, though it was nothing but a dream I had of your sweet worship last night.

Mons. Of my sweet worship! I warrant it was a sweet dream then :—what was it? ha! ha! ha!

Prue. Nay, indeed, I have told your worship enough already; you may guess the rest.

Mons. I cannot guess; ha! ha! ha! What should it be? prithee let's know the rest.

Prue. Would you have me so impudent?

Mons. Impudent! ha! ha! ha! Nay, prithee tell me; for I can't guess, da—

Prue. Nay, 'tis always so, for want of the men's guessing the poor women are forced to be impudent:—but I am still ashamed.

Mons. I will know it; speak.

Prue. Why then, methought last night you came up into my chamber in your shirt when I was in bed; and that you might easily do, for I have ne'er a lock to my door.—Now I warrant I am as red as my petticoat.

Mons. No, thou'rt as yellow as e'er thou wert.

Prue. Yellow, sir!

Mons. Ay, ay : but let s hear the dream out.

Prue. Why, can't you guess the rest now?

Mons. No, not I, I vow and swear : come, let's hear.

Prue. But can't you guess, in earnest?

Mons. Not I, the devil eat me!

Prue. Not guess yet ! why then, methought you came to bed to me.—Now am I as red as my petticoat again.

Mons. Ha ! ha ! ha !—well, and what then ? ha ! ha ! ha !

Prue. Nay, now I know by your worship's laughing you guess what you did. I'm sure I cried out, and waked all in tears, with these words in my mouth—" You have undone me ! you have undone me ! your worship has undone me ! "

Mons. Ha ! ha ! ha !—but you waked, and found it was but a dream.

Prue. Indeed it was so lively, I know not whether 'twas a dream, or no.—But if you were not there, I'll undertake you may come when you will, and do anything to me you will, I sleep so fast.

Mons. No, no ; I don't believe that.

Prue. Indeed you may, your worship—

Mons. It cannot be.

Prue. Insensible beast ! he will not understand me yet ; and one would think I speak plain enough.   [*Aside.*

Mons. Well, but, Prue, what art thou thinking of?

Prue. Of the dream, whether it were a dream or no.

Mons. 'Twas a dream, I warrant thee.

Prue. Was it ? I am hugeous glad it was a dream.

Mons. Ay, ay, it was a dream : and I am hugeous glad it was a dream too.

Prue. But now I have told your worship my door has neither lock nor latch to it, if you should be so naughty as to come one night, and prove the dream true—I am so afraid on't.

Mons. Ne'er fear it :—dreams go by the contraries.

Prue. Then, by that I should come into your worship's chamber, and come to bed to your worship.—Now am I as red as my petticoat again, I warrant.

Mons. No, thou art no redder than a brick unburnt, Prue.

Prue. But if I should do such a trick in my sleep,

your worship would not censure a poor harmless maid, I hope ?—for I am apt to walk in my sleep.

Mons. Well, then, Prue, because thou shalt not shame thyself, poor wench, I'll be sure to lock my door every night fast.

Prue. [*Aside.*] So ! so ! this way I find will not do :—I must come roundly and downright to the business, like other women, or—

Enter GERRARD.

Mons. O, the dancing-master !

Prue. Dear sir, I have something to say to you in your ear, which I am ashamed to speak aloud.

Mons. Another time, another time, Prue. But now go call your mistress to her dancing-master. Go, go.

Prue. Nay, pray hear me, sir, first.

Mons. Another time, another time, Prue ; prithee begone.

Prue. Nay, I beseech your worship hear me.

Mons. No ; prithee begone.

Prue. [*Aside.*] Nay, I am e'en well enough served for not speaking my mind when I had an opportunity.— Well, I must be playing the modest woman, forsooth ! a woman's hypocrisy in this case does only deceive herself.

                                                    [*Exit.*

Mons. O, the brave dancing-master ! the fine dancing-master ! Your servant, your servant.

Ger. Your servant, sir : I protest I did not know you at first.—[*Aside.*] I am afraid this fool should spoil all, notwithstanding Hippolita's care and management ; yet I ought to trust her :—but a secret is more safe with a treacherous knave than a talkative fool.

Mons. Come, sir, you must know a little brother dancing-master of yours—walking-master I should have said ; for he teaches me to walk and make legs, by-the-bye. Pray, know him, sir ; salute him, sir.—You Christian dancing-masters are so proud.

Ger. But, monsieur, what strange metamorphosis is this? You look like a Spaniard, and talk like an Englishman again, which I thought had been impossible.

Mons. Nothing impossible to love : I must do't, or lose my mistress, your pretty scholar; for 'tis I am to have her. You may remember I told you she was to be married to a great man, a man of honour and quality.

Ger. But does she enjoin you to this severe penance? —such I am sure it is to you.

Mons. No, no : 'tis by the compulsion of the starched fop her father, who is so arrant a Spaniard, he would kill you and his daughter, if he knew who you were : therefore have a special care to dissemble well.

[*Draws him aside.*

Ger. I warrant you.

Mons. Dear Gerrard—Go, little master, and call my cousin : tell her her dancing-master is here. [*Exit the* Black]— I say, dear Gerrard, faith, I'm obliged to you for the trouble you have had. When I sent you, I intended a jest indeed; but did not think it would have been so dangerous a jest : therefore pray forgive me.

Ger. I do, do heartily forgive you.

Mons. But can you forgive me for sending you at first, like a fool as I was? 'Twas ill done of me : can you forgive me?

Ger. Yes, yes, I do forgive you.

Mons. Well, thou art a generous man, I vow and swear, to come and take upon you all this trouble, danger, and shame, to be thought a paltry dancing-master; and all this to preserve a lady's honour and life, who intended to abuse you. But I take the obligation upon me.

Ger. Pish! pish! you are not obliged to me at all.

Mons. Faith, but I am strangely obliged to you.

Ger. Faith, but you are not.

Mons. I vow and swear but I am.

Ger. I swear you are not.

Mons. Nay, thou art so generous a dancing-master, ha! ha! ha!

Re-enter Don DIEGO, HIPPOLITA, Mrs. CAUTION, *and* PRUE.

Don. You shall not come in, sister.

Mrs. Caut. I will come in.

Don. You will not be civil.

Mrs. Caut. I'm sure they will not be civil, if I do not come in :—I must, I will.

Don. Well, honest friend, you are very punctual, which is a rare virtue in a dancing-master; I take notice of it, and will remember it; I will, look you.

Mons. So, silly, damned, politic Spanish uncle!—ha! ha! ha!   [*Aside.*

Ger. My fine scholar, sir, there, shall never have reason, as I have told you, sir, to say I am not a punctual man ; for I am more her servant than to any scholar I ever had.

Mons. Well said, i'faith !—[*Aside.*] Thou dost make a pretty fool of him, I vow and swear. But I wonder people can be made such fools of :—ha! ha! ha!

Hip. Well, master, I thank you ; and I hope I shall be a grateful, kind scholar to you.

Mons. Ha! ha! ha! cunning little jilt, what a fool she makes of him too! I wonder people can be made such fools of, I vow and swear :—ha! ha! ha!   [*Aside.*

Hip. Indeed, it shall go hard but I'll be a grateful, kind scholar to you.

Mrs. Caut. As kind as ever your mother was to your father, I warrant.

Don. How! again with your senseless suspicions.

Mons. Pish! pish! aunt.—[*Aside.*] Ha! ha! ha! she's a fool another way : she thinks she loves him, ha! ha! ha! Lord! that people should be such fools!

Mrs. Caut. Come, come, I cannot but speak : I tell you,

Wycherley.   I

beware in time ; for he is no dancing-master, but some
debauched person who will mump you of your daughter.

Don. Will you be wiser than I still ? Mump me of my
daughter ! I would I could see any one mump me of my
daughter.

Mrs. Caut. And mump you of your mistress too,
young Spaniard.

Mons. Ha ! ha ! ha ! will you be wiser than I too,
voto ? Mump me of my mistress ! I would I could see
any one mump me of my mistress.—[*Aside to* GERRARD
and HIPPOLITA.] I am afraid this damned old aunt
should discover us, I vow and swear: be careful therefore and resolute.

Mrs. Caut. He ! he does not go about his business
like a dancing-master. He'll ne'er teach her to dance ;
but he'll teach her no goodness soon enough, I warrant.
—He a dancing-master !

Mons. Ay, the devil eat me if he be not the best
dancing-master in England now !—[*Aside to* GERRARD
and HIPPOLITA.] Was not that well said, cousin ? was it
not ? for he's a gentleman dancing-master, you know.

Don. You know him, cousin, very well ? cousin, you
sent him to my daughter ?

Mons. Yes, yes, uncle :—know him !—[*Aside.*] We'll
ne'er be discovered, I warrant, ha ! ha ! ha !

Mrs. Caut. But will you be made a fool of too ?

Mons. Ay, ay, aunt, ne'er trouble yourself.

Don. Come, friend, about your business ; about with
my daughter.

Hip. Nay, pray, father, be pleased to go out a little,
and let us practise awhile, and then you shall see me
dance the whole dance to the violin.

Don. Tittle tattle ! more fooling still !—Did not you
say, when your master was here last, I should see you
dance to the violin when he came again ?

Hip. So I did, father : but let me practise a little first
before, that I may be perfect. Besides, my aunt is here,

and she will put me out; you know I cannot dance
before her.

Don. Fiddle faddle!

Mons. [*Aside.*] They're afraid to be discovered by
Gerrard's bungling, I see.—[*Aloud.*] Come, come, uncle
turn out! let 'em practise.

Don. I wont, *voto á St. Jago !* what a fooling's here.

Mons. Come, come, let 'em practise : turn out, turn
out, uncle.

Don. Why can't she practise it before me?

Mons. Come, dancers and singers are sometimes
humoursome; besides, 'twill be more grateful to you to
see it danced all at once to the violin. Come, turn out,
turn out, I say.

Don. What a fooling's here still among you, *voto !*

Mons. So, there he is with you, *voto !*—Turn out, turn
out; I vow and swear you shall turn out.

[*Takes him by the shoulder.*

Don. Well, shall I see her dance it to the violin at
last?

Ger. Yes, yes, sir; what do you think I teach her for?

Mons. Go, go, turn out.—[*Exit* Don DIEGO.] And
you too, aunt.

Mrs. Caut. Seriously, nephew, I shall not budge;
royally, I shall not.

Mons. Royally, you must, aunt: come.

Mrs. Caut. Pray hear me, nephew.

Mons. I will not hear you.

Mrs. Caut. 'Tis for your sake I stay: I must not
suffer you to be wronged.

Mons. Come, no wheedling, aunt: come away.

Mrs. Caut. That slippery fellow will do't.

Mons. Let him do't.

Mrs. Caut. Indeed he will do't; royally he will.

Mons. Well, let him do't, royally.

Mrs. Caut. He will wrong you.

Mons. Well, let him, I say; I have a mind to be

wronged : what's that to you ? I will be wronged, if you go there too, I vow and swear.

Mrs. Caut. You shall not be wronged.

Mons. I will.

Mrs. Caut. You shall not.

Re-enter Don DIEGO.

Don. What's the matter ? won't she be ruled ?—Come, come away : you shall not disturb 'em.

> [Don DIEGO *and* Monsieur *try to thrust* Mrs. CAUTION *out.*

Mrs. Caut. D'ye see how they laugh at you both?—Well, go to ; the troth-telling Trojan gentlewoman of old was ne'er believed till the town was taken, rummaged, and ransacked. Even, even so—

Mons. Ha! ha! ha! turn out.—[*Exeunt* Mrs. CAUTION *and* Don DIEGO.]—Lord, that people should be such arrant cuddens ![1] ha ! ha ! ha ! But I may stay, may I not ?

Hip. No, no ; I'd have you go out and hold the door, cousin ; or else my father will come in again before his time.

Mons. I will, I will then, sweet cousin.—'Tis well thought on ; that was well thought on, indeed, for me to hold the door.

Hip. But be sure you keep him out, cousin, till we knock.

Mons. I warrant you, cousin.—Lord, that people should be made such fools of ! Ha ! ha ! ha ! [*Exit.*

Ger. So, so :—to make him hold the door, while I steal his mistress, is not unpleasant.

Hip. Ay, but would you do so ill a thing, so treacherous a thing ? Faith 'tis not well.

Ger. Faith, I can't help it, since 'tis for your sake.—Come, sweetest, is not this our way into the gallery ?

Hip. Yes ; but it goes against my conscience to be accessory to so ill a thing.—You say you do it for my sake ?

---

[1] Cudden or cuddy : a clown ; a silly fellow.

Ger. Alas, poor miss! 'tis not against your conscience, but against your modesty, you think, to do it frankly.

Hip. Nay, if it be against my modesty, too, I can't do it indeed.

Ger. Come, come, miss, let us make haste :—all's ready.

Hip. Nay, faith, I can't satisfy my scruple.

Ger. Come, dearest, this is not a time for scruples nor modesty.—Modesty between lovers is as impertinent as ceremony between friends ; and modesty is now as unseasonable as on the wedding night.—Come away, my dearest.

Hip. Whither?

Ger. Nay, sure we have lost too much time already. Is that a proper question now? If you would know, come along; for I have all ready.

Hip. But I am not ready.

Ger. Truly, miss, we shall have your father come in upon us, and prevent us again, as he did in the morning.

Hip. 'Twas well for me he did :—for, on my conscience, if he had not come in, I had gone clear away with you when I was in the humour.

Ger. Come, dearest, you would frighten me, as if you were not yet in the same humour.—Come, come away; the coach and six is ready.

Hip. 'Tis too late to take the air, and I am not ready.

Ger. You were ready in the morning.

Hip. Ay, so I was.

Ger. Come, come, miss :—indeed the jest begins to be none.

Hip. What! I warrant you think me in jest then?

Ger. In jest, certainly ; but it begins to be troublesome.

Hip. But, sir, you could believe I was in earnest in the morning, when I but seemed to be ready to go with you ; and why won't you believe me now when I declare to the contrary?—I take it unkindly, that the longer I am acquainted with you, you should have the less confidence in me.

Ger. For Heaven's sake, miss, lose no more time thus; your father will come in upon us, as he did—

Hip. Let him if he will.

Ger. He'll hinder our design.

Hip. No, he will not; for mine is to stay here now.

Ger. Are you in earnest?

Hip. You'll find it so.

Ger. How! why, you confessed but now you would have gone with me in the morning.

Hip. I was in the humour then.

Ger. And I hope you are in the same still; you cannot change so soon.

Hip. Why, is it not a whole day ago?

Ger. What! are you not a day in the same humour?

Hip. Lord! that you who know the town, they say, should think any woman could be a whole day together in a humour!—ha! ha! ha!

Ger. Hey! this begins to be pleasant.—What! won't you go with me then after all?

Hip. No indeed, sir, I desire to be excused.

Ger. Then you have abused me all this while?

Hip. It may be so.

Ger. Could all that so natural innocency be dissembled?—faith, it could not, dearest miss.

Hip. Faith, it was, dear master.

Ger. Was it, faith?

Hip. Methinks you might believe me without an oath. You saw I could dissemble with my father, why should you think I could not with you?

Ger. So young a wheedle!

Hip. Ay, a mere damned jade I am.

Ger. And I have been abused, you say?

Hip. 'Tis well you can believe it at last.

Ger. And I must never hope for you?

Hip. Would you have me abuse you again?

Ger. Then you will not go with me?

Hip. No: but, for your comfort, your loss will not be

great ; and that you may not resent it, for once I'll be
ingenuous, and disabuse you.—I am no heiress, as I told
you, to twelve hundred pounds a-year ; I was only a
lying jade then.—Now will you part with me willingly, I
doubt not.

Ger. I wish I could.   [*Sighs.*

Hip. Come, now I find 'tis your turn to dissemble :—
but men use to dissemble for money ; will you dissemble for nothing?

Ger. 'Tis too late for me to dissemble.

Hip. Don't you dissemble, faith ?

Ger. Nay, this is too cruel.

Hip. What ! would you take me without the twelve
hundred pounds a-year ? would you be such a fool as to
steal a woman with nothing ?

Ger. I'll convince you ; for you shall go with me :—
and since you are twelve hundred pounds a-year the
lighter, you'll be the easier carried away.

                    [*He takes her in his arms, she struggles.*

Prue. What ! he takes her way against her will :—I
find I must knock for my master then.   [*She knocks.*

Re-enter Don DIEGO *and* Mrs. CAUTION.

Hip. My father ! my father is here !

Ger. Prevented again ! [GERRARD *sets her down again.*

Don. What, you have done I hope now, friend, for
good and all ?

Ger. Yes, yes ; we have done for good and all
indeed.

Don. How now !—you seem to be out of humour,
friend.

Ger. Yes, so I am ; I can't help it.

Mrs. Caut. He's a dissembler in his very throat,
brother.

Hip. Pray do not carry things so as to discover yourself, if it be but for my sake, good master.

                              [*Aside to* GERRARD.

Ger. She is grown impudent.   [*Aside.*

Mrs. Caut. See, see, they whisper, brother!—to steal a kiss under a whisper!—O the harlotry!

Don. What's the matter, friend?

Hip. I say, for my sake be in humour, and do not discover yourself, but be as patient as a dancing-master still.
[*Aside to* GERRARD.

Don. What, she is whispering to him indeed! What's the matter? I will know it, friend, look you.

Ger. Will you know it?

Don. Yes, I will know it.

Ger. Why, if you will know it then, she would not do as I would have her; and whispered me to desire me not to discover it to you.

Don. What, hussy, would you not do as he'd have you? I'll make you do as he'd have you.

Ger. I wish you would.

Mrs. Caut. 'Tis a lie; she'll do all he'll have her do, and more too, to my knowledge.

Don. Come, tell me what 'twas then she would not do —come, do it, hussy, or—Come, take her by the hand, friend. Come, begin:—let's see if she will not do anything now I'm here!

Hip. Come, pray be in humour, master.

Ger. I cannot dissemble like you.

Don. What, she can't dissemble already, can she?

Mrs. Caut. Yes, but she can: but 'tis with you she dissembles: for they are not fallen out, as we think. For I'll be sworn I saw her just now give him the languishing eye, as they call it, that is, the whiting's eye, of old called the sheep's eye:—I'll be sworn I saw it with these two eyes; that I did.

Hip. You'll betray us; have a care, good master.
[*Aside to* GERRARD.

Don. Hold your peace, I say, silly woman!—but does she dissemble already?—how do you mean?

Ger. She pretends she can't do what she should do;

and that she is not in humour.—The common excuse of women for not doing what they should do.

Don. Come, I'll put her in humour.—Dance, I say. —Come, about with her, master.

Ger. [*Aside.*] I am in a pretty humour to dance.—[*To* HIPPOLITA.] I cannot fool any longer, since you have fooled me.

Hip. You would not be so ungenerous as to betray the woman that hated you! I do not do that yet. For Heaven's sake! for this once be more obedient to my desires than your passion.   [*Aside to* GERRARD.

Don. What! is she humoursome still?—but methinks you look yourself as if you were in an ill-humour:—but about with her.

Ger. I am in no good dancing humour, indeed.

Re-enter Monsieur.

Mons. Well, how goes the dancing forward?—What, my aunt here to disturb 'em again?

Don. Come! come!   [GERRARD *leads her about.*

Mrs. Caut. I say, stand off:—thou shalt not come near. Avoid, Satan! as they say.

Don. Nay, then we shall have it:—nephew, hold her a little, that she may not disturb 'em.—Come, now away with her.

Ger. One, two, and a coupee.—[*Aside.*] Fooled and abused—

Mrs. Caut. Wilt thou lay violent hands upon thy own natural aunt, wretch?   [*To* Monsieur.

Don. Come, about with her.

Ger. One, two, three, four, and turn round—[*Aside.*] by such a piece of innocency!

Mrs. Caut. Dost thou see, fool, how he squeezes her hand?   [*To* Monsieur.

Mons. That won't do, aunt.

Hip. Pray, master, have patience, and let's mind our business.

Wycherley.   1*

Don. Why did you anger him then, hussy, look you?

Mrs. Caut. Do you see how she smiles in his face, and squeezes his hand now? [*To* Monsieur.

Mons. Your servant, aunt.—That won't do, I say.

Hip. Have patience, master.

Ger. [*Aside.*] I am become her sport!—[*Aloud.*] One, two, three—Death! hell! and the devil!

Don. Ay, they are three indeed!—But pray have patience.

Mrs. Caut. Do you see how she leers upon him, and clings to him? Can you suffer it? [*To* Monsieur.

Mons. Ay, ay.

Ger. One, two, three, and a slur.—Can you be so unconcerned after all?

Don. What! is she unconcerned?—Hussy, mind your business.

Ger. One, two, three, and turn round;—one, two, fall back—hell and damnation!

Don. Ay, people fall back indeed into hell and damnation, Heaven knows!

Ger. One, two, three, and your honour.—I can fool no longer!

Mrs. Caut. Nor will I be withheld any longer, like a poor hen in her pen, while the kite is carrying away her chicken before her face.

Don. What, have you done?—Well then, let's see her dance it now to the violin.

Mons. Ay, ay, let's see her dance it to the violin.

Ger. Another time, another time.

Don. Don't you believe that, friend:—these dancing-masters make no bones of breaking their words. Did not you promise just now, I should see her dance it to the violin? and that I will too, before I stir.

Ger. Let monsieur play then while I dance with her:—she can't dance alone.

Mons. I can't play at all; I'm but a learner:—but if you'll play, I'll dance with her.

Ger. I can't play neither.

Don. What! a dancing-master, and not play!

Mrs. Caut. Ay, you see what a dancing-master he is. 'Tis as I told you, I warrant.—A dancing-master, and not play upon the fiddle!

Don. How!

Hip. O you have betrayed us all! If you confess that, you undo us for ever.   [*Apart to* GERRARD.

Ger. I cannot play;—what would you have me say?
                            [*Apart to* HIPPOLITA.

Mons. I vow and swear we are all undone if you cannot play.   [*Apart to* GERRARD.

Don. What! are you a dancing-master, and cannot play? Umph—

Hip. He is only out of humour, sir.—Here, master, I know you will play for me yet;—for he has an excellent hand.   [*She offers* GERRARD *the violin.*

Mons. Ay, that he has.—[*Aside.*] At giving a box on

Don. Why does he not play, then?   [the ear.

Hip. Here, master, pray play for my sake.
                            [*Gives* GERRARD *the violin.*

Ger. What would you have me do with it?—I cannot play a stroke.   [*Apart to* HIPPOLITA.

Hip. No! stay—then seem to tune it, and break the strings.   [*Apart to* GERRARD.

Ger. Come then.—[*Aside.*] Next to the devil's, the invention of women! They'll no more want an excuse to cheat a father with, than an opportunity to abuse a husband.—[*Aloud.*] But what do you give me such a damned fiddle with rotten strings, for?

[*Winds up the strings till they break, and throws the violin on the ground.*

Don. Hey-day! the dancing-master is frantic.

Mons. Ha! ha! ha! That people should be made such fools of!   [*Aside.*

Mrs. Caut. He broke the strings on purpose, because he could not play.—You are blind, brother.

Don. What! will you see further than I, look you?

Hip. But pray, master, why in such haste?

[GERRARD *offers to go.*

Ger. Because you have done with me.

Don. But don't you intend to come to-morrow, again?

Ger. Your daughter does not desire it.

Don. No matter; I do: I must be your paymaster, I'm sure. I would have you come betimes too; not only to make her perfect, but since you have so good a hand upon the violin, to play your part with half-a-dozen of musicians more, whom I would have you bring with you: for we will have a very merry wedding, though a very private one.—You'll be sure to come?

Ger. Your daughter does not desire it.

Don. Come, come, baggage, you shall desire it of him; he is your master.

Hip. My father will have me desire it of you, it seems.

Ger. But you'll make a fool of me again if I should come; would you not?

Hip. If I should tell you so, you'd be sure not to come.

Don. Come, come, she shall not make a fool of you, upon my word. I'll secure you, she shall do what you will have her.

Mons. Ha! ha! ha! So, so, silly Don. [*Aside.*

Ger. But, madam, will you have me come?

Hip. I'd have you to know, for my part, I care not whether you come or no:—there are other dancing-masters to be had:—it is my father's request to you. All that I have to say to you is a little good advice, which, because I will not shame you, I'll give you in private.

[*Whispers* GERRARD.

Mrs. Caut. What! will you let her whisper with him too?

Don. Nay, if you find fault with it, they shall whisper, though I did not like it before:—I'll ha' nobody wiser than myself. But do you think, if 'twere any hurt, she would whisper it to him before us?

Mrs. Caut. If it be no hurt, why does she not speak aloud?

Don. Because she says she will not put the man out of countenance.

Mrs. Caut. Hey-day! put a dancing-master out of countenance!

Don. You say he is no dancing-master.

Mrs. Caut. Yes, for his impudence he may be a dancing-master.

Don. Well, well, let her whisper before me as much as she will to-night, since she is to be married to-morrow; —especially since her husband (that shall be) stands by consenting too.

Mons. Ay, ay, let 'em whisper, as you say, as much as they will before we marry.—[*Aside.*] She's making more sport with him, I warrant.—But I wonder how people can be fooled so.—Ha! ha! ha!

Don. Well, a penny for the secret, daughter.

Hip. Indeed, father, you shall have it for nothing to-morrow.

Don. Well, friend, you will not fail to come?

Ger. No, no, sir.—[*Aside.*] Yet I am a fool if I do.

Don. And be sure you bring the fiddlers with you, as I bid you.

Hip. Yes, be sure you bring the fiddlers with you, as I bid you.

Mrs. Caut. So, so: he'll fiddle your daughter out of the house.—Must you have fiddles, with a fiddle faddle?

Mons. Lord! that people should be made such fools of! Ha! ha!   [*Aside.*

      [*Exeunt* Don DIEGO, HIPPOLITA, Monsieur,
          Mrs. CAUTION, *and* PRUE.

Ger. Fortune we sooner may than woman trust:
     To her confiding gallant she is just;
     But falser woman only him deceives,
     Who to her tongue and eyes most credit gives.

                       [*Exit.*

ACT THE FIFTH.

SCENE I.—*A Room in* Don DIEGO'S *House.*

Enter Monsieur de PARIS *and the* Black, *stalking over the stage; to them* GERRARD.

ONS. Good morrow to thee, noble dancing-master:—ha! ha! ha! your little black brother here, my master, I see, is the more diligent man of the two. But why do you come so late? —What! you begin to neglect your scholar, do you?—Little black master, *con licencia*, pray get you out of the room.—[*Exit* Black.] What! out of humour, man! a dancing-master should be like his fiddle, always in tune. Come, my cousin has made an ass of thee; what then? I know it.

Ger. Does he know it!   [*Aside.*

Mons. But prithee don't be angry: 'twas agreed upon betwixt us, before I sent you, to make a fool of thee; —ha! ha! ha! ha!

Ger. Was it so?

Mons. I knew you would be apt to entertain vain hopes from the summons of a lady: but, faith, the design was but to make a fool of thee, as you find.

Ger. 'Tis very well.

Mons. But indeed I did not think the jest would have lasted so long, and that my cousin would have made a dancing-master of you, ha! ha! ha!

Ger. The fool has reason, I find, and I am the coxcomb while I thought him so.   [*Aside.*

Mons. Come, I see you are uneasy, and the jest of being a dancing-master grows tedious to you :—but have a little patience ; the parson is sent for, and when once my cousin and I are married, my uncle may know who you are.

Ger. I am certainly abused.   [*Aside.*

Mons. [*Listening.*] What do you say ?

Ger. Merely fooled !   [*Aside.*

Mons. Why do you doubt it ? ha ! ha ! ha !

Ger. Can it be ?   [*Aside.*

Mons. Pish ! pish ! she told me yesterday as soon as you were gone, that she had led you into a fool's paradise, and made you believe she would go away with you—ha ! ha ! ha !

Ger. Did she so ?—I am no longer to doubt it then.
                                                          [*Aside.*

Mons. Ay, ay, she makes a mere fool of thee, I vow and swear ; but don't be concerned, there's hardly a man of a thousand but has been made a fool of by some woman or other.—I have been made a fool of my-self, man, by the women; I have, I vow and swear I have.

Ger. Well, you have, I believe it, for you are a cox-comb.

Mons. Lord ! you need not be so touchy with one ; I tell you but the truth, for your good ; for though she docs, I would not fool you any longer ; but prithee don't be troubled at what can't be helped.   Women are made on purpose to fool men: when they are children, they fool their fathers ; and when they have taken their leaves of their hanging sleeves, they fool their gallants or dancing-masters,—ha ! ha ! ha !

Ger. Hark you, sir ! to be fooled by a woman, you say, is not to be helped ; but I will not be fooled by a fool.

Mons. You show your English breeding now ; an English rival is so dull and brutish as not to understand raillery; but what is spoken in your passion I'll take no notice of, for I am your friend, and would not have you my rival to make yourself ridiculous.—Come, prithee, prithee, don't be so concerned; for, as I was saying, women first fool their fathers, then their gallants, and then their husbands; so that it will be my turn to be fooled too (for your comfort); and when they come to be widows, they would fool the devil, I vow and swear. —Come, come, dear Gerrard, prithee don't be out of humour, and look so sillily.

Ger. Prithee do not talk so sillily.

Mons. Nay, faith, I am resolved to beat you out of this ill-humour.

Ger. Faith, I am afraid I shall first beat you into an ill-humour.

Mons. Ha! ha! ha! that thou shouldst be gulled so by a little gipsy, who left off her bib but yesterday!— faith I can't but laugh at thee.

Ger. Faith, then I shall make your mirth (as being too violent) conclude in some little misfortune to you. The fool begins to be tyrannical.

Mons. Ha! ha! ha! poor angry dancing-master! prithee match my Spanish pumps and legs with one of your best and newest sarabands; ha! ha! ha! come—

Ger. I will match your Spanish ear, thus, sir, and make you dance thus.   [*Strikes and kicks him.*

Mons. How! sa! sa! sa! then I'll make you dance thus.

[Monsieur *draws his sword and runs at him,
            but* GERRARD *drawing, he retires.*

Hold! hold a little!—[*Aside.*] A desperate disappointed lover will cut his own throat, then sure he will make nothing of cutting his rival's throat.

Ger. Consideration is an enemy to fighting; if you have a mind to revenge yourself, your sword's in your hand.

Mons. Pray, sir, hold your peace; I'll ne'er take my

rival's counsel, be't what 'twill.   I know what you would
be at; you are disappointed of your mistress, and could
hang yourself, and therefore will not fear hanging.   But
I am a successful lover, and need neither hang for you
nor my mistress : nay, if I should kill you, I know I
should do you a kindness; therefore e'en live, to die
daily with envy of my happiness.   But if you will needs
die, kill yourself, and be damned for me, I vow and swear.

Ger. But won't you fight for your mistress ?

Mons. I tell you, you shall not have the honour to be
killed for her ; besides I will not be hit in the teeth by
her as long as I live, with the great love you had for her.
Women speak well of their dead husbands; what will
they do of their dead gallants ?

Ger. But if you will not fight for her, you shall dance
for her, since you desired me to teach you to dance too :
—I'll teach you to dance thus—

[*Strikes his sword at his legs*, Monsieur *leaps.*

Mons. Nay, if it be for the sake of my mistress, there's
nothing I will refuse to do.

Ger. Nay, you must dance on.

Mons. Ay, ay, for my mistress, and sing too, la, la, la,
ra, la.

Enter HIPPOLITA *and* PRUE.

Hip. What ! swords drawn betwixt you two ! what's
the matter ?

Mons. [*Aside.*] Is she here ?—[*Aloud.*] Come, put up
your sword ; you see this is no place for us; but the
devil eat me if you shall not eat my sword, but—

Hip. What's the matter, cousin ?

Mons. Nothing, nothing, cousin, but your presence is
a sanctuary for my greatest enemy, or else, *tête non !*—

Hip. What, you have not hurt my cousin, sir, I hope ?

[*To* GERRARD.

Ger. How ! she's concerned for him ! nay, then I
need not doubt, my fears are true.   [*Aside.*

Mons. What was that you said, cousin ? hurt me !—
ha ! ha ! ha ! hurt me !—if any man hurt me, he must
do it basely; he shall ne'er do it when my sword's
drawn, sa ! sa ! sa !

Hip. Because you will ne'er draw your sword, perhaps.

Mons. [*Aside.*] Scurvily guessed.—[*Aloud.*] You ladies
may say anything ; but, cousin, pray do not you talk of
swords and fighting ; meddle with your guitar, and
talk of dancing with your dancing-master there, ha !
ha ! ha !

Hip. But I am afraid you have hurt my master,
cousin :—he says nothing ; can he draw his breath ?

Mons. No, 'tis you have hurt your master, cousin, in
the very heart, cousin, and therefore he would hurt me ;
for love is a disease makes people as malicious as the
plague does.

Hip. Indeed, poor master, something does ail you.

Mons. Nay, nay, cousin, faith don't abuse him any
longer ; he's an honest gentleman, and has been long of
my acquaintance, and a man of tolerable sense, to take
him out of his love ; but prithee, cousin, don't drive the
jest too far for my sake.

Ger. He counsels you well, pleasant, cunning, jilting
miss, for his sake ; for if I am your divertisement,
it shall be at his cost, since he's your gallant in favour.

Hip. I don't understand you.

Mons. But I do, a pox take him ! and the custom
that so orders it, forsooth ! that if a lady abuse or affront
a man, presently the gallant must be beaten ; nay, what's
more unreasonable, if a woman abuse her husband, the
poor cuckold must bear the shame as well as the injury.

[*Aside.*

Hip. But what's the matter, master ? what was it you
said ?

Ger. I say, pleasant, cunning, jilting lady, though you
make him a cuckold, it will not be revenge enough for
me upon him for marrying you.

Hip. How ! my surly, huffing, jealous, senseless, saucy master ?

Mons. Nay, nay, faith, give losers leave to speak, losers of mistresses especially, ha ! ha ! ha ! Besides, your anger is too great a favour for him ; I scorn to honour him with mine you see.

Hip. I tell you, my saucy master, my cousin shall never be made that monstrous thing you mention, by me.

Mons. Thank you, I vow and swear, cousin ; no, no, I never thought I should.

Ger. Sure you marry him by the sage maxim of your sex, which is, wittols make the best husbands, that is, cuckolds.

Hip. Indeed, master, whatsoever you think, I would sooner choose you for that purpose than him.

Mons. Ha ! ha ! ha ! there she was with him, i'faith ; —I thank you for that, cousin, I vow and swear.

Hip. Nay, he shall thank me for that too :—but how came you two to quarrel ? I thought, cousin, you had had more wit than to quarrel, or more kindness for me than to quarrel here. What if my father, hearing the bustle, should have come in ? he would have soon discovered our false dancing-master (for passion unmasks every man), and then the result of your quarrel had been my ruin.

Mons. Nay, you had both felt his desperate deadly daunting dagger :—there are your d's for you !

Hip. Go, go presently, therefore, and hinder my father from coming in, whilst I put my master into a better humour, that we may not be discovered, to the preven- tion of our wedding, or worse when he comes ; go, go.

Mons. Well, well, I will, cousin.

Hip. Be sure you let him not come in this good while.

Mons. No, no, I warrant you.—[*Goes out and returns.*] —But if he should come before I would have him, I'll come before him, and cough and hawk soundly, that you may not be surprised. Won't that do well, cousin?

Hip. Very well, pray begone. — [*Exit* Monsieur.] Well, master, since I find you are quarrelsome and melancholy, and would have taken me away without a portion, three infallible signs of a true lover, faith here's my hand now in earnest, to lead me a dance as long as I live.

Ger. How's this! you surprise me as much, as when first I found so much beauty and wit in company with so much innocency. But, dearest, I would be assured of what you say, and yet dare not ask the question. You h—— do not abuse me again? You h—— will fool me no more sure?

Hip. Yes, but I will sure.

Ger. How? nay, I was afraid on't.

Hip. For, I say, you are to be my husband, and you say husbands must be wittols, and some strange things to boot.

Ger. Well, I will take my fortune.

Hip. But have a care, rash man.

Ger. I will venture.

Hip. At your peril; remember I wished you to have a care: forewarned, fore-armed.

Prue. Indeed now, that's fair; for most men are fore-armed before they are warned.

Hip. Plain dealing is some kind of honesty however, and few women would have said so much.

Ger. None but those who would delight in a husband's jealousy, as the proof of his love and her honour.

Hip. Hold, sir, let us have a good understanding betwixt one another at first, that we may be long friends. I differ from you in the point; for a husband's jealousy, which cunning men would pass upon their wives for a compliment, is the worst can be made 'em; for indeed it is a compliment to their beauty, but an affront to their honour.

Ger. But madam—

Hip. So that upon the whole matter I conclude, jealousy in a gallant is humble true love, and the height of respect, and only an undervaluing of himself to over-value her; but in a husband 'tis arrant sauciness, cowardice, and ill-breeding, and not to be suffered.

Ger. I stand corrected, gracious miss.

Hip. Well, but have you brought the gentlemen fiddlers with you, as I desired?

Ger. They are below.

Hip. Are they armed well?

Ger. Yes, they have instruments too that are not of wood; but what will you do with them?

Hip. What did you think I intended to do with them? when I whispered you to bring gentlemen of your acquaintance instead of fiddlers, as my father desired you to bring, pray what did you think I intended?

Ger. Faith, e'en to make fools of the gentlemen fiddlers, as you had done of your gentleman dancing master.

Hip. I intended 'em for our guard and defence against my father's Spanish and Guinea force, when we were to make our retreat from hence; and to help us to take the keys from my aunt, who has been the watchful porter of this house this twelve-month; and this design (if your heart do not fail you) we will put in execution as soon as you have given your friends below instructions.

Ger. Are you sure your heart will stand right still? You flinched last night, when I little expected it, I am sure.

Hip. The time last night was not so proper for us as now, for reasons I will give you. But besides that, I confess I had a mind to try whether your interest did not sway you more than your love; whether the twelve hundred pounds a-year I told you of had not made a greater impression in your heart than Hippolita: but finding it otherwise—yet hold, perhaps upon consideration you are grown wiser; can you yet, as I said, be so desperate, so out of fashion, as to steal a woman with nothing?

Ger. With you I can want nothing, nor can be made by anything more rich or happy.

Hip. Think well again; can you take me without the twelve hundred pounds a-year, — the twelve hundred pounds a-year?

Ger. Indeed, miss, now you begin to be unkind again, and use me worse than e'er you did.

Hip. Well, though you are so modest a gentleman as to suffer a wife to be put upon you with nothing, I have more conscience than to do it. I have the twelve hundred pounds a-year out of my father's power, which is yours, and I am sorry it is not the Indies to mend your bargain.

Ger. Dear miss, you but increase my fears, and not my wealth. Pray let us make haste away; I desire but to be secure of you :—come, what are you thinking of?

Hip. I am thinking if some little, filching, inquisitive poet should get my story, and represent it to the stage, what those ladies who are never precise but at a play would say of me now ;—that I were a confident, coming piece, I warrant, and they would damn the poor poet for libelling the sex. But sure, though I give myself and fortune away frankly, without the consent of my friends, my confidence is less than theirs who stand off only for separate maintenance.

Ger. They would be widows before their time, have a husband and no husband :—but let us begone, lest fortune should recant my happiness, now you are fixed, my dearest miss.   [*He kisses her hand.*

Re-enter Monsieur, *coughing, followed by* Don Diego.

Hip. Oh, here's my father!

Don. How now, sir!—What, kissing her hand! what

means that, friend, ha?—Daughter, ha! do you permit this insolence, ha? *voto á mi honra!*

Ger. We are prevented again. [*Aside to* HIPPOLITA.

Hip. Ha! ha! ha! you are so full of your Spanish jealousy, father; why, you must know he is a city dancing-master, and they, forsooth, think it fine to kiss the hand at the honour before the corant.

Mons. Ay, ay, ay, uncle, don't you know that?

Don. Go to, go to, you are an easy French fool; there's more in it than so, look you.

Mons. I vow and swear there's nothing more in't, if you'll believe one.—[*Aside to* HIPPOLITA *and* GERRARD.] Did not I cough and hawk? a jealous, prudent husband could not cough and hawk louder at the approach of his wife's chamber in visiting time, and yet you would not hear me. He'll make now ado about nothing, and you'll be discovered both.

Don. Umph, umph,—no, no, I see it plain, he is no dancing-master: now I have found it out, and I think I can see as far into matters as another: I have found it now, look you.

Ger. My fear was prophetical. [*Aside to* HIPPOLITA.

Hip. What shall we do? — nay, pray, sir, do not stir yet. [GERRARD *offers to go out with her.*

Enter Mrs. CAUTION.

Mrs. Caut. What's the matter, brother? what's the matter?

Don. I have found it out, sister, I have found it out, sister; this villain here is no dancing-master—but a dishonourer of my house and daughter: I caught him kissing her hand.

Mons. Pish! pish! you are a strange Spanish kind of an uncle, that you are.—A dishonourer of your daughter, because he kissed her hand! pray how could he honour her more? he kissed her hand, you see, while he was making his honour to her.

Don. You are an unthinking, shallow French fop, *voto!*—But I tell you, sister, I have thought of it, and have found it out ; he is no dancing-master, sister. Do you remember the whispering last night ? I have found out the meaning of that too ; and I tell you, sister, he's no dancing-master, I have found it out.

Mrs. Caut. You found it out ! marry come up, did not I tell you always he was no dancing-master ?

Don. You tell me ! you silly woman, what then ? what of that ?—You tell me ! d'ye think I heeded what you told me ? but I tell you now I have found it out.

Mrs. Caut. I say I found it out.

Don. I say 'tis false, gossip, I found him out.

Mrs. Caut. I say I found him out first, say you what you will.

Don. Sister, mum, not such a word again, *guarda !*— You found him out !

Mrs. Caut. I must submit, or dissemble like other prudent women, or—　　　　　　　　　　　　　[*Aside.*

Don. Come, come, sister, take it from me, he is no dancing-master.

Mrs. Caut. O yes, he is a dancing-master.

Don. What ! will you be wiser than I every way ?— remember the whispering, I say.

Mrs. Caut. [*Aside.*] So, he thinks I speak in earnest, then I'll fit him still.—[*To* Don DIEGO.] But what do you talk of their whispering ! they would not whisper any ill before us, sure.

Don. Will you still be an idiot, a dolt, and see nothing ?

Mons. Lord ! you'll be wiser than all the world, will you ? are we not all against you ? pshaw ! pshaw ! I ne'er saw such a *donissimo* as you are, I vow and swear.

Don. No, sister, he's no dancing-master ; for now I think on't too, he could not play upon the fiddle.

Mrs. Caut. Pish ! pish ! what dancing-master can play upon a fiddle without strings ?

Don. Again, I tell you he broke them on purpose, because he could not play; I have found it out now, sister.

Mrs. Caut. Nay, you see farther than I, brother.

[GERRARD *offers to lead her out.*

Hip. For Heaven's sake stir not yet.

[*Aside to* GERRARD.

Don. Besides, if you remember, they were perpetually putting me out of the room; that was, sister, because they had a mind to be alone, I have found that out too: —now, sister, look you, he is no dancing-master.

Mrs. Caut. But has he not given her a lesson often before you?

Don. Ay, but sister, he did not go about his business like a dancing-master; but go, go down to the door, somebody rings. [*Exit* Mrs. CAUTION.

Mons. I vow and swear, uncle, he is a dancing-master; pray be appeased.—Lord! d'ye think I'd tell you a lie?

Don. If it prove to be a lie, and you do not confess it, though you are my next heir after my daughter, I will disown thee as much as I do her, for thy folly and treachery to thyself, as well as me.—You may have her, but never my estate, look you.

Mons. How! I must look to my hits then. [*Aside.*

Don. Look to't.

Mons. [*Aside.*] Then I had best confess all, before he discover all, which he will soon do.—

Enter Parson.

O here's the parson too! he won't be in choler, nor brandish toledo before the parson sure?—[*To* Don DIEGO.] Well, uncle, I must confess, rather than lose your favour, he is no dancing-master.

Don. No!

Ger. What! has the fool betrayed us then at last, nay, then 'tis time to be gone; come away, miss. [*Going out.*

Don. Nay, sir, if you pass this way, my toledo will pass that way, look you. [*Thrusts at him with his sword.*

Hip. O hold, Mr. Gerrard!—Hold father!

Mons. I tell you, uncle, he's an honest gentleman, means no hurt, and came hither but upon a frolic of mine and your daughter's. [*Stops* Don DIEGO.

Don. Ladron! traidor!

Mons. I tell you all's but a jest, a mere jest, I vow and swear.

Don. A jest!—jest with my honour, *voto!* ha! no family to dishonour but the grave, wise, noble, honourable, illustrious, puissant, and right worshipful family of the Formals!—Nay, I am contented to reprieve you, till you know who you have dishonoured, and convict you of the greatness of your crime before you die. We are descended, look you—

Mons. Nay, pray, uncle, hear me.

Don. I say, we are descended—

Mons. 'Tis no matter for that.

Don. And my great, great, great-grandfather was—

Mons. Well, well, I have something to say more to the purpose.

Don. My great, great, great-grandfather, I say, was—

Mons. Well, a pinmaker in—

Don. But he was a gentleman for all that, fop, for he was a sergeant to a company of the trainbands; and my great-great-grandfather was—

Mons. Was his son, what then? won't you let me clear this gentleman?

Don. He was, he was—

Mons. He was a felt-maker, his son a wine-cooper, your father a vintner, and so you came to be a Canary merchant.

Don. But we were still gentlemen, for our coat was, as the heralds say—was—

Mons. Was! your sign was the Three Tuns, and the field Canary; now let me tell you, this honest gentleman—

Don. Now, that you should dare to dishonour this

family!—by the graves of my ancestors in Great St. Helen's church—

Mons. Yard.

Don. Thou shalt die for't, *ladron!* [*Runs at* GERRARD.

Mons. Hold, hold, uncle, are you mad?

Hip. Oh! oh!—

Mons. Nay then, by your own Spanish rules of honour (though he be my rival), I must help him; [*Draws his sword.*] since I brought him into danger.—[*Aside.*] Sure he will not show his valour upon his nephew and son-in-law, otherwise I should be afraid of showing mine.— Here, Mr. Gerrard, go in here, nay, you shall go in, Mr. Gerrard, I'll secure you all; and, parson, do you go in too with 'em, for I see you are afraid of a sword and the other world, though you talk of it so familiarly, and make it so fine a place.

> [*Opens a door, and thrusts* GERRARD, HIPPO-
> LITA, Parson, *and* PRUE *in, then shuts it,
> and guards it with his sword.*

Don. Tu quoque, Brute!

Mons. Nay, now, uncle, you must understand reason.— What, you are not only a Don, but you are a Don Quixote too, I vow and swear!

Don. Thou spot, sploach [1] of my family and blood! I will have his blood, look you.

Mons. Pray, good Spanish uncle, have but patience to hear me. Suppose—I say, suppose he had done, done, done the feat to your daughter.

Don. How! done the feat! done the feat: done the feat! *en hora mala!*

Mons. I say, suppose, suppose—

Don. Suppose!

Mons. I say, suppose he had, for I do but suppose it; well, I am ready to marry her, however. Now marriage is as good a solder for cracked female honour as blood; and can't you suffer the shame but for a quarter of an hour,

[1] Blot.

till the parson has married us? and then if there be any shame, it becomes mine; for here in England, the father has nothing to do with the daughter's business, honour, what d'ye call't, when once she's married, d'ye see.

Don. England! what d'ye tell me of England? I'll be a Spaniard still, *voto à mi honra!* and I will be revenged. —Pedro! Juan! Sanchez! [*Calls at the door.*

Re-enter Mrs. CAUTION, *followed by* FLIRT *and* FLOUNCE, *in vizard masks.*

Mrs. Caut. What's the matter, brother?

Don. Pedro! Sanchez! Juan!— but who are these, sister? are they not men in women's clothes? what make they here?

Mrs. Caut. They are relations, they say, of my cousin's, who pressed in when I let in the parson; they say my cousin invited 'em to his wedding.

Mons. Two of my relations!—[*Aside.*] Ha! they are my cousins indeed of the other night; a pox take 'em!— but that's no curse for 'em; a plague take 'em then!— but how came they here?

Don. [*Aside.*] Now must I have witnesses too of the dishonour of my family; it were Spanish prudence to despatch 'em away out of the house, before I begin my revenge. [*To* FLIRT *and* FLOUNCE.] What are you? what make you here? who would you speak with?

Flirt. With monsieur.

Don. Here he is.

Mons. Now will these jades discredit me, and spoil my match just in the coupling minute. [*Aside.*

Don. Do you know 'em?

Mons. Yes, sir, sure, I know 'em.—[*Aside to them.*] Pray, ladies, say as I say, or you will spoil my wedding, for I am just going to be married; and if my uncle or mistress should know who you are, it might break off the match.

Flou. We come on purpose to break the match.

Mons. How !

Flirt. Why, d'ye think to marry, and leave us so in the lurch ?

Mons. What do the jades mean ?   [*Aside.*

Don. Come, who are they? what would they have ? If they come to the wedding, ladies, I assure you there will be none to-day here.

Mons. They won't trouble you, sir; they are going again.—Ladies, you hear what my uncle says ; I know you won't trouble him.—[*Aside.*] I wish I were well rid of 'em.

Flou. You shall not think to put us off so.   [*Aside.*

Don. Who are they ? what are their names ?

Flirt. We are, sir—

Mons. Nay, for Heaven's sake don't tell who you are, for you will undo me, and spoil my match infallibly.

[*Aside to them.*

Flou. We care not, 'tis our business to spoil matches.

Mons. You need not, for I believe married men are your best customers, for greedy bachelors take up with their wives.

Don. Come, pray ladies, if you have no business here, be pleased to retire ; for few of us are in humour to be so civil to you as you may deserve.

Mons. Ay, prithee, dear jades, get you gone.

Flirt. We will not stir.

Don. Who are they, I say, fool ? and why don't they go ?

Flou. We are, sir—

Mons. Hold ! hold !—They are persons of honour and quality, and—

Flirt. We are no persons of honour and quality, sir, we are—

Mons. They are modest ladies, and being in a kind of disguise, will not own their quality.

Flou. We modest ladies !

Mons. Why, sometimes you are in the humour to pass

for women of honour and quality; prithee, dear jades, let your modesty and greatness come upon you now.

[*Aside to them.*

Flirt. Come, sir, not to delude you, as he would have us, we are—

Mons. Hold! hold!—

Flirt. The other night at the French-house—

Mons. Hold, I say!—'Tis even true as Gerrard says, the women will tell, I see.

Flou. If you would have her silent, stop her mouth with that ring.

Mons. Will that do't? here, here—'Tis worth one hundred and fifty pounds.—[*Takes off his ring and gives it her.*] But I must not lose my match, I must not lose a trout for a fly.—That men should live to hire women to silence!

Re-enter GERRARD, HIPPOLITA, Parson, *and* PRUE.

Don. Oh, are you come again.

[*Draws his sword and runs at them,* Monsieur *holds him.*

Mons. Oh! hold! hold! uncle!—What, are you mad, Gerrard, to expose yourself to a new danger? why would you come out yet?

Ger. Because our danger now is over, I thank the parson there. And now we must beg—

[GERRARD *and* HIPPOLITA *kneel.*

Mons. Nay, faith, uncle, forgive him now, since he asks you forgiveness upon his knees, and my poor cousin too.

Hip. You are mistaken, cousin; we ask him blessing, and you forgiveness.

Mons. How, how, how! what do you talk of blessing? what, do you ask your father blessing and he ask me forgiveness? but why should he ask me forgiveness?

Hip. Because he asks my father's blessing.

Mons. Pish! pish! I don't understand you, I vow and swear.

Hip. The parson will expound it to you, cousin.

Mons. Hey! what say you to it, parson?

Par. They are married, sir.

Mons. Married!

Mrs. Caut. Married! so, I told you what 'twould come to.

Don. You told us!—

Mons. Nay, she is setting up for the reputation of a witch.

Don. Married!—Juan, Sanchez, Pedro, arm! arm! arm!

Mrs. Caut. A witch! a witch!

Hip. Nay, indeed, father, now we are married, you had better call the fiddlers.—Call 'em, Prue, quickly.

[*Exit* PRUE.

Mons. Who do you say, married, man?

Par. Was I not sent for on purpose to marry 'em? why should you wonder at it?

Mons. No, no, you were to marry me, man, to her; I knew there was a mistake in't somehow; you were merely mistaken, therefore you must do your business over again for me now.—The parson was mistaken, uncle, it seems, ha! ha! ha!

Mrs. Caut. I suppose five or six guineas made him make the mistake, which will not be rectified now, nephew. They'll marry all that come near 'em, and, for a guinea or two, care not what mischief they do, nephew.

Don. Married!—Pedro! Sanchez!

Mons. How! and must she be his wife then for ever and ever? have I held the door then for this, like a fool as I was?

Mrs. Caut. Yes, indeed!

Mons. Have I worn *golilla* here for this? little breeches for this?

Mrs. Caut. Yes, truly.

Mons. And put on the Spanish honour with the habit, in defending my rival? nay then, I'll have another turn of honour in revenge. Come, uncle, I'm of your side now, sa! sa! sa! but let's stay for our force; Sanchez, Juan, Pedro, arm! arm! arm!

Enter two Blacks *and a* Spaniard, *followed by* PRUE, MARTIN, *and five other gentlemen-like* Fiddlers.

Don. Murder the villain! kill him!

[*Running all upon* GERRARD.

Mar. Hold! hold! sir!

Don. How now! who sent for you, friends?

Mar. We fiddlers, sir, often come unsent for.

Don. And you are often kicked down stairs for't too.

Mar. No, sir, our company was never kicked, I think.

Don. Fiddlers, and not kicked! then to preserve your virgin honour, get you down stairs quickly; for we are not at present disposed much for mirth, *voto!*

Mons. [*Peeping.*] A pox! is it you, is it you, Martin?— Nay, uncle, then 'tis in vain; for they won't be kicked down stairs, to my knowledge. They are gentlemen fiddlers, forsooth! A pox on all gentlemen fiddlers and gentlemen dancing-masters! say I.

Don. How! ha!   [*Pausing.*

Mons. Well, Flirt, now I am a match for thee: now I may keep you.—And there's little difference betwixt keeping a wench and marriage; only marriage is a little the cheaper; but the other is the more honourable now, *vert* and *bleu!* Nay, now I may swear a French oath too. Come, come, I am thine; let us strike up the bargain: thine, according to the honourable institution of keeping.—Come.

Flirt. Nay, hold, sir; two words to the bargain; first, I have ne'er a lawyer here to draw articles and settlements.

Mons. How! is the world come to that? A man cannot keep a wench without articles and settlements! Nay, then 'tis e'en as bad as marriage, indeed, and there's no difference betwixt a wife and a wench.

Flirt. Only in cohabitation ; for the first article shall be against cohabitation :—we mistresses suffer no co-habitation.

Mons. Nor wives neither now.

Flirt. Then separate maintenance, in case you should take a wife, or I a new friend.

Mons. How! that too ! then you are every whit as bad as a wife.

Flirt. Then my house in town and yours in the country, if you will.

Mons. A mere wife !

Flirt. Then my coach apart, as well as my bed apart.

Mons. As bad as a wife still !

Flirt. But take notice, I will have no little, dirty, second-hand chariot new furbished, but a large, sociable, well-painted coach ; nor will I keep it till it be as well known as myself, and it come to be called Flirt-coach ; nor will I have such pitiful horses as cannot carry me every night to the Park ; for I will not miss a night in the Park, I'd have you to know.

Mons. 'Tis very well : you must have your great, gilt, fine painted coaches. I'm sure they are grown so common already amongst you, that ladies of quality begin to take up with hackneys again, *jarni !*—But what else ?

Flirt. Then, that you do not think I will be served by a little dirty boy in a bonnet, but a couple of handsome, lusty, cleanly footmen, fit to serve ladies of quality, and do their business as they should do.

Mons. What then ?

Flirt. Then, that you never grow jealous of them.

Mons. Why, will you make so much of them ?

Flirt. I delight to be kind to my servants.

Mons. Well, is this all ?

Flirt. No.—Then, that when you come to my house, you never presume to touch a key, lift up a latch, or thrust a door, without knocking beforehand : and that you ask no questions, if you see a stray piece of plate-cabinet, or looking-glass, in my house.

Mons. Just a wife in everything.—But what else?

Flirt. Then, that you take no acquaintance with me abroad, nor bring me home any when you are drunk, whom you will not be willing to see there when you are sober.

Mons. But what allowance? let's come to the main business; the money.

Flirt. Stay, let me think : first for advance-money, five hundred pounds for pins.

Mons. A very wife!

Flirt. Then you must take the lease of my house, and furnish it as becomes one of my quality; for don't you think we'll take up with your old Queen Elizabeth furniture, as your wives do.

Mons. Indeed there she is least like a wife, as she says.

Flirt. Then for house-keeping, servants' wages, clothes, and the rest, I'll be contented with a thousand pounds a year present maintenance, and but three hundred pounds a year separate maintenance for my life, when your love grows cold.   But I am contented with a thousand pounds a year, because for pendants, neck-laces, and all sorts of jewels, and such trifles, nay, and some plate, I will shift myself as I can ; make shifts, which you shall not take any notice of.

Mons. A thousand pounds a year! what will wenching come to?   Time was a man might have fared as well at a much cheaper rate, and a lady of one's affections, instead of a house, would have been contented with a little chamber, three pair of stairs backward, with a little closet or ladder to't ; and instead of variety of new gowns and rich petticoats, with her *deshabillé*, or flame-colour gown called Indian, and slippers of the same, would have been contented for a twelvemonth ; and instead of visits and gadding to plays, would have entertained herself at home

with "St. George for England," "The Knight of the
Sun," or "The Practice of Piety;" and instead of sending her wine and meat from the French-houses, would
have been contented, if you had given her, poor wretch,
but credit at the next chandler's and chequered cellar;[1]
and then, instead of a coach, would have been well satisfied to have gone out and taken the air for three or four
hours in the evening in the balcony, poor soul. Well,
Flirt, however, we'll agree:—'tis but three hundred
pounds a year separate maintenance, you say, when I am
weary of thee and the charge.

Don. [*Aside.*]—Robbed of my honour, my daughter,
and my revenge too! O my dear honour! Nothing
vexes me, but that the world should say I had not
Spanish policy enough to keep my daughter from being
debauched from me. But methinks my Spanish policy
might help me yet. I have it—so—I will cheat 'em all;
for I will declare I understood the whole plot and contrivance, and connived at it, finding my cousin a fool, and
not answering my expectation. Well, but then if I
approve of the match, I must give this mock-dancing-
master my estate, especially since half he would have in
right of my daughter, and in spite of me. Well, I am resolved to turn the cheat upon themselves, and give them
my consent and estate.

Mons. Come, come, ne'er be troubled, uncle: 'twas a
combination, you see, of all these heads and your
daughter's, you know what I mean, uncle, not to be
thwarted or governed by all the Spanish policy in Christendom. I'm sure my French policy would not have
governed her: so since I have 'scaped her, I am glad I
have 'scaped her, *jarni!*

Mrs. Caut. Come, brother, you are wiser than I, you
see: ay, ay.

Don. No, you think you are wiser than I now, in

[1] The "Checkers" was a common sign of public houses; from
the game of checkers, or draughts.

earnest : but know, while I was thought a gull, I gulled you all, and made them and you think I knew nothing of the contrivance. Confess, did not you think verily that I knew nothing of it, and that I was a gull?

Mrs. Caut. Yes indeed, brother, I did think verily you were a gull.

Hip. How's this?   [*Listening.*

Don. Alas, alas ! all the sputter I made was but to make this young man, my cousin, believe, when the thing should be effected, that it was not with my connivance or consent ; but since he is so well satisfied, I own it. For do you think I would ever have suffered her to marry a monsieur, a monsieur ? *guarda !*—besides, it had been but a beastly incestuous kind of a match, *voto !*—

Mrs. Caut. Nay, then I see, brother, you are wiser than I indeed.

Ger. So, so.

Mrs. Caut. Nay, young man, you have danced a fair dance for yourself, royally ; and now you may go jig it together till you are both weary. And though you were so eager to have him, Mrs. Minx, you'll soon have your bellyful of him, let me tell you, mistress.

Prue. Ha ! ha !

Mons. How, uncle ! what was't you said ? Nay, if I had your Spanish policy against me, it was no wonder I missed of my aim, *ma foi !*

Don. I was resolved too my daughter should not marry a coward, therefore made the more the more ado to try you, sir. But I find you are a brisk man of honour, firm stiff Spanish honour ; and that you may see I deceived you all along, and you not me, ay, and am able to deceive you still, for I know now you think that I will give you little or nothing with my daughter, like other fathers, since you have married her without my consent—but, I say, I'll deceive you now ; for you shall have the most part of my estate in present, and the rest at my death.— There's for you: I think I have deceived you now, look you.

Ger. No, indeed, sir, you have not deceived me ; for I never suspected your love to your daughter, nor your generosity.

Don. How, sir ! have a care of saying I have not deceived you, lest I deceive you another way, *guarda !*— Pray, gentlemen, do not think any man could deceive me, look you ; that any man could steal my daughter, look you, without my connivance :—

> The less we speak, the more we think ;
> And he sees most, that seems to wink.

Hip. So, so, now I could give you my blessing, father ; now you are a good complaisant father, indeed :—

> When children marry, parents should obey,
> Since love claims more obedience far than they.

[Exeunt.

EPILOGUE

SPOKEN BY FLIRT.

The ladies first I am to compliment,
Whom (if he could) the poet would content,
But to their pleasure then they must consent ;
Most spoil their sport still by their modesty,
And when they should be pleased, cry out, " O fy ! "
And the least smutty jest will ne'er pass by.
But city damsel ne'er had confidence
At smutty play to take the least offence,
But mercy shows, to show her innocence.
Yet lest the merchants' daughters should to-day
Be scandalised, not at our harmless play,

But our Hippolita, since she's like one
Of us bold flirts of t'other end o' th' town;
Our poet sending to you (though unknown)
His best respects by me, does frankly own
The character to be unnatural;
Hippolita is not like you at all:
You, while your lovers court you, still look grum,
And far from wooing, when they woo, cry mum
And if some of you e'er were stol'n away,
Your portion's fault 'twas only, I dare say.
Thus much for him the poet bid me speak;
Now to the men I my own mind will break.
You good men o' th' Exchange, on whom alone
We must depend, when sparks to sea are gone;
Into the pit already you are come,
'Tis but a step more to our tiring-room;
Where none of us but will be wondrous sweet
Upon an able love of Lombard-street.
You we had rather see between our scenes,
Than spendthrift fops with better clothes and miens;
Instead of laced coats, belts, and pantaloons,
Your velvet jumps,[1] gold chains, and grave fur gowns;
Instead of periwigs, and broad cocked hats,
Your satin caps, small cuffs, and vast cravats.
For you are fair and square in all your dealings,
You never cheat your doxies with gilt shillings;
You ne'er will break our windows; then you are
Fit to make love, while our huzzas make war;
And since all gentlemen must pack to sea,
Our gallants and our judges you must be!
We, therefore, and our poet, do submit,
To all the camlet cloaks now i' the pit.

[1] Jump : a short coat.

THE COUNTRY WIFE.

Indignor quidquam reprehendi, non quia crasse
Compositum illepideve putetur, sed quia nuper :
Nec veniam antiquis, sed honorem et præmia posci.[1]

HORAT.

I am out of patience when anything is blamed, not because it is thought coarsely and inelegantly composed, but because it is new : when for the ancients not indulgence, but honour and rewards are demanded.—*Epist.* II. i. 76-8.

HE COUNTRY WIFE was written, according to its author's own statement, about the year 1671 or 1672. Its production upon the stage was subsequent to that of *The Gentleman Dancing-Master*, to which allusion is made in the prologue, and antecedent to that of the earlier-written *Plain Dealer*, in the second act of which the author inserted some critical observations upon *The Country Wife*. The first performance of *The Plain Dealer*, as will afterwards appear, admits not of a later date than that of March, or the very beginning of April, 1674; it follows then that *The Country Wife* was brought forward some time between the early spring of 1672 and that of 1674. It was acted by the King's Company, established during these two years at the theatre in Portugal Street, Lincoln's Inn Fields, and was published in the year 1675.

If we can overlook the immorality which, in this play, is more offensive and pronounced than in any of Wycherley's other dramas, we shall find in *The Country Wife* a brilliantly written and skilfully constructed comedy, superior to either of the preceding dramas from the same pen, and surpassed, among comedies of the Restoration, only by its author's own masterpiece, *The Plain Dealer*. The plot of *The Country Wife* is partly based upon two comedies by Molière—*L'Ecole des Femmes* and *L'Ecole des Maris*. From the former of these Wycherley derived his conception of the jealous man who keeps under close restraint a young and ignorant woman, with the vain hope of thereby securing her fidelity to him. Agnes's innocent confessions to Arnolphe of her lover's stratagems and her own esteem for him find a counterpart in the Country Wife's frankness on a similar occasion, but beyond these points of coincidence there is little resemblance between the two plays. From *L'Ecole des Maris*, again, Wycherley has borrowed one or two incidents : the imprisoned girl's device of making her would-be husband (in the English play, her actual husband) the bearer of a letter to her gallant, and the trick by which Isabella causes her tyrant, under the impression that she is another woman, to consign her with his own hands to his rival.

Steele has published, in the *Tatler* of April 16, 1709, a very just criticism upon this play, which, as it cannot fail to interest the reader, I venture to subjoin.

"Will's Coffee-house, April 14.

"This evening the Comedy, called *The Country Wife*, was acted in Drury Lane, for the benefit of Mrs. Bignell. The part which gives name to the Play was performed by herself. Through the whole action she made a very pretty figure, and exactly entered into the nature of the part. Her husband, in the Drama, is represented to be one of those debauchees who run through the vices of the town, and believe, when they think fit, they can marry and settle at their ease. His own knowledge of the iniquity of the age makes him choose a wife wholly ignorant of it, and place his security in her want of skill to abuse him. The Poet, on many occasions, where the propriety of the character will admit of it, insinuates that there is no defence against vice but the contempt of it : and has, in the natural ideas of an untainted innocent, shown the gradual steps to ruin and destruction which persons of condition run into, without the help of a good education to form their conduct. The torment of a jealous coxcomb, which arises from his own false maxims, and the aggravation of his pain by the very words in which he sees her innocence, makes a very pleasant and instructive satire. The character of Horner, and the design of it, is a good representation of the age in which that Comedy was written:

at which time love and wenching were the business of life, and the gallant manner of pursuing women was the best recommendation at Court. To this only it is to be imputed that a Gentleman of Mr. Wycherley's character and sense condescends to represent the insults done to the honour of the bed without just reproof ; but to have drawn a man of probity with regard to such considerations had been a monster, and a Poet had at that time discovered his want of knowing the manners of the Court he lived in, by a virtuous character in his fine gentleman, as he would show his ignorance by drawing a vicious one to please the present audience."

PROLOGUE

SPOKEN BY MR. HART.[1]

POETS, like cudgelled bullies, never do
At first or second blow submit to you ;
But will provoke you still, and ne'er have done,
Till you are weary first with laying on.
The late so baffled scribbler of this day,
Though he stands trembling, bids me boldly say,
What we before most plays are used to do,
For poets out of fear first draw on you ;
In a fierce prologue the still pit defy,
And, ere you speak, like Castril [2] give the lie.
But though our Bayes's battles oft I've fought,
And with bruised knuckles their dear conquests bought ;
Nay, never yet feared odds upon the stage,
In prologue dare not hector with the age ;
But would take quarter from your saving hands,
Though Bayes within all yielding countermands,
Says, you confederate wits no quarter give,
Therefore his play shan't ask your leave to live.
Well, let the vain rash fop, by huffing so,
Think to obtain the better terms of you ;
But we, the actors, humbly will submit,
Now, and at any time, to a full pit ;
Nay, often we anticipate your rage,
And murder poets for you on our stage :
We set no guards upon our tiring-room,
But when with flying colours there you come,
We patiently, you see, give up to you
Our poets, virgins, nay, our matrons too.

---

[1] Charles Hart, grandson of Shakespeare's sister, Joan Hart, was one of the most distinguished actors of his time. He excelled chiefly in tragedy, and it was said of him that he " might teach any king on earth how to comport himself." He retired from the stage in 1682, and died in the following year.

[2] A character in Ben Jonson's comedy, *The Alchemist.*

Mr. HORNER.
Mr. HARCOURT.
Mr. DORILANT.
Mr. PINCHWIFE.
Mr. SPARKISH.
Sir JASPER FIDGET.
A Boy.
A Quack.
Waiters, Servants, and Attendants.

Mrs. MARGERY PINCHWIFE.
ALITHEA, Sister of PINCHWIFE.
Lady FIDGET.
Mrs. DAINTY FIDGET, Sister of Sir JASPER.
Mrs. SQUEAMISH.
Old Lady SQUEAMISH.
LUCY, ALITHEA'S Maid.

SCENE—LONDON.

THE COUNTRY WIFE.

ACT THE FIRST.

SCENE I.—HORNER'S *Lodging*.

Enter HORNER, *and* Quack *following him at a distance*

HORN. [*Aside.*] A quack is as fit for a pimp, as a midwife for a bawd; they are still but in their way, both helpers of nature.—[*Aloud.*] Well, my dear doctor, hast thou done what I desired?

Quack. I have undone you for ever with the women, and reported you throughout the whole town as bad as an eunuch, with as much trouble as if I had made you one in earnest.

Horn. But have you told all the midwives you know, the orange wenches at the playhouses, the city husbands, and old fumbling keepers of this end of the town? for they'll be the readiest to report it.

Quack. I have told all the chambermaids, waiting-women, tire-women, and old women of my acquaintance; nay, and whispered it as a secret to 'em, and to the whisperers of Whitehall; so that you need not doubt 'twill spread, and you will be as odious to the handsome young women, as—

Horn. As the small-pox. Well—

Quack. And to the married women of this end of the town, as—

Horn. As the great one; nay, as their own husbands.

Quack. And to the city dames, as aniseed Robin, of filthy and contemptible memory; and they will frighten their children with your name, especially their females.

Horn. And cry, Horner's coming to carry you away. I am only afraid 'twill not be believed. You told 'em it was by an English-French disaster, and an English-French chirurgeon, who has given me at once not only a cure, but an antidote for the future against that damned malady, and that worse distemper, love, and all other women's evils?

Quack. Your late journey into France has made it the more credible, and your being here a fortnight before you appeared in public, looks as if you apprehended the shame, which I wonder you do not. Well, I have been hired by young gallants to belie 'em t'other way; but you are the first would be thought a man unfit for women.

Horn. Dear Mr. Doctor, let vain rogues be contented only to be thought abler men than they are, generally 'tis all the pleasure they have; but mine lies another way.

Quack. You take, methinks, a very preposterous way to it, and as ridiculous as if we operators in physic should put forth bills to disparage our medicaments, with hopes to gain customers.

Horn. Doctor, there are quacks in love as well as physic, who get but the fewer and worse patients for their boasting; a good name is seldom got by giving it one's self; and women, no more than honour, are compassed by bragging. Come, come, Doctor, the wisest lawyer never discovers the merits of his cause till the trial; the wealthiest man conceals his riches, and the cunning gamester his play. Shy husbands and keepers, like old rooks, are not to be cheated but by a new unpractised trick: false friendship will pass now no more than false dice upon 'em; no, not in the city.

Enter Boy.

Boy. There are two ladies and a gentleman coming up.
[*Exit.*

Horn. A pox! some unbelieving sisters of my former
acquaintance, who, I am afraid, expect their sense should
be satisfied of the falsity of the report.   No—this formal
fool and women!

Enter Sir JASPER FIDGET, Lady FIDGET, *and* Mrs.
DAINTY FIDGET.

Quack. His wife and sister.

Sir Jasp. My coach breaking just now before your
door, sir, I look upon as an occasional reprimand to
me, sir, for not kissing your hands, sir, since your coming
out of France, sir; and so my disaster, sir, has been my
good fortune, sir; and this is my wife and sister, sir.

Horn. What then, sir?

Sir Jasp. My lady, and sister, sir.—Wife, this is Master
Horner.

Lady Fid. Master Horner, husband!

Sir Jasp. My lady, my Lady Fidget, sir.

Horn. So, sir.

Sir Jasp. Won't you be acquainted with her, sir?—
[*Aside.*] So, the report is true, I find, by his coldness or
aversion to the sex; but I'll play the wag with him.—
[*Aloud.*] Pray salute my wife, my lady, sir.

Horn. I will kiss no man's wife, sir, for him, sir; I
have taken my eternal leave, sir, of the sex already, sir.

Sir Jasp. [*Aside.*] Ha! ha! ha! I'll plague him yet.—
[*Aloud.*] Not know my wife, sir?

Horn. I do know your wife, sir; she's a woman, sir,
and consequently a monster, sir, a greater monster than
a husband, sir.

Sir Jasp. A husband! how, sir?

Horn. So, sir; but I make no more cuckolds, sir.

[*Makes horns.*

Sir Jasp. Ha! ha! ha! Mercury! Mercury!

Lady Fid. Pray, Sir Jasper, let us be gone from this rude fellow.

Mrs. Dain. Who, by his breeding, would think he had ever been in France?

Lady Fid. Foh! he's but too much a French fellow, such as hate women of quality and virtue for their love to their husbands. Sir Jasper, a woman is hated by 'em as much for loving her husband as for loving their money. But pray let's be gone.

Horn. You do well, madam; for I have nothing that you came for. I have brought over not so much as a bawdy picture, no new postures, nor the second part of the *Ecole des Filles ;* nor—

Quack. Hold, for shame, sir! what d'ye mean? you'll ruin yourself for ever with the sex— [*Apart to* HORNER.

Sir Jasp. Ha! ha! ha! he hates women perfectly, I find.

Mrs. Dain. What pity 'tis he should!

Lady Fid. Ay, he's a base fellow for't. But affectation makes not a woman more odious to them than virtue.

Horn. Because your virtue is your greatest affectation, madam.

Lady Fid. How, you saucy fellow! would you wrong my honour?

Horn. If I could.

Lady Fid. How d'ye mean, sir?

Sir Jasp. Ha! ha! ha! no, he can't wrong your lady-ship's honour, upon my honour. He, poor man—hark you in your ear—a mere eunuch.   [*Whispers.*

Lady Fid. O filthy French beast! foh! foh! why do we stay? let's be gone: I can't endure the sight of him.

Sir Jasp. Stay but till the chairs come; they'll be here presently.

Lady Fid. No,

Sir Jasp. Nor can I stay longer. 'Tis, let me see, a quarter and half quarter of a minute past eleven. The council will be sat; I must away. Business must be preferred always before love and ceremony with the wise, Mr. Horner.

Horn. And the impotent, Sir Jasper.

Sir Jasp. Ay, ay, the impotent, Master Horner; hah! hah! hah!

Lady Fid. What, leave us with a filthy man alone in his lodgings?

Sir Jasp. He's an innocent man now, you know. Pray stay, I'll hasten the chairs to you.—Mr. Horner, your servant; I should be glad to see you at my house. Pray come and dine with me, and play at cards with my wife after dinner; you are fit for women at that game yet, ha! ha!—[*Aside.*] 'Tis as much a husband's prudence to provide innocent diversion for a wife as to hinder her unlawful pleasures; and he had better employ her than let her employ herself.—[*Aloud.*] Farewell.

Horn. Your servant, Sir Jasper.   [*Exit* Sir JASPER.

Lady Fid. I will not stay with him, foh!—

Horn. Nay, madam, I beseech you stay, if it be but to see I can be as civil to ladies yet as they would desire.

Lady Fid. No, no, foh! you cannot be civil to ladies.

Mrs. Dain. You as civil as ladies would desire?

Lady Fid. No, no, no, foh! foh! foh!

[*Exeunt* Lady FIDGET *and* Mrs. DAINTY FIDGET.

Quack. Now, I think, I, or you yourself, rather, have done your business with the women.

Horn. Thou art an ass. Don't you see already, upon the report, and my carriage, this grave man of business leaves his wife in my lodgings, invites me to his house and wife, who before would not be acquainted with me out of jealousy?

Quack. Nay, by this means you may be the more acquainted with the husbands, but the less with the wives.

Horn. Let me alone; if I can but abuse the husbands, I'll soon disabuse the wives. Stay—I'll reckon you up the advantages I am like to have by my stratagem. First, I shall be rid of all my old acquaintances, the most insatiable sort of duns, that invade our lodgings in a morning; and next to the pleasure of making a new mistress is that of being rid of an old one, and of all old debts. Love, when it comes to be so, is paid the most unwillingly.

Quack. Well, you may be so rid of your old acquaintances; but how will you get any new ones?

Horn. Doctor, thou wilt never make a good chemist, thou art so incredulous and impatient. Ask but all the young fellows of the town if they do not lose more time, like huntsmen, in starting the game, than in running it down. One knows not where to find 'em; who will or will not. Women of quality are so civil, you can hardly distinguish love from good breeding, and a man is often mistaken: but now I can be sure she that shows an aversion to me loves the sport, as those women that are gone, whom I warrant to be right. And then the next thing is, your women of honour, as you call 'em, are only chary of their reputations, not their persons; and 'tis scandal they would avoid, not men. Now may I have, by the reputation of an eunuch, the privileges of one, and be seen in a lady's chamber in a morning as early as her husband; kiss virgins before their parents or lovers; and may be, in short, the *passe-partout* of the town. Now, doctor.

Quack. Nay, now you shall be the doctor; and your process is so new that we do not know but it may succeed.

Horn. Not so new neither; *probatum est,* doctor.

Quack. Well, I wish you luck, and many patients, whilst I go to mine. [*Exit.*

Enter HARCOURT *and* DORILANT.

Har. Come, your appearance at the play yesterday, has, I hope, hardened you for the future against the women's contempt, and the men's raillery ; and now you'll abroad as you were wont.

Horn. Did I not bear it bravely ?

Dor. With a most theatrical impudence, nay, more than the orange-wenches show there, or a drunken vizard-mask, or a great-bellied actress ; nay, or the most impudent of creatures, an ill poet; or what is yet more impudent, a second-hand critic.

Horn. But what say the ladies ? have they no pity ?

Har. What ladies ? The vizard-masks, you know, never pity a man when all's gone, though in their service.

Dor. And for the women in the boxes, you'd never pity them when 'twas in your power.

Har. They say 'tis pity but all that deal with common women should be served so.

Dor. Nay, I dare swear they won't admit you to play at cards with them, go to plays with 'em, or do the little duties which other shadows of men are wont to do for 'em.

Horn. What do you call shadows of men ?

Dor. Half-men.

Horn. What, boys ?

Dor. Ay, your old boys, old *beaux garçons*, who, like superannuated stallions, are suffered to run, feed, and whinny with the mares as long as they live, though they can do nothing else.

Horn. Well, a pox on love and wenching ! Women serve but to keep a man from better company. Though I can't enjoy them, I shall you the more. Good fellowship and friendship are lasting, rational, and manly pleasures.

Har. For all that, give me some of those pleasures you call effeminate too ; they help to relish one another.

Horn. They disturb one another.

Har. No, mistresses are like books. If you pore upon them too much, they doze you, and make you unfit for company ; but if used discreetly, you are the fitter for conversation by 'em.

Dor. A mistress should be like a little country retreat near the town ; not to dwell in constantly, but only for a night and away, to taste the town the better when a man returns.

Horn. I tell you, 'tis as hard to be a good fellow, a good friend, and a lover of women, as 'tis to be a good fellow, a good friend, and a lover of money. You cannot follow both, then choose your side. Wine gives you liberty, love takes it away.

Dor. Gad, he's in the right on't.

Horn. Wine gives you joy; love, grief and tortures, besides surgeons. Wine makes us witty; love, only sots. Wine makes us sleep ; love breaks it.

Dor. By the world he has reason, Harcourt.

Horn. Wine makes—

Dor. Ay, wine makes us—makes us princes; love makes us beggars, poor rogues, egad—and wine—

Horn. So, there's one converted.—No, no, love and wine, oil and vinegar.

Har. I grant it ; love will still be uppermost.

Horn. Come, for my part, I will have only those glorious manly pleasures of being very drunk and very slovenly.

Enter Boy.

Boy. Mr. Sparkish is below, sir.   [*Exit.*

Har. What, my dear friend ! a rogue that is fond of me only, I think, for abusing him.

Dor. No, he can no more think the men laugh at him than that women jilt him ; his opinion of himself is so good.

Horn. Well, there's another pleasure by drinking I thought not of,—I shall lose his acquaintance, because he cannot drink : and you know 'tis a very hard thing to be rid of him ; for he's one of those nauseous offerers at wit, who, like the worst fiddlers, run themselves into all companies.

Har. One that, by being in the company of men of sense, would pass for one.

Horn. And may so to the short-sighted world ; as a false jewel amongst true ones is not discerned at a distance. His company is as troublesome to us as a cuckold's when you have a mind to his wife's.

Har. No, the rogue will not let us enjoy one another, but ravishes our conversation ; though he signifies no more to't than Sir Martin Mar-all's[1] gaping, and awkward thrumming upon the lute, does to his man's voice and music.

Dor. And to pass for a wit in town shows himself a fool every night to us, that are guilty of the plot.

Horn. Such wits as he are, to a company of reasonable men, like rooks to the gamesters ; who only fill a room at the table, but are so far from contributing to the play, that they only serve to spoil the fancy of those that do.

Dor. Nay, they are used like rooks too, snubbed, checked, and abused ; yet the rogues will hang on.

Horn. A pox on 'em, and all that force nature, and would be still what she forbids 'em ! Affectation is her greatest monster.

Har. Most men are the contraries to that they would seem. Your bully, you see, is a coward with a long sword ; the little humbly-fawning physician, with his ebony cane, is he that destroys men.

Dor. The usurer, a poor rogue, possessed of mouldy bonds and mortgages ; and we they call spendthrifts, are only wealthy, who lay out his money upon daily new purchases of pleasure.

Horn. Ay, your arrantest cheat is your trustee or executor ; your jealous man, the greatest cuckold ; your

---

[1] *Sir Martin Mar-all* is the title of a comedy by Dryden, first produced in 1667. In the scene referred to, Sir Martin serenades his mistress, going through the motions of singing and accompanying himself with the lute, while the actual performance is that of his man, who is concealed behind him. The lady discovers the imposition, through Sir Martin's failing to leave off at the right time.

churchman the greatest atheist; and your noisy pert rogue of a wit, the greatest fop, dullest ass, and worst company, as you shall see; for here he comes.

Enter SPARKISH.

Spark. How is't, sparks? how is't? Well, faith, Harry, I must rally thee a little, ha! ha! ha! upon the report in town of thee, ha! ha! ha! I can't hold i'faith; shall I speak?

Horn. Yes; but you'll be so bitter then.

Spark. Honest Dick and Frank here shall answer for me; I will not be extreme bitter, by the universe.

Har. We will be bound in a ten thousand pound bond, he shall not be bitter at all.

Dor. Nor sharp, nor sweet.

Horn. What, not downright insipid?

Spark. Nay then, since you are so brisk, and provoke me, take what follows. You must know, I was discoursing and rallying with some ladies yesterday, and they happened to talk of the fine new signs in town—

Horn. Very fine ladies, I believe.

Spark. Said I, I know where the best new sign is.— Where? says one of the ladies.—In Covent-Garden, I replied.—Said another, In what street?—In Russel-street, answered I.—Lord, says another, I'm sure there was never a fine new sign there yesterday.—Yes, but there was, said I again; and it came out of France, and has been there a fortnight.

Dor. A pox! I can hear no more, prithee.

Horn. No, hear him out; let him tune his crowd a while.

Har. The worst music, the greatest preparation.

Spark. Nay, faith, I'll make you laugh.—It cannot be, says a third lady.—Yes, yes, quoth I again.—Says a fourth lady—

Horn. Look to't, we'll have no more ladies.

Spark. No—then mark, mark, now. Said I to the

fourth, Did you never see Mr. Horner? he lodges in Russel-street, and he's a sign of a man, you know, since he came out of France; ha! ha! ha!

Horn. But the devil take me if thine be the sign of a jest.

Spark. With that they all fell a-laughing, till they be-pissed themselves. What, but it does not move you, me-thinks? Well, I see one had as good go to law without a witness, as break a jest without a laugher on one's side. —Come, come, sparks, but where do we dine? I have left at Whitehall an earl, to dine with you.

Dor. Why, I thought thou hadst loved a man with a title, better than a suit with a French trimming to't.

Har. Go to him again.

Spark. No, sir, a wit to me is the greatest title in the world.

Horn. But go dine with your earl, sir; he may be ex-ceptious. We are your friends, and will not take it ill to be left, I do assure you.

Har. Nay, faith, he shall go to him.

Spark. Nay, pray, gentlemen.

Dor. We'll thrust you out, if you won't; what, dis-appoint anybody for us?

Spark. Nay, dear gentlemen, hear me.

Horn. No, no, sir, by no means; pray go, sir.

Spark. Why, dear rogues—

Dor. No, no.   [*They all thrust him out of the room.*

All. Ha! ha! ha!

Re-enter SPARKISH.

Spark. But, sparks, pray hear me. What, d'ye think I'll eat then with gay shallow fops and silent coxcombs? I think wit as necessary at dinner, as a glass of good wine; and that's the reason I never have any stomach when I eat alone.—Come, but where do we dine?

Horn. Even where you will.

Spark. At Chateline's?

Dor. Yes, if you will.

Spark. Or at the Cock?

Dor. Yes, if you please.

Spark. Or at the Dog and Partridge?

Horn. Ay, if you have a mind to't; for we shall dine at neither.

Spark. Pshaw! with your fooling we shall lose the new play; and I would no more miss seeing a new play the first day, than I would miss sitting in the wit's row. Therefore I'll go fetch my mistress, and away.   [*Exit.*

Enter PINCHWIFE.

Horn. Who have we here? Pinchwife?

Pinch. Gentlemen, your humble servant.

Horn. Well, Jack, by thy long absence from the town, the grumness of thy countenance, and the slovenliness of thy habit, I should give thee joy, should I not, of marriage?

Pinch. [*Aside.*] Death! does he know I'm married too? I thought to have concealed it from him at least. —[*Aloud.*] My long stay in the country will excuse my dress; and I have a suit of law that brings me up to town, that puts me out of humour. Besides, I must give Sparkish to-morrow five thousand pounds to lie with my sister.

Horn. Nay, you country gentlemen, rather than not purchase, will buy anything; and he is a cracked title, if we may quibble. Well, but am I to give thee joy? I heard thou wert married.

Pinch. What then?

Horn. Why, the next thing that is to be heard, is, thou'rt a cuckold.

¹ Chatelain's was a famous French ordinary in Covent Garden, much frequented by wits and men of fashion. It is mentioned by Pepys, and often referred to by Shadwell in his plays. The Cock Tavern was in Bow Street, near where Wycherley and his first wife, the Countess of Droghtda, lodged; and it was here that the windows had to be left open when Wycherley frequented it, that the countess might see there were no ladies in the company.

Pinch. Insupportable name !   [*Aside.*

Horn. But I did not expect marriage from such a whoremaster as you; one that knew the town so much, and women so well.

Pinch. Why, I have married no London wife.

Horn. Pshaw ! that's all one. That grave circumspection in marrying a country wife, is like refusing a deceitful pampered Smithfield jade, to go and be cheated by a friend in the country.

Pinch. [*Aside.*] A pox on him and his simile !—[*Aloud.*] At least we are a little surer of the breed there, know what her keeping has been, whether foiled or unsound.

Horn. Come, come, I have known a clap gotten in Wales ; and there are cousins, justices' clerks, and chaplains in the country, I won't say coachmen. But she's handsome and young?

Pinch. [*Aside.*] I'll answer as I should do.—[*Aloud.*] No, no; she has no beauty but her youth, no attraction but her modesty: wholesome, homely, and huswifely; that's all.

Dor. He talks as like a grazier as he looks.

Pinch. She's too awkward, ill-favoured, and silly to bring to town.

Har. Then methinks you should bring her to be taught breeding.

Pinch. To be taught ! no, sir, I thank you. Good wives and private soldiers should be ignorant—I'll keep her from your instructions, I warrant you.

Har. The rogue is as jealous as if his wife were not ignorant.   [*Aside.*

Horn. Why, if she be ill-favoured, there will be less danger here for you than by leaving her in the country. We have such variety of dainties that we are seldom hungry.

Dor. But they have always coarse, constant, swingeing stomachs in the country.

Har. Foul feeders indeed !

Dor. And your hospitality is great there.

Har. Open house; every man's welcome.

Pinch. So, so, gentlemen.

Horn. But prithee, why shouldst thou marry her? If she be ugly, ill-bred, and silly, she must be rich then.

Pinch. As rich as if she brought me twenty thousand pound out of this town; for she'll be as sure not to spend her moderate portion, as a London baggage would be to spend hers, let it be what it would: so 'tis all one. Then, because she's ugly, she's the likelier to be my own; and being ill-bred, she'll hate conversation; and since silly and innocent, will not know the difference betwixt a man of one-and-twenty and one of forty.

Horn. Nine—to my knowledge. But if she be silly, she'll expect as much from a man of forty-nine, as from him of one-and-twenty. But methinks wit is more necessary than beauty; and I think no young woman ugly that has it, and no handsome woman agreeable without it.

Pinch. 'Tis my maxim, he's a fool that marries; but he's a greater that does not marry a fool. What is wit in a wife good for, but to make a man a cuckold?

Horn. Yes, to keep it from his knowledge.

Pinch. A fool cannot contrive to make her husband a cuckold.

Horn. No; but she'll club with a man that can: and what is worse, if she cannot make her husband a cuckold, she'll make him jealous, and pass for one: and then 'tis all one.

Pinch. Well, well, I'll take care for one. My wife shall make me no cuckold, though she had your help, Mr. Horner. I understand the town, sir.

Dor. His help!   [*Aside.*

Har. He's come newly to town, it seems, and has not heard how things are with him.   [*Aside.*

Horn. But tell me, has marriage cured thee of whoring, which it seldom does?

Har. 'Tis more than age can do.

Horn. No, the word is, I'll marry and live honest: but a marriage vow is like a penitent gamester's oath, and entering into bonds and penalties to stint himself to such a particular small sum at play for the future, which makes him but the more eager; and not being able to hold out, loses his money again, and his forfeit to boot.

Dor. Ay, ay, a gamester will be a gamester whilst his money lasts, and a whoremaster whilst his vigour.

Har. Nay, I have known 'em, when they are broke, and can lose no more, keep a fumbling with the box in their hands to fool with only, and hinder other gamesters.

Dor. That had wherewithal to make lusty stakes.

Pinch. Well, gentlemen, you may laugh at me; but you shall never lie with my wife: I know the town.

Horn. But prithee, was not the way you were in better? is not keeping better than marriage?

Pinch. A pox on't! the jades would jilt me, I could never keep a whore to myself.

Horn. So, then you only married to keep a whore to yourself. Well, but let me tell you, women, as you say, are like soldiers, made constant and loyal by good pay, rather than by oaths and covenants. Therefore I'd advise my friends to keep rather than marry, since too I find, by your example, it does not serve one's turn; for I saw you yesterday in the eighteenpenny place with a pretty country-wench.

Pinch. How the devil! did he see my wife then? I sat there that she might not be seen. But she shall never go to a play again. [*Aside.*

Horn. What! dost thou blush, at nine-and-forty, for having been seen with a wench?

Dor. No, faith, I warrant 'twas his wife, which he seated there out of sight; for he's a cunning rogue, and understands the town.

Har. He blushes. Then 'twas his wife; for men are now more ashamed to be seen with them in public than with a wench.

Pinch. Hell and damnation! I'm undone, since Horner has seen her, and they know 'twas she.

[*Aside.*

Horn. But prithee, was it thy wife? She was exceeding pretty : I was in love with her at that distance.

Pinch. You are like never to be nearer to her. Your servant, gentlemen.   [*Offers to go.*

Horn. Nay, prithee stay.

Pinch. I cannot; I will not.

Horn. Come, you shall dine with us.

Pinch. I have dined already.

Horn. Come, I know thou hast not : I'll treat thee, dear rogue ; thou sha't spend none of thy Hampshire money to-day.

Pinch. Treat me! So, he uses me already like his cuckold.   [*Aside.*

Horn. Nay, you shall not go.

Pinch. I must ; I have business at home.   [*Exit.*

Har. To beat his wife. He's as jealous of her, as a Cheapside husband of a Covent-garden wife.

Horn. Why, 'tis as hard to find an old whoremaster without jealousy and the gout, as a young one without fear, or the pox :—

As gout in age from pox in youth proceeds,

So wenching past, then jealousy succeeds ;

The worst disease that love and wenching breeds.

[*Exeunt.*

ACT THE SECOND.

SCENE I.—*A Room in* PINCHWIFE'S *House.*

Mrs. MARGERY PINCHWIFE *and* ALITHEA. PINCHWIFE
peeping behind at the door.

RS. PINCH. Pray, sister, where are the
best fields and woods to walk in, in
London?

Alith. [*Aside.*] A pretty question!
—[*Aloud.*] Why, sister, Mulberry-
garden and St. James's-park; and, for
close walks, the New Exchange.[1]

Mrs. Pinch. Pray, sister, tell me why my husband
looks so grum here in town, and keeps me up so close,
and will not let me go a-walking, nor let me wear my best
gown yesterday.

Alith. O, he's jealous, sister.

Mrs. Pinch. Jealous! what's that?

Alith. He's afraid you should love another man.

Mrs. Pinch. How should he be afraid of my loving
another man, when he will not let me see any but
himself?

Alith. Did he not carry you yesterday to a play?

Mrs. Pinch. Ay; but we sat amongst ugly people.
He would not let me come near the gentry, who sat under
us, so that I could not see 'em. He told me, none but
naughty women sat there, whom they toused and moused.
But I would have ventured, for all that.

---

[1] See note, *ante*, p. 48.

Alith. But how did you like the play ?

Mrs. Pinch. Indeed I was weary of the play; but I liked hugeously the actors. They are the goodliest, properest men, sister !

Alith. O, but you must not like the actors, sister.

Mrs. Pinch. Ay, how should I help it, sister ? Pray, sister, when my husband comes in, will you ask leave for me to go a-walking ?

Alith. A-walking ! ha ! ha ! Lord, a country-gentle-woman's pleasure is the drudgery of a footpost ; and she requires as much airing as her husband's horses.—[*Aside.*] But here comes your husband : I'll ask, though I'm sure he'll not grant it.

Mrs. Pinch. He says he won't let me go abroad for fear of catching the pox.

Alith. Fy ! the small-pox you should say.

Enter PINCHWIFE.

Mrs. Pinch. O my dear, dear bud, welcome home ! Why dost thou look so fropish ? who has nangered thee ?

Pinch. You're a fool.

[*Mrs.* PINCHWIFE *goes aside, and cries.*

Alith. Faith, so she is, for crying for no fault, poor tender creature !

Pinch. What, you would have her as impudent as yourself, as arrant a jilflirt, a gadder, a magpie ; and to say all, a mere notorious town-woman?

Alith. Brother, you are my only censurer ; and the honour of your family will sooner suffer in your wife there than in me, though I take the innocent liberty of the town.

Pinch. Hark you, mistress, do not talk so before my wife.—The innocent liberty of the town !

Alith. Why, pray, who boasts of any intrigue with me ? what lampoon has made my name notorious ? what ill women frequent my lodgings? I keep no company with any women of scandalous reputations.

Pinch. No, you keep the men of scandalous reputations company.

Alith. Where? would you not have me civil? answer 'em in a box at the plays, in the drawing-room at Whitehall, in St. James'-park, Mulberry-garden, or—

Pinch. Hold, hold! Do not teach my wife where the men are to be found: I believe she's the worse for your town-documents already. I bid you keep her in ignorance, as I do

Mrs. Pinch. Indeed, be not angry with her, bud, she will tell me nothing of the town, though I ask her a thousand times a day.

Pinch. Then you are very inquisitive to know, I find?

Mrs. Pinch. Not I indeed, dear; I hate London. Our place-house in the country is worth a thousand of't: would I were there again!

Pinch. So you shall, I warrant. But were you not talking of plays and players when I came in?— [*To* ALITHEA.] You are her encourager in such discourses.

Mrs. Pinch. No, indeed, dear; she chid me just now for liking the playermen.

Pinch. [*Aside.*] Nay, if she be so innocent as to own to me her liking them, there is no hurt in't.—[*Aloud.*] Come, my poor rogue, but thou likest none better than me?

Mrs. Pinch. Yes, indeed, but I do. The playermen are finer folks.

Pinch. But you love none better than me?

Mrs. Pinch. You are my own dear bud, and I know you. I hate a stranger.

Pinch. Ay, my dear, you must love me only; and not be like the naughty town-women, who only hate their husbands, and love every man else; love plays, visits, fine coaches, fine clothes, fiddles, balls, treats, and so lead a wicked town-life.

Mrs. Pinch. Nay, if to enjoy all these things be a town-life, London is not so bad a place, dear.

Pinch. How! if you love me, you must hate London.

Alith. The fool has forbid me discovering to her the pleasures of the town, and he is now setting her agog upon them himself.   [*Aside.*

Mrs. Pinch. But, husband, do the town-women love the playermen too?

Pinch. Yes, I warrant you.

Mrs. Pinch. Ay, I warrant you.

Pinch. Why, you do not, I hope?

Mrs. Pinch. No, no, bud. But why have we no player-men in the country?

Pinch. Ha!—Mrs. Minx, ask me no more to go to a play.

Mrs. Pinch. Nay, why, love? I did not care for going: but when you forbid me, you make me, as 'twere, desire it

Alith. So 'twill be in other things, I warrant.   [*Aside.*

Mrs. Pinch. Pray let me go to a play, dear.

Pinch. Hold your peace, I wo' not.

Mrs. Pinch. Why, love?

Pinch. Why, I'll tell you.

Alith. Nay, if he tell her, she'll give him more cause to forbid her that place.   [*Aside.*

Mrs. Pinch. Pray why, dear?

Pinch. First, you like the actors; and the gallants may like you.

Mrs. Pinch. What, a homely country girl! No, bud, nobody will like me.

Pinch. I tell you yes, they may.

Mrs. Pinch. No, no, you jest—I won't believe you: I will go.

Pinch. I tell you then, that one of the lewdest fellows in town, who saw you there, told me he was in love with you.

Mrs. Pinch. Indeed! who, who, pray who was't?

Pinch. I've gone too far, and slipped before I was aware ; how overjoyed she is ! [*Aside.*

Mrs. Pinch. Was it any Hampshire gallant, any of our neighbours ? I promise you, I am beholden to him.

Pinch. I promise you, you lie ; for he would but ruin you, as he has done hundreds. He has no other love for women but that ; such as he look upon women, like basilisks, but to destroy 'em.

Mrs. Pinch. Ay, but if he loves me, why should he ruin me ? answer me to that. Methinks he should not, I would do him no harm.

Alith. Ha ! ha ! ha !

Pinch. 'Tis very well ; but I'll keep him from doing you any harm, or me either. But here comes company ; get you in, get you in.

Mrs. Pinch. But, pray, husband, is he a pretty gentleman that loves me ?

Pinch. In, baggage, in.

[*Thrusts her in, and shuts the door.*

Enter SPARKISH *and* HARCOURT.

What, all the lewd libertines of the town brought to my lodging by this easy coxcomb ! 'sdeath, I'll not suffer it.

Spark. Here, Harcourt, do you approve my choice ?— [*To* ALITHEA.] Dear little rogue, I told you I'd bring you acquainted with all my friends, the wits and—

[HARCOURT *salutes her.*

Pinch. Ay, they shall know her, as well as you yourself will, I warrant you.

Spark. This is one of those, my pretty rogue, that are to dance at your wedding to-morrow ; and him you must bid welcome ever, to what you and I have.

Pinch. Monstrous ! [*Aside.*

Spark. Harcourt, how dost thou like her, faith ? Nay, dear, do not look down ; I should hate to have a wife of mine out of countenance at anything.

Pinch. Wonderful ! [*Aside.*

Spark. Tell me, I say, Harcourt, how dost thou like her? Thou hast stared upon her enough, to resolve me.

Har. So infinitely well, that I could wish I had a mistress too, that might differ from her in nothing but her love and engagement to you.

Alith. Sir, Master Sparkish has often told me that his acquaintance were all wits and raillieurs, and now I find it.

Spark. No, by the universe, madam, he does not rally now; you may believe him. I do assure you, he is the honestest, worthiest, true-hearted gentlemen—a man of such perfect honour, he would say nothing to a lady he does not mean.

Pinch. Praising another man to his mistress! [*Aside.*

Har. Sir, you are so beyond expectation obliging, that—

Spark. Nay, egad, I am sure you do admire her extremely; I see't in your eyes.—He does admire you, madam.—By the world, don't you?

Har. Yes, above the world, or the most glorious part of it, her whole sex: and till now I never thought I should have envied you, or any man about to marry, but you have the best excuse for marriage I ever knew.

Alith. Nay, now, sir, I'm satisfied you are of the society of the wits and raillieurs, since you cannot spare your friend, even when he is but too civil to you; but the surest sign is, since you are an enemy to marriage,—for that I hear you hate as much as business or bad wine.

Har. Truly, madam, I was never an enemy to marriage till now, because marriage was never an enemy to me before.

Alith. But why, sir, is marriage an enemy to you now? because it robs you of your friend here? for you look upon a friend married, as one gone into a monastery, that is, dead to the world.

Har. 'Tis indeed, because you marry him ; I see, madam, you can guess my meaning. I do confess heartily and openly, I wish it were in my power to break the match ; by Heavens I would.

Spark. Poor Frank !

Alith. Would you be so unkind to me ?

Har. No, no, 'tis not because I would be unkind to you.

Spark. Poor Frank ! no gad, 'tis only his kindness to me.

Pinch. Great kindness to you indeed ! Insensible fop, let a man make love to his wife to his face !   [*Aside.*

Spark. Come, dear Frank, for all my wife there, that shall be, thou shalt enjoy me sometimes, dear rogue. By my honour, we men of wit condole for our deceased brother in marriage, as much as for one dead in earnest : I think that was prettily said of me, ha, Harcourt ?—But come, Frank, be not melancholy for me.

Har. No, I assure you, I am not melancholy for you.

Spark. Prithee, Frank, dost think my wife that shall be there, a fine person ?

Har. I could gaze upon her till I became as blind as you are.

Spark. How as I am ? how ?

Har. Because you are a lover, and true lovers are blind, stock blind.

Spark. True, true ; but by the world she has wit too, as well as beauty : go, go with her into a corner, and try if she has wit ; talk to her anything, she's bashful before me.

Har. Indeed if a woman wants wit in a corner, she has it nowhere.

Alith. Sir, you dispose of me a little before your time—   [*Aside to* SPARKISH.

Spark. Nay, nay, madam, let me have an earnest of your obedience, or—go, go, madam—

[HARCOURT *courts* ALITHEA *aside.*

Pinch. How, sir! if you are not concerned for the
honour of a wife, I am for that of a sister; he shall not
debauch her. Be a pander to your own wife! bring men
to her! let 'em make love before your face! thrust 'em
into a corner together, then leave 'em in private! is this
your town wit and conduct?

Spark. Ha! ha! ha! a silly wise rogue would make
one laugh more than a stark fool, ha! ha! I shall burst.
Nay, you shall not disturb 'em; I'll vex thee, by the world.

[*Struggles with* PINCHWIFE *to keep him from* HAR-
COURT *and* ALITHEA.

Alith. The writings are drawn, sir, settlements made;
'tis too late, sir, and past all revocation.

Har. Then so is my death.

Alith. I would not be unjust to him.

Har. Then why to me so?

Alith. I have no obligation to you.

Har. My love.

Alith. I had his before.

Har. You never had it; he wants, you see, jealousy,
the only infallible sign of it.

Alith. Love proceeds from esteem; he cannot distrust
my virtue: besides, he loves me, or he would not marry
me.

Har. Marrying you is no more sign of his love than
bribing your woman, that he may marry you, is a sign of
his generosity. Marriage is rather a sign of interest than
love; and he that marries a fortune covets a mistress, not
loves her. But if you take marriage for a sign of love,
take it from me immediately.

Alith. No, now you have put a scruple in my head;
but in short, sir, to end our dispute, I must marry him.
my reputation would suffer in the world else.

Har. No; if you do marry him, with your pardon,
madam, your reputation suffers in the world, and you
would be thought in necessity for a cloak.

Alith. Nay, now you are rude, sir.—Mr. Sparkish,

·pray come hither, your friend here is very troublesome, and very loving.

Har. Hold! hold!—   [*Aside to* ALITHEA.

Pinch. D'ye hear that?

Spark. Why, d'ye think I'll seem to be jealous, like a country bumpkin?

Pinch. No, rather be a cuckold, like a credulous cit.

Har. Madam, you would not have been so little generous as to have told him.

Alith. Yes, since you could be so little generous as to wrong him.

Har. Wrong him! no man can do't, he's beneath an injury: a bubble, a coward, a senseless idiot, a wretch so contemptible to all the world but you, that—

Alith. Hold, do not rail at him, for since he is like to be my husband, I am resolved to like him: nay, I think I am obliged to tell him you are not his friend.—Master Sparkish, Master Sparkish!

Spark. What, what?—[*To* HARCOURT.] Now, dear rogue, has not she wit?

Har. Not so much as I thought, and hoped she had.

        [*Speaks surlily.*

Alith. Mr. Sparkish, do you bring people to rail at you?

Har. Madam—

Spark. How! no; but if he does rail at me, 'tis but in jest, I warrant: what we wits do for one another, and never take any notice of it.

Alith. He spoke so scurrilously of you, I had no patience to hear him; besides, he has been making love to me.

Har. True, damned tell-tale woman!   [*Aside.*

Spark. Pshaw! to show his parts—we wits rail and make love often, but to show our parts: as we have no affections, so we have no malice, we—

Alith. He said you were a wretch below an injury—

Spark. Pshaw!

Har. Damned, senseless, impudent, virtuous jade!

Well, since she won't let me have her, she'll do as good, she'll make me hate her. [*Aside.*

Alith. A common bubble—

Spark. Pshaw !

Alith. A coward—

Spark. Pshaw, pshaw !

Alith. A senseless, drivelling idiot—

Spark. How ! did he disparage my parts ? Nay, then, my honour's concerned, I can't put up that, sir, by the world—brother, help me to kill him—[*Aside*] I may draw now, since we have the odds of him :—'tis a good occasion, too, before my mistress— [*Offers to draw.*

Alith. Hold, hold !

Spark. What, what ?

Alith. [*Aside.*] I must not let 'em kill the gentleman neither, for his kindness to me : I am so far from hating him, that I wish my gallant had his person and understanding. Nay, if my honour—

Spark. I'll be thy death.

Alith. Hold, hold ! Indeed, to tell the truth, the gentleman said after all, that what he spoke was but out of friendship to you.

Spark. How ! say, I am, I am a fool, that is, no wit, out of friendship to me ?

Alith. Yes, to try whether I was concerned enough for you ; and made love to me only to be satisfied of my virtue, for your sake.

Har. Kind, however. [*Aside.*

Spark. Nay, if it were so, my dear rogue, I ask thee pardon ; but why would not you tell me so, faith ?

Har. Because I did not think on't, faith.

Spark. Come, Horner does not come ; Harcourt, let's be gone to the new play.—Come, madam.

Alith. I will not go, if you intend to leave me alone in the box, and run into the pit, as you use to do.

Spark. Pshaw ! I'll leave Harcourt with you in the box to entertain you, and that's as good ; if I sat in the

box, I should be thought no judge but of trimmings.—
Come away, Harcourt, lead her down.

　　　　　[*Exeunt* SPARKISH, HARCOURT, *and* ALITHEA.

　Pinch. Well, go thy ways, for the flower of the true
town fops, such as spend their estates before they come
to 'em, and are cuckolds before they're married. But
let me go look to my own freehold.—How!

Enter Lady FIDGET, Mrs. DAINTY FIDGET, *and* Mrs.
SQUEAMISH.

　Lady Fid. Your servant, sir : where is your lady? We
are come to wait upon her to the new play.

　Pinch. New play!

　Lady Fid. And my husband will wait upon you
presently.

　Pinch. [*Aside.*] Damn your civility.—[*Aloud.*] Madam,
by no means ; I will not see Sir Jasper here, till I have
waited upon him at home ; nor shall my wife see you till
she has waited upon your ladyship at your lodgings.

　Lady Fid. Now we are here, sir?

　Pinch. No, Madam.

　Mrs. Dain. Pray, let us see her.

　Mrs. Squeam. We will not stir till we see her.

　Pinch. [*Aside.*] A pox on you all!—[*Goes to the door,
and returns.*] She has locked the door, and is gone
abroad.

　Lady Fid. No, you have locked the door, and she's
within.

　Mrs. Dain. They told us below she was here.

　Pinch. [*Aside.*] Will nothing do?—[*Aloud.*] Well, it
must out then. To tell you the truth, ladies, which I was
afraid to let you know before, lest it might endanger your
lives, my wife has just now the small-pox come out upon
her ; do not be frightened ; but pray be gone, ladies ;
you shall not stay here in danger of your lives ; pray get
you gone, ladies.

　Lady Fid. No, no, we have all had 'em.

Mrs. Squeam. Alack, alack !

Mrs. Dain. Come, come, we must see how it goes with her; I understand the disease.

Lady Fid. Come !

Pinch. [*Aside.*] Well, there is no being too hard for women at their own weapon, lying, therefore I'll quit the field.   [*Exit.*

Mrs. Squeam. Here's an example of jealousy !

Lady Fid. Indeed, as the world goes, I wonder there are no more jealous, since wives are so neglected.

Mrs. Dain. Pshaw ! as the world goes, to what end should they be jealous ?

Lady Fid. Foh ! 'tis a nasty world.

Mrs. Squeam. That men of parts, great acquaintance, and quality, should take up with and spend themselves and fortunes in keeping little playhouse creatures, foh !

Lady Fid. Nay, that women of understanding, great acquaintance, and good quality, should fall a-keeping too of little creatures, foh !

Mrs. Squeam. Why, 'tis the men of quality's fault ; they never visit women of honour and reputation as they used to do ; and have not so much as common civility for ladies of our rank, but use us with the same indifferency and ill-breeding as if we were all married to 'em.

Lady Fid. She says true ; 'tis an arrant shame women of quality should be so slighted; methinks birth — birth should go for something; I have known men admired, courted, and followed for their titles only.

Mrs. Squeam. Ay, one would think men of honour should not love, no more than marry, out of their own rank.

Mrs. Dain. Fy, fy, upon 'em ! they are come to think cross breeding for themselves best, as well as for their dogs and horses.

Lady Fid. They are dogs and horses for't.

Mrs. Squeam. One would think, it not for love, for vanity a little.

Mrs. Dain. Nay, they do satisfy their vanity upon us sometimes; and are kind to us in their report, tell all the world they lie with us.

Lady Fid. Damned rascals, that we should be only wronged by 'em! To report a man has had a person, when he has not had a person, is the greatest wrong in the whole world that can be done to a person.

Mrs. Squeam. Well, 'tis an arrant shame noble persons should be so wronged and neglected.

Lady Fid. But still 'tis an arranter shame for a noble person to neglect her own honour, and defame her own noble person with little inconsiderable fellows, foh!

Mrs. Dain. I suppose the crime against our honour is the same with a man of quality as with another.

Lady Fid. How! no sure, the man of quality is likest one's husband, and therefore the fault should be the less.

Mrs. Dain. But then the pleasure should be the less.

Lady Fid. Fy, fy, fy, for shame, sister! whither shall we ramble? Be continent in your discourse, or I shall hate you.

Mrs. Dain. Besides, an intrigue is so much the more notorious for the man's quality.

Mrs. Squeam. 'Tis true that nobody takes notice of a private man, and therefore with him 'tis more secret; and the crime's the less when 'tis not known.

Lady Fid. You say true; i'faith, I think you are in the right on't: 'tis not an injury to a husband, till it be an injury to our honours; so that a woman of honour loses no honour with a private person; and to say truth—

Mrs. Dain. So, the little fellow is grown a private person —with her— [*Apart to* Mrs. SQUEAMISH.

Lady Fid. But still my dear, dear honour—

Enter Sir JASPER FIDGET, HORNER, *and* DORILANT.

Sir Jasp. Ay, my dear, dear of honour, thou hast still so much honour in thy mouth—

Horn. That she has none elsewhere. [*Aside.*

Wycherley

L*

Lady Fid. Oh, what d'ye mean to bring in these upon us ?

Mrs. Dain. Foh! these are as bad as wits.

Mrs. Squeam. Foh !

Lady Fid. Let us leave the room.

Sir Jasp. Stay, stay; faith, to tell you the naked truth—

Lady Fid. Fy, Sir Jasper! do not use that word naked.

Sir Jasp. Well, well, in short I have business at White-hall, and cannot go to the play with you, therefore would have you go—

Lady Fid. With those two to a play ?

Sir Jasp. No, not with t'other, but with Mr. Horner; there can be no more scandal to go with him than with Mr. Tattle, or Master Limberham.

Lady Fid. With that nasty fellow ! no—no.

Sir Jasp. Nay, prithee, dear, hear me.

[*Whispers to* Lady FIDGET.

Horn. Ladies—

[HORNER *and* DORILANT *draw near* Mrs. SQUEAMISH *and* Mrs. DAINTY FIDGET.

Mrs. Dain. Stand off.

Mrs. Squeam. Do not approach us.

Mrs. Dain. You herd with the wits, you are obscenity all over.

Mrs. Squeam. And I would as soon look upon a picture of Adam and Eve, without fig-leaves, as any of you, if I could help it; therefore keep off, and do not make us sick.

Dor. What a devil are these ?

Horn. Why, these are pretenders to honour, as critics to wit, only by censuring others; and as every raw, peevish, out-of-humoured, affected, dull, tea-drinking, arithmetical fop, sets up for a wit by railing at men of sense, so these for honour, by railing at the court, and ladies of as great honour as quality.

Sir Jasp. Come, Mr. Horner, I must desire you to go with these ladies to the play, sir.

Horn. I, sir?

Sir Jasp. Ay, ay, come, sir.

Horn. I must beg your pardon, sir, and theirs; I will not be seen in women's company in public again for the world.

Sir Jasp. Ha, ha, strange aversion!

Mrs. Squeam. No, he's for women's company in private.

Sir Jasp. He—poor man—he—ha! ha! ha!

Mrs. Dain. 'Tis a greater shame amongst lewd fellows to be seen in virtuous women's company, than for the women to be seen with them.

Horn. Indeed, madam, the time was I only hated virtuous women, but now I hate the other too; I beg your pardon, ladies.

Lady Fid. You are very obliging, sir, because we would not be troubled with you.

Sir Jasp. In sober sadness, he shall go.

Dor. Nay, if he wo' not, I am ready to wait upon the ladies, and I think I am the fitter man.

Sir Jasp. You sir! no, I thank you for that.   Master Horner is a privileged man amongst the virtuous ladies, 'twill be a great while before you are so; he! he! he! he's my wife's gallant; he! he! he! No, pray withdraw, sir, for as I take it, the virtuous ladies have no business with you.

Dor. And I am sure he can have none with them. 'Tis strange a man can't come amongst virtuous women now, but upon the same terms as men are admitted into the Great Turk's seraglio.   But heavens keep me from being an ombre player with 'em!—But where is Pinchwife?

[*Exit.*

Sir Jasp. Come, come, man; what, avoid the sweet society of womankind? that sweet, soft, gentle, tame, noble creature, woman, made for man's companion—

Horn. So is that soft, gentle, tame, and more noble creature a spaniel, and has all their tricks ; can fawn, lie down, suffer beating, and fawn the more ; barks at your friends when they come to see you, makes your bed hard, gives you fleas, and the mange sometimes. And all the difference is, the spaniel's the more faithful animal, and fawns but upon one master.

Sir Jasp. He ! he ! he !

Mrs. Squeam. O the rude beast !

Mrs. Dain. Insolent brute !

Lady Fid. Brute ! stinking, mortified, rotten French wether, to dare—

Sir Jasp. Hold, an't please your ladyship.—For shame, Master Horner ! your mother was a woman—[*Aside.*] Now shall I never reconcile 'em.—[*Aside to* Lady Fidget.] Hark you, madam, take my advice in your anger. You know you often want one to make up your drolling pack of ombre players, and you may cheat him easily ; for he's an ill gamester, and consequently loves play. Besides, you know you have but two old civil gentlemen (with stinking breaths too) to wait upon you abroad ; take in the third into your service. The other are but crazy ; and a lady should have a supernumerary gentleman-usher as a supernumerary coach-horse, lest sometimes you should be forced to stay at home.

Lady Fid. But are you sure he loves play, and has money ?

Sir Jasp. He loves play as much as you, and has money as much as I.

Lady Fid. Then I am contented to make him pay for his scurrility. Money makes up in a measure all other wants in men.—Those whom we cannot make hold for gallants, we make fine.   [*Aside.*

Sir Jasp. [*Aside.*] So, so ; now to mollify, wheedle him.—[*Aside to* Horner.] Master Horner, will you never keep civil company ? methinks 'tis time now, since you are only fit for them. Come, come, man, you must e'en fall to visiting our wives, eating at our tables, drinking tea with our virtuous relations after dinner, dealing cards to 'em, reading plays and gazettes to 'em, picking fleas out of their smocks for 'em, collecting receipts, new songs, women, pages, and footmen for 'em.

Horn. I hope they'll afford me better employment, sir.

Sir Jasp. He! he! he! 'tis fit you know your work before you come into your place. And since you are unprovided of a lady to flatter, and a good house to eat at, pray frequent mine, and call my wife mistress, and she shall call you gallant, according to the custom.

Horn. Who, I?

Sir Jasp. Faith, thou sha't for my sake; come, for my sake only.

Horn. For your sake—

Sir Jasp. Come, come, here's a gamester for you; let him be a little familiar sometimes; nay, what if a little rude? Gamesters may be rude with ladies, you know.

Lady Fid. Yes; losing gamesters have a privilege with women.

Horn. I always thought the contrary, that the winning gamester had most privilege with women; for when you have lost your money to a man, you'll lose anything you have, all you have, they say, and he may use you as he pleases.

Sir Jasp. He! he! he! well, win or lose, you shall have your liberty with her.

Lady Fid. As he behaves himself; and for your sake I'll give him admittance and freedom.

Horn. All sorts of freedom, madam?

Sir Jasp. Ay, ay, ay, all sorts of freedom thou canst take. And so go to her, begin thy new employment; wheedle her, jest with her, and be better acquainted one with another.

Horn. [*Aside.*] I think I know her already; therefore may venture with her my secret for hers.

[HORNER *and* Lady FIDGET *whisper.*

Sir Jasp. Sister cuz, I have provided an innocent play-fellow for you there.

Mrs. Dain. Who, he?

Mrs. Squeam. There's a playfellow, indeed!

Sir Jasp. Yes sure.—What, he is good enough to play at cards, blindman's-buff, or the fool with, sometimes!

Mrs. Squeam. Foh! we'll have no such playfellows.

Mrs. Dain. No, sir; you shan't choose playfellows for us, we thank you.

Sir Jasp. Nay, pray hear me.   [*Whispering to them.*

Lady Fid. But, poor gentleman, could you be so generous, so truly a man of honour, as for the sakes of us women of honour, to cause yourself to be reported no man? No man! and to suffer yourself the greatest shame that could fall upon a man, that none might fall upon us women by your conversation? but, indeed, sir, as perfectly, perfectly the same man as before your going into France, sir? as perfectly, perfectly, sir?

Horn. As perfectly, perfectly, madam. Nay, I scorn you should take my word; I desire to be tried only, madam.

Lady Fid. Well, that's spoken again like a man of honour: all men of honour desire to come to the test. But, indeed, generally you men report such things of yourselves, one does not know how or whom to believe; and it is come to that pass, we dare not take your words no more than your tailor's, without some staid servant of yours be bound with you. But I have so strong a faith in your honour, dear, dear, noble sir, that I'd forfeit mine for yours, at any time, dear sir.

Horn. No, madam, you should not need to forfeit it for me; I have given you security already to save you harmless, my late reputation being so well known in the world, madam.

Lady Fid. But if upon any future falling-out, or upon a suspicion of my taking the trust out of your hands, to employ some other, you yourself should betray your trust, dear sir? I mean, if you'll give me leave to speak obscenely, you might tell, dear sir.

Horn. If I did, nobody would believe me. The reputation of impotency is as hardly recovered again in the world as that of cowardice, dear madam.

Lady Fid. Nay, then, as one may say, you may do your worst, dear, dear sir.

Sir Jasp. Come, is your ladyship reconciled to him yet? have you agreed on matters? for I must be gone to Whitehall.

Lady Fid. Why, indeed, Sir Jasper, Master Horner is a thousand, thousand times a better man than I thought him. Cousin Squeamish, sister Dainty, I can name him now. Truly, not long ago, you know, I thought his very name obscenity; and I would as soon have lain with him as have named him.

Sir Jasp. Very likely, poor madam.

Mrs. Dain. I believe it.

Mrs. Squeam. No doubt on't.

Sir Jasp. Well, well—that your ladyship is as virtuous as any she, I know, and him all the town knows—he! he! he! therefore now you like him, get you gone to your business together, go, go to your business, I say, pleasure, whilst I go to my pleasure, business.

Lady Fid. Come, then, dear gallant.

Horn. Come away, my dearest mistress.

Sir Jasp. So, so; why, 'tis as I'd have it.   [*Exit.*

Horn. And as I'd have it.

Lady Fid. Who for his business from his wife will run,
Takes the best care to have her business done.
                                          [*Exeunt.*

ACT THE THIRD.

SCENE I.—*A Room in* PINCHWIFE'S *House.*

Enter ALITHEA *and* MRS. PINCHWIFE.

LITH. Sister, what ails you? you are grown melancholy.

Mrs. Pinch. Would it not make any one melancholy to see you go every day fluttering about abroad, whilst I must stay at home like a poor lonely sullen bird in a cage?

Alith. Ay, sister; but you came young, and just from the nest to your cage: so that I thought you liked it, and could be as cheerful in't as others that took their flight themselves early, and are hopping abroad in the open air.

Mrs. Pinch. Nay, I confess I was quiet enough till my husband told me what pure lives the London ladies live abroad, with their dancing, meetings, and junketings, and dressed every day in their best gowns; and I warrant you, play at nine-pins every day of the week, so they do.

Enter PINCHWIFE.

Pinch. Come, what's here to do? you are putting the town-pleasures in her head, and setting her a-longing.

Alith. Yes, after nine-pins. You suffer none to give her those longings you mean but yourself.

Pinch. I tell her of the vanities of the town like a confessor.

Alith. A confessor ! just such a confessor as he that, by forbidding a silly ostler to grease the horse's teeth, taught him to do't.

Pinch. Come, Mrs. Flippant, good precepts are lost when bad examples are still before us : the liberty you take abroad makes her hanker after it, and out of humour at home. Poor wretch ! she desired not to come to London ; I would bring her.

Alith. Very well.

Pinch. She has been this week in town, and never desired till this afternoon to go abroad.

Alith. Was she not at a play yesterday ?

Pinch. Yes ; but she ne'er asked me ; I was myself the cause of her going.

Alith. Then if she ask you again, you are the cause of her asking, and not my example.

Pinch. Well, to-morrow night I shall be rid of you ; and the next day, before 'tis light, she and I'll be rid of the town, and my dreadful apprehensions.—Come, be not melancholy ; for thou sha't go into the country after to-morrow, dearest.

Alith. Great comfort !

Mrs. Pinch. Pish ! what d'ye tell me of the country for ?

Pinch. How's this ! what, pish at the country ?

Mrs. Pinch. Let me alone ; I am not well.

Pinch. O, if that be all—what ails my dearest ?

Mrs. Pinch. Truly, I don't know : but I have not been well since you told me there was a gallant at the play in love with me.

Pinch. Ha !—

Alith. That's by my example too !

Pinch. Nay, if you are not well, but are so concerned, because a lewd fellow chanced to lie, and say he liked you, you'll make me sick too.

Mrs. Pinch. Of what sickness ?

Pinch. O, of that which is worse than the plague, jealousy.

Mrs. Pinch. Pish, you jeer! I'm sure there's no such disease in our receipt-book at home.

Pinch. No, thou never met'st with it, poor innocent.—Well, if thou cuckold me, 'twill be my own fault—for cuckolds and bastards are generally makers of their own fortune.   [*Aside.*

Mrs. Pinch. Well, but pray, bud, let's go to a play to-night.

Pinch. 'Tis just done, she comes from it.   But why are you so eager to see a play?

Mrs. Pinch. Faith, dear, not that I care one pin for their talk there; but I like to look upon the player-men, and would see, if I could, the gallant you say loves me: that's all, dear bud.

Pinch. Is that all, dear bud?

Alith. This proceeds from my example!

Mrs. Pinch. But if the play be done, let's go abroad, however, dear bud.

Pinch. Come have a little patience and thou shalt go into the country on Friday.

Mrs. Pinch. Therefore I would see first some sights to tell my neighbours of.   Nay, I will go abroad, that's once.

Alith. I'm the cause of this desire too!

Pinch. But now I think on't, who, who was the cause of Horner's coming to my lodgings to-day?   That was you.

Alith. No, you, because you would not let him see your handsome wife out of your lodging.

Mrs. Pinch. Why, O Lord! did the gentleman come hither to see me indeed?

Pinch. No, no.—You are not the cause of that damned question too, Mistress Alithea?—[*Aside.*] Well, she's in the right of it.   He is in love with my wife—and comes after her—'tis so—but I'll nip his love in the bud; lest he should follow us into the country, and break his chariot-wheel near our house, on purpose for an excuse to come to't.   But I think I know the town.

Mrs. Pinch. Come, pray, bud, let's go abroad before 'tis late; for I will go, that's flat and plain.

Pinch. [*Aside.*] So! the obstinacy already of the town-wife; and I must, whilst she's here, humour her like one. —[*Aloud.*] Sister, how shall we do, that she may not be seen, or known?

Alith. Let her put on her mask.

Pinch. Pshaw! a mask makes people but the more inquisitive, and is as ridiculous a disguise as a stage-beard: her shape, stature, habit will be known. And if we should meet with Horner, he would be sure to take acquaintance with us, must wish her joy, kiss her, talk to her, leer upon her, and the devil and all. No, I'll not use her to a mask, 'tis dangerous; for masks have made more cuckolds than the best faces that ever were known.

Alith. How will you do then?

Mrs. Pinch. Nay, shall we go? The Exchange will be shut, and I have a mind to see that.

Pinch. So—I have it—I'll dress her up in the suit we are to carry down to her brother, little Sir James; nay, I understand the town-tricks. Come, let's go dress her. A mask! no—a woman masked, like a covered dish, gives a man curiosity and appetite; when, it may be, uncovered, 'twould turn his stomach: no, no.

Alith. Indeed your comparison is something a greasy one: but I had a gentle gallant used to say, A beauty masked, like the sun in eclipse, gathers together more gazers than if it shined out. [*Exeunt.*

SCENE II.—*The New Exchange.*

Enter HORNER, HARCOURT, *and* DORILANT.

Dor. Engaged to women, and not sup with us!

Horn. Ay, a pox on 'em all!

Har. You were much a more reasonable man in the

morning, and had as noble resolutions against 'em, as a widower of a week's liberty.

Dor. Did I ever think to see you keep company with women in vain?

Horn. In vain : no—'tis since I can't love 'em, to be revenged on 'em.

Har. Now your sting is gone, you looked in the box amongst all those women like a drone in the hive ; all upon you, shoved and ill-used by 'em all, and thrust from one side to t'other.

Dor. Yet he must be buzzing amongst 'em still, like other beetle-headed liquorish drones. Avoid 'em, and hate 'em, as they hate you.

Horn. Because I do hate 'em, and would hate 'em yet more, I'll frequent 'em. You may see by marriage, nothing makes a man hate a woman more than her constant conversation. In short, I converse with 'em, as you do with rich fools, to laugh at 'em and use 'em ill.

Dor. But I would no more sup with women, unless I could lie with 'em, than sup with a rich coxcomb, unless I could cheat him.

Horn. Yes, I have known thee sup with a fool for his drinking ; if he could set out your hand that way only, you were satisfied, and if he were a wine-swallowing mouth, 'twas enough.

Har. Yes, a man drinks often with a fool, as he tosses with a marker, only to keep his hand in use. But do the ladies drink?

Horn. Yes, sir ; and I shall have the pleasure at least of laying 'em flat with a bottle, and bring as much scandal that way upon 'em as formerly t'other.

Har. Perhaps you may prove as weak a brother among 'em that way as t'other.

Dor. Foh! drinking with women is as unnatural as scolding with 'em. But 'tis a pleasure of decayed forni-cators, and the basest way of quenching love.

Har. Nay, 'tis drowning love, instead of quenching it. But leave us for civil women too !

Dor. Ay, when he can't be the better for 'em. We hardly pardon a man that leaves his friend for a wench, and that's a pretty lawful call.

Horn. Faith, I would not leave you for 'em, if they would not drink.

Dor. Who would disappoint his company at Lewis's for a gossiping ?

Har. Foh ! Wine and women, good apart, together are as nauseous as sack and sugar. But hark you, sir, before you go, a little of your advice; an old maimed general, when unfit for action, is fittest for counsel. I have other designs upon women than eating and drinking with them ; I am in love with Sparkish's mistress, whom he is to marry to-morrow : now how shall I get her ?

Enter SPARKISH, *looking about.*

Horn. Why, here comes one will help you to her.

Har. He ! he, I tell you, is my rival, and will hinder my love.

Horn. No ; a foolish rival and a jealous husband assist their rival's designs ; for they are sure to make their women hate them, which is the first step to their love for another man.

Har. But I cannot come near his mistress but in his company.

Horn. Still the better for you ; for fools are most easily cheated when they themselves are accessaries : and he is to be bubbled of his mistress as of his money, the common mistress, by keeping him company.

Spark. Who is that that is to be bubbled ? Faith, let me snack ; I han't met with a bubble since Christmas. 'Gad, I think bubbles are like their brother woodcocks, go out with the cold weather.

Har. A pox ! he did not hear all, I hope.

[*Apart to* HORNER.

Spark. Come, you bubbling rogues you, where do we sup?—Oh, Harcourt, my mistress tells me you have been making fierce love to her all the play long: ha! ha!—But I—

Har. I make love to her!

Spark. Nay, I forgive thee, for I think I know thee, and I know her; but I am sure I know myself.

Har. Did she tell you so? I see all women are like these of the Exchange; who, to enhance the prize of their commodities, report to their fond customers offers which were never made 'em.

Horn. Ay, women are apt to tell before the intrigue, as men after it, and so show themselves the vainer sex. But hast thou a mistress, Sparkish? 'Tis as hard for me to believe it, as that thou ever hadst a bubble, as you bragged just now.

Spark. O, your servant, sir: are you at your raillery, sir? But we are some of us beforehand with you to-day at the play. The wits were something bold with you, sir; did you not hear us laugh?

Horn. Yes; but I thought you had gone to plays, to laugh at the poet's wit, not at your own.

Spark. Your servant, sir: no, I thank you. 'Gad I go to a play as to a country treat; I carry my own wine to one, and my own wit to t'other, or else I'm sure I should not be merry at either. And the reason why we are so often louder than the players, is, because we think we speak more wit, and so become the poet's rivals in his audience: for to tell you the truth, we hate the silly rogues; nay, so much, that we find fault even with their bawdy upon the stage, whilst we talk nothing else in the pit as loud.

Horn. But why shouldst thou hate the silly poets? Thou hast too much wit to be one; and they, like whores, are only hated by each other: and thou dost scorn writing, I'm sure.

Spark. Yes; I'd have you to know I scorn writing:

but women, women, that make men do all foolish things, make 'em write songs too. Everybody does it. 'Tis even as common with lovers, as playing with fans ; and you can no more help rhyming to your Phillis, than drinking to your Phillis.

Har. Nay, poetry in love is no more to be avoided than jealousy.

Dor. But the poets damned your songs, did they ?

Spark. Damn the poets ! they have turned 'em into burlesque, as they call it. That burlesque is a hocus-pocus trick they have got, which, by the virtue of *Hictius doctius topsy turvy*, they make a wise and witty man in the world, a fool upon the stage you know not how : and 'tis therefore I hate 'em too, for I know not but it may be my own case ; for they'll put a man into a play for looking asquint. Their predecessors were contented to make serving-men only their stage-fools : but these rogues must have gentlemen, with a pox to 'em, nay, knights ; and, indeed, you shall hardly see a fool upon the stage but he's a knight. And to tell you the truth, they have kept me these six years from being a knight in earnest, for fear of being knighted in a play, and dubbed a fool.

Dor. Blame 'em not, they must follow their copy, the age.

Har. But why shouldst thou be afraid of being in a play, who expose yourself every day in the play-houses, and at public places ?

Horn. 'Tis but being on the stage, instead of standing on a bench in the pit.

Dor. Don't you give money to painters to draw you like ? and are you afraid of your pictures at length in a playhouse, where all your mistresses may see you ?

Spark. A pox ! painters don't draw the small-pox or pimples in one's face. Come, damn all your silly authors whatever, all books and booksellers, by the world ; and all readers, courteous or uncourteous !

Har. But who comes here, Sparkish ?

Enter PINCHWIFE *and* Mrs. PINCHWIFE *in man's clothes*,
ALITHEA *and* LUCY.

Spark. Oh, hide me ! There's my mistress too.

          [SPARKISH *hides himself behind* HARCOURT.

Har. She sees you.

Spark. But I will not see her. 'Tis time to go to
Whitehall, and I must not fail the drawing-room.

Har. Pray, first carry me, and reconcile me to her.

Spark. Another time. Faith, the king will have
supped.

Har. Not with the worse stomach for thy absence.
Thou art one of those fools that think their attendance
at the king's meals as necessary as his physicians, when
you are more troublesome to him than his doctors or his
dogs.

Spark. Pshaw ! I know my interest. sir. Prithee hide
me.

Horn. Your servant, Pinchwife.—What, he knows us
not !

Pinch. Come along.   [*To his* Wife *aside.*

Mrs. Pinch. Pray, have you any ballads ? give me six-
penny worth.

Bookseller. We have no ballads.

Mrs. Pinch. Then give me " Covent Garden Drollery,"
and a play or two—Oh, here's " Tarugo's Wiles," and
" The Slighted Maiden " ;[1] I'll have them.

Pinch. No ; plays are not for your reading. Come
along ; will you discover yourself ?   [*Apart to her.*

Horn. Who is that pretty youth with him, Sparkish ?

---

[1] " Covent Garden Drolery, Or a Colection of all the Choice
Songs, Poems, Prologues, and Epilogues (Sung and Spoken at
Courts and Theaters) never in Print before. Written by the re-
fined'st Witts of the Age. And Collected by R[ichard] B[rome]
Servant to His Majestie. London, Printed for James Magnes neer
the Piazza in Russel-Street, 1672."—*Tarugo's Wiles, or the Coffee
House ;* a comedy by Sir Thomas St. Serle, produced in 1668.—
The Slighted Maid, a comedy by Sir Robert Stapleton, produced in
1663.

Spark. I believe his wife's brother, because he's something like her : but I never saw her but once.

Horn. Extremely handsome ; I have seen a face like it too. Let us follow 'em.

> [*Exeunt* PINCHWIFE, MRS. PINCHWIFE, ALITHEA,
> *and* LUCY ; HORNER *and* DORILANT *following them.*

Har. Come, Sparkish, your mistress saw you, and will be angry you go not to her. Besides, I would fain be reconciled to her, which none but you can do, dear friend.

Spark. Well, that's a better reason, dear friend. I would not go near her now for her's or my own sake ; but I can deny you nothing : for though I have known thee a great while, never go, if I do not love thee as well as a new acquaintance.

Har. I am obliged to you indeed, dear friend. I would be well with her, only to be well with thee still ; for these ties to wives usually dissolve all ties to friends. I would be contented she should enjoy you a-nights, but I would have you to myself a-days as I have had, dear friend.

Spark. And thou shalt enjoy me a-days, dear, dear friend, never stir : and I'll be divorced from her, sooner than from thee. Come along.

Har. [*Aside.*] So, we are hard put to't, when we make our rival our procurer ; but neither she nor her brother would let me come near her now. When all's done, a rival is the best cloak to steal to a mistress under, without suspicion ; and when we have once got to her as we desire, we throw him off like other cloaks.

> [*Exit* SPARKISH, HARCOURT *following him.*

Re-enter PINCHWIFE *and* MRS. PINCHWIFE.

Pinch. [*To* ALITHEA.] Sister, if you will not go, we must leave you.—[*Aside.*] The fool her gallant and she will muster up all the young saunterers of this place, and they will leave their dear sempstresses to follow us. What a swarm of cuckolds and cuckold-makers are here!—Come, let's be gone, Mistress Margery.

Mrs. Pinch. Don't you believe that; I han't half my bellyfull of sights yet.

Pinch. Then walk this way.

Mrs. Pinch. Lord, what a power of brave signs are here! stay—the Bull's-Head, the Ram's-Head, and the Stag's-Head, dear—

Pinch. Nay, if every husband's proper sign here were visible, they would be all alike.

Mrs. Pinch. What d'ye mean by that, bud?

Pinch. 'Tis no matter—no matter, bud.

Mrs. Pinch. Pray tell me: nay, I will know.

Pinch. They would be all Bulls, Stags, and Rams-heads.   [*Exeunt* PINCHWIFE *and* Mrs. PINCHWIFE.

Re-enter SPARKISH, HARCOURT, ALITHEA, *and* LUCY, *at the other side.*

Spark. Come, dear madam, for my sake you shall be reconciled to him.

Alith. For your sake I hate him.

Har. That's something too cruel, madam, to hate me for his sake.

Spark. Ay indeed, madam, too, too cruel to me, to hate my friend for my sake.

Alith. I hate him because he is your enemy; and you ought to hate him too, for making love to me, if you love me.

Spark. That's a good one! I hate a man for loving you! If he did love you, 'tis but what he can't help; and 'tis your fault, not his, if he admires you. I hate a man for being of my opinion! I'll n'er do't, by the world.

Alith. Is it for your honour, or mine, to suffer a man to make love to me, who am to marry you to-morrow?

Spark. Is it for your honour, or mine, to have me jealous? That he makes love to you, is a sign you are handsome; and that I am not jealous, is a sign you are virtuous. That I think is for your honour.

Alith. But 'tis your honour too I am concerned for.

Har. But why, dearest madam, will you be more concerned for his honour than he is himself? Let his honour alone, for my sake and his. He! he has no honour—

Spark. How's that?

Har. But what my dear friend can guard himself.

Spark. O ho—that's right again.

Har. Your care of his honour argues his neglect of it, which is no honour to my dear friend here. Therefore once more, let his honour go which way it will, dear madam.

Spark. Ay, ay; were it for my honour to marry a woman whose virtue I suspected, and could not trust her in a friend's hands?

Alith. Are you not afraid to lose me?

Har. He afraid to lose you, madam! No, no—you may see how the most estimable and most glorious creature in the world is valued by him. Will you not see it?

Spark. Right, honest Frank, I have that noble value for her that I cannot be jealous of her.

Alith. You mistake him. He means, you care not for me, nor who has me.

Spark. Lord, madam, I see you are jealous! Will you wrest a poor man's meaning from his words?

Alith. You astonish me, sir, with your want of jealousy.

Spark. And you make me giddy, madam, with your jealousy and fears, and virtue and honour. 'Gad, I see virtue makes a woman as troublesome as a little reading or learning.

Alith. Monstrous!

Lucy. Well, to see what easy husbands these women of quality can meet with! a poor chambermaid can never have such ladylike luck. Besides, he's thrown away upon her. She'll make no use of her fortune, her blessing,

none to a gentleman, for a pure cuckold; for it requires good breeding to be a cuckold.   [*Aside.*

Alith. I tell you then plainly, he pursues me to marry me.

Spark. Pshaw!

Har. Come, madam, you see you strive in vain to make him jealous of me.   My dear friend is the kindest creature in the world to me.

Spark. Poor fellow!

Har. But his kindness only is not enough for me, without your favour, your good opinion, dear madam: 'tis that must perfect my happiness.   Good gentleman, he believes all I say: would you would do so! Jealous of me!   I would not wrong him nor you for the world.

Spark. Look you there.   Hear him, hear him, and do not walk away so.   [ALITHEA *walks carelessly to and fro.*

Har. I love you, madam, so—

Spark. How's that?   Nay, now you begin to go too far indeed.

Har. So much, I confess, I say, I love you, that I would not have you miserable, and cast yourself away upon so unworthy and inconsiderable a thing as what you see here.
     [*Clapping his hand on his breast, points at* SPARKISH.

Spark. No, faith, I believe thou wouldst not: now his meaning is plain; but I knew before thou wouldst not wrong me, nor her.

Har. No, no, Heavens forbid the glory of her sex should fall so low, as into the embraces of such a contemptible wretch, the least of mankind—my friend here— I injure him!   [*Embracing* SPARKISH.

Alith. Very well.

Spark. No, no, dear friend, I knew it.—Madam, you see he will rather wrong himself than me, in giving himself such names.

Alith. Do not you understand him yet?

Spark. Yes: how modestly he speaks of himself, poor fellow!

Alith. Methinks he speaks impudently of yourself, since—before yourself too; insomuch that I can no longer suffer his scurrilous abusiveness to you, no more than his love to me.   [*Offers to go.*

Spark. Nay, nay, madam, pray stay—his love to you ! Lord, madam, has he not spoke yet plain enough ?

Alith. Yes, indeed, I should think so,

Spark. Well then, by the world, a man can't speak civilly to a woman now, but presently she says, he makes love to her.   Nay, madam, you shall stay, with your pardon, since you have not yet understood him, till he has made an eclaircissement of his love to you, that is, what kind of love it is.   Answer to thy catechism, friend ; do you love my mistress here ?

Har. Yes, I wish she would not doubt it

Spark. But how do you love her ?

Har. With all my soul.

Alith. I thank him, methinks he speaks plain enough now.

Spark. [*To* ALITHEA.] You are out still.—But with what kind of love, Harcourt ?

Har. With the best and the truest love in the world.

Spark. Look you there then, that is with no matrimonial love, I'm sure.

Alith. How's that ? do you say matrimonial love is not best ?

Spark. 'Gad, I went too far ere I was aware.   But speak for thyself, Harcourt, you said you would not wrong me nor her.

Har. No, no, madam, e'en take him for Heaven's sake.

Spark. Look you there, madam.

Har. Who should in all justice be yours, he that loves you most.   [*Claps his hand on his breast.*

Alith. Look you there, Mr. Sparkish, who's that ?

Spark. Who should it be ?—Go on, Harcourt.

Har. Who loves you more than women titles, or fortune fools.   [*Points at* SPARKISH.

Spark. Look you there, he means me still, for he points at me.

Alith. Ridiculous !

Har. Who can only match your faith and constancy in love.

Spark. Ay.

Har. Who knows, if it be possible, how to value so much beauty and virtue.

Spark. Ay.

Har. Whose love can no more be equalled in the world, than that heavenly form of yours.

Spark. No.

Har. Who could no more suffer a rival, than your absence, and yet could no more suspect your virtue, than his own constancy in his love to you.

Spark. No.

Har. Who, in fine, loves you better than his eyes, that first made him love you.

Spark. Ay—Nay, madam, faith, you shan't go till—

Alith. Have a care, lest you make me stay too long.

Spark. But till he has saluted you ; that I may be assured you are friends, after his honest advice and declaration. Come, pray, madam, be friends with him.

Re-enter PINCHWIFE *and* Mrs. PINCHWIFE.

Alith. You must pardon me, sir, that I am not yet so obedient to you.

Pinch. What, invite your wife to kiss men? Monstrous! are you not ashamed ? I will never forgive you.

Spark. Are you not ashamed, that I should have more confidence in the chastity of your family than you have ? You must not teach me, I am a man of honour, sir, though I am frank and free ; I am frank, sir—

Pinch. Very frank, sir, to share your wife with your friends.

Spark. He is an humble, menial friend, such as reconciles the differences of the marriage bed ; you know man

. and wife do not always agree; I design him for that use, therefore would have him well with my wife.

Pinch. A menial friend!—you will get a great many menial friends, by showing your wife as you do.

Spark. What then? It may be I have a pleasure in't, as I have to show fine cloths at a play-house, the first day, and count money before poor rogues.

Pinch. He that shows his wife or money, will be in danger of having them borrowed sometimes.

Spark. I love to be envied, and would not marry a wife that I alone could love; loving alone is as dull as eating alone. Is it not a frank age? and I am a frank person; and to tell you the truth, it may be, I love to have rivals in a wife, they make her seem to a man still but as a kept mistress; and so good night, for I must to Whitehall.— Madam, I hope you are now reconciled to my friend; and so I wish you a good night, madam, and sleep if you can: for to-morrow you know I must visit you early with a canonical gentleman. Good night, dear Harcourt.

[*Exit.*

Har. Madam, I hope you will not refuse my visit to-morrow, if it should be earlier with a canonical gentleman than Mr. Sparkish's.

Pinch. This gentlewoman is yet under my care, therefore you must yet forbear your freedom with her, sir.

[*Coming between* ALITHEA *and* HARCOURT.

Har. Must, sir?

Pinch. Yes, sir, she is my sister.

Har. 'Tis well she is, sir—for I must be her servant, sir.—Madam—

Pinch. Come away, sister, we had been gone, if it had not been for you, and so avoided these lewd rake-hells, who seem to haunt us.

Re-enter HORNER *and* DORILANT.

Horn. How now, Pinchwife!

Pinch. Your servant.

Horn. What! I see a little time in the country makes a man turn wild and unsociable, and only fit to converse with his horses, dogs, and his herds.

Pinch. I have business, sir, and must mind it; your business is pleasure, therefore you and I must go different ways.

Horn. Well, you may go on, but this pretty young gentleman— [*Takes hold of* Mrs. PINCHWIFE.

Har. The lady—

Dor. And the maid—

Horn. Shall stay with us; for I suppose their business is the same with ours, pleasure.

Pinch. 'Sdeath, he knows her, she carries it so sillily! yet if he does not, I should be more silly to discover it first. [*Aside.*

Alith. Pray, let us go, sir.

Pinch. Come, come—

Horn. [*To* Mrs. PINCHWIFE.] Had you not rather stay with us?—Prithee, Pinchwife, who is this pretty young gentleman?

Pinch. One to whom I'm a guardian.—[*Aside.*] I wish I could keep her out of your hands.

Horn. Who is he? I never saw anything so pretty in all my life.

Pinch. Pshaw! do not look upon him so much, he's a poor bashful youth, you'll put him out of countenance.— Come away, brother. [*Offers to take her away.*

Horn. O, your brother!

Pinch. Yes, my wife's brother.—Come, come, she'll stay supper for us.

Horn. I thought so, for he is very like her I saw you at the play with, whom I told you I was in love with.

Mrs. Pinch. [*Aside.*] O jeminy! is that he that was in love with me? I am glad on't, I vow, for he's a curious fine gentleman, and I love him already, too.—[*To* PINCHWIFE.] Is this he, bud?

Pinch. Come away, come away. [*To his* Wife.

Horn. Why, what haste are you in? why wont you let me talk with him?

Pinch. Because you'll debauch him; he's yet young and innocent, and I would not have him debauched for anything in the world.—[*Aside.*] How she gazes on him! the devil!

Horn. Harcourt, Dorilant, look you here, this is the likeness of that dowdy he told us of, his wife; did you ever see a lovelier creature? The rogue has reason to be jealous of his wife, since she is like him, for she would make all that see her in love with her.

Har. And, as I remember now, she is as like him here as can be.

Dor. She is indeed very pretty, if she be like him.

Horn. Very pretty? a very pretty commendation!— she is a glorious creature, beautiful beyond all things I ever beheld.

Pinch. So, so.

Har. More beautiful than a poet's first mistress of imagination.

Horn. Or another man's last mistress of flesh and blood.

Mrs. Pinch. Nay, now you jeer, sir; pray don't jeer me.

Pinch. Come, come.—[*Aside.*] By Heavens, she'll discover herself!

Horn. I speak of your sister, sir.

Pinch. Ay, but saying she was handsome, if like him, made him blush.—[*Aside.*] I am upon a rack!

Horn. Methinks he is so handsome he should not be a man.

Pinch. [*Aside.*] O, there 'tis out! he has discovered her! I am not able to suffer any longer.—[*To his* Wife.] Come, come away, I say.

Horn. Nay, by your leave, sir, he shall not go yet.— [*Aside to them.*] Harcourt, Dorilant, let us torment this jealous rogue a little.

Wycherley.

M

Har. Dor. How?

Horn. I'll show you.

Pinch. Come, pray let him go, I cannot stay fooling any longer; I tell you his sister stays supper for us.

Horn. Does she? Come then, we'll all go to sup with he and thee.

Pinch. No, now I think on't, having stayed so long for us, I warrant she's gone to bed.—[*Aside.*] I wish she and I were well out of their hands.—[*To his* Wife.] Come, I must rise early to-morrow, come.

Horn. Well then, if she be gone to bed, I wish her and you a good night. But pray, young gentleman, present my humble service to her.

Mrs. Pinch. Thank you heartily, sir.

Pinch. [*Aside.*] 'Sdeath, she will discover herself yet in spite of me—[*Aloud.*] He is something more civil to you, for your kindness to his sister, than I am, it seems.

Horn. Tell her, dear sweet little gentleman, for all your brother there, that you have revived the love I had for her at first sight in the playhouse.

Mrs. Pinch. But did you love her indeed, and indeed?

Pinch. [*Aside.*] So, so.—[*Aloud.*] Away, I say.

Horn. Nay, stay.—Yes, indeed, and indeed, pray do you tell her so, and give her this kiss from me.

[*Kisses her.*

Pinch. [*Aside.*] O Heavens! what do I suffer? Now 'tis too plain he knows her, and yet—

Horn. And this, and this—   [*Kisses her again.*

Mrs. Pinch. What do you kiss me for? I am no woman.

Pinch. [*Aside.*] So, there, 'tis out.—[*Aloud.*] Come, I cannot, nor will stay any longer.

Horn. Nay, they shall send your lady a kiss too. Here, Harcourt, Dorilant, will you not?   [*They kiss her.*

Pinch. [*Aside.*] How! do I suffer this? Was I not accusing another just now for this rascally patience, in permitting his wife to be kissed before his face? Ten thousand ulcers gnaw away their lips.—[*Aloud.*] Come, come.

Horn. Good night, dear little gentleman; madam, good night; farewell, Pinchwife.—[*Apart to* HARCOURT *and* DORILANT.] Did not I tell you I would raise his jealous gall?

[*Exeunt* HORNER, HARCOURT *and* DORILANT.

Pinch. So, they are gone at last; stay, let me see first if the coach be at this door. [*Exit.*

Re-enter HORNER, HARCOURT, *and* DORILANT.

Horn. What, not gone yet? Will you be sure to do as I desired you, sweet sir?

Mrs. Pinch. Sweet sir, but what will you give me then?

Horn. Anything. Come away into the next walk.

[*Exit, haling away* Mrs. PINCHWIFE.

Alith. Hold! hold! what d'ye do?

Lucy. Stay, stay, hold—

Har. Hold, madam, hold, let him present him—he'll come presently; nay, I will never let you go till you answer my question.

Lucy. For God's sake, sir, I must follow 'em.

[ALITHEA *and* LUCY, *struggling with* HARCOURT *and* DORILANT.

Dor. No, I have something to present you with too, you shan't follow them.

Re-enter PINCHWIFE.

Pinch. Where?—how— what's become of?—gone!— whither?

Lucy. He's only gone with the gentleman, who will give him something, an't please your worship.

Pinch. Something!—give him something, with a pox!— where are they?

Alith. In the next walk only, brother.

Pinch. Only, only! where, where?

[*Exit and returns presently, then goes out again*

Har. What's the matter with him? why so much concerned? But, dearest madam—

Alith. Pray let me go, sir; I have said and suffered enough already.

Har. Then you will not look upon, nor pity, my sufferings?

Alith. To look upon 'em, when I cannot help 'em, were cruelty, not pity; therefore, I will never see you more.

Har. Let me then, madam, have my privilege of a banished lover, complaining or railing, and giving you but a farewell reason why, if you cannot condescend to marry me, you should not take that wretch, my rival.

Alith. He only, not you, since my honour is engaged so far to him, can give me a reason why I should not marry him; but if he be true, and what I think him to me, I must be so to him. Your servant, sir.

Har. Have women only constancy when 'tis a vice, and are, like Fortune, only true to fools?

Dor. Thou sha't not stir, thou robust creature; you see I can deal with you, therefore you should stay the rather, and be kind.

[*To* LUCY, *who struggles to get from him.*

Re-enter PINCHWIFE.

Pinch. Gone, gone, not to be found! quite gone! ten thousand plagues go with 'em! Which way went they?

Alith. But into t'other walk, brother.

Lucy. Their business will be done presently sure, an't please your worship; it can't be long in doing, I'm sure on't.

Alith. Are they not there?

Pinch. No, you know where they are, you infamous wretch, eternal shame of your family, which you do not dishonour enough yourself you think, but you must help her to do it too, thou legion of bawds!

Alith. Good brother—

Pinch. Damned, damned sister !

Alith. Look you here, she's coming.

Re-enter Mrs. PINCHWIFE *running, with her hat full of oranges and dried fruit under her arm,* HORNER *following.*

Mrs. Pinch. O dear bud, look you here what I have got, see !

Pinch. And what I have got here too, which you can't see.   [*Aside, rubbing his forehead.*

Mrs. Pinch. The fine gentleman has given me better things yet.

Pinch. Has he so ?—[*Aside.*] Out of breath and coloured !—I must hold yet.

Horn. I have only given your little brother an orange, sir.

Pinch. [*To* HORNER.] Thank you, sir.—[*Aside.*] You have only squeezed my orange, I suppose, and given it me again ; yet I must have a city patience.— [*To his Wife.*] Come, come away.

Mrs. Pinch. Stay, till I have put up my fine things, bud.

Enter Sir JASPER FIDGET.

Sir Jasp. O, Master Horner, come, come, the ladies stay for you ; your mistress, my wife, wonders you make not more haste to her.

Horn. I have stayed this half hour for you here, and 'tis your fault I am not now with your wife.

Sir Jasp. But, pray, don't let her know so much ; the truth on't is, I was advancing a certain project to his majesty about—I'll tell you.

Horn. No, let's go, and hear it at your house. Good night, sweet little gentleman ; one kiss more, you'll remember me now, I hope.   [*Kisses her.*

Dor. What, Sir Jasper, will you separate friends ? He promised to sup with us, and if you take him to your house, you'll be in danger of our company too.

Sir Jasp. Alas! gentlemen, my house is not fit for you; there are none but civil women there, which are not for your turn. He, you know, can bear with the society of civil women now, ha! ha! ha! besides, he's one of my family—he's—he! he! he!

Dor. What is he?

Sir Jasp. Faith, my eunuch, since you'll have it; he! he! he! [*Exeunt* Sir JASPER FIDGET *and* HORNER.

Dor. I rather wish thou wert his or my cuckold. Harcourt, what a good cuckold is lost there for want of a man to make him one? Thee and I cannot have Horner's privilege, who can make use of it.

Har. Ay, to poor Horner 'tis like coming to an estate at threescore, when a man can't be the better for't.

Pinch. Come.

Mrs. Pinch. Presently, bud.

Dor. Come, let us go too.—[*To* ALITHEA.] Madam, your servant.—[*To* LUCY.] Good night, strapper.

Har. Madam, though you will not let me have a good day or night, I wish you one; but dare not name the other half of my wish.

Alith. Good night, sir, for ever.

Mrs. Pinch. I don't know where to put this here, dear bud, you shall eat it; nay, you shall have part of the fine gentleman's good things, or treat, as you call it, when we come home.

Pinch. Indeed, I deserve it, since I furnished the best part of it. [*Strikes away the orange.*

The gallant treats presents, and gives the ball;
But 'tis the absent cuckold pays for all. [*Exeunt.*

ACT THE FOURTH.

SCENE I.—PINCHWIFE'S *House in the morning.*

Enter ALITHEA *dressed in new clothes, and* LUCY.

LUCY. Well — madam, now have I dressed you, and set you out with so many ornaments, and spent upon you ounces of essence and pulvillio;[1] and all this for no other purpose but as people adorn and perfume a corpse for a stinking second-hand grave : such, or as bad, I think Master Sparkish's bed.

Alith. Hold your peace.

Lucy. Nay, madam, I will ask you the reason why you would banish poor Master Harcourt for ever from your sight; how could you be so hard-hearted?

Alith. 'Twas because I was not hard-hearted.

Lucy. No, no; 'twas stark love and kindness, I warrant.

Alith. It was so; I would see him no more because I love him.

Lucy. Hey day, a very pretty reason!

Alith. You do not understand me.

Lucy. I wish you may yourself.

Alith. I was engaged to marry, you see, another man, whom my justice will not suffer me to deceive or injure.

---

[1] A sweet-scented powder.

Lucy. Can there be a greater cheat or wrong done to a man than to give him your person without your heart? I should make a conscience of it.

Alith. I'll retrieve it for him after I am married a while.

Lucy. The woman that marries to love better, will be as much mistaken as the wencher that marries to live better. No, madam, marrying to increase love is like gaming to become rich; alas! you only lose what little stock you had before.

Alith. I find by your rhetoric you have been bribed to betray me.

Lucy. Only by his merit, that has bribed your heart, you see, against your word and rigid honour. But what a devil is this honour! 'tis sure a disease in the head, like the megrim or falling-sickness, that always hurries people away to do themselves mischief. Men lose their lives by it; women, what's dearer to 'em, their love, the life of life.

Alith. Come, pray talk you no more of honour, nor Master Harcourt; I wish the other would come to secure my fidelity to him and his right in me.

Lucy. You will marry him then?

Alith. Certainly, I have given him already my word, and will my hand too, to make it good, when he comes.

Lucy. Well, I wish I may never stick pin more, if he be not an arrant natural, to t'other fine gentleman.

Alith. I own he wants the wit of Harcourt, which I will dispense withal for another want he has, which is want of jealousy, which men of wit seldom want.

Lucy. Lord, madam, what should you do with a fool to your husband? You intend to be honest, don't you? then that husbandly virtue, credulity, is thrown away upon you.

Alith. He only that could suspect my virtue should have cause to do it; 'tis Sparkish's confidence in my truth that obliges me to be so faithful to him.

Lucy. You are not sure his opinion may last.

Alith. I am satisfied, 'tis impossible for him to be jealous after the proofs I have had of him. Jealousy in a husband—Heaven defend me from it! it begets a thousand plagues to a poor woman, the loss of her honour, her quiet, and her—

Lucy. And her pleasure.

Alith. What d'ye mean, impertinent?

Lucy. Liberty is a great pleasure, madam.

Alith. I say, loss of her honour, her quiet, nay, her life sometimes ; and what's as bad almost, the loss of this town ; that is, she is sent into the country, which is the last ill-usage of a husband to a wife, I think.

Lucy. [*Aside.*] O, does the wind lie there?—[*Aloud.*] Then of necessity, madam, you think a man must carry his wife into the country, if he be wise. The country is as terrible, I find, to our young English ladies, as a monastery to those abroad ; and on my virginity, I think they would rather marry a London jailer, than a high sheriff of a county, since neither can stir from his employment. Formerly women of wit married fools for a great estate, a fine seat, or the like ; but now 'tis for a pretty seat only in Lincoln's-Inn-Fields, St. James's-Fields, or the Pall-Mall.

Enter SPARKISH, *and* HARCOURT, *dressed like a* Parson.

Spark. Madam, your humble servant, a happy day to you, and to us all.

Har. Amen.

Alith. Who have we here?

Spark. My chaplain, faith——O madam, poor Harcourt remembers his humble service to you ; and, in obedience to your last commands, refrains coming into your sight.

Alith. Is not that he?

Spark. No, fy, no ; but to show that he ne'er intended to hinder our match, has sent his brother here to join our hands. When I get me a wife, I must get her a chaplain, according to the custom; that is his brother, and my chaplain.

Alith. His brother!

Lucy. And your chaplain, to preach in your pulpit then— 　　　　　　　　　　　　　　　　　[*Aside.*

Alith. His brother!

Spark. Nay, I knew you would not believe it.—I told you, sir, she would take you for your brother Frank.

Alith. Believe it!

Lucy. His brother! ha! ha! he! he has a trick left still, it seems. 　　　　　　　　　　　　　　[*Aside.*

Spark. Come, my dearest, pray let us go to church before the canonical hour is past.

Alith. For shame, you are abused still.

Spark. By the world, 'tis strange now you are so incredulous.

Alith. 'Tis strange you are so credulous.

Spark. Dearest of my life, hear me. I tell you this is Ned Harcourt of Cambridge, by the world; you see he has a sneaking college look. 'Tis true he's something like his brother Frank; and they differ from each other no more than in their age, for they were twins.

Lucy. Ha! ha! ha!

Alith. Your servant, sir; I cannot be so deceived, though you are. But come, let's hear, how do you know what you affirm so confidently?

Spark. Why, I'll tell you all. Frank Harcourt coming to me this morning to wish me joy, and present his service to you, I asked him if he could help me to a parson. Whereupon he told me, he had a brother in town who was in orders; and he went straight away, and sent him, you see there, to me.

Alith. Yes, Frank goes and puts on a black coat, then tells you he is Ned; that's all you have for't.

Spark. Pshaw! pshaw! I tell you, by the same token, the midwife put her garter about Frank's neck, to know 'em asunder, they were so like

Alith. Frank tells you this too?

Spark. Ay, and Ned there too: nay, they are both in a story.

Alith. So, so; very foolish.

Spark. Lord, if you won't believe one, you had best try him by your chambermaid there; for chambermaids must needs know chaplains from other men, they are so used to 'em.

Lucy. Let's see: nay, I'll be sworn he has the canonical smirk, and the filthy clammy palm of a chaplain.

Alith. Well, most reverend doctor, pray let us make an end of this fooling.

Har. With all my soul, divine heavenly creature, when you please.

Alith. He speaks like a chaplain indeed.

Spark. Why, was there not soul, divine, heavenly, in what he said?

Alith. Once more, most impertinent black coat, cease your persecution, and let us have a conclusion of this ridiculous love.

Har. I had forgot, I must suit my style to my coat, or I wear it in vain.   [*Aside.*

Alith. I have no more patience left; let us make once an end of this troublesome love, I say.

Har. So be it, seraphic lady, when your honour shall think it meet and convenient so to do.

Spark. 'Gad I'm sure none but a chaplain could speak so, I think.

Alith. Let me tell you, sir, this dull trick will not serve your turn; though you delay our marriage, you shall not hinder it.

Har. Far be it from me, munificent patroness, to delay your marriage; I desire nothing more than to marry you presently, which I might do, if you yourself would; for my noble, good-natured, and thrice generous patron here would not hinder it.

Spark. No, poor man, not I, faith.

Har. And now, madam, let me tell you plainly nobody else shall marry you ; by Heavens ! I'll die first, for I'm sure I should die after it.

Lucy. How his love has made him forget his function, as I have seen it in real parsons !

Alith. That was spoken like a chaplain too ? now you understand him, I hope.

Spark. Poor man, he takes it heinously to be refused ; I can't blame him, 'tis putting an indignity upon him, not to be suffered ; but you'll pardon me, madam, it shan't be ; he shall marry us ; come away, pray madam.

Lucy. Ha ! ha ! he ! more ado ! 'tis late.

Alith. Invincible stupidity ! I tell you, he would marry me as your rival, not as your chaplain.

Spark. Come, come, madam.   [*Pulling her away.*

Lucy. I pray, madam, do not refuse this reverend divine the honour and satisfaction of marrying you ; for I dare say, he has set his heart upon't, good doctor.

Alith. What can you hope or design by this ?

Har. I could answer her, a reprieve for a day only, often revokes a hasty doom. At worst, if she will not take mercy on me, and let me marry her, I have at least the lover's second pleasure, hindering my rival's enjoyment, though but for a time.   [*Aside.*

Spark. Come, madam, 'tis e'en twelve o'clock, and my mother charged me never to be married out of the canonical hours. Come, come ; Lord, here's such a deal of modesty, I warrant, the first day.

Lucy. Yes, an't please your worship, married women show all their modesty the first day, because married men show all their love the first day.   [*Exeunt.*

SCENE II.--*A Bedchamber in* PINCHWIFE'S *House.*

PINCHWIFE *and* Mrs. PINCHWIFE *discovered.*

Pinch. Come, tell me, I say.

Mrs. Pinch. Lord! han't I told it a hundred times over?

Pinch. [*Aside.*] I would try, if in the repetition of the ungrateful tale, I could find her altering it in the least circumstance; for if her story be false, she is so too.—— [*Aloud.*] Come, how was't, baggage?

Mrs. Pinch. Lord, what pleasure you take to hear it sure!

Pinch. No, you take more in telling it I find; but speak, how was't?

Mrs. Pinch. He carried me up into the house next to the Exchange.

Pinch. So, and you two were only in the room!

Mrs. Pinch. Yes, for he sent away a youth that was there, for some dried fruit, and China oranges.

Pinch. Did he so? Damn him for it—and for—

Mrs. Pinch. But presently came up the gentlewoman of the house.

Pinch. O, 'twas well she did; but what did he do whilst the fruit came?

Mrs. Pinch. He kissed me a hundred times, and told me he fancied he kissed my fine sister, meaning me, you know, whom he said he loved with all his soul, and bid me be sure to tell her so, and to desire her to be at her window, by eleven of the clock this morning, and he would walk under it at that time.

Pinch. And he was as good as his word, very punctual; a pox reward him for't. [*Aside.*

Mrs. Pinch. Well, and he said if you were not within, he would come up to her, meaning me, you know, bud, still.

Pinch. [*Aside.*] So—he knew her certainly: but for

this confession, I am obliged to her simplicity.—[*Aloud.*] But what, you stood very still when he kissed you?

Mrs. Pinch. Yes, I warrant you; would you have had me discovered myself?

Pinch. But you told me he did some beastliness to you, as you call it; what was't?

Mrs. Pinch. Why, he put—

Pinch. What?

Mrs. Pinch. Why, he put the tip of his tongue between my lips, and so mousled me—and I said, I'd bite it.

Pinch. An eternal canker seize it, for a dog!

Mrs. Pinch. Nay, you need not be so angry with him neither, for to say truth, he has the sweetest breath I ever knew.

Pinch. The devil! you were satisfied with it then, and would do it again?

Mrs. Pinch. Not unless he should force me.

Pinch. Force you, changeling! I tell you, no woman can be forced.

Mrs. Pinch. Yes, but she may sure, by such a one as he, for he's a proper, goodly, strong man; 'tis hard, let me tell you, to resist him.

Pinch. [*Aside.*] So, 'tis plain she loves him, yet she has not love enough to make her conceal it from me; but the sight of him will increase her aversion for me and love for him; and that love instruct her how to deceive me and satisfy him, all idiot as she is. Love! 'twas he gave women first their craft, their art of deluding. Out of Nature's hands they came plain, open, silly, and fit for slaves, as she and Heaven intended 'em; but damned Love—well—I must strangle that little monster whilst I can deal with him.—[*Aloud.*] Go fetch pen, ink, and paper out of the next room.

Mrs. Pinch. Yes, bud. [*Exit.*

Pinch. Why should women have more invention in love than men? It can only be, because they have more desires, more soliciting passions, more lust, and more of the devil.

Re-enter Mrs. PINCHWIFE.

Come, minx, sit down and write.

Mrs. Pinch. Ay, dear bud, but I can't do't very well.

Pinch. I wish you could not at all.

Mrs. Pinch. But what should I write for?

Pinch. I'll have you write a letter to your lover.

Mrs. Pinch. O Lord, to the fine gentleman a letter!

Pinch. Yes, to the fine gentleman.

Mrs. Pinch. Lord, you do but jeer: sure you jest.

Pinch. I am not so merry: come, write as I bid you.

Mrs. Pinch. What, do you think I am a fool?

Pinch. [*Aside.*] She's afraid I would not dictate any love to him, therefore she's unwilling.—[*Aloud.*] But you had best begin.

Mrs. Pinch. Indeed, and indeed, but I won't, so I won't.

Pinch. Why?

Mrs. Pinch. Because he's in town; you may send for him if you will.

Pinch. Very well, you would have him brought to you; is it come to this? I say, take the pen and write, or you'll provoke me.

Mrs. Pinch. Lord, what d'ye make a fool of me for? Don't I know that letters are never writ but from the country to London, and from London into the country? Now he's in town, and I am in town too; therefore I can't write to him, you know.

Pinch. [*Aside.*] So, I am glad it is no worse; she is innocent enough yet.—[*Aloud.*] Yes, you may, when your husband bids you, write letters to people that are in town.

Mrs. Pinch. O, may I so? then I'm satisfied.

Pinch. Come, begin:—"Sir"—   [*Dictates.*

Mrs. Pinch. Shan't I say, " Dear Sir ? "—You know one says always something more than bare " sir."

Pinch. Write as I bid you, or I will write whore with this penknife in your face.

Mrs. Pinch. Nay, good bud—" Sir "—   [*Writes.*

Pinch. " Though I suffered last night your nauseous, loathed kisses and embraces "—Write !

Mrs. Pinch. Nay, why should I say so ?   You know I told you he had a sweet breath.

Pinch. Write !

Mrs. Pinch. Let me but put out " loathed."

Pinch. Write, I say !

Mrs. Pinch. Well then.   [*Writes.*

Pinch. Let's see, what have you writ ?—[*Takes the paper and reads.*] " Though I suffered last night your kisses and embraces "—Thou impudent creature ! where is " nauseous" and " loathed ? "

Mrs. Pinch. I can't abide to write such filthy words.

Pinch. Once more write as I'd have you, and question it not, or I will spoil thy writing with this.   I will stab out those eyes that cause my mischief.

[*Holds up the penknife.*

Mrs. Pinch. O Lord ! I will.

Pinch. So—so—let's see now.—[*Reads.*]   " Though I suffered last night your nauseous, loathed kisses and embraces "—go on—" yet I would not have you presume that you shall ever repeat them "—so—   [*She writes.*

Mrs. Pinch. I have writ it.

Pinch. On, then—" I then concealed myself from your knowledge, to avoid your insolencies."—   [*She writes.*

Mrs. Pinch. So—

Pinch. " The same reason, now I am out of your hands—"   [*She writes.*

Mrs. Pinch. So—

Pinch. " Makes me own to you my unfortunate, though innocent frolic, of being in man's clothes "— [*She writes.*

Mrs. Pinch. So—

Pinch. "That you may for evermore cease to pursue her, who hates and detests you"—   [*She writes on.*

Mrs. Pinch. So—heigh !   [*Sighs.*

Pinch. What, do you sigh ?—" detests you—as much as she loves her husband and her honour—"

Mrs. Pinch. I vow, husband, he'll ne'er believe I should write such a letter.

Pinch. What, he'd expect a kinder from you ? Come, now your name only.

Mrs. Pinch. What, shan't I say " Your most faithful humble servant till death ? "

Pinch. No, tormenting fiend !—[*Aside.*] Her style, I find, would be very soft.—[*Aloud.*] Come, wrap it up now, whilst I go fetch wax and a candle ; and write on the backside, " For Mr. Horner."   [*Exit.*

Mrs. Pinch. " For Mr. Horner."—So, I am glad he has told me his name. Dear Mr. Horner ! but why should I send thee such a letter that will vex thee, and make thee angry with me ?—Well, I will not send it.— Ay, but then my husband will kill me—for I see plainly he won't let me love Mr. Horner—but what care I for my husband ?—I won't, so I won't, send poor Mr. Horner such a letter—But then my husband—but oh, what if I writ at bottom my husband made me write it ?— Ay, but then my husband would see't—Can one have no shift ? ah, a London woman would have had a hundred presently. Stay—what if I should write a letter, and wrap it up like this, and write upon't too ? Ay, but then my husband would see't—I don't know what to do.— But yet evads I'll try, so I will—for I will not send this letter to poor Mr. Horner, come what will on't.

" Dear, sweet Mr. Horner "—[*Writes and repeats what she writes.*]—so—" my husband would have me send you a base, rude, unmannerly letter; but I won't "—so— " and would have me forbid you loving me ; but I won't " —so—" and would have me say to you, I hate you, poor Mr. Horner ; but I won't tell a lie for him "—there—

"for I'm sure if you and I were in the country at cards together"—so—" I could not help treading on your toe under the table "—so—" or rubbing knees with you, and staring in your face, till you saw me "—very well—" and then looking down, and blushing for an hour together" —so—" but I must make haste before my husband comes : and now he has taught me to write letters, you shall have longer ones from me, who am, dear, dear, poor, dear Mr. Horner, your most humble friend, and servant to command till death,—Margery Pinchwife."

Stay, I must give him a hint at bottom—so—now wrap it up just like t'other—so—now write " For Mr. Horner " —But oh now, what shall I do with it ? for here comes my husband.

Re-enter PINCHWIFE.

Pinch. [*Aside.*] I have been detained by a sparkish coxcomb, who pretended a visit to me ; but I fear 'twas to my wife—[*Aloud.*] What, have you done?

Mrs. Pinch. Ay, ay, bud, just now.

Pinch. Let's see't : what d'ye tremble for ? what, you would not have it go?

Mrs. Pinch. Here—[*Aside.*] No, I must not give him that : so I had been served if I had given him this.

[*He opens and reads the first letter.*

Pinch. Come, where's the wax and seal?

Mrs. Pinch. [*Aside.*] Lord, what shall I do now? Nay, then I have it—[*Aloud.*] Pray let me see't. Lord, you think me so arrant a fool, I cannot seal a letter; I will do't, so I will.

[*Snatches the letter from him, changes it for the other, seals it, and delivers it to him.*

Pinch. Nay, I believe you will learn that, and other things too, which I would not have you.

Mrs. Pinch. So, han't I done it curiously [1]?—[*Aside.*]

---

[1] Carefully.

I think I have; there's my letter going to Mr. Horner, since he'll needs have me send letters to folks.

Pinch. 'Tis very well; but I warrant, you would not have it go now?

Mrs. Pinch. Yes, indeed, but I would, bud, now.

Pinch. Well, you are a good girl then. Come, let me lock you up in your chamber, till I come back; and be sure you come not within three strides of the window when I am gone, for I have a spy in the street.—[*Exit* Mrs. PINCHWIFE, PINCHWIFE *locks the door.*] At least, 'tis fit she think so. If we do not cheat women, they'll cheat us, and fraud may be justly used with secret enemies, of which a wife is the most dangerous; and he that has a handsome one to keep, and a frontier town, must provide against treachery, rather than open force. Now I have secured all within, I'll deal with the foe without, with false intelligence.

[*Holds up the letter. Exit.*

SCENE III.—HORNER'S *Lodging*

Enter HORNER *and* Quack.

Quack. Well, sir, how fadges[1] the new design? have you not the luck of all your brother projectors, to deceive only yourself at last?

Horn. No, good domine doctor, I deceive you, it seems, and others too; for the grave matrons, and old, rigid husbands think me as unfit for love, as they are; but their wives, sisters, and daughters know, some of 'em, better things already.

Quack. Already!

Horn. Already, I say. Last night I was drunk with half-a-dozen of ·our civil persons, as you call 'em, and

---

[1] Succeeds.

people of honour, and so was made free of their society and dressing-rooms for ever hereafter; and am already come to the privileges of sleeping upon their pallets, warming smocks, tying shoes and garters, and the like, doctor, already, already, doctor.

Quack. You have made good use of your time, sir.

Horn. I tell thee, I am now no more interruption to 'em, when they sing, or talk bawdy, than a little squab French page who speaks no English.

Quack. But do civil persons and women of honour drink, and sing bawdy songs?

Horn. O, amongst friends, amongst friends. For your bigots in honour are just like those in religion; they fear the eye of the world more than the eye of Heaven; and think there is no virtue, but railing at vice, and no sin, but giving scandal. They rail at a poor, little, kept player, and keep themselves some young, modest pulpit comedian to be privy to their sins in their closets, not to tell 'em of them in their chapels.

Quack. Nay, the truth on't is, priests, amongst the women now, have quite got the better of us lay-confessors, physicians.

Horn. And they are rather their patients; but—

Enter Lady FIDGET, *looking about her.*

Now we talk of women of honour, here comes one. Step behind the screen there, and but observe, if I have not particular privileges with the women of reputation already, doctor, already. [Quack *retires.*

Lady Fid. Well, Horner, am not I a woman of honour? you see, I'm as good as my word.

Horn. And you shall see, madam, I'll not be behind-hand with you in honour; and I'll be as good as my word too, if you please but to withdraw into the next room.

Lady Fid. But first, my dear sir, you must promise to have a care of my dear honour.

Horn. If you talk a word more of your honour, you'll make me incapable to wrong it. To talk of honour in the mysteries of love, is like talking of Heaven or the Deity, in an operation of witchcraft, just when you are employing the devil: it makes the charm impotent.

Lady Fid. Nay, fy! let us not be smutty. But you talk of mysteries and bewitching to me; I don't understand you.

Horn. I tell you, madam, the word money in a mistress's mouth, at such a nick of time, is not a more disheartening sound to a younger brother, than that of honour to an eager lover like myself.

Lady Fid. But you can't blame a lady of my reputation to be chary.

Horn. Chary! I have been chary of it already, by the report I have caused of myself.

Lady Fid. Ay, but if you should ever let other women know that dear secret, it would come out. Nay, you must have a great care of your conduct; for my acquaintance are so censorious, (oh, 'tis a wicked, censorious world, Mr. Horner!) I say, are so censorious, and detracting, that perhaps they'll talk to the prejudice of my honour, though you should not let them know the dear secret.

Horn. Nay, madam, rather than they shall prejudice your honour, I'll prejudice theirs; and, to serve you, I'll lie with 'em all, make the secret their own, and then they'll keep it. I am a Machiavel in love, madam.

Lady Fid. O, no sir, not that way.

Horn. Nay, the devil take me, if censorious women are to be silenced any other way.

Lady Fid. A secret is better kept, I hope, by a single person than a multitude; therefore pray do not trust anybody else with it, dear, dear Mr. Horner.

[*Embracing him.*

Enter Sir JASPER FIDGET.

Sir Jasp. How now!

Lady Fid. [*Aside.*] O my husband!—prevented—and what's almost as bad, found with my arms about another man—that will appear too much—what shall I say?— [*Aloud.*] Sir Jasper, come hither: I am trying if Mr. Horner were ticklish, and he's as ticklish as can be. I love to torment the confounded toad; let you and I tickle him.

Sir Jasp. No, your ladyship will tickle him better without me, I suppose. But is this your buying china? I thought you had been at the china-house.

Horn. [*Aside.*] China-house! that's my cue, I must take it.—[*Aloud.*] A pox! can't you keep your impertinent wives at home? Some men are troubled with the husbands, but I with the wives; but I'd have you to know, since I cannot be your journeyman by night, I will not be your drudge by day, to squire your wife about, and be your man of straw, or scarecrow only to pies and jays, that would be nibbling at your forbidden fruit; I shall be shortly the hackney gentleman-usher of the town.

Sir Jasp. [*Aside.*] He! he! he! poor fellow, he's in the right on't, faith. To squire women about for other folks, is as ungrateful an employment, as to tell money for other folks.—[*Aloud.*] He! he! he! be'n't angry, Horner.

Lady Fid. No, 'tis I have more reason to be angry, who am left by you, to go abroad indecently alone; or, what is more indecent, to pin myself upon such ill-bred people of your acquaintance as this is.

Sir Jasp. Nay, prithee, what has he done?

Lady Fid. Nay, he has done nothing.

Sir Jasp. But what d'ye take ill, if he has done nothing?

Lady Fid. Ha! ha! ha! faith, I can't but laugh however; why, d'ye think the unmannerly toad would come

down to me to the coach? I was fain to come up to
fetch him, or go without him, which I was resolved not
to do; for he knows china very well, and has himself
very good, but will not let me see it, lest I should beg
some; but I will find it out, and have what I came for
yet.

Horn. [*Apart to* Lady FIDGET, *as he follows her to the
door.*] Lock the door, madam.—[*Exit* Lady FIDGET, *and
locks the door.*]—[*Aloud.*] So, she has got into my
chamber and locked me out. Oh the impertinency of
woman-kind! Well, Sir Jasper, plain-dealing is a jewel;
if ever you suffer your wife to trouble me again here, she
shall carry you home a pair of horns; by my lord mayor
she shall; though I cannot furnish you myself, you are
sure, yet I'll find a way.

Sir Jasp. Ha! ha! he!—[*Aside.*] At my first coming
in, and finding her arms about him, tickling him it seems,
I was half jealous, but now I see my folly.—[*Aloud.*]
He! he! he! poor Horner.

Horn. Nay, though you laugh now, 'twill be my turn
ere long. Oh women, more impertinent, more cunning,
and more mischievous than their monkeys, and to me
almost as ugly!—Now is she throwing my things about
and rifling all I have; but I'll get into her the back way,
and so rifle her for it.

Sir Jasp. Ha! ha! ha! poor angry Horner.

Horn. Stay here a little, I'll ferret her out to you
presently, I warrant. [*Exit at the other door.*

[Sir JASPER *talks through the door to his* Wife,
she answers from within.

Sir Jasp. Wife! my Lady Fidget! wife! he is coming
in to you the back way.

Lady Fid. Let him come, and welcome, which way he
will.

Sir Jasp. He'll catch you, and use you roughly, and
be too strong for you.

L. Fid. Don't you trouble yourself, let him if he can.

Quack. [*Aside.*] This indeed I could not have believed from him, nor any but my own eyes.

Enter Mrs. SQUEAMISH.

Mrs. Squeam. Where's this woman-hater, this toad, this ugly, greasy, dirty sloven?

Sir Jasp. [*Aside.*] So, the women all will have him ugly: methinks he is a comely person, but his wants make his form contemptible to 'em; and 'tis e'en as my wife said yesterday, talking of him, that a proper handsome eunuch was as ridiculous a thing as a gigantic coward.

Mrs. Squeam. Sir Jasper, your servant: where is the odious beast?

Sir Jasp. He's within in his chamber, with my wife; she's playing the wag with him.

Mrs. Squeam. Is she so? and he's a clownish beast, he'll give her no quarter, he'll play the wag with her again, let me tell you: come, let's go help her —What, the door's locked?

Sir Jasp. Ay, my wife locked it.

Mrs. Squeam. Did she so? let's break it open then.

Sir Jasp. No, no, he'll do her no hurt.

Mrs. Squeam. [*Aside.*] But is there no other way to get in to 'em? whither goes this? I will disturb 'em.

[*Exit at another door.*

Enter Old Lady SQUEAMISH.

L. Squeam. Where is this harlotry, this impudent baggage, this rambling tomrigg?[1] O Sir Jasper, I'm glad to see you here; did you not see my vile grandchild come in hither just now?

Sir Jasp. Yes.

L. Squeam. Ay, but where is she then? where is she? Lord, Sir Jasper, I have e'en rattled myself to pieces in pursuit of her: but can you tell what she makes here? they say below, no woman lodges here.

---

[1] Romp; tomboy.

Sir Jasp. No.

L. Squeam. No! what does she here then? say, if it be not a woman's lodging, what makes she here? But are you sure no woman lodges here?

Sir Jasp. No, nor no man neither, this is Mr. Horner's lodging.

L. Squeam. Is it so, are you sure?

Sir Jasp. Yes, yes.

L. Squeam. So; then there's no hurt in't, I hope. But where is he?

Sir Jasp. He's in the next room with my wife.

L. Squeam. Nay, if you trust him with your wife, I may with my Biddy. They say, he's a merry harmless man now, e'en as harmless a man as ever came out of Italy with a good voice, and as pretty, harmless company for a lady, as a snake without his teeth.

Sir Jasp. Ay, ay, poor man.

Re-enter Mrs. SQUEAMISH.

Mrs. Squeam. I can't find 'em.—Oh, are you here, grandmother? I followed, you must know, my Lady Fidget hither; 'tis the prettiest lodging, and I have been staring on the prettiest pictures —

Re-enter Lady FIDGET *with a piece of china in her hand, and* HORNER *following.*

L. Fid. And I have been toiling and moiling for the prettiest piece of china, my dear.

Horn. Nay, she has been too hard for me, do what I could.

Mrs. Squeam. Oh, lord, I'll have some china too. Good Mr. Horner, don't think to give other people china and me none; come in with me too.

Horn. Upon my honour, I have none left now.

Mrs. Squeam. Nay, nay, I have known you deny your china before now, but you shan't put me off so. Come.

Horn. This lady had the last there.

L. Fid. Yes indeed, madam, to my certain knowledge, he has no more left.

Mrs. Squeam. O, but it may be he may have some you could not find.

L. Fid. What, d'ye think if he had had any left, I would not have had it too? for we women of quality never think we have china enough.

Horn. Do not take it ill, I cannot make china for you all, but I will have a roll-waggon for you too, another time.

Mrs. Squeam. Thank you, dear toad.

L. Fid. What do you mean by that promise?
[Aside to HORNER.

Horn. Alas, she has an innocent, literal understanding.
[Aside to Lady FIDGET.

L. Squeam. Poor Mr. Horner! he has enough to do to please you all, I see.

Horn. Ay, madam, you see how they use me.

L. Squeam. Poor gentleman, I pity you.

Horn. I thank you, madam: I could never find pity, but from such reverend ladies as you are; the young ones will never spare a man.

Mrs. Squeam. Come, come, beast, and go dine with us; for we shall want a man at ombre after dinner.

Horn. That's all their use of me, madam, you see.

Mrs. Squeam. Come, sloven, I'll lead you, to be sure of you. [*Pulls him by the cravat.*

L. Squeam. Alas, poor man, how she tugs him! Kiss, kiss her; that's the way to make such nice women quiet.

Horn. No, madam, that remedy is worse than the torment; they know I dare suffer anything rather than do it.

L. Squeam. Prithee kiss her, and I'll give you her picture in little, that you admired so last night; prithee do.

Horn. Well, nothing but that could bribe me: I love a woman only in effigy, and good painting as much as I hate them.—I'll do't, for I could adore the devil well painted. [*Kisses Mrs. SQUEAMISH.*

Mrs. Squeam. Foh, you filthy toad! nay, now I've done jesting.

L. Squeam. Ha! ha! ha! I told you so.

Mrs. Squeam. Foh! a kiss of his—

Sir Jasp. Has no more hurt in't than one of my spaniel's.

Mrs. Squeam. Nor no more good neither.

Quack. I will now believe anything he tells me. [*Aside.*

Enter PINCHWIFE.

L. Fid. O lord, here's a man! Sir Jasper, my mask, my mask! I would not be seen here for the world.

Sir Jasp. What, not when I am with you?

L. Fid. No, no, my honour—let's be gone.

Mrs. Squeam. Oh grandmother, let's be gone; make haste, make haste, I know not how he may censure us.

L. Fid. Be found in the lodging of anything like a man!—Away.

[*Exeunt* Sir JASPER FIDGET, Lady FIDGET, Old Lady SQUEAMISH, *and* Mrs. SQUEAMISH.

Quack. What's here? another cuckold? he looks like one, and none else sure have any business with him. [*Aside.*

Horn. Well, what brings my dear friend hither?

Pinch. Your impertinency.

Horn. My impertinency!—why, you gentlemen that have got handsome wives, think you have a privilege of saying anything to your friends, and are as brutish as if you were our creditors.

Pinch. No, sir, I'll ne'er trust you any way.

Horn. But why not, dear Jack? why diffide in me thou know'st so well?

Pinch. Because I do know you so well.

Horn. Han't I been always thy friend, honest Jack, always ready to serve thee, in love or battle, before thou wert married, and am so still?

Pinch. I believe so, you would be my second now, indeed.

Horn. Well then, dear Jack, why so unkind, so grum, so strange to me? Come, prithee kiss me, dear rogue: gad I was always, I say, and am still as much thy servant as—

Pinch. As I am yours, sir. What, you would send a kiss to my wife, is that it?

Horn. So, there 'tis—a man can't show his friendship to a married man, but presently he talks of his wife to you. Prithee, let thy wife alone, and let thee and I be all one, as we were wont. What, thou art as shy of my kindness, as a Lombard-street alderman of a courtier's civility at Locket's![1]

Pinch. But you are over-kind to me, as kind as if I were your cuckold already; yet I must confess you ought to be kind and civil to me, since I am so kind, so civil to you, as to bring you this: look you there, sir.

[*Delivers him a letter.*

Horn. What is't?

Pinch. Only a love-letter, sir.

Horn. From whom?—how! this is from your wife— hum—and hum—   [*Reads.*

Pinch. Even from my wife, sir: am I not wondrous kind and civil to you now too?—[*Aside.*] But you'll not think her so.

Horn. Ha! is this a trick of his or hers?   [*Aside.*

Pinch. The gentleman's surprised I find.—What, you expected a kinder letter?

Horn. No faith, not I, how could I?

Pinch. Yes, yes, I'm sure you did. A man so well made as you are, must needs be disappointed, if the women declare not their passion at first sight or opportunity.

Horn. [*Aside.*] But what should this mean? Stay, the postscript.—[*Reads aside.*] "Be sure you love me, whatsoever my husband says to the contrary, and let him not

---

[1] A well frequented ordinary near Charing Cross, on the site of Drummond's Bank.

see this, lest he should come home and pinch me, or kill my squirrel."—It seems he knows not what the letter contains.

Pinch. Come, ne'er wonder at it so much.

Horn. Faith, I can't help it.

Pinch. Now, I think I have deserved your infinite friendship and kindness, and have showed myself sufficiently an obliging kind friend and husband; am I not so, to bring a letter from my wife to her gallant?

Horn. Ay, the devil take me, art thou, the most obliging, kind friend and husband in the world, ha! ha!

Pinch. Well, you may be merry, sir; but in short I must tell you, sir, my honour will suffer no jesting.

Horn. What dost thou mean?

Pinch. Does the letter want a comment? Then, know, sir, though I have been so civil a husband, as to bring you a letter from my wife, to let you kiss and court her to my face, I will not be a cuckold, sir, I will not.

Horn. Thou art mad with jealousy. I never saw thy wife in my life but at the play yesterday, and I know not if it were she or no. I court her, kiss her!

Pinch. I will not be a cuckold, I say; there will be danger in making me a cuckold.

Horn. Why, wert thou not well cured of thy last clap?

Pinch. I wear a sword.

Horn. It should be taken from thee, lest thou shouldst do thyself a mischief with it; thou art mad, man.

Pinch. As mad as I am, and as merry as you are, I must have more reason from you ere we part. I say again, though you kissed and courted last night my wife in man's clothes, as she confesses in her letter—

Horn. Ha! [*Aside.*

Pinch. Both she and I say, you must not design it again, for you have mistaken your woman, as you have done your man.

Horn. [*Aside.*] O—I understand something now— [*Aloud.*] Was that thy wife! Why wouldst thou not tell

me 'twas she? Faith, my freedom with her was your
fault, not mine.

Pinch. Faith, so 'twas.   [*Aside.*

Horn. Fy! I'd never do't to a woman before her
husband's face, sure.

Pinch. But I had rather you should do't to my wife
before my face, than behind my back; and that you shall
never do.

Horn. No—you will hinder me.

Pinch. If I would not hinder you, you see by her letter
she would.

Horn. Well, I must e'en acquiesce then, and be contented with what she writes.

Pinch. I'll assure you 'twas voluntarily writ; I had no
hand in't you may believe me.

Horn. I do believe thee, faith.

Pinch. And believe her too, for she's an innocent
creature, has no dissembling in her: and so fare you
well, sir.

Horn. Pray, however, present my humble service to
her, and tell her, I will obey her letter to a tittle, and
fulfil her desires, be what they will, or with what difficulty
soever I do't; and you shall be no more jealous of me, I
warrant her, and you.

Pinch. Well then, fare you well; and play with any
man's honour but mine, kiss any man's wife but mine, and
welcome.   [*Exit.*

Horn. Ha! ha! ha! doctor.

Quack. It seems, he has not heard the report of you,
or does not believe it.

Horn. Ha! ha!—now, doctor, what think you?

Quack. Pray let's see the letter—hum—" for—dear—
love you—"   [*Reads the letter.*

Horn. I wonder how she could contrive it! What
say'st thou to't? 'tis an original.

Quack. So are your cuckolds too originals: for they
are like no other common cuckolds, and I will henceforth

believe it not impossible for you to cuckold the Grand
Signior amidst his guards of eunuchs, that I say.

Horn. And I say for the letter, 'tis the first love-letter
that ever was without flames, darts, fates, destinies, lying
and dissembling in't.

Enter SPARKISH *pulling in* PINCHWIFE.

Spark. Come back, you are a pretty brother-in-law,
neither go to church nor to dinner with your sister bride !

Pinch. My sister denies her marriage, and you see is
gone away from you dissatisfied.

Spark. Pshaw ! upon a foolish scruple, that our parson
was not in lawful orders, and did not say all the common-
prayer ; but 'tis her modesty only I believe. But let all
women be never so modest the first day, they'll be sure to
come to themselves by night, and I shall have enough of
her then. In the mean time, Harry Horner, you must
dine with me : I keep my wedding at my aunt's in the
Piazza.[1]

Horn. Thy wedding ! what stale maid has lived to
despair of a husband, or what young one of a gallant ?

Spark. O, your servant, sir—this gentleman's sister
then,—no stale maid.

Horn. I'm sorry for't.

Pinch. How comes he so concerned for her ?   [*Aside.*

Spark. You sorry for't ? why, do you know any ill by
her ?

Horn. No, I know none but by thee ; 'tis for her sake,

[1] In Wycherley's time the square of Covent Garden must have
presented an elegant appearance. The Piazza, designed by Inigo
Jones, extended, like the modern piazza, along the northern and
eastern sides ; on the west stood St. Paul's Church, built by the
same famous architect, and on the south the square was bordered
by the gardens of Bedford House. "The area was inclosed with
railings, at sixty feet from the buildings ; and in the centre was a
dial, with a gilt ball, raised upon a column." *Timbs' Curiosities of
London.* In 1671 the market was established, but was held, originally, only on the southern side of the square, under the wall of
Bedford Gardens. The houses within the Piazza were then occupied
by persons of rank and fashion.

not yours, and another man's sake that might have hoped, I thought.

Spark. Another man! another man! what is his name?

Horn. Nay, since 'tis past, he shall be nameless.— [*Aside.*] Poor Harcourt! I am sorry thou hast missed her.

Pinch. He seems to be much troubled at the match.

[*Aside.*

Spark. Prithee, tell me—Nay, you shan't go, brother.

Pinch. I must of necessity, but I'll come to you to dinner.   [*Exit.*

Spark. But, Harry, what, have I a rival in my wife already? But with all my heart, for he may be of use to me hereafter; for though my hunger is now my sauce, and I can fall on heartily without, the time will come, when a rival will be as good sauce for a married man to a wife, as an orange to veal.

Horn. O thou damned rogue! thou hast set my teeth on edge with thy orange.

Spark. Then let's to dinner—there I was with you again. Come.

Horn. But who dines with thee?

Spark. My friends and relations, my brother Pinchwife, you see, of your acquaintance.

Horn. And his wife?

Spark. No, 'gad, he'll ne'er let her come amongst us good fellows; your stingy country coxcomb keeps his wife from his friends, as he does his little firkin of ale, for his own drinking, and a gentleman can't get a smack on't; but his servants, when his back is turned, broach it at their pleasures, and dust it away, ha! ha! ha!—'Gad, I am witty, I think, considering I was married to-day, by the world; but come—

Horn. No, I will not dine with you, unless you can fetch her too.

Spark. Pshaw! what pleasure canst thou have with women now, Harry?

Horn. My eyes are not gone; I love a good prospect yet, and will not dine with you unless she does too; go fetch her, therefore, but do not tell her husband 'tis for my sake.

Spark. Well, I'll go try what I can do; in the meantime, come away to my aunt's lodging, 'tis in the way to Pinchwife's.

Horn. The poor woman has called for aid, and stretched forth her hand, doctor; I cannot but help her over the pale out of the briars. [*Exeunt.*

SCENE IV.—*A Room in* PINCHWIFE'S *House.*

Mrs. PINCHWIFE *alone, leaning on her elbow.—A table, pen, ink and paper.*

Mrs. Pinch. Well, 'tis e'en so, I have got the London disease they call love; I am sick of my husband, and for my gallant. I have heard this distemper called a fever, but methinks 'tis like an ague; for when I think of my husband, I tremble, and am in a cold sweat, and have inclinations to vomit; but when I think of my gallant, dear Mr. Horner, my hot fit comes, and I am all in a fever indeed; and, as in other fevers, my own chamber is tedious to me, and I would fain be removed to his, and then methinks I should be well. Ah, poor Mr. Horner! Well, I cannot, will not stay here; therefore I'll make an end of my letter to him, which shall be a finer letter than my last, because I have studied it like anything. Oh sick, sick! [*Takes the pen and writes.*

Enter PINCHWIFE, *who seeing her writing, steals softly behind her and looking over her shoulder, snatches the paper from her.*

Pinch. What, writing more letters?

Mrs. Pinch. O Lord, bud, why d'ye fright me so?

[*She offers to run out; he stops her, and reads.*

Pinch. How's this? nay, you shall not stir, madam:—
"Dear, dear, dear Mr. Horner"—very well—I have
taught you to write letters to good purpose—but let us
see't. "First, I am to beg your pardon for my boldness in
writing to you, which I'd have you to know I would not
have done, had not you said first you loved me so
extremely, which if you do, you will never suffer me to
lie in the arms of another man whom I loathe, nauseate,
and detest."—Now you can write these filthy words.
But what follows?—"Therefore, I hope you will speedily
find some way to free me from this unfortunate match,
which was never, I assure you, of my choice, but I'm
afraid 'tis already too far gone; however, if you love me,
as I do you, you will try what you can do; but you
must help me away before to-morrow, or else, alas! I
shall be for ever out of your reach, for I can defer no
longer our—our—" what is to follow "our"?—speak,
what—our journey into the country I suppose—Oh
woman, damned woman! and Love, damned Love, their
old tempter! for this is one of his miracles; in a moment
he can make those blind that could see, and those see
that were blind, those dumb that could speak, and those
prattle who were dumb before; nay, what is more than
all, make these dough-baked, senseless, indocile animals,
women, too hard for us their politic lords and rulers, in a
moment. But make an end of your letter, and then I'll
make an end of you thus, and all my plagues together.

[*Draws his sword.*

Mrs. Pinch. O Lord, O Lord, you are such a passionate
man, bud!

Enter SPARKISH.

Spark. How now, what's here to do?

Pinch. This fool here now!

Spark. What! drawn upon your wife? You should
never do that, but at night in the dark, when you can't

hurt her.   This is my sister-in-law, is it not? ay, faith, e'en our country Margery ; [*Pulls aside her handkerchief*] one may know her.   Come, she and you must go dine with me ; dinner's ready, come.   But where's my wife? is she not come home yet ? where is she ?

Pinch. Making you a cuckold; 'tis that they all do, as soon as they can.

Spark. What, the wedding-day? no, a wife that designs to make a cully of her husband will be sure to let him win the first stake of love, by the world.   But come, they stay dinner for us : come, I'll lead down our Margery.

Pinch. No—sir, go, we'll follow you.

Spark. I will not wag without you.

Pinch. This coxcomb is a sensible torment to me amidst the greatest in the world.   [*Aside.*

Spark. Come, come, Madam Margery.

Pinch. No ; I'll lead her my way : what, would you treat your friends with mine, for want of your own wife?— [*Leads her to the other door, and locks her in and returns.*] I am contented my rage should take breath—   [*Aside.*

Spark. I told Horner this.

Pinch. Come now.

Spark. Lord, how shy you are of your wife ! but let me tell you, brother, we men of wit have amongst us a saying, that cuckolding, like the small-pox, comes with a fear ; and you may keep your wife as much as you will out of danger of infection, but if her constitution incline her to't, she'll have it sooner or later, by the world, say they.

Pinch. [*Aside.*] What a thing is a cuckold, that every fool can make him ridiculous !—[*Aloud.*] Well, sir—but let me advise you, now you are come to be concerned, because you suspect the danger, not to neglect the means to prevent it, especially when the greatest share of the malady will light upon your own head, for

Hows'e'er the kind wife's belly comes to swell,
The husband breeds for her, and first is ill.
                                                  [*Exeunt.*

ACT THE FIFTH.

SCENE I.—PINCHWIFE'S *House.*

Enter PINCHWIFE *and* MRS. PINCHWIFE. *A table and candle.*

INCH. Come, take the pen and make an end of the letter, just as you intended; if you are false in a tittle, I shall soon perceive it, and punish you as you deserve.—[*Lays his hand on his sword.*] Write what was to follow—let's see—"You must make haste, and help me away before to-morrow, or else I shall be for ever out of your reach, for I can defer no longer our "—What follows " our " ?

Mrs. Pinch. Must all out, then, bud?—Look you there, then. [Mrs. PINCHWIFE *takes the pen and writes.*

Pinch. Let's see—" For I can defer no longer our—wedding—Your slighted Alithea."—What's the meaning of this? my sister's name to't? speak, unriddle.

Mrs. Pinch. Yes, indeed, bud.

Pinch. But why her name to't? speak—speak, I say.

Mrs. Pinch. Ay, but you'll tell her then again. If you would not tell her again—

Pinch. I will not :—I am stunned, my head turns round.—Speak.

Mrs. Pinch. Won't you tell her, indeed, and indeed?

Pinch. No; speak, I say.

Mrs. Pinch. She'll be angry with me; but I had rather she should be angry with me than you, bud;

And, to tell you the truth, 'twas she made me write the letter, and taught me what I should write.

Pinch. [*Aside.*] Ha!— I thought the style was somewhat better than her own.—[*Aloud.*] Could she come to you to teach you, since I had locked you up alone?

Mrs. Pinch. O, through the key-hole, bud.

Pinch. But why should she make you write a letter for her to him, since she can write herself?

Mrs. Pinch. Why, she said because—for I was unwilling to do it—

Pinch. Because what—because?

Mrs. Pinch. Because, lest Mr. Horner should be cruel, and refuse her; or be vain afterwards, and show the letter, she might disown it, the hand not being hers.

Pinch. [*Aside.*] How's this? Ha!—then I think I shall come to myself again.—This changeling could not invent this lie: but if she could, why should she? she might think I should soon discover it.—Stay—now I think on't too, Horner said he was sorry she had married Sparkish; and her disowning her marriage to me makes me think she has evaded it for Horner's sake: yet why should she take this course? But men in love are fools; women may well be so—[*Aloud.*] But hark you, madam, your sister went out in the morning, and I have not seen her within since.

Mrs. Pinch. Alack-a-day, she has been crying all day above, it seems, in a corner.

Pinch. Where is she? let me speak with her.

Mrs. Pinch. [*Aside.*] O Lord, then she'll discover all!—[*Aloud.*] Pray hold, bud; what, d'ye mean to discover me? she'll know I have told you then. Pray, bud, let me talk with her first.

Pinch. I must speak with her, to know whether Horner ever made her any promise, and whether she be married to Sparkish or no.

Mrs. Pinch. Pray, dear bud, don't, till I have spoken

with her, and told her that I have told you all ; for she'll
kill me else.

Pinch. Go then, and bid her come out to me.

Mrs. Pinch. Yes, yes, bud.

Pinch. Let me see—   [*Pausing.*

Mrs. Pinch. [*Aside.*] I'll go, but she is not within to
come to him : I have just got time to know of Lucy her
maid, who first set me on work, what lie I shall tell next;
for I am e'en at my wit's end.   [*Exit.*

Pinch. Well, I resolve it, Horner shall have her : I'd
rather give him my sister than lend him my wife ; and
such an alliance will prevent his pretensions to my wife,
sure. I'll make him of kin to her, and then he won't care
for her.

Re-enter Mrs. PINCHWIFE.

Mrs. Pinch. O Lord, bud ! I told you what anger you
would make me with my sister.

Pinch. Won't she come hither ?

Mrs. Pinch. No, no. Lack-a-day, she's ashamed to
look you in the face : and she says, if you go in to her,
she'll run away down stairs, and shamefully go herself to
Mr. Horner, who has promised her marriage, she says ;
and she will have no other, so she won't.

Pinch. Did he so ?—promise her marriage !—then she
shall have no other. Go tell her so; and if she will come
and discourse with me a little concerning the means, I will
about it immediately. Go.—[*Exit* Mrs. PINCHWIFE.] His
estate is equal to Sparkish's, and his extraction as much
better than his, as his parts are ; but my chief reason is,
I'd rather be akin to him by the name of brother-in-law
than that of cuckold.

Re-enter Mrs. PINCHWIFE.

Well, what says she now?

Mrs. Pinch. Why, she says, she would only have you
lead her to Horner's lodging ; with whom she first will
discourse the matter before she talks with you, which yet

she cannot do; for alack, poor creature, she says she can't so much as look you in the face, therefore she'll come to you in a mask. And you must excuse her, if she make you no answer to any question of yours, till you have brought her to Mr. Horner; and if you will not chide her, nor question her, she'll come out to you immediately.

Pinch. Let her come: I will not speak a word to her, nor require a word from her.

Mrs. Pinch. Oh, I forgot: besides she says, she cannot look you in the face, though through a mask; therefore would desire you to put out the candle.

Pinch. I agree to all. Let her make haste.—There, 'tis out—[*Puts out the candle. Exit* Mrs. PINCHWIFE.] My case is something better: I'd rather fight with Horner for not lying with my sister, than for lying with my wife; and of the two, I had rather find my sister too forward than my wife. I expected no other from her free education, as she calls it, and her passion for the town. Well, wife and sister are names which make us expect love and duty, pleasure and comfort; but we find 'em plagues and torments, and are equally, though differently, troublesome to their keeper; for we have as much ado to get people to lie with our sisters as to keep 'em from lying with our wives.

Re-enter Mrs. PINCHWIFE *masked, and in hoods and scarfs, and a night-gown and petticoat of* ALITHEA'S.

What, are you come, sister? let us go then.— But first, let me lock up my wife. Mrs. Margery, where are you?

Mrs. Pinch. Here, bud.

Pinch. Come hither, that I may lock you up: get you in.—[*Locks the door.*] Come, sister, where are you now?

> [Mrs. PINCHWIFE *gives him her hand; but when he lets her go, she steals softly on to the other side of him, and is led away by him for his* Sister, ALITHEA.

SCENE II.—Horner's *Lodging.*

Horner *and* Quack.

Quack. What, all alone? not so much as one of your cuckolds here, nor one of their wives! They use to take their turns with you, as if they were to watch you.

Horn. Yes, it often happens that a cuckold is but his wife's spy, and is more upon family duty when he is with her gallant abroad, hindering his pleasure, than when he is at home with her playing the gallant. But the hardest duty a married woman imposes upon a lover is keeping her husband company always.

Quack. And his fondness wearies you almost as soon as hers.

Horn. A pox! keeping a cuckold company, after you have had his wife, is as tiresome as the company of a country squire to a witty fellow of the town, when he has got all his money.

Quack. And as at first a man makes a friend of the husband to get the wife, so at last you are fain to fall out with the wife to be rid of the husband.

Horn. Ay, most cuckold-makers are true courtiers; when once a poor man has cracked his credit for 'em, they can't abide to come near him.

Quack. But at first, to draw him in, are so sweet, so kind, so dear! just as you are to Pinchwife. But what becomes of that intrigue with his wife?

Horn. A pox! he's as surly as an alderman that has been bit; and since he's so coy, his wife's kindness is in vain, for she's a silly innocent.

Quack. Did she not send you a letter by him?

Horn. Yes; but that's a riddle I have not yet solved. Allow the poor creature to be willing, she is silly too, and ne keeps her up so close—

Quack. Yes, so close, that he makes her but the more willing, and adds but revenge to her love; which two, when met, seldom fail of satisfying each other one way or other.

Horn. What! here's the man we are talking of, I think.

Enter PINCHWIFE, *leading in his* Wife *masked, muffled, and in her* Sister's *gown.*

Pshaw!

Quack. Bringing his wife to you is the next thing to bringing a love-letter from her.

Horn. What means this?

Pinch. The last time, you know, sir, I brought you a love-letter; now, you see, a mistress; I think you'll say I am a civil man to you.

Horn. Ay, the devil take me, will I say thou art the civilest man I ever met with; and I have known some. I fancy I understand thee now better than I did the letter. But, hark thee, in thy ear—

Pinch. What?

Horn. Nothing but the usual question, man: is she sound, on thy word?

Pinch. What, you take her for a wench, and me for a pimp?

Horn. Pshaw! wench and pimp, paw[1] words; I know thou art an honest fellow, and hast a great acquaintance among the ladies, and perhaps hast made love for me, rather than let me make love to thy wife.

Pinch. Come, sir, in short, I am for no fooling.

Horn. Nor I neither: therefore prithee, let's see her face presently. Make her show, man: art thou sure I don't know her?

Pinch. I am sure you do know her.

Horn. A pox! why dost thou bring her to me then?

Pinch. Because she's a relation of mine—

Horn. Is she, faith, man? then thou art still more civil and obliging, dear rogue.

[1] Paw, adj. naughty. An affected word fashionable in the latter half of the seventeenth century.—*Wright.*

Pinch. Who desired me to bring her to you.

Horn. Then she is obliging, dear rogue.

Pinch. You'll make her welcome for my sake, I hope.

Horn. I hope she is handsome enough to make herself welcome.   Prithee let her unmask.

Pinch. Do you speak to her ; she would never be ruled by me.

Horn. Madam — [Mrs. PINCHWIFE *whispers to* HORNER.] She says she must speak with me in private. Withdraw, prithee.

Pinch. [*Aside.*] She's unwilling, it seems, I should know all her indecent conduct in this business—[*Aloud.*] Well then, I'll leave you together, and hope when I am gone, you'll agree ; if not, you and I shan't agree, sir.

Horn. What means the fool ? if she and I agree 'tis no matter what you and I do.

[*Whispers to* Mrs. PINCHWIFE, *who makes signs with her hand for him to be gone.*

Pinch. In the mean time I'll fetch a parson, and find out Sparkish, and disabuse him.   You would have me fetch a parson, would you not? Well then—now I think I am rid of her, and shall have no more trouble with her—our sisters and daughters, like usurers' money, are safest when put out ; but our wives, like their writings, never safe, but in our closets under lock and key. [*Exit.*

Enter Boy.

Boy. Sir Jasper Fidget, sir, is coming up.   [*Exit.*

Horn. Here's the trouble of a cuckold now we are talking of.   A pox on him ! has he not enough to do to hinder his wife's sport, but he must other women's too ?— Step in here, madam.   [*Exit* Mrs. PINCHWIFE.

Enter Sir JASPER FIDGET.

Sir Jasp. My best and dearest friend.

Horn. [*Aside to* Quack.] The old style, doctor.—

[*Aloud.*] Well, be short, for I am busy. What would your impertinent wife have now?

Sir Jasp. Well guessed, i'faith; for I do come from her.

Horn. To invite me to supper! Tell her, I can't come: go.

Sir Jasp. Nay, now you are out, faith; for my lady, and the whole knot of the virtuous gang, as they call themselves, are resolved upon a frolic of coming to you to-night in masquerade, and are all dressed already.

Horn. I shan't be at home.

Sir Jasp. [*Aside.*] Lord, how churlish he is to women! —[*Aloud.*] Nay, prithee don't disappoint 'em; they'll think 'tis my fault: prithee don't. I'll send in the banquet and the fiddles. But make no noise on't; for the poor virtuous rogues would not have it known, for the world, that they go a-masquerading; and they would come to no man's ball but yours.

Horn. Well, well—get you gone; and tell 'em, if they come, 'will be at the peril of their honour and yours.

Sir Jasp. He! he! he!—we'll trust you for that: fare-well. [*Exit.*

Horn. Doctor, anon you too shall be my guest,

But now I'm going to a private feast. [*Exeunt.*

SCENE III.—*The Piazza of Covent Garden.*

Enter SPARKISH *with a letter in his hand,* PINCHWIFE *following.*

Spark. But who would have thought a woman could nave been false to me? By the world, I could not have thought it.

Pinch. You were for giving and taking liberty: she has taken it only, sir, now you find in that letter. You are a frank person, and so is she, you see there.

Spark. Nay, if this be her hand—for I never saw it.

Pinch. 'Tis no matter whether that be her hand or no; I am sure this hand, at her desire, led her to Mr. Horner, with whom I left her just now, to go fetch a parson to 'em at their desire too, to deprive you of her for ever; for it seems yours was but a mock marriage.

Spark. Indeed, she would needs have it that 'twas Harcourt himself, in a parson's habit, that married us; but I'm sure he told me 'twas his brother Ned.

Pinch. O, there 'tis out; and you were deceived, not she: for you are such a frank person. But I must be gone.—You'll find her at Mr. Horner's. Go, and believe your eyes.   [*Exit.*

Spark. Nay, I'll to her, and call her as many crocodiles, sirens, harpies, and other heathenish names, as a poet would do a mistress who had refused to hear his suit, nay more, his verses on her. — But stay, is not that she following a torch at t'other end of the Piazza? and from Horner's certainly—'tis so.

Enter ALITHEA *following a torch, and* LUCY *behind.*

You are well met, madam, though you don't think so. What, you have made a short visit to Mr. Horner? but I suppose you'll return to him presently, by that time the parson can be with him.

Alith. Mr. Horner and the parson, sir!

Spark. Come, madam, no more dissembling, no more jilting; for I am no more a frank person.

Alith. How's this?

Lucy. So, 'twill work, I see.   [*Aside*

Spark. Could you find out no easy country fool to abuse? none but me, a gentleman of wit and pleasure about the town? But it was your pride to be too hard for a man of parts, unworthy false woman! false as a friend that lends a man money to lose; false as dice, who undo those that trust all they have to 'em.

Lucy. He has been a great bubble, by his similes, as they say.   [*Aside.*

Alith. You have been too merry, sir, at your wedding-dinner, sure.

Spark. What, d'ye mock me too?

Alith. Or you have been deluded.

Spark. By you.

Alith. Let me understand you.

Spark. Have you the confidence, (I should call it something else, since you know your guilt,) to stand my just reproaches? you did not write an impudent letter to Mr. Horner? who I find now has clubbed with you in deluding me with his aversion for women, that I might not, forsooth, suspect him for my rival.

Lucy. D'ye think the gentleman can be jealous now, madam?   [*Aside.*

Alith. I write a letter to Mr. Horner!

Spark. Nay, madam, do not deny it. Your brother showed it me just now; and told me likewise, he left you at Horner's lodging to fetch a parson to marry you to him: and I wish you joy, madam, joy, joy; and to him too, much joy; and to myself more joy, for not marrying you.

Alith. [*Aside.*] So, I find my brother would break off the match; and I can consent to't, since I see this gentleman can be made jealous.—[*Aloud.*] O Lucy, by his rude usage and jealousy, he makes me almost afraid I am married to him. Art thou sure 'twas Harcourt himself, and no parson, that married us?

Spark. No, madam, I thank you. I suppose, that was a contrivance too of Mr. Horner's and yours, to make Harcourt play the parson; but I would as little as you have him one now, no, not for the world. For, shall I tell you another truth? I never had any passion for you till now, for now I hate you. 'Tis true, I might have married your portion, as other men of parts of the town do sometimes: and so, your servant. And to show my unconcernedness, I'll come to your wedding, and resign you with as much joy, as I would a stale wench to a new

cully; nay, with as much joy as I would after the first
night, if I had been married to you. There's for you;
and so your servant, servant. [*Exit.*

Alith. How was I deceived in a man!

Lucy. You'll believe then a fool may be made jealous
now? for that easiness in him that suffers him to be led
by a wife, will likewise permit him to be persuaded
against her by others.

Alith. But marry Mr. Horner! my brother does not
intend it, sure: if I thought he did, I would take thy
advice, and Mr. Harcourt for my husband. And now I
wish, that if there be any over-wise woman of the town,
who, like me, would marry a fool for fortune, liberty, or
title, first, that her husband may love play, and be a cully
to all the town but her, and suffer none but Fortune to
be mistress of his purse; then, if for liberty, that he may
send her into the country, under the conduct of some
huswifely mother-in-law; and if for title, may the world
give 'em none but that of cuckold.

Lucy. And for her greater curse, madam, may he not
deserve it.

Alith. Away, impertinent! Is not this my old Lady
Lanterlu's?[1]

Lucy. Yes, madam.—[*Aside.*] And here I hope we
shall find Mr. Harcourt. [*Exeunt.*

SCENE IV.—HORNER's *Lodging. A table, banquet,
and bottles.*

Enter HORNER, Lady FIDGET, Mrs. DAINTY FIDGET,
and Mrs. SQUEAMISH.

Horn. A pox! they are come too soon—before I have
sent back my new mistress. All that I have now to do
is to lock her in, that they may not see her. [*Aside.*

[1] "Lanterloo" or "langteraloo" was the name of a game at
cards.

L. Fid. That we may be sure of our welcome, we have brought our entertainment with us, and are resolved to treat thee, dear toad.

Mrs. Dain. And that we may be merry to purpose, have left Sir Jasper and my old Lady Squeamish, quarrelling at home at backgammon.

Mrs. Squeam. Therefore let us make use of our time, lest they should chance to interrupt us.

L. Fid. Let us sit then.

Horn. First, that you may be private, let me lock this door and that, and I'll wait upon you presently.

L. Fid. No, sir, shut 'em only, and your lips for ever ; for we must trust you as much as our women.

Horn. You know all vanity's killed in me ; I have no occasion for talking.

L. Fid. Now, ladies, supposing we had drank each of us our two bottles, let us speak the truth of our hearts.

Mrs. Dain. and Mrs. Squeam. Agreed.

L. Fid. By this brimmer, for truth is nowhere else to be found—[*Aside to* HORNER.] not in thy heart, false man !

Horn. You have found me a true man, I'm sure.

[*Aside to* Lady FIDGET.

L. Fid. [*Aside to* HORNER.] Not every way.—But let us sit and be merry. [*Sings.*

Why should our damned tyrants oblige us to live
On the pittance of pleasure which they only give ?
     We must not rejoice
     With wine and with noise :
In vain we must wake in a dull bed alone,
Whilst to our warm rival the bottle they're gone.
     Then lay aside charms,
     And take up these arms.[1]
'Tis wine only gives 'em their courage and wit :
Because we live sober, to men we submit.
     If for beauties you'd pass,
     Take a lick of the glass,

[1] The glasses.

'Twill mend your complexions, and when they are gone,
 The best red we have is the red of the grape :
Then, sisters, lay't on,
   And damn a good shape.

Mrs. Dain. Dear brimmer ! Well, in token of our
openness and plain-dealing, let us throw our masks over
our heads.

Horn. So, 'twill come to the glasses anon. [*Aside.*

Mrs. Squeam. Lovely brimmer ! let me enjoy him first.

L. Fid. No, I never part with a gallant till I've tried
him. Dear brimmer ! that makest our husbands short-
sighted.

Mrs. Dain. And our bashful gallants bold.

Mrs. Squeam. And, for want of a gallant, the butler
lovely in our eyes.—Drink, eunuch.

L. Fid. Drink, thou representative of a husband.—
Damn a husband !

Mrs. Dain. And, as it were a husband, an old keeper.

Mrs. Squeam. And an old grandmother.

Horn. And an English bawd, and a French surgeon.

L. Fid. Ay, we have all reason to curse 'em.

Horn. For my sake, ladies ?

L. Fid. No, for our own ; for the first spoils all young
gallants' industry.

Mrs. Dain. And the other's art makes 'em bold only
with common women.

Mrs. Squeam. And rather run the hazard of the vile
distemper amongst them, than of a denial amongst us.

Mrs. Dain. The filthy toads choose mistresses now as
they do stuffs, for having been fancied and worn by
others.

Mrs. Squeam. For being common and cheap.

L. Fid. Whilst women of quality, like the richest
stuffs, lie untumbled, and unasked for.

Horn. Ay, neat, and cheap, and new, often they think
best.

Mrs. Dain. No, sir, the beasts will be known by a mistress longer than by a suit.

Mrs. Squeam. And 'tis not for cheapness neither.

L. Fid. No; for the vain fops will take up druggets, and embroider 'em. But I wonder at the depraved appetites of witty men; they use to be out of the common road, and hate imitation. Pray tell me, beast, when you were a man, why you rather chose to club with a multitude in a common house for an entertainment, than to be the only guest at a good table.

Horn. Why, faith, ceremony and expectation are unsufferable to those that are sharp bent. People always eat with the best stomach at an ordinary, where every man is snatching for the best bit.

L. Fid. Though he get a cut over the fingers.—But I have heard, that people eat most heartily of another man's meat, that is, what they do not pay for.

Horn. When they are sure of their welcome and freedom; for ceremony in love and eating is as ridiculous as in fighting: falling on briskly is all should be done on those occasions.

L. Fid. Well then, let me tell you, sir, there is no where more freedom than in our houses; and we take freedom from a young person as a sign of good breeding; and a person may be as free as he pleases with us, as frolic, as gamesome, as wild as he will.

Horn. Han't I heard you all declaim against wild men?

L. Fid. Yes; but for all that, we think wildness in a man as desirable a quality as in a duck or rabbit: a tame man! foh!

Horn. I know not, but your reputations frightened me as much as your faces invited me.

L. Fid. Our reputation! Lord, why should you not think that we women make use of our reputation, as you men of yours, only to deceive the world with less suspicion? Our virtue is like the statesman's religion, the quaker's word, the gamester's oath, and the great man's honour; but to cheat those that trust us.

Mrs. Squeam. And that demureness, coyness, and modesty, that you see in our faces in the boxes at plays, is as much a sign of a kind woman, as a vizard-mask in the pit.

Mrs. Dain. For, I assure you, women are least masked when they have the velvet vizard on.

L. Fid. You would have found us modest women in our denials only.

Mrs. Squeam. Our bashfulness is only the reflection of the men's.

Mrs. Dain. We blush when they are shamefaced.

Horn. I beg your pardon, ladies, I was deceived in you devilishly. But why that mighty pretence to honour?

L. Fid. We have told you; but sometimes 'twas for the same reason you men pretend business often, to avoid ill company, to enjoy the better and more privately those you love.

Horn. But why would you ne'er give a friend a wink then?

L. Fid. Faith, your reputation frightened us, as much as ours did you, you were so notoriously lewd.

Horn. And you so seemingly honest.

L. Fid. Was that all that deterred you?

Horn. And so expensive—you allow freedom, you say.

L. Fid. Ay, ay.

Horn. That I was afraid of losing my little money, as well as my little time, both which my other pleasures required.

L. Fid. Money! foh! you talk like a little fellow now: do such as we expect money?

Horn. I beg your pardon, madam, I must confess, I have heard that great ladies, like great merchants, set but the higher prices upon what they have, because they are not in necessity of taking the first offer.

Mrs. Dain. Such as we make sale of our hearts?

Mrs. Squeam. We bribed for our love? foh!

Horn. With your pardon ladies, I know, like great men in offices, you seem to exact flattery and attendance only from your followers; but you have receivers about you, and such fees to pay, a man is afraid to pass your grants. Besides, we must let you win at cards, or we lose your hearts; and if you make an assignation, 'tis at a goldsmith's, jeweller's, or china-house; where for your honour you deposit to him, he must pawn his to the punctual cit, and so paying for what you take up, pays for what he takes up.

Mrs. Dain. Would you not have us assured of our gallants' love?

Mrs. Squeam. For love is better known by liberality than by jealousy.

L. Fid. For one may be dissembled, the other not.— [*Aside.*] But my jealousy can be no longer dissembled, and they are telling ripe.—[*Aloud.*]—Come, here's to our gallants in waiting, whom we must name, and I'll begin. This is my false rogue. [*Claps him on the back.*

Mrs. Squeam. How!

Horn. So, all will out now. [*Aside.*

Mrs. Squeam. Did you not tell me, 'twas for my sake only you reported yourself no man? [*Aside to* HORNER.

Mrs. Dain. Oh, wretch! did you not swear to me, 'twas for my love and honour you passed for that thing you do? [*Aside to* HORNER.

Horn. So, so.

L. Fid. Come, speak, ladies: this is my false villain.

Mrs. Squeam. And mine too.

Mrs. Dain. And mine.

Horn. Well then, you are all three my false rogues too, and there's an end on't.

L. Fid. Well then, there's no remedy; sister sharers, let us not fall out, but have a care of our honour. Though we get no presents, no jewels of him, we are savers of our honour, the jewel of most value and use, which shines yet to the world unsuspected, though it be counterfeit.

Horn. Nay, and is e'en as good as if it were true, provided the world think so ; for honour, like beauty now, only depends on the opinion of others.

L. Fid. Well, Harry Common, I hope you can be true to three. Swear ; but 'tis to no purpose to require your oath, for you are as often forsworn as you swear to new women.

Horn. Come, faith, madam, let us e'en pardon one another ; for all the difference I find betwixt we men and you women, we forswear ourselves at the beginning of an amour, you as long as it lasts.

Enter Sir JASPER FIDGET, *and* Old Lady SQUEAMISH.

Sir Jasp. Oh, my Lady Fidget, was this your cunning, to come to Mr. Horner without me ? but you have been nowhere else, I hope.

L. Fid. No, Sir Jasper.

L. Squeam. And you came straight hither, Biddy ?

Mrs. Squeam. Yes, indeed, lady grandmother.

Sir Jasp. 'Tis well, 'tis well ; I knew when once they were thoroughly acquainted with poor Horner, they'd ne'er be from him : you may let her masquerade it with my wife and Horner, and I warrant her reputation safe.

Enter Boy.

Boy. O, sir, here's the gentleman come, whom you bid me not suffer to come up, without giving you notice, with a lady too, and other gentlemen.

Horn. Do you all go in there, whilst I send 'em away; and, boy, do you desire 'em to stay below till I come, which shall be immediately.

> [*Exeunt* Sir JASPER FIDGET, Lady FIDGET,
> Lady SQUEAMISH, Mrs. SQUEAMISH, *and*
> Mrs. DAINTY FIDGET.

Boy. Yes, sir. [*Exit.*

[*Exit* HORNER *at the other door, and returns
with* Mrs. PINCHWIFE.

Horn. You would not take my advice, to be gone
home before your husband came back, he'll now discover
all; yet pray, my dearest, be persuaded to go home, and
leave the rest to my management; I'll let you down the
back way.

Mrs. Pinch. I don't know the way home, so I don't.

Horn. My man shall wait upon you.

Mrs. Pinch. No, don't you believe that I'll go at all;
what, are you weary of me already?

Horn. No, my life, 'tis that I may love you long, 'tis
to secure my love, and your reputation with your husband; he'll never receive you again else.

Mrs. Pinch. What care I? d'ye think to frighten me
with that? I don't intend to go to him again; you shall
be my husband now.

Horn. I cannot be your husband, dearest, since you
are married to him.

Mrs. Pinch. O, would you make me believe that?
Don't I see every day at London here, women leave
their first husbands, and go and live with other men as
their wives? pish, pshaw! you'd make me angry, but
that I love you so mainly.

Horn. So, they are coming up—In again, in, I hear
'em.—[*Exit* Mrs. PINCHWIFE.] Well, a silly mistress is
like a weak place, soon got, soon lost, a man has scarce
time for plunder; she betrays her husband first to her
gallant, and then her gallant to her husband.

Enter PINCHWIFE, ALITHEA, HARCOURT, SPARKISH,
LUCY, *and a* Parson.

Pinch. Come, madam, 'tis not the sudden change of
your dress, the confidence of your asseverations, and
your false witness there, shall persuade me I did not
bring you hither just now; here's my witness, who can-

not deny it, since you must be confronted.—Mr. Horner, did not I bring this lady to you just now?

Horn. Now must I wrong one woman for another's sake,—but that's no new thing with me, for in these cases I am still on the criminal's side against the innocent. [*Aside.*

Alith. Pray speak, sir.

Horn. It must be so. I must be impudent, and try my luck; impudence uses to be too hard for truth.

[*Aside.*

Pinch. What, you are studying an evasion or excuse for her! Speak, sir.

Horn. No, faith, I am something backward only to speak in women's affairs or disputes.

Pinch. She bids you speak.

Alith. Ay, pray, sir, do, pray satisfy him.

Horn. Then truly, you did bring that lady to me just now.

Pinch. O ho!

Alith. How, sir?

Har. How, Horner?

Alith. What mean you, sir? I always took you for a man of honour.

Horn. Ay, so much a man of honour, that I must save my mistress, I thank you, come what will on't. [*Aside.*

Spark. So, if I had had her, she'd have made me believe the moon had been made of a Christmas pie.

Lucy. Now could I speak, if I durst, and solve the riddle, who am the author of it. [*Aside.*

Alith. O unfortunate woman! A combination against my honour! which most concerns me now, because you share in my disgrace, sir, and it is your censure, which I must now suffer, that troubles me, not theirs.

Har. Madam, then have no trouble, you shall now see 'tis possible for me to love too, without being jealous; I will not only believe your innocence myself,

but make all the world believe it.—[*Aside to* HORNER.]
Horner, I must now be concerned for this lady's honour.

Horn. And I must be concerned for a lady's honour
too.

Har. This lady has her honour, and I will protect it.

Horn. My lady has not her honour, but has given it
me to keep, and I will preserve it.

Har. I understand you not.

Horn. I would not have you.

Mrs. Pinch. What's the matter with 'em all?

[*Peeping in behind.*

Pinch. Come, come, Mr. Horner, no more disputing;
here's the parson, I brought him not in vain.

Har. No, sir, I'll employ him, if this lady please.

Pinch. How! what d'ye mean?

Spark. Ay, what does he mean?

Horn. Why, I have resigned your sister to him, he has
my consent.

Pinch. But he has not mine, sir; a woman's injured
honour, no more than a man's, can be repaired or satisfied by any but him that first wronged it; and you shall
marry her presently, or—   [*Lays his hand on his sword.*

Re-enter Mrs. PINCHWIFE.

Mrs. Pinch. O Lord, they'll kill poor Mr. Horner!
besides, he shan't marry her whilst I stand by, and look
on; I'll not lose my second husband so.

Pinch. What do I see?

Alith. My sister in my clothes!

Spark. Ha!

Mrs. Pinch. Nay, pray now don't quarrel about finding
work for the parson, he shall marry me to Mr. Horner;
or now, I believe, you have enough of me.

[*To* PINCHWIFE.

Horn. Damned, damned loving changeling!   [*Aside.*

Mrs. Pinch. Pray, sister, pardon me for telling so
many lies of you.

Horn. I suppose the riddle is plain now.

Lucy. No, that must be my work.—Good sir, hear me.

> [*Kneels to* PINCHWIFE, *who stands doggedly with his hat over his eyes.*

Pinch. I will never hear woman again, but make 'em all silent thus—   [*Offers to draw upon his* Wife.

Horn. No, that must not be.

Pinch. You then shall go first, 'tis all one to me.

> [*Offers to draw on* HORNER, *but is stopped by* HARCOURT.

Har. Hold!

Re-enter Sir JASPER FIDGET, Lady FIDGET, Lady SQUEAMISH, Mrs. DAINTY FIDGET, *and* Mrs. SQUEAMISH.

Sir Jasp. What's the matter? what's the matter? pray, what's the matter, sir? I beseech you communicate, sir.

Pinch. Why, my wife has communicated, sir, as your wife may have done too, sir, if she knows him, sir.

Sir Jasp. Pshaw, with him! ha! ha! he!

Pinch. D'ye mock me, sir? a cuckold is a kind of a wild beast; have a care, sir.

Sir Jasp. No, sure, you mock me, sir. He cuckold you! it can't be, ha! ha! he! why, I'll tell you, sir—

> [*Offers to whisper.*

Pinch. I tell you again, he has whored my wife, and yours too, if he knows her, and all the women he comes near; 'tis not his dissembling, his hypocrisy, can wheedle me.

Sir Jasp. How! does he dissemble? is he a hypocrite? Nay, then—how—wife—sister, is he a hypocrite?

L. Squeam. A hypocrite! a dissembler! Speak, young harlotry, speak, how?

Sir Jasp. Nay, then—O my head too!—O thou libidinous lady!

L. Squeam. O thou harloting harlotry! hast thou done't then?

Sir Jasp. Speak, good Horner, art thou a dissembler, a rogue? hast thou—

Horn. So!

Lucy. I'll fetch you off, and her too, if she will but hold her tongue. [*Apart to* HORNER.

Horn. Canst thou? I'll give thee— [*Apart to* LUCY.

Lucy. [*To* PINCHWIFE.] Pray have but patience to hear me, sir, who am the unfortunate cause of all this confusion. Your wife is innocent, I only culpable; for I put her upon telling you all these lies concerning my mistress, in order to the breaking off the match between Mr. Sparkish and her, to make way for Mr. Harcourt.

Spark. Did you so, eternal rotten tooth? Then, it seems, my mistress was not false to me, I was only deceived by you. Brother, that should have been, now man of conduct, who is a frank person now, to bring your wife to her lover, ha?

Lucy. I assure you, sir, she came not to Mr. Horner out of love, for she loves him no more—

Mrs. Pinch. Hold, I told lies for you, but you shall tell none for me, for I do love Mr. Horner with all my soul, and nobody shall say me nay; pray, don't you go to make poor Mr. Horner believe to the contrary; 'tis spitefully done of you, I'm sure.

Horn. Peace, dear idiot. [*Aside to* Mrs. PINCHWIFE.

Mrs. Pinch. Nay, I will not peace.

Pinch. Not till I make you.

Enter DORILANT *and* QUACK.

Dor. Horner, your servant; I am the doctor's guest, he must excuse our intrusion.

Quack. But what's the matter, gentlemen? for Heaven's sake, what's the matter?

Horn. Oh, 'tis well you are come. 'Tis a censorious world we live in; you may have brought me a reprieve, or else I had died for a crime I never committed, and these innocent ladies had suffered with me; therefore,

pray satisfy these worthy, honourable, jealous gentlemen
—that—   [*Whispers.*

Quack. O, I understand you, is that all?—Sir Jasper,
by Heavens, and upon the word of a physician, sir—

[*Whispers to* Sir JASPER.

Sir Jasp. Nay, I do believe you truly.—Pardon me,
my virtuous lady, and dear of honour.

L. Squeam. What, then all's right again?

Sir Jasp. Ay, ay, and now let us satisfy him too.

[*They whisper with* PINCHWIFE.

Pinch. An eunuch! Pray, no fooling with me.

Quack. I'll bring half the chirurgeons in town to
swear it.

Pinch. They!—they'll swear a man that bled to death
through his wounds, died of an apoplexy.

Quack. Pray, hear me, sir—why, all the town has
heard the report of him.

Pinch. But does all the town believe it?

Quack. Pray, inquire a little, and first of all these.

Pinch. I'm sure when I left the town, he was the
lewdest fellow in't.

Quack. I tell you, sir, he has been in France since;
pray, ask but these ladies and gentlemen, your friend Mr.
Dorilant. Gentlemen and ladies, han't you all heard the
late sad report of poor Mr. Horner?

All the Ladies. Ay, ay, ay.

Dor. Why, thou jealous fool, dost thou doubt it? he's
an arrant French capon.

Mrs. Pinch. 'Tis false, sir, you shall not disparage
poor Mr. Horner, for to my certain knowledge—

Lucy. O, hold!

Mrs. Squeam. Stop her mouth!   [*Aside to* LUCY.

L. Fid. Upon my honour, sir, 'tis as true—

[*To* PINCHWIFE.

Mrs. Dain. D'ye think we would have been seen in his
company?

Mrs. Squeam. Trust our unspotted reputations with him?

1. Fid. This you get, and we too, by trusting your secret to a fool. [*Aside to* HORNER.

Horn. Peace, madam. — [*Aside to* Quack.] Well, doctor, is not this a good design, that carries a man on unsuspected, and brings him off safe?

Pinch. Well, if this were true—but my wife— [*Aside.*
[DORILANT *whispers with* Mrs. PINCHWIFE.

Alith. Come, brother, your wife is yet innocent, you see; but have a care of too strong an imagination, lest, like an over-concerned timorous gamester, by fancying an unlucky cast, it should come. Women and fortune are truest still to those that trust 'em.

Lucy. And any wild thing grows but the more fierce and hungry for being kept up, and more dangerous to the keeper.

Alith. There's doctrine for all husbands, Mr. Harcourt.

Har. I edify, madam, so much, that I am impatient till I am one.

Dor. And I edify so much by example, I will never be one.

Spark. And because I will not disparage my parts, I'll ne'er be one.

Horn. And I, alas! can't be one.

Pinch. But I must be one—against my will to a country wife, with a country murrain to me!

Mrs. Pinch. And I must be a country wife still too, I find; for I can't, like a city one, be rid of my musty husband, and do what I list. [*Aside.*

Horn. Now, sir, I must pronounce your wife innocent, though I blush whilst I do it; and I am the only man by her now exposed to shame, which I will straight drown in wine, as you shall your suspicion; and the ladies' troubles we'll divert with a ballad.—Doctor, where are your maskers?

Lucy. Indeed, she's innocent, sir, I am her witness; and her end of coming out was but to see her sister's wedding; and what she has said to your face of her love to

Mr. Horner, was but the usual innocent revenge on a husband's jealousy;—was it not, madam, speak?

Mrs. Pinch. [*Aside to* LUCY *and* HORNER.] Since you'll have me tell more lies—[*Aloud.*] Yes, indeed, bud.

Pinch. For my own sake fain I would all believe;
Cuckolds, like lovers, should themselves deceive.
But—   [*Sighs.*
His honour is least safe (too late I find)
Who trusts it with a foolish wife or friend.

A Dance of Cuckolds.

Horn. Vain fops but court and dress, and keep a pother,
To pass for women's men with one another;
But he who aims by women to be prized,
First by the men, you see, must be despised. [*Exeunt.*

EPILOGUE.

SPOKEN BY MRS. KNEP.[1]

Now you the vigorous, who daily here
O'er vizard-mask in public domineer,
And what you'd do to her, if in place where;
Nay, have the confidence to cry, " Come out!"
Yet when she says, " Lead on!" you are not stout;
But to your well-dressed brother straight turn round,
And cry " Pox on her, Ned, she can't be sound!"
Then slink away, a fresh one to engage,
With so much seeming heat and loving rage,

---

[1] Or Knipp, the friend of Mr. Pepys. She played the part of Lady Fidget.

You'd frighten listening actress on the stage;
Till she at last has seen you huffing come,
And talk of keeping in the tiring-room,
Yet cannot be provoked to lead her home.
Next, you Falstaffs of fifty, who beset
Your buckram maidenheads, which your friends get
And whilst to them you of achievements boast,
They share the booty, and laugh at your cost.
In fine, you essenced boys, both old and young,
Who would be thought so eager, brisk, and strong,
Yet do the ladies, not their husbands wrong;
Whose purses for your manhood make excuse,
And keep your Flanders mares for show not use;
Encouraged by our woman's man to-day,
A Horner's part may vainly think to play;
And may intrigues so bashfully disown,
That they may doubted be by few or none;
May kiss the cards at picquet, ombre, loo,
And so be taught to kiss the lady too;
But, gallants, have a care, faith, what you do.
The world, which to no man his due will give,
You by experience know you can deceive,
And men may still believe you vigorous,
But then we women—there's no cozening us.

THE PLAIN DEALER.

Ridiculum acri
Fortius et melius magnas plerumque secat res.[1]—HORAT.

[1] Ridicule commonly decides great matters more forcibly and better than severity.—*Sat.* i. 10, 14—15.

 CCORDING to Wycherley's own statement *The Plain Dealer* was written when
the author was twenty-five years of age—
i.e., in the year 1665-6.[1] Its first performance on the stage cannot have taken place
later than the spring of 1674, as there is an
interesting allusion to it in the preface to Dryden's *State of
Innocence*, which was registered at Stationers' Hall, April 17,
1674. Dryden writes in terms of noble eulogy : "The author
of *The Plain Dealer*, whom I am proud to call my friend,
has obliged all honest and virtuous men by one of the most
bold, most general, and most useful satires, which has ever
been presented on the English theatre." *The Plain Dealer*
was brought forward by the King's Company, probably, like
The Country Wife, at the house in Lincoln's Inn Fields, as
the new theatre, in Drury Lane, was not opened until
March 26 of that year. It was published three years later,
in 1677, the title-page bearing the *imprimatur*—" Licensed
Jan. 9, 1676, Roger L'Estrange." The license, of course,
was for printing, not for acting ; the date, in new style,
would be 1677.

We shall have, I think, little difficulty in accepting
Wycherley's statement as to the year in which this play was
written, if we suppose, as would almost certainly be the case,
that it was revised and altered before its production on the
stage. The critique on *The Country Wife*, in particular,
cannot have been written earlier than 1672 or 1673, in one of
which years that comedy was first acted.

Of our author's four comedies *The Plain Dealer* is, questionless, the most powerful. From the mock dedication to

---

[1] It cannot have been earlier than the latter year, as *Le Misanthrope*, upon which Wycherley's play is based, did not appear until
1666.

the epilogue "the satire, wit, and strength, of manly Wycherley"[1] are everywhere conspicuous and triumphant. The main purport of the plot, as well as the particular design of certain scenes, is borrowed from *Le Misanthrope* of Molière, but it is almost a truism that the most original writers are frequently the most extensive plagiarists, and Wycherley has so overlaid his appropriations with the colouring of his own brilliant individuality, that his play appears almost equally a masterpiece of orginality as of ingenuity. It is scarcely too much to say that in *The Plain Dealer* we are conscious of a fertility of invention, a richness of wit and satire, which make even *Le Misanthrope* seem tame in comparison. Voltaire has justly contrasted the two plays. "All Wycherley's strokes," he writes, "are stronger and bolder than those of our *Misanthrope*, but then they are less delicate, and the Rules of Decorum are not so well observed in this Play."[2]

The scene in the second act, between Olivia, her cousin, and the two "pretty fellows," Novel and Plausible, was suggested by a dialogue between Célimène and her admirers, in the second act of *Le Misanthrope*, but the detail is almost entirely Wycherley's own, and is enlivened with such diverting antitheses and such brilliant fancy that, perhaps, few scenes more masterly are to be found in the entire range of English comedy from the time of the Restoration downwards. In this scene occurs the critique upon *The Country Wife*, of which the hint was taken from Molière's *Critique de l'École des Femmes*. It is here introduced with great felicity, and the contrast between the affected prudery of the vicious Olivia and the simple candour of the truly modest Eliza is both just and edifying. Again, the discovery by Novel and Plausible of the duplicity of Olivia, by means of an exchange of letters, is borrowed from the *dénouement* of *Le Misanthrope;* but the scene in which it occurs owes little to Molière beyond the incident ; and the humorous device of making each letter, *mutato nomine*, the exact counterpart of the other, belongs to Wycherley alone. One or two more particular coincidences between *The Plain Dealer* and *Le Misanthrope* will be pointed out in the notes.

[1] Dryden.
[2] *Letters concerning the English Nation.* London, 1733.

The admirably conceived character of the Widow Black-acre has been described as a copy of that of the Countess in Racine's comedy, *Les Plaideurs*, surely, in the first instance, by one of those critics with whom "most authors steal their works, or buy." There is a litigious old woman in *Les Plaideurs*, there is a litigious old woman in *The Plain Dealer;* and here the likeness begins and ends.[1] Voltaire calls the Widow Blackacre "the most comical character that was ever brought upon the stage." Lastly, although Fidelia is imitated from Shakespeare's Viola, and although the imitation is immeasurably and at all points inferior to the original, it must be admitted, nevertheless, that she fills her place in the play with perfect propriety, and is even drawn with some not inconsiderable degree of sweetness and pathos.

[1] It is, to say the least, doubtful if *Les Plaideurs* were written before *The Plain Dealer.* The former was produced in 1668. This supposed discovery of a non-existent coincidence appears to have arisen from a misinterpretation of Voltaire's words in the French edition of his *Letters concerning the English Nation :* "On a encore lardé cette pièce (*The Plain Dealer*) d'une Comtesse de Pimbesche, vieille plaideuse." But Voltaire clearly employs the title of "Comtesse de Pimbesche" only as a generic term for a litigious female.

TO MY LADY B——.[1]

Madam,—

HOUGH I never had the honour to receive a favour from you, nay, or be known to you, I take the confidence of an author to write to you a *billet-doux* dedicatory ;—which is no new thing. For by most dedications it appears that authors, though they praise their patrons from top to toe, and seem to turn 'em inside out, know 'em as little as sometimes their patrons their books, though they read them out ; and if the poetical daubers did not write the name of the man or woman on top of the picture, 'twere impossible to guess whose it were. But you, madam, without the help of a poet, have made yourself known and famous in the world ; and because you do not want it, are therefore most worthy of an epistle dedicatory. And this play claims naturally your protection, since it has lost its reputation with the ladies of stricter lives in the play-house ; and, you know, when men's endeavours are discountenanced and refused by the nice coy women of honour, they come to you :—to you, the great and noble patroness of rejected and bashful men (of which number I profess myself to be one, though a poet, a dedicating poet), to you, I say, madam, who have as discerning a judgment, in what's obscene or not, as any quick-sighted civil person of 'em all, and can make as much of a double-meaning saying as the best of 'em ; yet would not, as some do, make nonsense of a poet's jest, rather than not make it bawdy ; by which they show, they as little value wit in a play as in a lover, provided they can bring t'other thing about. Their sense, indeed, lies all one way, and therefore are only for that in a poet, which is moving, as they say. But what do they mean by that word "moving?" Well, I must not put 'em to the blush,

---

[1] Mother Bennet, a noted procuress. "The ironical commendation of the industry and charity of these antiquated ladies, these directors of Sin, after they can no longer commit it, makes up the beauty of the inimitable dedication to *The Plain Dealer*, and is a masterpiece of raillery on this vice."—Steele, in the *Spectator*, No. 266.

since I find I can do't. In short, madam, you would not be one of those who ravish a poet's innocent words, and make 'em guilty of their own naughtiness (as 'tis termed) in spite of his teeth. Nay, nothing is secure from the power of their imaginations, no, not their husbands, whom they cuckold with themselves, by thinking of other men ; and so make the lawful matrimonial embraces adultery, wrong husbands and poets in thought and word, to keep their own reputations. But your ladyship's justice, I know, would think a woman's arraigning and damning a poet for her own obscenity like her crying out a rape, and hanging a man for giving her pleasure, only that she might be thought not to consent to't ; and so to vindicate her honour, forfeits her modesty. But you, madam, have too much modesty to pretend to't, though you have as much to say for your modesty as many a nicer she : for you never were seen at this play, no, not the first day ; and 'tis no matter what people's lives have been, they are unquestionably modest who frequent not this play. For, as Mr. Bayes says of his, "That it is the only touchstone of men's wit and understanding ;" mine is, it seems, the only touchstone of women's virtue and modesty. But hold, that touchstone is equivocal, and, by the strength of a lady's imagination, may become something that is not civil : but your ladyship, I know, scorns to misapply a touchstone.

And, madam, though you have not seen this play, I hope (like other nice ladies) you will the rather read it. Yet, lest the chambermaid or page should not be trusted, and their indulgence could gain no further admittance for it than to their ladies' lobbies or outward rooms, take it into your care and protection ; for by your recommendation and procurement, it may have the honour to get into their closets ; for what they renounce in public, often entertains 'em there, with your help especially. In fine, madam, for these and many other reasons, you are the fittest patroness or judge of this play ; for you show no partiality to this or that author. For from some many ladies will take a broad jest as cheerfully as from the watermen, and sit at some downright filthy plays (as they call 'em) as well satisfied, and as still, as a poet could wish 'em elsewhere. Therefore it must be the doubtful obscenity of my play alone they take exceptions at, because it is too bashful for 'em : and, indeed, most women hate men for attempting by halves on their chastity ; and bawdy, I find, like satire, should be home, not to have it taken notice of. But, now I mention satire, some there are who say, "'Tis the plain-dealing of the play, not the obscenity ; 'tis taking off the ladies' masks, not offering at their petticoats, which offends 'em :"—and generally they are not the handsomest, or most innocent, who are the most angry at their being discovered :—

> " Nihil est audacius illis
> Deprensis ; iram atque animos a crimine sumunt." [1]

Pardon, madam, the quotation ; for a dedication can no more be without ends of Latin, than flattery : and 'tis no matter whom it is writ to ; for an author can as easily, I hope, suppose people to have more understanding and languages than they have, as well as more virtues. But why, the devil, should any of the few modest and handsome be alarmed ?— for some there are, who, as well as any, deserve those attributes, yet refrain not from seeing this play, nor think it any addition to their virtue to set up for it in a playhouse, lest there it should look too much like acting—but why, I say, should any at all of the truly virtuous be concerned, if those who are not so are distinguished from 'em ? for by that mask of modesty which women wear promiscuously in public, they are all alike ; and you can no more know a kept wench from a woman of honour by her looks than by her dress. For those who are of quality without honour (if any such there are) they have their quality to set off their false modesty, as well as their false jewels ; and you must no more suspect their countenances for counterfeit than their pendants, though as the plain dealer Montaigne says, " *Els envoy leur conscience au bordel, et tiennent leur continence en règle.*" But those who act as they look, ought not to be scandalised at the reprehension of others' faults, lest they tax themselves with 'em, and by too delicate and quick an apprehension not only make that obscene which I meant innocent, but that satire on all, which was intended only on those who deserved it.

But, madam, I beg your pardon for this digression to civil women and ladies of honour, since you and I shall never be the better for 'em : for a comic poet and a lady of your pro-

---

[1] Nothing is bolder than they who are detected ; the sense of their own infamy gives them anger and spirit.

fession make most of the other sort ; and the stage and your houses, like our plantations, are propagated by the least nice women ; and, as with the ministers of justice, the vices of the age are our best business. But now I mention public persons, I can no longer defer doing you the justice of a dedication, and telling you your own, who are, of all public-spirited people, the most necessary, most communicative, most generous and hospitable. Your house has been the house of the people ; your sleep still disturbed for the public ; and when you arose, 'twas that others might lie down and you waked that others might rest ; the good you have done is unspeakable. How many young inexperienced heirs have you kept from rash foolish marriages, and from being jilted for their lives by the worst sort of jilts, wives ! How many unbewitched widowers' children have you preserved from the tyranny of stepmothers ! How many old doters from cuckoldage, and keeping other men's wenches and children ! How many adulteries and unnatural sins have you prevented ! In fine, you have been a constant scourge to the old lecher, and often a terror to the young : you have made concupiscence its own punishment, and extinguished lust with lust, like blowing up of houses to stop the fire.

> " Nimirum propter continentiam, incontinentia
> Necessaria est, incendium ignibus exstinguitur." [1]

There's Latin for you again, madam : I protest to you, as I am an author, I cannot help it : nay, I can hardly keep myself from quoting Aristotle and Horace, and talking to you of the rules of writing (like the French authors), to show you and my reader I understand 'em, in my epistle, lest neither of you should find it out by the play. And according to the rules of dedications, 'tis no matter whether you understand or no what I quote or say to you of writing ; for an author can as easily make any one a judge or critic in an epistle, as a hero in his play. But, madam, that this may prove to the end a true epistle dedicatory, I'd have you to know 'tis not without a design upon you, which is in the behalf of the fraternity of Parnassus ; that songs and sonnets may go at your houses, and in your liberties, for guineas and half-guineas ; and that wit, at least with you, as of old, may

---

Indeed, excess is needful for continency's sake. Fire is with fire extinguished.

be the price of beauty, and so you will prove a true encourager of poetry ; for love is a better help to it than wine ; and poets, like painters, draw better after the life than by fancy. Nay, in justice, madam, I think a poet ought to be as free of your houses, as of the play-houses ; since he contributes to the support of both, and is as necessary to such as you, as a ballad-singer to a pick-purse, in convening the cullies at the theatres, to be picked up and carried to supper and bed at your houses. And, madam, the reason of this motion of mine is, because poor poets can get no favour in the tiring-rooms, for they are no keepers, you know ; and folly and money, the old enemies of wit, are even too hard for it on its own dunghill : and for other ladies, a poet can least go to the price of them. Besides, his wit, which ought to recommend him to 'em, is as much an obstruction to his love, as to his wealth or preferment ; for most women now-a-days apprehend wit in a lover, as much as in a husband ; they hate a man that knows 'em, they must have a blind easy fool, whom they can lead by the nose ; and, as the Scythian women of old, must baffle a man, and put out his eyes, ere they will lie with him ; and then too like thieves, when they have plundered and stripped a man, leave him. But if there should be one of a hundred of those ladies generous enough to give herself to a man that has more wit than money, (all things considered,) he would think it cheaper coming to you for a mistress, though you made him pay his guinea ; as a man in a journey (out of good husbandry), had better pay for what he has at an inn, than lie on free-cost at a gentleman's house.

In fine, madam, like a faithful dedicator, I hope I have done myself right in the first place : then you, and your profession, which in the wisest and most religious government in the world is honoured with the public allowance ; and in those that are thought the most uncivilised and barbarous is protected and supported by the ministers of justice. And of you, madam, I ought to say no more here, for your virtues deserve a poem rather than an epistle, or a volume entire to give the world your memoirs, or life at large ; and which (upon the word of an author that has a mind to make an end of his dedication) I promise to do, when I write the annals of our British love, which shall be dedicated to the ladies concerned, if they will not think them something too obscene too; when your life, compared with many that are thought innocent, I doubt not, may vindicate you, and me, to the world, for the confidence I have taken in this address to you; which then may be thought neither impertinent nor immodest; and whatsoever your amorous misfortunes have been, none can charge you with that heinous, and worst of women's crimes, hypocrisy; nay, in spite of misfortunes or age, you are the same woman still; though most of your sex grow Magdalens at fifty, and as a solid French author has it—

> "Après le plaisir, vient la peine;
> Après la peine, la vertu."

But sure an old sinner's continency is much like a gamester's forswearing play, when he had lost all his money; and modesty is a kind of a youthful dress, which, as it makes a young woman more amiable, makes an old one more nauseous: a bashful old woman is like a hopeful old man; and the affected chastity of antiquated beauties is rather a reproach than an honour to 'em; for it shows the men's virtue only, not theirs. But you, in fine, madam, are no more a hypocrite than I am when I praise you; therefore I doubt not will be thought (even by yours and the play's enemies, the nicest ladies) to be the fittest patroness for,

Madam,

Your ladyship's most obedient, faithful, humble servant, and

THE PLAIN DEALER.

PROLOGUE.

SPOKEN BY THE PLAIN DEALER.

I the Plain Dealer am to act to-day,
And my rough part begins before the play.
First, you who scribble, yet hate all that write,
And keep each other company in spite,
As rivals in your common mistress, fame,
And with faint praises one another damn;
'Tis a good play, we know, you can't forgive,
But grudge yourselves the pleasure you receive:

Our scribbler therefore bluntly bid me say,
He would not have the wits pleased here to-day
Next, you, the fine, loud gentlemen o' th' pit,
Who damn all plays, yet, if y'ave any wit,
'Tis but what here you spunge and daily get ;
Poets, like friends to whom you are in debt,
You hate ; and so rooks laugh, to see undone
Those pushing gamesters whom they live upon.
Well, you are sparks, and still will be i' th' fashion ;
Rail then at plays, to hide your obligation.
Now, you shrewd judges, who the boxes sway,
Leading the ladies' hearts and sense astray,
And, for their sakes, see all, and hear no play ;
Correct your cravats, foretops, lock behind :
The dress and breeding of the play ne'er mind ;
Plain dealing is, you'll say, quite out of fashion ;
You'll hate it here, as in a dedication :
And your fair neighbours, in a limning poet
No more than in a painter will allow it.
Pictures too like the ladies will not please ;
They must be drawn too here like goddesses.
You, as at Lely's too, would truncheon wield,
And look like heroes in a painted field.
But the coarse dauber of the coming scenes
To follow life and nature only means,
Displays you as you are, makes his fine woman
A mercenary jilt, and true to no man :
His men of wit and pleasure of the age
Are as dull rogues as ever cumber'd stage :
He draws a friend only to custom just,
And makes him naturally break his trust.
I, only, act a part like none of you,
And yet you'll say, it is a fool's part too :
An honest man who, like you, never winks
At faults ; but, unlike you, speaks what he thinks :
The only fool who ne'er found patron yet,
For truth is now a fault as well as wit.
And where else, but on stages, do we see
Truth pleasing, or rewarded honesty ?
Which our bold poet does this day in me.
If not to th' honest, be to th' prosperous kind,
Some friends at court let the Plain Dealer find

Wycherley.

O*

MANLY, of an honest, surly, nice humour, supposed first, in the time of the Dutch war, to have procured the command of a ship, out of honour, not interest ; and choosing a sea-life only to avoid the world.

FREEMAN, MANLY'S Lieutenant, a gentleman well educated, but of a broken fortune, a complier with the age.

VERNISH, MANLY'S bosom and only friend.

NOVEL, a pert railing Coxcomb, and an admirer of novelties, makes love to OLIVIA.

Major OLDFOX, an old impertinent Fop, given to scribbling, makes love to the Widow BLACKACRE.

Lord PLAUSIBLE, a ceremonious, supple, commending Coxcomb, in love with OLIVIA.

JERRY BLACKACRE, a true raw Squire, under age, and his mother's government, bred to the law.

Lawyers, Knights of the Post, Bailiffs and Aldermen, a Bookseller's Apprentice, a Foot-boy, Sailors, Waiters, and Attendants.

OLIVIA, MANLY'S Mistress.

FIDELIA, in love with MANLY, and follows him to sea in man's clothes.

ELIZA, Cousin of OLIVIA.

LETTICE, OLIVIA'S Woman.

Widow BLACKACRE, a petulant, litigious Widow, always in law, and Mother of Squire JERRY.

SCENE—LONDON.

THE PLAIN DEALER.

ACT THE FIRST.

SCENE I.—MANLY'S *Lodging*.

Enter MANLY, *surlily*, Lord PLAUSIBLE, *following him;
and two* Sailors *behind*.

AN. Tell not me, my good Lord Plausible, of your decorums, supercilious forms, and slavish ceremonies! your little tricks, which you, the spaniels of the world, do daily over and over, for and to one another; not out of love or duty, but your servile fear.

L. Plau. Nay, i' faith, i' faith, you are too passionate; and I must humbly beg your pardon and leave to tell you, they are the arts and rules the prudent of the world walk by.

Man. Let 'em. But I'll have no leading-strings; I can walk alone: I hate a harness, and will not tug on in a faction, kissing my leader behind, that another slave may do the like to me.

L. Plau. What, will you be singular then, like nobody? follow, love, and esteem nobody?

Man. Rather than be general, like you, follow everybody; court and kiss everybody; though perhaps at the same time you hate everybody.

L. Plau. Why, seriously, with your pardon, my dear friend—

Man. With your pardon, my no friend, I will not, as you do, whisper my hatred or my scorn; call a man fool or knave by signs or mouths over his shoulder, whilst you have him in your arms.—For such as you, like common whores and pickpockets, are only dangerous to those you embrace.

L. Plau. Such as I! Heavens defend me!—upon my honour—

Man. Upon your title, my lord, if you'd have me believe you.

L. Plau. Well, then, as I am a person of honour, I never attempted to abuse or lessen any person in my life.

Man. What, you were afraid?

L. Plau. No; but seriously, I hate to do a rude thing: no, faith, I speak well of all mankind.

Man. I thought so: but know, that speaking well of all mankind is the worst kind of detraction; for it takes away the reputation of the few good men in the world, by making all alike. Now, I speak ill of most men, because they deserve it; I that can do a rude thing, rather than an unjust thing.

L. Plau. Well, tell not me, my dear friend, what people deserve; I ne'er mind that. I, like an author in a dedication, never speak well of a man for his sake, but my own; I will not disparage any man, to disparage myself: for to speak ill of people behind their backs, is not like a person of honour; and, truly, to speak ill of 'em to their faces, is not like a complaisant person. But if I did say or do an ill thing to anybody, it should be sure to be behind their backs, out of pure good manners.

Man. Very well; but I, that am an unmannerly sea-fellow, if I ever speak well of people, (which is very seldom indeed,) it should be sure to be behind their backs; and if I would say or do ill to any, it should be to their faces. I would jostle a proud, strutting, over-looking coxcomb, at the head of his sycophants, rather than put out my tongue at him when he were past me; would frown in the arrogant, big, dull face of an over-grown knave of business, rather than vent my spleen against him when his back were turned; would give fawning slaves the lie whilst they embrace or commend me; cowards whilst they brag; call a rascal by no other title, though his father had left him a duke's; laugh at fools aloud before their mistresses; and must desire people to leave me, when their visits grow at last as troublesome as they were at first impertinent.

L. Plau. I would not have my visits troublesome.

Man. The only way to be sure not to have 'em trouble-some, is to make 'em when people are not at home; for your visits, like other good turns, are most obliging when made or done to a man in his absence. A pox! why should any one, because he has nothing to do, go and disturb another man's business?

L. Plau. I beg your pardon, my dear friend.—What, you have business?

Man. If you have any, I would not detain your lord-ship.

L. Plau. Detain me, dear sir!—I can never have enough of your company.

Man. I'm afraid I should be tiresome: I know not what you think.

L. Plau. Well, dear sir, I see you'd have me gone.

[*Aside.*

Man. But I see you won't.

L. Plau. Your most faithful—

Man. God be w'ye, my lord.

L. Plau. Your most humble—

Man. Farewell.

L. Plau. And eternally—

Man. And eternally ceremony— [*Aside.*] Then the devil take thee eternally.

L. Plau. You shall use no ceremony, by my life.

Man. I do not intend it.

L. Plau. Why do you stir then?

Man. Only to see you out of doors, that I may shut 'em against more welcomes.

L. Plau. Nay, faith, that shall not pass upon your most faithful humble servant.

Man. Nor this any more upon me.   [*Aside.*

L. Plau. Well, you are too strong for me.

Man. [*Aside.*] I'd sooner be visited by the plague; for that only would keep a man from visits, and his doors shut.   [*Exit thrusting out* Lord PLAUSIBLE.

1st Sail. Here's a finical fellow, Jack! What a brave fair-weather captain of a ship he would make!

2nd Sail. He a captain of a ship! it must be when she's in the dock then; for he looks like one of those that get the king's commissions for hulls to sell a king's ship, when a brave fellow has fought her almost to a long-boat.

1st Sail. On my conscience then, Jack, that's the reason our bully tar sunk our ship; not only that the Dutch might not have her; but that the courtiers, who laugh at wooden legs, might not make her prize.

2nd Sail. A pox of his sinking, Tom! we have made a base, broken, short voyage of it.

1st Sail. Ay, your brisk dealers in honour always make quick returns with their ships to the dock, and their men to the hospitals. 'Tis, let me see, just a month since we set out of the river, and the wind was almost as cross to us as the Dutch.

2nd Sail. Well, I forgive him sinking my own poor truck, if he would but have given me time and leave to have saved black Kate of Wapping's small venture.

1st Sail. Faith, I forgive him, since, as the purser told me, he sunk the value of five or six thousand pound of his own, with which he was to settle himself somewhere in the Indies; for our merry lieutenant was to succeed him in his commission for the ship back; for he was resolved never to return again for England.

2nd Sail. So it seemed, by his fighting.

1st Sail. No; but he was a-weary of this side of the world here, they say.

2nd Sail. Ay, or else he would not have bid so fair for a passage into t'other.

1st Sail. Jack, thou thinkest thyself in the forecastle, thou'rt so waggish. But I tell you, then, he had a mind to go live and bask himself on the sunny side of the globe.

2nd Sail. What, out of any discontent? for he's always as dogged as an old tarpaulin, when hindered of a voyage by a young pantaloon captain.

1st Sail. 'Tis true I never saw him pleased but in the fight; and then he looked like one of us coming from the pay-table, with a new lining to our hats under our arms.

2nd Sail. A pox! he's like the Bay of Biscay, rough and angry, let the wind blow where 'twill.

1st Sail. Nay, there's no more dealing with him, than with the land in a storm, no near—

2nd Sail. 'Tis a hurry-durry blade. Dost thou remember after we had tugged hard the old leaky long-boat to save his life, when I welcomed him ashore, he gave me a box on the ear, and called me fawning water-dog?

Re-enter MANLY *with* FREEMAN.

1st Sail. Hold thy peace, Jack, and stand by; the foul weather's coming.

Man. You rascals! dogs! how could this tame thing get through you?

1st Sail. Faith, to tell your honour the truth, we were at hob in the hall,[1] and whilst my brother and I were quarrelling about a cast, he slunk by us.

---

[1] Hob in the Hall: the name of a game.

2nd Sail. He's a sneaking fellow I warrant for't.

Man. Have more care for the future, you slaves. Go, and with drawn cutlasses stand at the stair-foot and keep all that ask for me from coming up ; suppose you were guarding the scuttle to the powder-room. Let none enter here, at your and their peril.

1st Sail. No, for the danger would be the same : you would blow them and us up, if we should.

2nd Sail. Must no one come to you, sir ?

Man. No man, sir.

1st Sail. No man, sir ; but a woman then, an't like your honour—

Man. No woman neither, you impertinent dog ! Would you be pimping ? sea-pimp is the strangest monster she has.

2nd Sail. Indeed, an't like your honour, 'twill be hard for us to deny a woman anything, since we are so newly come on shore.

1st Sail. We'll let no old woman come up, though it were our trusting landlady at Wapping.

Man. Would you be witty, you brandy casks you ? you become a jest as ill as you do a horse. Begone, you dogs ! I hear a noise on the stairs.   [*Exeunt* Sailors.

Free. Faith, I am sorry you would let the fop go, I intended to have had some sport with him.

Man. Sport with him ! A pox ! then, why did you not stay ? You should have enjoyed your coxcomb, and had him to yourself for me.

Free. No, I should not have cared for him without you neither ; for the pleasure which fops afford is like that of drinking, only good when 'tis shared ; and a fool, like a bottle, which would make you merry in company, will make you dull alone. But how the devil could you turn a man of his quality down stairs ? You use a lord with very little ceremony, it seems.

Man. A lord ! What, thou art one of those who esteem men only by the marks and value fortune has set upon 'em, and never consider intrinsic worth! but counterfeit honour will not be current with me : I weigh the man, not his title; 'tis not the king's stamp can make the metal better or heavier. Your lord is a leaden shilling, which you bend every way, and debases the stamp he bears, instead of being raised by it.—Here again, you slaves!

Re-enter Sailors.

1st Sail. Only to receive farther instructions, an't like your honour.—What if a man should bring you money, should we turn him back?

Man. All men, I say : must I be pestered with you too?—You dogs, away!

2nd Sail. Nay, I know one man your honour would not have us hinder coming to you, I'm sure.

Man. Who's that? speak quickly, slaves.

2nd Sail. Why, a man that should bring you a challenge. For though you refuse money, I'm sure you love fighting too well to refuse that.

Man. Rogue! rascal! dog!   [*Kicks the* Sailors *out.*

Free. Nay, let the poor rogues have their forecastle jests : they cannot help 'em in a fight, scarce when a ship's sinking.

Man. Damn their untimely jests! a servant's jest is more sauciness than his counsel.

Free. But what, will you see nobody? not your friends?

Man. Friends!—I have but one, and he, I hear, is not in town; nay, can have but one friend, for a true heart admits but of one friendship, as of one love. But in having that friend, I have a thousand; for he has the courage of men in despair, yet the diffidency and caution of cowards; the secrecy of the revengeful, and the constancy of martyrs; one fit to advise, to keep a secret, to fight and die for his friend. Such I think him; for I have trusted him with my mistress in my absence : and the trust of beauty is sure the greatest we can show.

Free. Well, but all your good thoughts are not for him alone, I hope? Pray, what d'ye think of me for a friend?

Man. Of thee! Why, thou art a latitudinarian in friendship, that is, no friend ; thou dost side with all mankind, but wilt suffer for none.   Thou art indeed like your Lord Plausible, the pink of courtesy, therefore hast no friendship : for ceremony and great professing renders friendship as much suspected as it does religion.

Free. And no professing, no ceremony at all in friendship, were as unnatural and as undecent as in religion : and there is hardly such a thing as an honest hypocrite, who professes himself to be worse than he is, unless it be yourself; for though I could never get you to say you were my friend, I know you'll prove so.

Man. I must confess, I am so much your friend, I would not deceive you ; therefore must tell you, not only because my heart is taken up, but according to your rules of friendship, I cannot be your friend.[1]

Free. Pray, why?

Man. Because he that is, you'll say, a true friend to a man, is a friend to all his friends.   But you must pardon me, I cannot wish well to pimps, flatterers, detractors, and cowards, stiff nodding knaves, and supple, pliant, kissing fools.   Now, all these I have seen you use like the dearest friends in the world.

Free. Ha! ha! ha!—What, you observed me, I warrant, in the galleries at Whitehall, doing the business of the place? Pshaw! Court-professions, like court promises, go for nothing, man.   But, faith, could you think I was a friend to all those I hugged, kissed, flattered, bowed to?   Ha! ha!—

Man. You told 'em so, and swore it too ; I heard you.

[1] Compare the ensuing dialogue with *Le Misanthrope*, act I, scene I.

Free. Ay, but when their backs were turned, did not I tell you they were rogues, villains, rascals, whom I despised and hated?

Man. Very fine! But what reason had I to believe you spoke your heart to me, since you professed deceiving so many?

Free. Why, don't you know, good captain, that telling truth is a quality as prejudicial to a man that would thrive in the world, as square play to a cheat, or true love to a whore? Would you have a man speak truth to his ruin? You are severer than the law, which requires no man to swear against himself. You would have me speak truth against myself I warrant, and tell my promising friend the courtier, he has a bad memory.

Man. Yes.

Free. And so make him remember to forget my business? And I should tell the great lawyer too, that he takes oftener fees to hold his tongue, than to speak?

Man. No doubt on't.

Free. Ay, and have him hang or ruin me, when he should come to be a judge, and I before him? And you would have me tell the new officer, who bought his employment lately, that he is a coward?

Man. Ay.

Free. And so get myself cashiered, not him, he having the better friends, though I the better sword? And I should tell the scribbler of honour, that heraldry were a prettier and fitter study for so fine a gentleman than poetry?

Man. Certainly.

Free. And so find myself mauled in his next hired lampoon? And you would have me tell the holy lady, too, she lies with her chaplain?

Man. No doubt on't.

Free. And so draw the clergy upon my back, and want a good table to dine at sometimes? And by the same reason too, I should tell you that the world thinks you a mad man, a brutal, and have you cut my throat, or worse, hate me. What other good success of all my plain-dealing could I have, than what I've mentioned?

Man. Why, first, your promising courtier would keep his word out of fear of more reproaches, or at least would give you no more vain hopes : your lawyer would serve you more faithfully ; for he, having no honour but his interest, is truest still to him he knows suspects him : the new officer would provoke thee to make him a coward, and so be cashiered, that thou, or some other honest fellow, who had more courage than money, might get his place : the noble sonnetteer would trouble thee no more with his madrigals : the praying lady would leave off railing at wenching before thee, and not turn away her chambermaid for her own known frailty with thee : and I, instead of hating thee, should love thee for thy plain dealing ; and in lieu of being mortified, am proud that the world and I think not well of one another.

Free. Well, doctors differ. You are for plain dealing, I find : but against your particular notions, I have the practice of the whole world. Observe but any morning what people do when they get together on the Exchange, in Westminster-hall, or the galleries in Whitehall.

Man. I must confess, there they seem to rehearse Bayes's grand dance. Here you see a bishop bowing low to a gaudy atheist ; a judge to a door-keeper ; a great lord to a fishmonger, or scrivener with a jack-chain about his neck ; a lawyer to a sergeant-at-arms ; a velvet physician to a threadbare chemist ; and a supple gentleman-usher to a surly beefeater : and so tread round in a preposterous huddle of ceremony to each other, whilst they can hardly hold their solemn false countenances.

Free. Well, they understand the world.

Man. Which I do not, I confess.

Free. But, sir, pray believe the friendship I promise you real, whatsoever I have professed to others : try me, at least.

Man. Why, what would you do for me?

Free. I would fight for you.

Man. That you would do for your own honour.   But what else?

Free. I would lend you money, if I had it.

Man. To borrow more of me another time. That were putting your money to interest; a usurer would be as good a friend.—But what other piece of friendship?

Free. I would speak well of you to your enemies.

Man. To encourage others to be your friends, by a show of gratitude.—But what else?

Free. Nay, I would not hear you ill spoken of behind your back by my friend.

Man. Nay, then, thou'rt a friend, indeed.—But it were unreasonable to expect it from thee, as the world goes now, when new friends, like new mistresses, are got by disparaging old ones.

Enter FIDELIA.

But here comes another, will say as much at least.—Dost thou not love me devilishly too, my little volunteer, as well as he or any man can?

Fid. Better than any man can love you, my dear captain.

Man. Look you there, I told you so.

Fid. As well as you do truth or honour, sir; as well.

Man. Nay, good young gentleman, enough, for shame! Thou hast been a page, by thy flattering and lying, to one of those praying ladies who love flattery so well they are jealous of it; and wert turned away for saying the same things to the old housekeeper for sweetmeats, as you did to your lady; for thou flatterest everything and everybody alike.

Fid. You, dear sir, should not suspect the truth of what I say of you, though to you.   Fame, the old liar, is believed when she speaks wonders of you: you cannot be flattered, sir, your merit is unspeakable.

Man. Hold, hold, sir, or I shall suspect worse of you, that you have been a cushion-bearer to some state-hypocrite, and turned away by the chaplains, for out-flattering their probation-sermons for a benefice.

Fid. Suspect me for anything, sir, but the want of love, faith, and duty to you, the bravest, worthiest of mankind ; believe me, I could die for you, sir.

Man. Nay, there you lie, sir ; did not I see thee more afraid in the fight than the chaplain of the ship, or the purser that bought his place ?

Fid. Can he be said to be afraid, that ventures to sea with you ?

Man. Fy ! fy ! no more ; I shall hate thy flattery worse than thy cowardice, nay, than thy bragging.

Fid. Well, I own then I was afraid, mightily afraid ; yet for you I would be afraid again, a hundred times afraid. Dying is ceasing to be afraid, and that I could do sure for you, and you'll believe me one day. [*Weeps.*

Free. Poor youth ! believe his eyes, if not his tongue : he seems to speak truth with them.

Man. What, does he cry ? A pox on't ! a maudlin flatterer is as nauseously troublesome as a maudlin drunkard.—No more, you little milksop, do not cry, I'll never make thee afraid again ; for of all men, if I had occasion, thou shouldst not be my second ; and when I go to sea again, thou shalt venture thy life no more with me.

Fid. Why, will you leave me behind then ?— [*Aside.*] If you would preserve my life, I'm sure you should not.

Man. Leave thee behind ! ay, ay, thou art a hopeful youth for the shore only. Here thou wilt live to be cherished by fortune and the great ones ; for thou mayst easily come to outflatter a dull poet, outlie a coffee-house or gazette-writer, outswear a knight of the post,[1] out-watch a pimp, outfawn a rook, outpromise a lover, outrail a wit, and outbrag a sea-captain :—all this thou canst do,

---

[1] One who gave false bail or evidence, for hire.

because thou'rt a coward, a thing I hate ; therefore thou'lt do better with the world than with me, and these are the good courses you must take in the world. There's good advice, at least, at parting ; go, and be happy with't.

Fid. Parting, sir ! O let me not hear that dismal word.

Man. If my words frighten thee, begone the sooner ; for to be plain with thee, cowardice and I cannot dwell together.

Fid. And cruelty and courage never dwelt together sure, sir. Do not turn me off to shame and misery, for I am helpless and friendless.

Man. Friendless ! there are half a score friends for thee then.—[*Offers her gold.*] I leave myself no more : they'll help thee a little. Begone, go, I must be cruel to thee (if thou callest it so) out of pity.

Fid. If you would be cruelly pitiful, sir, let it be with your sword, not gold. [*Exit.*

Re-enter 1st Sailor.

1st Sail. We have, with much ado, turned away two gentlemen, who told us, forty times over, their names were Mr. Novel and Major Oldfox.

Man. Well, to your post again.—[*Exit* Sailor.] But how come those puppies coupled always together?

Free. O, the coxcombs keep each other company, to show each other, as Novel calls it ; or, as Oldfox says, like two knives, to whet one another.

Man. And set other people's teeth on edge.

Re-enter 2nd Sailor.

2nd Sail. Here is a woman, an't like your honour, scolds and bustles with us, to come in, as much as a seaman's widow at the Navy office : her name is Mrs. Blackacre.

Man. That fiend too !

Free. The Widow Blackacre, is it not ? that litigious she petty-fogger, who is at law and difference with all the

world; but I wish I could make her agree with me in
the church. They say she has fifteen hundred pounds a
year jointure, and the care of her son, that is, the
destruction of his estate.

Man. Her lawyers, attorneys, and solicitors, have
fifteen hundred pounds a year, whilst she is contented to
be poor, to make other people so. For she is as
vexatious as her father was, the great attorney, nay, as a
dozen Norfolk attorneys, and as implacable an adversary
as a wife suing for alimony, or a parson for his tithes ;
and she loves an Easter term, or any term, not as other
country ladies do, to come up to be fine, cuckold their
husbands, and take their pleasure ; for she has no
pleasure but in vexing others, and is usually clothed and
daggled [1] like a bawd in disguise, pursued through alleys
by sergeants. When she is in town, she lodges in one of
the inns of Chancery, where she breeds her son, and is
herself his tutoress in law-French ; and for her country
abode, though she has no estate there, she chooses
Norfolk.—But, bid her come in, with a pox to her ! she
is Olivia's kinswoman, and may make me amends for her
visit, by some discourse of that dear woman.

[Exit Sailor.

Enter Widow BLACKACRE, *with a mantle and a green
bag, and several papers in the other hand :* JERRY
BLACKACRE *in a gown, laden with green bags,
following her.*

Wid. I never had so much to do with a judge's door-
keeper, as with yours ; but——

Man. But the incomparable Olivia, how does she
since I went ?

Wid. Since you went, my suit—

Man. Olivia, I say, is she well ?

Wid. My suit, if you had not returned—

Man. Damn your suit ! how does your cousin Olivia ?

[1] *i.e.* Draggled : bespattered with mud.

Wid. My suit, I say, had been quite lost; but now—

Man. But now, where is Olivia? in town? for—

Wid. For to-morrow we are to have a hearing.

Man. Would you would let me have a hearing to-day!

Wid. But why won't you hear me?

Man. I am no judge, and you talk of nothing but suits; but, pray tell me, when did you see Olivia?

Wid. I am no visiter, but a woman of business; or if I ever visit, 'tis only the Chancery-lane ladies, ladies towards the law; and not any of your lazy, good-for-nothing flirts, who cannot read law-French, though a gallant writ it. But as I was telling you, my suit—

Man. Damn these impertinent vexatious people of business, of all sexes! they are still troubling the world with the tedious recitals of their lawsuits: and one can no more stop their mouths than a wit's when he talks of himself, or an intelligencer's when he talks of other people.

Wid. And a pox of all vexatious, impertinent lovers! they are still perplexing the world with the tedious narrations of their love-suits, and discourses of their mistresses! You are as troublesome to a poor widow of business, as a young coxcombly rhyming lover.

Man. And thou art as troublesome to me, as a rook to a losing gamester, or a young putter of cases to his mistress or sempstress, who has love in her head for another.

Wid. Nay, since you talk of putting of cases, and will not hear me speak, hear our Jerry a little; let him put our case to you, for the trial's to-morrow: and since you are my chief witness, I would have your memory refreshed and your judgment informed, that you may not give your evidence improperly.—Speak out, child.

Jer. Yes, forsooth. Hem! hem! John-a-Stiles—

Man. You may talk, young lawyer, but I shall no more mind you, than a hungry judge does a cause after the clock has struck one.

Free. Nay, you'll find him as peevish too.

Wid. No matter. Jerry, go on.—Do you observe it then, sir; for I think I have seen you in a gown once. Lord, I could hear our Jerry put cases all day long.— Mark him, sir.

Jer. John-a-Stiles—no—there are first, Fitz, Pere, and Ayle,—no, no, Ayle, Pere, and Fitz; Ayle is seised in fee of Blackacre; John-a-Stiles disseises Ayle; Ayle makes claim, and the disseisor dies; then the Ayle—no, the Fitz—

Wid. No, the Pere, sirrah.

Jer. Oh, the Pere! ay, the Pere, sir, and the Fitz—no, the Ayle,—no, the Pere and the Fitz, sir, and—

Man. Damn Pere, Mere, and Fitz, sir!

Wid. No, you are out, child.—Hear me, captain, then. There are Ayle, Pere, and Fitz; Ayle is seised in fee of Blackacre; and, being so seised, John-a-Stiles disseises the Ayle, Ayle makes claim, and the disseisor dies; and then the Pere re-enters, the Pere, sirrah, the Pere—[*to* JERRY] and the Fitz enters upon the Pere, and the Ayle brings his writ of disseisin in the post; and the Pere brings his writ of disseisin in the Pere, and—

Man. Canst thou hear this stuff, Freeman? I could as soon suffer a whole noise of flatterers at a great man's levee in a morning; but thou hast servile complacency enough to listen to a quibbling statesman in disgrace, nay, and be beforehand with him, in laughing at his dull no-jest; but I— [*Offering to go out.*

Wid. Nay, sir, hold! Where's the subpœna, Jerry? I must serve you, sir. You are required by this, to give your testimony—

Man. I'll be forsworn to be revenged on thee.

[*Exit, throwing away the subpœna.*

Wid. Get you gone, for a lawless companion!—Come, Jerry, I had almost forgot, we were to meet at the master's at three: let us mind our business still, child.

Jer. Ay, forsooth, e'en so let's.

Free. Nay, madam, now I would beg you to hear me a little, a little of my business.

Wid. I have business of my own calls me away, sir.

Free. My business would prove yours too, dear madam.

Wid. Yours would be some sweet business, I warrant. What, 'tis no Westminster Hall business? would you have my advice?

Free. No, faith, 'tis a little Westminster Abbey business; I would have your consent.

Wid. O fy, fy, sir! to me such discourse, before my dear minor there!

Jer. Ay, ay, mother, he would be taking livery and seisin of your jointure by digging the turf, but I'll watch your waters,[1] bully, i'fac.—Come away, mother.

[*Exit, haling away his* Mother.

Re-enter FIDELIA.

Fid. Dear sir, you have pity; beget but some in our captain for me.

Free. Where is he?

Fid. Within; swearing as much as he did in the great storm, and cursing you, and sometimes sinks into calms and sighs, and talks of his Olivia.

Free. He would never trust me to see her.—Is she handsome?

Fid. No, if you'll take my word: but I am not a proper judge.

Free. What is she?

Fid. A gentlewoman, I suppose, but of as mean a fortune as beauty; but her relations would not suffer her to go with him to the Indies: and his aversion to this side of the world, together with the late opportunity of commanding the convoy, would not let him stay here longer, though to enjoy her.

---

[1] To keep a strict watch on anyone's actions. *Grose: Lexicon Balatronicum.*

Free. He loves her mightily then?

Fid. Yes, so well, that the remainder of his fortune (I hear about five or six thousand pounds) he has left her, in case he had died by the way, or before she could prevail with her friends to follow him; which he expected she should do, and has left behind him his great bosom friend to be her convoy to him.

Free. What charms has she for him, if she be not handsome?

Fid. He fancies her, I suppose, the only woman of truth and sincerity in the world.

Free. No common beauty, I confess.

Fid. Or else sure he would not have trusted her with so great a share of his fortune, in his absence, I suppose (since his late loss) all he has.

Free. Why, has he left it in her own custody?

Fid. I am told so.

Free. Then he has showed love to her indeed, in leaving her, like an old husband that dies as soon as he has made his wife a good jointure.—But I'll go in to him, and speak for you, and know more from him of his Olivia.   [*Exit.*

Fid. His Olivia, indeed, his happy Olivia!
Yet she was left behind, when I was with him:
But she was ne'er out of his mind or heart.
She has told him she loved him; I have show'd it,
And durst not tell him so, till I had done,
Under this habit, such convincing acts
Of loving friendship for him, that through it
He first might find out both my sex and love;
And, when I'd had him from his fair Olivia,
And this bright world of artful beauties here,
Might then have hoped, he would have look'd on me,
Amongst the sooty Indians; and I could,
To choose, there live his wife, where wives are forced
To live no longer, when their husbands die;
Nay, what's yet worse, to share 'em whilst they live

With many rival wives.   But here he comes,
And I must yet keep out of his sight, not
To lose it for ever.   [*Exit*

Re-enter MANLY *and* FREEMAN.

Free. But pray what strange charms has she that could
make you love?

Man. Strange charms indeed! she has beauty enough
to call in question her wit or virtue, and her form would
make a starved hermit a ravisher; yet her virtue and
conduct would preserve her from the subtle lust of a
pampered prelate.   She is so perfect a beauty, that art
could not better it, nor affectation deform it.   Yet all
this is nothing.   Her tongue as well as face ne'er knew
artifice; nor ever did her words or looks contradict her
heart.   She is all truth, and hates the lying, masking,
daubing world, as I do: for which I love her, and for
which I think she dislikes not me.   For she has often
shut out of her conversation for mine, the gaudy fluttering parrots of the town, apes and echoes of men only,
and refused their common-place pert chat, flattery and
submissions, to be entertained with my sullen bluntness,
and honest love: and, last of all, swore to me, since her
parents would not suffer her to go with me, she would
stay behind for no other man; but follow me without
their leave, if not to be obtained.   Which oath—

Free. Did you think she would keep?

Man. Yes; for she is not (I tell you) like other
women, but can keep her promise, though she has sworn
to keep it.   But, that she might the better keep it, I left
her the value of five or six thousand pounds: for women's
wants are generally the most importunate solicitors to
love or marriage.

Free. And money summons lovers more than beauty,
and augments but their importunity, and their number;
so makes it the harder for a woman to deny 'em.   For
my part, I am for the French maxim:—" If you would

have your female subjects loyal, keep 'em poor."—But in short, that your mistress may not marry, you have given her a portion.

Man. She had given me her heart first, and I am satisfied with the security; I can never doubt her truth and constancy.

Free. It seems you do, since you are fain to bribe it with money. But how come you to be so diffident of the man that says he loves you, and not doubt the woman that says it?

Man. I should, I confess, doubt the love of any other woman but her, as I do the friendship of any other man but him I have trusted; but I have such proofs of their faith as cannot deceive me.

Free. Cannot!

Man. Not but I know that generally no man can be a great enemy but under the name of friend; and if you are a cuckold, it is your friend only that makes you so, for your enemy is not admitted to your house : if you are cheated in your fortune, 'tis your friend that does it, for your enemy is not made your trustee : if your honour or good name be injured, 'tis your friend that does it still, because your enemy is not believed against you. Therefore, I rather choose to go where honest, downright barbarity is professed, where men devour one another like generous hungry lions and tigers, not like crocodiles ; where they think the devil white, of our complexion ; and I am already so far an Indian. But if your weak faith doubts this miracle of a woman, come along with me, and believe ; and thou wilt find her so handsome, that thou, who art so much my friend, wilt have a mind to lie with her, and so wilt not fail to discover what her faith and thine is to me.

> When we're in love, the great adversity,
> Our friends and mistresses at once we try.

[Exeunt.

ACT THE SECOND.

SCENE I.—OLIVIA's *Lodging*.

Enter OLIVIA, ELIZA, *and* LETTICE.

Oliv. Ah, cousin, what a world 'tis we live in! I am so weary of it.

Eliza. Truly, cousin, I can find no fault with it, but that we cannot always live in't, for I can never be weary of it.

Oliv. O hideous! you cannot be in earnest sure, when you say you like the filthy world.

Eliza. You cannot be in earnest sure, when you say you dislike it.

Oliv. You are a very censorious creature, I find.

Eliza. I must confess, I think we women as often discover where we love by railing, as men when they lie by their swearing; and the world is but a constant keeping gallant, whom we fail not to quarrel with when anything crosses us, yet cannot part with't for our hearts.

Let. A gallant indeed, madam, whom ladies first make jealous, and then quarrel with it for being so; for if, by her indiscretion, a lady be talked of for a man, she cries presently, "'Tis a censorious world!" if by her vanity the intrigue be found out, "'Tis a prying malicious world!" if by her over-fondness the gallant proves unconstant, "'Tis a false world!" and if by her niggardli

ness the chambermaid tells, "'Tis a perfidious world!"
But that, I'm sure, your ladyship cannot say of the world
yet, as bad as 'tis.

Oliv. But I may say, "'Tis a very impertinent world!"
—Hold your peace.—And, cousin, if the world be a
gallant, 'tis such a one as is my aversion. Pray name it
no more.

Eliza. But is it possible the world, which has such
variety of charms for other women, can have none for
you? Let's see—first, what d'ye think of dressing and
fine clothes?

Oliv. Dressing! Fy, fy, 'tis my aversion.—[*To* Lettice.] But come hither, you dowdy; methinks you might
have opened this toure better; O hideous! I cannot
suffer it! D'ye see how't sits?

Eliza. Well enough, cousin, if dressing be your aversion.

Oliv. 'Tis so : and for variety of rich clothes, they are
more my aversion.

Let. Ay, 'tis because your ladyship wears 'em too long;
for indeed a gown, like a gallant, grows one's aversion by
having too much of it.

Oliv. Insatiable creature! I'll be sworn I have had
this not above three days, cousin, and within this month
have made some six more.

Eliza. Then your aversion to 'em is not altogether so
great.

Oliv. Alas! 'tis for my woman only I wear 'em,
cousin.

Let. If it be for me only, madam, pray do not wear
em.

Eliza. But what d'ye think of visits—balls?

Oliv. O, I detest 'em!

Eliza. Of plays?

Oliv. I abominate 'em ; filthy, obscene, hideous things.

Eliza. What say you to masquerading in the winter,
and Hyde Park in the summer?

Oliv. Insipid pleasures I taste not.

Eliza. Nay, if you are for more solid pleasures, what think you of a rich young husband?

Oliv. O horrid! marriage! what a pleasure you have found out! I nauseate it of all things.

Let. But what does your ladyship think then of a liberal handsome young lover?

Oliv. A handsome young fellow, you impudent! begone out of my sight. Name a handsome young fellow to me! foh, a hideous handsome young fellow I abominate! [*Spits.*

Eliza. Indeed! But let's see—will nothing please you? what d'ye think of the court?

Oliv. How, the court! the court, cousin! my aversion, my aversion, my aversion of all aversions!

Eliza. How, the court! where—

Oliv. Where sincerity is a quality as much out of fashion and as unprosperous as bashfulness: I could not laugh at a quibble, though it were a fat privy-counsellor's; nor praise a lord's ill verses, though I were myself the subject; nor an old lady's young looks, though I were her woman; nor sit to a vain young smile-maker, though he flattered me. In short, I could not glout[1] upon a man when he comes into a room, and laugh at him when he goes out: I cannot rail at the absent to flatter the standers-by; I—

Eliza. Well, but railing now is so common, that 'tis no more malice, but the fashion; and the absent think they are no more the worse for being railed at, than the present think they're the better for being flattered. And for the court—

Oliv. Nay, do not defend the court; for you'll make me rail at it like a trusting citizen's widow.

Eliza. Or like a Holborn lady, who could not get in to the last ball, or was out of countenance in the drawing-room the last Sunday of her appearance there. For

---

[1] Look sullen.

none rail at the court but those who cannot get into it, or else who are ridiculous when they are there ; and I shall suspect you were laughed at when you were last there, or would be a maid of honour.

Oliv. I a maid of honour ! To be a maid of honour, were yet of all things my aversion.

Eliza. In what sense am I to understand you ? But in fine, by the word aversion, I'm sure you dissemble ; for I never knew woman yet used it who did not. Come, our tongues belie our hearts more than our pocket-glasses do our faces. But methinks we ought to leave off dissembling, since 'tis grown of no use to us ; for all wise observers understand us now-a-days, as they do dreams, almanacs, and Dutch gazettes, by the contrary : and a man no more believes a woman, when she says she has an aversion for him, than when she says she'll cry out.

Oliv. O filthy ! hideous ! Peace, cousin, or your discourse will be my aversion : and you may believe me.

Eliza. Yes ; for if anything be a woman's aversion, 'tis plain dealing from another woman : and perhaps that's your quarrel to the world ; for that will talk, as your woman says.

Oliv. Talk ? not of me sure ; for what men do I converse with ? what visits do I admit ?

Enter Boy.

Boy. Here's the gentleman to wait upon you, madam.

Oliv. On me ! you little unthinking fop ; d'ye know what you say ?

Boy. Yes, madam, 'tis the gentleman that comes every day to you, who—

Oliv. Hold your peace, you heedless little animal, and get you gone.—[*Exit* Boy.] This country boy, cousin, takes my dancing-master, tailor, or the spruce milliner, for visitors.

Let. No, madam; 'tis Mr. Novel, I'm sure, by his talking so loud : I know his voice too, madam.

Oliv. You know nothing, you buffle-headed stupid creature you : you would make my cousin believe I receive visits. But if it be Mr.—what did you call him ?

Let. Mr. Novel, madam ; he that—

Oliv. Hold your peace ; I'll hear no more of him. But if it be your Mr.—(I cannot think of his name again) I suppose he has followed my cousin hither.

Eliza. No, cousin, I will not rob you of the honour of the visit: 'tis to you, cousin ; for I know him not.

Oliv. Nor did I ever hear of him before, upon my honour, cousin ; besides, han't I told you, that visits, and the business of visits, flattery and detraction, are my aversion? D'ye think then I would admit such a coxcomb as he is ? who rather than not rail, will rail at the dead, whom none speak ill of; rather than not flatter, will flatter the poets of the age, whom none will flatter; who affects novelty as much as the fashion, and is as fantastical as changeable, and as well known as the fashion ; who likes nothing but what is new, nay, would choose to have his friend or his title a new one. In fine, he is my aversion.

Eliza. I find you do know him, cousin ; at least, have heard of him.

Oliv. Yes, now I remember, I have heard of him.

Eliza. Well ; but since he is such a coxcomb, for Heaven's sake, let him not come up. Tell him, Mrs. Lettice, your lady it not within.

Oliv. No, Lettice, tell him my cousin is here, and that he may come up. For notwithstanding I detest the sight of him, you may like his conversation ; and though I would use him scurvily, I will not be rude to you in my own lodging : since he has followed you hither, let him come up, I say.

Eliza. Very fine ! pray let him go to the devil, I say,

for me : I know him not, nor desire it.   Send him away, Mrs. Lettice.

Oliv. Upon my word, she shan't : I must disobey your commands, to comply with your desires.   Call him up, Lettice.

Eliza. Nay, I'll swear she shall not stir on that errand.
[*Holds* LETTICE.

Oliv. Well then, I'll call him myself for you, since you will have it so.—[*Calls out at the door.*] Mr. Novel, sir, sir !

Enter NOVEL.

Nov. Madam, I beg your pardon ; perhaps you were busy : I did not think you had company with you.

Eliza. Yet he comes to me, cousin !

[*Aside to* OLIVIA.

Oliv. Chairs there.   [*They sit.*

Nov. Well ; but, madam, d'ye know whence I come now ?

Oliv. From some melancholy place, I warrant, sir, since they have lost your good company.

Eliza. So !

Nov. From a place where they have treated me at dinner with so much civility and kindness, a pox on them ! that I could hardly get away to you, dear madam.

Oliv. You have a way with you so new and obliging, sir !

Eliza. You hate flattery, cousin !   [*Apart to* OLIVIA.

Nov. Nay, faith, madam, d'ye think my way new ? Then you are obliging, madam.   I must confess, I hate imitation, to do anything like other people.   All that know me do me the honour to say, I am an original, faith.   But, as I was saying, madam, I have been treated to-day with all the ceremony and kindness imaginable at my Lady Autumn's.   But, the nauseous old woman at the upper end of her table—

Oliv. Revives the old Grecian custom, of serving in a death's head with their banquets.

Nov. Ha! ha! fine, just, i'faith, nay, and new. 'Tis like eating with the ghost in "The Libertine:"[1] she would frighten a man from her dinner with her hollow invitations, and spoil one's stomach—

Oliv. To meat or women. I detest her hollow cherry cheeks: she looks like an old coach new painted; affecting an unseemly smugness, whilst she is ready to drop in pieces.

Eliza. You hate detraction, I see, cousin.

[*Apart to* OLIVIA.

Nov. But the silly old fury, whilst she affects to look like a woman of this age, talks—

Oliv. Like one of the last; and as passionately as an old courtier who has outlived his office.

Nov. Yes, madam; but pray let me give you her character. Then she never counts her age by the years, but—

Oliv. By the masques she has lived to see.

Nov. Nay then, madam, I see you think a little harmless railing too great a pleasure for any but yourself; and therefore I've done.

Oliv. Nay, faith, you shall tell me who you had there at dinner.

Nov. If you would hear me, madam.

Oliv. Most patiently; speak, sir.

Nov. Then, we had her daughter—

Oliv. Ay, her daughter; the very disgrace to good clothes, which she always wears but to heighten her deformity, not mend it: for she is still most splendidly, gallantly ugly, and looks like an ill piece of daubing in a rich frame.

Nov. So! But have you done with her, madam? and can you spare her to me a little now?

---

[1] A tragedy by Thomas Shadwell, produced in 1676, partly based on Molière's *Le Festin de Pierre.* This allusion must have been inserted after the production of *The Plain Dealer.*

Oliv. Ay, ay, sir.

Nov. Then, she is like—

Oliv. She is, you'd say, like a city bride ; the greater fortune, but not the greater beauty, for her dress.

Nov. Well : yet have you done, madam ? Then she—

Oliv. Then she bestows as unfortunately on her face all the graces in fashion, as the languishing eye, the hanging or pouting lip. But as the fool is never more provoking than when he aims at wit, the ill-favoured of our sex are never more nauseous than when they would be beauties, adding to their natural deformity the artificial ugliness of affectation.

Eliza. So, cousin, I find one may have a collection of all one's acquaintance's pictures as well at your house as at Mr. Lely's.[1] Only the difference is, there we find 'em much handsomer than they are, and like ; here much uglier, and like : and you are the first of the profession of picture-drawing I ever knew without flattery.

Oliv. I draw after the life ; do nobody wrong, cousin.

Eliza. No, you hate flattery and detraction.

Oliv. But, Mr. Novel, who had you besides at dinner ?

Nov. Nay, the devil take me if I tell you, unless you will allow me the privilege of railing in my turn.—But, now I think on't, the women ought to be your province, as the men are mine : and you must know we had him whom—

Oliv. Him, whom—

Nov. What, invading me already ? and giving the character before you know the man ?

Eliza. No, that is not fair, though it be usual.

Oliv. I beg your pardon, Mr. Novel ; pray go on.

Nov. Then, I say, we had that familiar coxcomb who is at home wheresoe'er he comes.

Oliv. Ay, that fool—

Nov. Nay then, madam, your servant ; I'm gone.

[1] Afterwards Sir Peter Lely, painter of the beauties of the Court of Charles II.

Taking the fool out of one's mouth is worse than taking the bread out of one's mouth.

Oliv. I've done; your pardon, Mr. Novel: pray proceed.

Nov. I say, the rogue, that he may be the only wit in company, will let nobody else talk, and—

Oliv. Ay, those fops who love to talk all themselves are of all things my aversion.

Nov. Then you'll let me speak, madam, sure. The rogue, I say, will force his jest upon you; and I hate a jest that's forced upon a man, as much as a glass.

Eliza. Why, I hope, sir, he does not expect a man of your temperance in jesting should do him reason?

Nov. What! interruption from this side too? I must then—   [*Offers to rise.* OLIVIA *holds him.*

Oliv. No, sir.—You must know, cousin, that fop he means, though he talks only to be commended, will not give you leave to do't.

Nov. But, madam—

Oliv. He a wit! Hang him; he's only an adopter of straggling jests and fatherless lampoons; by the credit of which he eats at good tables, and so, like the barren beggar-woman, lives by borrowed children.

Nov. Madam—

Oliv. And never was author of anything but his news: but that is still all his own.

Nov. Madam, pray—

Oliv. An eternal babbler; and makes no more use of his ears, than a man that sits at a play by his mistress, or in Fop-corner. He's, in fine, a base detracting fellow, and is my aversion.—But who else, prithee Mr. Novel, was there with you? Nay, you shan't stir.

Nov. I beg your pardon, madam; I cannot stay in any place where I'm not allowed a little christian liberty of ra'ling.

Oliv. Nay, prithee Mr. Novel, stay: and though you should rail at me, I would hear you with patience. Prithee, who else was there with you?

Nov. Your servant, madam.

Oliv. Nay, prithee tell us, Mr. Novel, prithee do.

Nov. We had nobody else.

Oliv. Nay, faith, I know you had. Come, my Lord Plausible was there too ; who is, cousin, a—

Eliza. You need not tell me what he is, cousin ; for I know him to be a civil, good-natured, harmless gentleman, that speaks well of all the world, and is always in good-humour ; and—

Oliv. Hold, cousin, hold ; I hate detraction. But I must tell you, cousin, his civility is cowardice, his good-nature want of wit ; and he has neither courage nor sense to rail : and for his being always in humour, 'tis because he is never dissatisfied with himself. In fine, he is my aversion ; and I never admit his visits beyond my hall.

Nov. No, he visit you ! Damn him, cringing grinning rogue ! if I should see him coming up to you, I would make bold to kick him down again.—Ha !

Enter Lord PLAUSIBLE.

My dear lord, your most humble servant.

[*Rises and salutes* Lord PLAUSIBLE, *and kisses him.*

Eliza. So, I find kissing and railing succeed each other with the angry men as well as with the angry women ; and their quarrels are like love-quarrels, since absence is the only cause of them ; for as soon as the man appears again, they are over. [*Aside.*

L. Plau. Your most faithful humble servant, generous Mr. Novel. And, madam, I am your eternal slave, and kiss your fair hands ; which I had done sooner, according to your commands, but—

Oliv. No excuses, my lord.

Eliza. What, you sent for him then, cousin ?

[*Apart to* OLIVIA.

Nov. Ha ! invited ! [*Aside.*

Oliv. I know you must divide yourself ; for your good

company is too general a good to be engrossed by any particular friend.

L. Plau. O Lord, madam, my company! your most obliged, faithful, humble servant. But I could have brought you good company indeed; for I parted at your door with two of the worthiest, bravest men—

Oliv. Who were they, my lord?

Nov. Who do you call the worthiest, bravest men, pray?

L. Plau. O, the wisest, bravest gentlemen! men of such honour and virtue! of such good qualities! ah—

Eliza. This is a coxcomb that speaks ill of all people a different way, and libels everybody with dull praise, and commonly in the wrong place; so makes his panegyrics abusive lampoons.   [*Aside.*

Oliv. But pray let me know who they were?

L. Plau. Ah! such patterns of heroic virtue! such —

Nov. Well: but who the devil were they?

L. Plau. The honour of our nation! the glory of our age! Ah, I could dwell a twelvemonth on their praise; which indeed I might spare by telling their names; Sir John Current and Sir Richard Court-Title.

Nov. Court-Title! ha! ha!

Oliv. And Sir John Current! Why will you keep such a wretch company, my lord?

L. Plau. O madam, seriously you are a little too severe; for he is a man of unquestioned reputation in everything.

Oliv. Yes, because he endeavours only with the women to pass for a man of courage, and with the bullies for a wit; with the wits for a man of business, and with the men of business for a favourite at court; and at court for city-security.

Nov. And for Sir Richard, he—

L. Plau. He loves your choice picked company, persons that—

Oliv. He loves a lord indeed; but—

Nov. Pray, dear madam, let me have but a bold stroke or two at his picture. He loves a lord, as you say, though-

Oliv. Though he borrowed his money, and ne'er paid him again.

Nov. And would bespeak a place three days before at the back-end of a lord's coach to Hyde Park.

L. Plau. Nay, i'faith, i'faith, you are both too severe.

Oliv. Then to show yet more his passion for quality, he makes love to that fulsome coach-load of honour, my Lady Goodly, for he's always at her lodging.

L. Plau. Because it is the conventicle-gallant, the meeting-house of all the fair ladies, and glorious superfine beauties of the town.

Nov. Very fine ladies! there's first—

Oliv. Her honour, as fat as an hostess.

L. Plau. She is something plump indeed, a goodly, comely, graceful person.

Nov. Then there's my Lady Frances—what d'ye call her? as ugly—

Oliv. As a citizen's lawfully begotten daughter.

L. Plau. She has wit in abundance, and the handsomest heel, elbow, and tip of an ear, you ever saw.

Nov. Heel and elbow! ha! ha! And there's my Lady Betty, you know—

Oliv. As sluttish and slatternly as an Irish woman bred in France.

L. Plau. Ah! all she has hangs with a loose air, indeed, and becoming negligence.

Eliza. You see all faults with lovers' eyes, I find, my lord.

L. Plau. Ah, madam, your most obliged, faithful, humble servant to command! But you can say nothing sure against the superfine mistress—

Oliv. I know who you mean. She is as censorious and detracting a jade as a superannuated sinner.

L. Plau. She has a smart way of raillery, 'tis confessed.

Nov. And then for Mrs. Grideline—

L. Plau. She, I'm sure is—

Oliv. One that never spoke ill of anybody, 'tis confessed.   For she is as silent in conversation as a country
lover, and no better company than a clock, or a weather-
glass : for if she sounds, 'tis but once an hour to put you
in mind of the time of day, or to tell you 'twill be cold or
hot, rain or snow.

L. Plau. Ah, poor creature ! she's extremely good and
modest.

Nov. And for Mrs. Bridlechin, she's—

Oliv. As proud as a churchman's wife.

L. Plau. She's a woman of great spirit and honour,
and will not make herself cheap, 'tis true.

Nov. Then Mrs. Hoyden, that calls all people by their
surnames, and is—

Oliv. As familiar a duck—

Nov. As an actress in the tiring room.   There I was
once beforehand with you, madam.

L. Plau. Mrs. Hoyden ! a poor, affable, good-natured
soul.   But the divine Mrs. Trifle comes thither too.
Sure her beauty, virtue, and conduct, you can say
nothing to.

Oliv. No !

Nov. No !—Pray let me speak, madam.

Oliv. First, can any one be called beautiful that
squints ?

L. Plau. Her eyes languish a little, I own.

Nov. Languish ! ha ! ha !

Oliv. Languish !—Then, for her conduct, she was
seen at the " Country Wife " after the first day.   There's
for you, my lord.

L. Plau. But, madam, she was not seen to use her
fan all the play long, turn aside her head, or by a
conscious blush discover more guilt than modesty.

Oliv. Very fine !   Then you think a woman modest
that sees the hideous " Country Wife " without blushing
or publishing her detestation of it ?   D'ye hear him,
cousin ?

Eliza. Yes, and am, I must confess, something of his opinion ; and think, that as an over-conscious fool at a play, by endeavouring to show the author's want of wit, exposes his own to more censure, so may a lady call her own modesty in question, by publicly cavilling with the poet's.   For all those grimaces of honour and artificial modesty disparage a woman's real virtue, as much as the use of white and red does the natural complexion : and you must use very, very little, if you would have it thought your own.

Oliv. Then you would have a woman of honour with passive looks, ears, and tongue, undergo all the hideous obscenity she hears at nasty plays.

Eliza. Truly, I think a woman betrays her want of modesty, by showing it publicly in a playhouse, as much as a man does his want of courage by a quarrel there ; for the truly modest and stout say least, and are least exceptious, especially in public.

Oliv. O hideous, cousin ! this cannot be your opinion. But you are one of those who have the confidence to pardon the filthy play.

Eliza. Why, what is there of ill in't, say you ?

Oliv. O fy ! fy ! fy ! would you put me to the blush anew ? call all the blood into my face again ?   But to satisfy you then ; first, the clandestine obscenity in the very name of Horner.

Eliza. Truly, 'tis so hidden, I cannot find it out, I confess.

Oliv. O horrid !   Does it not give you the rank conception or image of a goat, or town-bull, or a satyr ? nay, what is yet a filthier image than all the rest, that of an eunuch ?

Eliza. What then ?   I can think of a goat, a bull, or a satyr, without any hurt.

Oliv. Ay : but cousin, one cannot stop there.

Eliza. I can, cousin.

Oliv. O no ; for when you have those filthy creatures

in your head once, the next thing you think, is what they do; as their defiling of honest men's beds and couches, rapes upon sleeping and waking country virgins under hedges, and on haycocks. Nay, farther—

Eliza. Nay, no farther, cousin. We have enough of your comment on the play, which will make me more ashamed than the play itself.

Oliv. O, believe me, 'tis a filthy play! and you may take my word for a filthy play as soon as another's. But the filthiest thing in that play, or any other play, is—

Eliza. Pray keep it to yourself, if it be so.

Oliv. No, faith, you shall know it; I'm resolved to make you out of love with the play. I say, the lewdest, filthiest thing is his china; nay, I will never forgive the beastly author his china. He has quite taken away the reputation of poor china itself, and sullied the most innocent and pretty furniture of a lady's chamber; insomuch that I was fain to break all my defiled vessels. You see I have none left; nor you, I hope.

Eliza. You'll pardon me, I cannot think the worse of my china for that of the playhouse.

Oliv. Why, you will not keep any now, sure! 'Tis now as unfit an ornament for a lady's chamber as the pictures that come from Italy and other hot countries; as appears by their nudities, which I always cover, or scratch out, whereso'er I find 'em. But china! out upon't, filthy china! nasty debauched china!

Eliza. All this will not put me out of conceit with china, nor the play, which is acted to-day, or another of the same beastly author's, as you call him, which I'll go see.

Oliv. You will not, sure! nay, you sha' not venture your reputation by going, and mine by leaving me alone with two men here: nay, you'll disoblige me for ever, if—

[*Pulls her back.*

Eliza. I stay!—your servant. [*Exit.*

Oliv. Well—but, my lord, though you justify every-body, you cannot in earnest uphold so beastly a writer, whose ink is so smutty as one may say.

L. Plau. Faith, I dare swear the poor man did not think to disoblige the ladies, by any amorous, soft, passionate, luscious saying in his play.

Oliv. Fy, my lord! But what think you, Mr. Novel, of the play? though I know you are a friend to all that are new.

Nov. Faith, madam, I must confess, the new plays would not be the worse for my advice, but I could never get the silly rogues, the poets, to mind what I say; but I'll tell you what counsel I gave the surly fool you spake of.

Oliv. What was't?

Nov. Faith, to put his play into rhyme; for rhyme, you know, often makes mystical nonsense pass with the critics for wit, and a double-meaning saying with the ladies, for soft, tender, and moving passion. But now I talk of passion, I saw your old lover this morning— Captain—   [*Whispers.*

Enter MANLY, FREEMAN, *and* FIDELIA *standing behind.*

Oliv. Whom?—nay, you need not whisper.

Man. We are luckily got hither unobserved!—How! in a close conversation with these supple rascals, the out-casts of sempstresses' shops!

Free. Faith, pardon her, captain, that, since she could no longer be entertained with your manly bluntness and honest love, she takes up with the pert chat and common-place flattery of these fluttering parrots of the town, apes and echoes of men only.

Man. Do not you, sir, play the echo too, mock me, dally with my own words, and show yourself as imperti-nent as they are.

Free. Nay, captain—

Fid. Nay, lieutenant, do not excuse her; methinks she

looks very kindly upon 'em both, and seems to be pleased with what that fool there says to her.

Man. You lie, sir ! and hold your peace, that I may not be provoked to give you a worse reply.

Oliv. Manly returned, d'ye say ! and is he safe ?

Nov. My lord saw him too.—Hark you, my lord.

[*Whispers to* Lord PLAUSIBLE.

Man. She yet seems concerned for my safety, and perhaps they are admitted now here but for their news of me : for intelligence indeed is the common passport of nauseous fools, when they go their round of good tables and houses.   [*Aside.*

Oliv. I heard of his fighting only, without particulars, and confess I always loved his brutal courage, because it made me hope it might rid me of his more brutal love.

Man. What's that ?   [*Aside.*

Oliv. But is he at last returned, d'ye say, unhurt ?

Nov. Ay, faith, without doing his business ; for the rogue has been these two years pretending to a wooden leg, which he would take from fortune as kindly as the staff of a marshal of France, and rather read his name in a gazette—

Oliv. Than in the entail of a good estate.

Man. So !   [*Aside.*

Nov. I have an ambition, I must confess, of losing my heart before such a fair enemy as yourself, madam ; but that silly rogues should be ambitious of losing their arms, and—

Oliv. Looking like a pair of compasses.

Nov. But he has no use of his arms but to set 'em on kimbow, for he never pulls off his hat, at least not to me, I'm sure ; for you must know, madam, he has a fanatical hatred to good company : he can't abide me.

L. Plau. O, be not so severe to him, as to say he hates good company : for I assure you he has a great respect, esteem and kindness for me.

Man. That kind, civil rogue has spoken yet ten thousand times worse of me than t'other.   [*Aside.*

Oliv. Well, if he be returned, Mr. Novel, then shall I be pestered again with his boisterous sea-love ; have my alcove smell like a cabin, my chamber perfumed with his tarpaulin Brandenburgh ; and hear volleys of brandy-sighs, enough to make a fog in one's room. Foh ! I hate a lover that smells like Thames Street !

Man. [*Aside.*] I can bear no longer, and need hear no more.—[*To* OLIVIA.] But since you have these two pulvillio[1] boxes, these essence-bottles, this pair of musk-cats here, I hope I may venture to come yet nearer you.

Oliv. Overheard us then !

Nov. I hope he heard me not.   [*Aside.*

L. Plau. Most noble and heroic captain, your most obliged, faithful, humble servant.

Nov. Dear tar, thy humble servant.

Man. Away !—[*Thrusts* NOVEL *and* Lord PLAUSIBLE *on each side.*] Madam—

Oliv. Nay, I think I have fitted[2] you for listening.

Man. You have fitted me for believing you could not be fickle, though you were young ; could not dissemble love, though 'twas your interest ; nor be vain, though you were handsome ; nor break your promise, though to a parting lover ; nor abuse your best friend, though you had wit : but I take not your contempt of me worse than your esteem, or civility for these things here, though you know 'em.

Nov. Things !

L. Plau. Let the captain rally a little.

Man. Yes, things ! Canst thou be angry, thou thing ?
          [*Coming up to* NOVEL.

Nov. No, since my lord says you speak in raillery ; for though your sea-raillery be something rough, yet, I confess,

---

[1] A sweet-scented powder.   [2] Been even with.

we use one another too **as** bad **every** day at Locket's,[1] and never quarrel for the matter.

L. Plau. Nay, noble captain, be not angry with him. —A word with you, I beseech you—

[*Whispers to* MANLY.

Oliv. Well, we women, like the rest of the cheats of the world, when our cullies or creditors have found us out, and will or can trust no longer, pay debts and satisfy obligations with a quarrel, the kindest present a man can make to his mistress, when he can make no more presents. For oftentimes in love, as at cards, we are forced to play foul, only to give over the game; and use our lovers like the cards, when we can get no more by them, throw 'em up in a pet upon the first dispute.

[*Aside.*

Man. My lord, all that you have made me know by your whispering, which I knew not before, is, that you have a stinking breath; there's a secret for your secret.

L. Plau. Pshaw! pshaw!

Man. But, madam, tell me, pray, what was't about this spark could take you? Was it the merit of his fashionable impudence; the briskness of his noise, the wit of his laugh, his judgment, or fancy in his garniture? or was it a well-trimmed glove, or the scent of it, that charmed you?

Nov. Very well, sir : 'gad these sea-captains make nothing of dressing. But let me tell you, sir, a man by his dress, as much as by anything, shows his wit and judgment; nay, and his courage too.

Free. How, his courage, Mr. Novel?

Nov. Why, for example, by red breeches, tucked-up hair or peruke, a greasy broad belt, and now-a-days a short sword.

Man. Thy courage will appear more by thy belt than thy sword, I dare swear.—Then, madam, for this gentle piece of courtesy, this man of tame honour, what could

---

[1] See note *ante*, p. 328.

you find in him ? Was it his languishing affected tone ? his mannerly look ? his second-hand flattery ? the refuse of the playhouse tiring-rooms ? or his slavish obsequious-ness in watching at the door of your box at the playhouse, for your hand to your chair ? or his jaunty way of playing with your fan ? or was it the gunpowder spot on his hand, or the jewel in his ear, that purchased your heart ?

Oliv. Good jealous captain, no more of your—

L. Plau. No, let him go on, madam, for perhaps he may make you laugh : and I would contribute to your pleasure any way.

Man. Gentle rogue !

Oliv. No, noble captain, you cannot sure think any-thing could take me more than that heroic title of yours, captain ; for you know we women love honour inordi-nately.

Nov. Ha ! ha ! faith, she is with thee, bully, for thy raillery.

Man. Faith, so shall I be with you, no bully, for your grinning. [*Aside to* NOVEL.

Oliv. Then that noble lion-like mien of yours, that soldier-like, weather-beaten complexion, and that manly roughness of your voice ; how can they otherwise than charm us women, who hate effeminacy !

Nov. Ha ! ha ! faith I can't hold from laughing.

Man. Nor shall I from kicking anon. [*Aside to* NOVEL.

Oliv. And then, that captain-like carelessness in your dress, but especially your scarf ; 'twas just such another, only a little higher tied, made me in love with my tailor as he passed by my window the last training-day ; for we women adore a martial man, and you have nothing want-ing to make you more one, or more agreeable, but a wooden leg.

L. Plau. Nay, i'faith, there your ladyship was a wag, and it was fine, just, and well rallied.

Nov. Ay, ay, madam, with you ladies too martial men must needs be very killing.

Man. Peace, you Bartholomew-fair buffoons! And be not you vain that these laugh on your side, for they will laugh at their own dull jests; but no more of 'em, for I will only suffer now this lady to be witty and merry.

Oliv. You would not have your panegyric interrupted. I go on then to your humour. Is there anything more agreeable than the pretty sullenness of that? than the greatness of your courage, which most of all appears in your spirit of contradiction? for you dare give all mankind the lie; and your opinion is your only mistress, for you renounce that too, when it becomes another man's.[1]

Nov. Ha! ha! I cannot hold, I must laugh at thee, tar, faith!

L. Plau. And i'faith, dear captain, I beg your pardon, and leave to laugh at you too, though I protest I mean you no hurt; but when a lady rallies, a stander-by must be complaisant, and do her reason in laughing: ha! ha!

Man. Why, you impudent, pitiful wretches, you presume sure upon your effeminacy to urge me; for you are in all things so like women, that you may think it in me a kind of cowardice to beat you.

Oliv. No hectoring, good captain.

Man. Or, perhaps, you think this lady's presence secures you; but have a care, she has talked herself out of all the respect I had for her; and by using me ill before you, has given me a privilege of using you so before her: but if you would preserve your respect to her, and not be beaten before her, go, begone immediately.

Nov. Begone! what?

L. Plau. Nay, worthy, noble, generous, captain—

Man. Begone, I say!

> L'honneur de contredire a pour lui tant de charmes,
> Qu'il prend contre lui-même assez souvent les armes
> Et ses vrais sentiments sont combattus par lui,
> Aussitôt qu'il les voit dans la bouche d'autrui.
>
> *Le Misanthrope*, act 2, scene 5.

Nov. Begone again ! to us begone !

Man. No chattering, baboons, instantly begone, or—

[*Puts them out of the room :* NOVEL *struts,*
Lord PLAUSIBLE *cringes.*

Nov. Well, madam, we'll go make the cards ready in your bedchamber : sure you will not stay long with him.

[*Exeunt* Lord PLAUSIBLE *and* NOVEL.

Oliv. Turn hither your rage, good captain Swagger-huff, and be saucy with your mistress, like a true captain ; but be civil to your rivals and betters, and do not threaten anything but me here ; no, not so much as my windows ; nor do not think yourself in the lodgings of one of your suburb mistresses beyond the Tower.

Man. Do not give me cause to think so ; for those less infamous women part with their lovers, just as you did from me, with unforced vows of constancy and floods of willing tears ; but the same winds bear away their lovers and their vows : and for their grief, if the credulous unexpected fools return, they find new comforters, fresh cullies, such as I found here. The mercenary love of those women too suffers shipwreck with their gallants' fortunes ; now you have heard chance has used me scurvily, therefore you do too. Well, persevere in your ingratitude, falsehood, and disdain ; have constancy in something, and I promise you to be as just to your real scorn as I was to your feigned love ; and henceforward will despise, contemn, hate, loathe, and detest you most faithfully.

Enter LETTICE.

Oliv. Get the ombre-cards ready in the next room, Lettice, and—   [*Whispers to* LETTICE, *who goes out.*

Free. Bravely resolved, captain !

Fid. And you'll be sure to keep your word, I hope, sir?

Man. I hope so too.

Fid. Do you but hope it, sir ? If you are not as good as your word, 'twill be the first time you ever bragged, sure.

Man. She has restored my reason with my heart.

Free. But now you talk of restoring, captain, there are other things, which next to one's heart one would not part with; I mean your jewels and money, which it seems she has, sir.

Man. What's that to you, sir?

Free. Pardon me, whatsoever is yours I have a share in't I'm sure, which I will not lose for asking, though you may be too generous or too angry now to do't yourself.

Fid. Nay, then I'll make bold to make my claim too.

[*Both going towards* OLIVIA.

Man. Hold, you impertinent, officious fops—[*Aside.*] How have I been deceived!

Free. Madam, there are certain appurtenances to a lover's heart, called jewels, which always go along with it.

Fid. And which, with lovers, have no value in themselves, but from the heart they come with. Our captain's, madam, it seems you scorn to keep, and much more will those worthless things without it, I am confident.

Oliv. A gentleman so well made as you are, may be confident—us easy women could not deny you anything you ask, if 'twere for yourself; but, since 'tis for another, I beg your leave to give him my answer.—[*Aside.*] An agreeable young fellow this—and would not be my aversion.—[*Aloud.*] Captain, your young friend here has a very persuading face, I confess; yet you might have asked me yourself for those trifles you left with me, which (hark you a little, for I dare trust you with the secret; you are a man of so much honour, I'm sure) I say then, not expecting your return, or hoping ever to see you again, I have delivered your jewels to—

Man. Whom?

Oliv. My husband.

Man. Your husband!

Oliv. Ay, my husband. For since you could leave me, I am lately and privately married to one, who is a man of so much honour and experience in the world, that I dare not ask him for your jewels again to restore 'em to you; lest he should conclude you never would have parted with 'em to me on any other score but the exchange of my honour : which rather than you'd let me lose, you'd lose I'm sure yourself, those trifles of yours.

Man. Triumphant impudence ! but married too !

Oliv. O, speak not so loud, my servants know it not : I am married , there's no resisting one's destiny or love, you know.

Man. Why, did you love him too ?

Oliv. Most passionately ; nay, love him now, though I have married him, and he me : which mutual love I hope you are too good, too generous a man to disturb, by any future claim, or visits to me. 'Tis true, he is now absent in the country, but returns shortly ; therefore I beg of you, for your own ease and quiet, and my honour, you will never see me more.

Man. I wish I never had seen you.

Oliv. But if you should ever have anything to say to me hereafter, let that young gentleman there be your messenger.

Man. You would be kinder to him ; I find he should be welcome.

Oliv. Alas ! his youth would keep my husband from suspicions, and his visits from scandal ; for we women may have pity for such as he, but no love : and I already think you do not well to spirit him away to sea ; and the sea is already but too rich with the spoils of the shore.

Man. True perfect woman ! If I could say anything more injurious to her now, I would ; for I could outrail a bilked whore, or a kicked coward ; but now I think on't, that were rather to discover my love than hatred ; and I must not talk, for something I must do.

[*Aside.*

Oliv. I think I have given him enough of me now, never to be troubled with him again. [*Aside.*

Re-enter LETTICE.

Well, Lettice, are the cards and all ready within? I come then.—Captain, I beg your pardon: you will not make one at ombre?

Man. No, madam, but I'll wish you a little good luck before you go.

Oliv. No, if you would have me thrive, curse me: for that you'll do heartily, I suppose.

Man. Then if you will have it so, may all the curses light upon you, women ought to fear, and you deserve!— First, may the curse of loving play attend your sordid covetousness, and fortune cheat you, by trusting to her, as you have cheated me; the curse of pride, or a good reputation, fall on your lust; the curse of affectation on your beauty; the curse of your husband's company on your pleasures; and the curse of your gallant's disappointments in his absence; and the curse of scorn, jealousy, or despair on your love; and then the curse of loving on!

Oliv. And to requite all your curses, I will only return you your last; may the curse of loving me still fall upon your proud hard heart, that could be so cruel to me in these horrid curses! but heaven forgive you! [*Exit.*

Man. Hell and the devil reward thee!

Free. Well, you see now, mistresses, like friends, are lost by letting 'em handle your money; and most women are such kind of witches, who can have no power over a man, unless you give 'em money: but when once they have got any from you, they never leave you till they have all. Therefore I never give a woman a farthing.

Man. Well, there is yet this comfort by losing one's money with one's mistress, a man is out of danger of getting another; of being made prize again by love, who, like a pirate, takes you by spreading false colours: but when once you have run your ship a-ground, the

treacherous picaroon[1] loots; so by your ruin you save
yourself from slavery at least.

Enter Boy.

Boy. Mrs. Lettice, here's Madam Blackacre come to
wait upon her honour.   [*Exeunt* LETTICE *and* Boy.

Man. D'ye hear that? Let us be gone before she
comes: for henceforth I'll avoid the whole damned sex
for ever, and woman as a sinking ship.

[*Exeunt* MANLY *and* FIDELIA.

Free. And I'll stay, to revenge on her your quarrel to
the sex: for out of love to her jointure, and hatred to
business, I would marry her, to make an end of her
thousand suits, and my thousand engagements, to the
comfort of two unfortunate sort of people, my plaintiffs
and her defendants, my creditors and her adversaries.

Enter Widow BLACKACRE, *led in by* Major OLDFOX, *and*
JERRY BLACKACRE *following, laden with green bags.*

Wid. 'Tis an arrant sea-ruffian; but I am glad I met
with him at last, to serve him again, major; for the
last service was not good in law. Boy, duck, Jerry,
where is my paper of memorandums? Give me, child:
so. Where is my cousin Olivia now, my kind relation?

Free. Here is one that would be your kind relation,
madam.

Wid. What mean you, sir?

Free. Why, faith, (to be short) to marry you, widow.

Wid. Is not this the wild rude person we saw at
Captain Manly's?

Jer. Ay, forsooth, an't please.

Wid. What would you? what are you? Marry me!

Free. Ay, faith; for I am a younger brother, and you
are a widow.

Wid. You are an impertinent person; and go about
your business.

---

[1] "Picaroon," a rogue, from Spanish *picaro.*

Free. I have none, but to marry thee, widow.

Wid. But I have other business, I'd have you to know.

Free. But you have no business a-nights, widow; and I'll make you pleasanter business than any you have. For a-nights, I assure you, I am a man of great business; for the business—

Wid. Go, I'm sure you're an idle fellow.

Free. Try me but, widow, and employ me as you find my abilities and industry.

Old. Pray be civil to the lady, Mr. —— she is a person of quality, a person that is no person—

Free. Yes, but she's a person that is a widow. Be you mannerly to her, because you are to pretend only to be her squire, to arm her to her lawyer's chambers: but I will be impudent and bawdy; for she must love and marry me.

Wid. Marry come up, you saucy familiar Jack! You think, with us widows, 'tis no more than up, and ride. Gad forgive me! now-a-days, every idle, young, hectoring, roaring companion, with a pair of turned red breeches, and a broad back, thinks to carry away any widow of the best degree. But I'd have you to know, sir, all widows are not got, like places at court, by impudence and importunity only.

Old. No, no, soft, soft, you are a young man, and not fit—

Free. For a widow? yes sure, old man, the fitter.

Old. Go to, go to; if others had not laid in their claims before you—

Free. Not you, I hope.

Old. Why not I, sir? sure I am a much more proportionable match for her than you, sir; I, who am an elder brother, of a comfortable fortune, and of equal years with her.

Wid. How's that, you unmannerly person? I'd have you to know, I was born but in *Ann' undec' Caroli prim'*.

Old. Your pardon, lady, your pardon : be not offended
with your very humble servant—But, I say, sir, you are
a beggarly younger brother, twenty years younger than
her, without any land or stock, but your great stock of
impudence : therefore what pretension can you have to
her?

Free. You have made it for me : first, because I am a
younger brother.

Wid. Why, is that a sufficient plea to a relict? how
appears it, sir? by what foolish custom?

Free. By custom time out of mind only. Then, sir,
because I have nothing to keep me after her death, I am
the likelier to take care of her life. And for my being
twenty years younger than her, and having a sufficient
stock of impudence, I leave it to her whether they will be
valid exceptions to me in her widow's law or equity.

Old. Well, she has been so long in chancery, that I'll
stand to her equity and decree between us. Come, lady,
pray snap up this young snap [1] at first, or we shall be
troubled with him. Give him a city-widow's answer, that
is, with all the ill-breeding imaginable.—[*Aside to* Widow
Blackacre.] Come, madam.

Wid. Well then, to make an end of this foolish wooing,
for nothing interrupts business more : first for you,
major—

Old. You declare in my favour, then?

Free. What, direct the court! come, young lawyer,
thou shalt be a counsel for me.   [*To* Jerry.

Jer. Gad, I shall betray your cause then, as well as an
older lawyer ; never stir.

Wid. First, I say, for you, major, my walking hospital
of an ancient foundation ; thou bag of mummy, that
wouldst fall asunder, if 'twere not for thy cerecloths—

Old. How, lady !

Free. Ha ! ha !—

Jer. Hey, brave mother! use all suitors thus, for my
sake.

----
[1] A pert young fellow.

Wid. Thou withered, hobbling, distorted cripple; nay, thou art a cripple all over: wouldst thou make me the staff of thy age, the crutch of thy decrepidness? me—

Free. Well said, widow! Faith, thou wouldst make a man love thee now, without dissembling.

Wid. Thou senseless, impertinent, quibbling, drivelling, feeble, paralytic, impotent, fumbling, frigid nincompoop!

Jer. Hey, brave mother, for calling of names, i'fac!

Wid. Wouldst thou make a caudle-maker, a nurse of me? can't you be bedrid without a bed-fellow? won't your swan-skins, furs, flannels, and the scorched trencher, keep you warm there? would you have me your Scotch warming-pan,[1] with a pox to you! me—

Old. O Heavens!

Free. I told you I should be thought the fitter man, major.

Jer. Ay, you old fobus, and you would have been my guardian, would you, to have taken care of my estate, that half of't should never come to me, by letting long leases at pepper-corn rents?

Wid. If I would have married an old man, 'tis well known I might have married an earl, nay, what's more, a judge, and been covered the winter nights with the lamb-skins, which I prefer to the ermines of nobles. And dost thou think I would wrong my poor minor there for you?

Free. Your minor is a chopping minor, God bless him!
                                [*Strokes* JERRY *on the head.*

Old. Your minor may be a major of horse or foot, for his bigness; and it seems you will have the cheating of your minor to yourself.

Wid. Pray, sir, bear witness:—cheat my minor! I'll bring my action of the case for the slander.

Free. Nay, I would bear false witness for thee now,

---

[1] Scotch warming-pan: a wench. *Grose: Lex. Balat.*

widow, since you have done me justice, and have thought
me the fitter man for you.

Wid. Fair and softly, sir, 'tis my minor's case, more
than my own; and I must do him justice now on you.

Free. How!

Old. So then.

Wid. You are, first, (I warrant,) some renegado from
the inns of court and the law; and thou'lt come to suffer
for't by the law, that is, be hanged.

Jer. Not about your neck, forsooth, I hope.

Free. But, madam—

Old. Hear the court.

Wid. Thou art some debauched, drunken, lewd,
hectoring, gaming companion, and wantest some widow's
old gold to nick ¹ upon; but I thank you, sir, that's for
my lawyers.

Free. Faith, we should ne'er quarrel about that; for
guineas would serve my turn.² But, widow—

Wid. Thou art a foul-mouthed boaster of thy lust, a
mere bragadochio of thy strength for wine and women,
and wilt belie thyself more than thou dost women, and
art every way a base deceiver of women; and would
deceive me too, would you?

Free. Nay, faith, widow, this is judging without seeing
the evidence.

Wid. I say, you are a worn-out whoremaster at five-
and-twenty, both in body and fortune, and cannot be
trusted by the common wenches of the town, lest you
should not pay 'em; nor by the wives of the town lest
you should pay 'em: so you want women, and would
have me your bawd to procure 'em for you.

Free. Faith, if you had any good acquaintance, widow,
'twould be civilly done of thee; for I am just come from
sea.

---

¹ Cheat: gamble.
² The point of the antithesis lies in the opposition of the *new*
guinea to the *old* gold. Guineas were not coined before the year
1662.

Wid. I mean, you would have me keep you, that you might turn keeper; for poor widows are only used like bawds by you: you go to church with us, but to get other women to lie with. In fine, you are a cheating, cozening spendthrift; and having sold your own annuity, would waste my jointure.

Jer. And make havoc of our estate personal, and all our gilt plate; I should soon be picking up all our mortgaged apostle-spoons, bowls, and beakers, out of most of the ale-houses betwixt Hercules-pillars [1] and the Boatswain in Wapping; nay, and you'd be scouring amongst my trees, and make 'em knock down one another, like routed reeling watchmen at midnight; would you so, bully?

Free. Nay, prithee, widow, hear me.

Wid. No, sir; I'd have you to know, thou pitiful, paltry, lath-backed fellow, if I would have married a young man, 'tis well known I could have had any young heir in Norfolk, nay, the hopefullest young man this day at the King's-bench bar; I that am a relict and executrix of known plentiful assets and parts, who understand myself and the law. And would you have me under covert-baron [2] again? No, sir, no covert-baron for me.

Free. But, dear widow, hear me. I value you only, not your jointure.

Wid. Nay, sir, hold there; I know your love to a widow is covetousness of her jointure: and a widow, a little striken in years, with a good jointure, is like an old mansion-house in a good purchase, never valued, but take one, take t'other: and perhaps, when you are in possession, you'd neglect it, let it drop to the ground, for want of necessary repairs or expenses upon't.

Free. No, widow, one would be sure to keep all tight, when one is to forfeit one's lease by dilapidation.

---

[1] Hercules' Pillars was the name of a tavern in Fleet Street, mentioned by Pepys; also of one at Hyde Park Corner, immortalised in the pages of *Tom Jones*.

[2] A law-term, signifying under the protection of a husband.

Wid. Fy! fy! I neglect my business with this foolish discourse of love. Jerry, child, let me see the list of the jury: I'm sure my cousin Olivia has some relations amongst them. But where is she?

Free. Nay, widow, but hear me one word only.

Wid. Nay, sir, no more, pray. I will no more hearken to your foolish love-motions, than to offers of arbitration.

[*Exeunt* Widow BLACKACRE *and* JERRY.

Free. Well, I'll follow thee yet; for he that has a pretension at court, or to a widow, must never give over for a little ill-usage.

Old. Therefore, I'll get her by assiduity, patience, and long sufferings, which you will not undergo; for you idle young fellows leave off love when it comes to be business; and industry gets more women than love.

Free. Ay, industry, the fool's and old man's merit.— But I'll be industrious too, and make a business on't, and get her by law, wrangling, and contests, and not by sufferings: and, because you are no dangerous rival, I'll give thee counsel, major:—

> If you litigious widow e'er would gain,
> Sigh not to her, but by the law complain;
> To her, as to a bawd, defendant sue
> With statutes, and make justice pimp for you.

[*Exeunt*

ACT THE THIRD.

SCENE I.—*Westminster Hall.*

Enter MANLY *and* FREEMAN, *two* Sailors *behind.*

AN. I hate this place worse than a man that has inherited a chancery suit: I wish I were well out on't again.

Free. Why, you need not be afraid of this place: for a man without money needs no more fear a crowd of lawyers than a crowd of pickpockets.

Man. This, the reverend of the law would have thought the palace or residence of Justice; but, if it be, she lives here with the state of a Turkish emperor, rarely seen ; and besieged rather than defended by her numerous black-guard here.

Free. Methinks 'tis like one of their own halls in Christmas time, whither from all parts fools bring their money, to try by the dice (not the worst judges) whether it shall be their own or no : but after a tedious fretting and wrangling, they drop away all their money on both sides ; and, finding neither the better, at last go emptily and lovingly away together to the tavern, joining their curses against the young lawyer's box, that sweeps all, like the old ones.

Man. Spoken like a revelling Christmas lawyer.

Free. Yes, I was one, I confess, but was fain to leave

the law, out of conscience, and fall to making false
musters : rather choose to cheat the king than his subjects ; plunder rather than take fees.

Man. Well, a plague and a purse-famine light on the
law ; and that female limb of it who dragged me hither
to-day ! But prithee go see if, in that crowd of daggled
gowns there, [*Pointing to a crowd of* Lawyers *at the end of
the stage,*] thou canst find her.   [*Exit* FREEMAN.

> How hard it is to be a hypocrite !
> At least to me, who am but newly so.
> I thought it once a kind of knavery,
> Nay, cowardice, to hide one's fault ; but now
> The common frailty, love, becomes my shame.
> He must not know I love the ungrateful still,
> Lest he contemn me more than she ; for I,
> It seems, can undergo a woman's scorn,
> But not a man's—

Enter FIDELIA.

Fid. Sir, good sir, generous captain.

Man. Prithee, kind impertinence, leave me. Why
should'st thou follow me, flatter my generosity now, since
thou knowest I have no money left ? if I had it, I'd give
it thee, to buy my quiet.

Fid. I never followed yet, sir, reward or fame, but you
alone ; nor do I now beg anything but leave to share
your miseries. You should not be a niggard of 'em,
since, methinks, you have enough to spare. Let me
follow you now, because you hate me, as you have often
said.

Man. I ever hated a coward's company, I must
confess.

Fid. Let me follow you till I am none, then ; for you,
I'm sure, will go through such worlds of dangers, that,
I shall be inured to 'em ; nay, I shall be afraid of your
anger more than danger, and so turn valiant out of fear.
Dear captain, do not cast me off till you have tried

me once more : do not, do not go to sea again without me.

Man. Thou to sea ! to court, thou fool ; remember the advice I gave thee : thou art a handsome spaniel, and canst fawn naturally : go, busk about and run thyself into the next great man's lobby ; first fawn upon the slaves without, and then run into the lady's bedchamber ; thou mayst be admitted at last to tumble her bed. Go seek, I say, and lose me ; for I am not able to keep thee ; I have not bread for myself.

Fid. Therefore I will not go, because then I may help and serve you.

Man. Thou !

Fid. I warrant you, sir ; for, at worst, I could beg or steal for you.

Man. Nay, more bragging ! Dost thou not know there's venturing your life in stealing ? Go, prithee, away : thou art as hard to shake off as that flattering, effeminating mischief, love.

Fid. Love did you name ? Why, you are not so miserable as to be yet in love, sure ?

Man. No, no, prithee away, begone, or—[*Aside.*] I had almost discovered my love and shame ; well, if I had, that thing could not think the worse of me—or if he did—no—yes, he shall know it—he shall—but then I must never leave him, for they are such secrets, that make parasites and pimps lords of their masters : for any slavery or tyranny is easier than love's.—[*Aloud.*] Come hither, since thou art so forward to serve me : hast thou but resolution enough to endure the torture of a secret ? for such to some is insupportable.

Fid. I would keep it as safe as if your dear, precious life depended on't.

Man. Damn your dearness ! It concerns more than my life,—my honour.

Fid. Doubt it not, sir.

Man. And do not discover it, by too much fear of

discovering it; but have a great care you let not Freeman find it out.

Fid. I warrant you, sir, I am already all joy with the
hopes of your commands; and shall be all wings in the
execution of 'em: speak quickly, sir.

Man. You said you'd beg for me.

Fid. I did, sir.

Man. Then you shall beg for me.

Fid. With all my heart, sir.

Man. That is, pimp for me.

Fid. How, sir?

Man. D'ye start! Thinkest thou, thou couldst do me
any other service? Come, no dissembling honour: I
know you can do it handsomely, thou wert made for't.
You have lost your time with me at sea, you must recover it.

Fid. Do not, sir, beget yourself more reasons for your
aversion to me, and make my obedience to you a fault;
I am the unfittest in the world to do you such a service.

Man. Your cunning arguing against it shows but how
fit you are for it. No more dissembling; here, I say,
you must go use it for me to Olivia.

Fid. To her, sir?

Man. Go flatter, lie, kneel, promise, anything to get
her for me: I cannot live unless I have her. Didst thou
not say thou wouldst do anything to save my life? and
she said you had a persuading face.

Fid. But did you not say, sir, your honour was dearer
to you than your life? and would you have me contribute to the loss of that, and carry love from you to the
most infamous, most false, and—

Man. And most beautiful!—   [*Sighs aside.*

Fid. Most ungrateful woman that ever lived; for sure
she must be so, that could desert you so soon, use you
so basely, and so lately too: do not, do not forget it,
sir, and think—

Man. No, I will not forget it, but think of revenge;

I will lie with her out of revenge. Go, begone, and prevail for me, or never see me more.

Fid. You scorned her last night.

Man. I know not what I did last night; I dissembled last night.

Fid. Heavens!

Man. Begone, I say, and bring me love or compliance back, or hopes at least, or I'll never see thy face again, by—

Fid. O, do not swear, sir! first hear me.

Man. I'm impatient, away! you'll find me here till twelve.   [*Turns away.*

Fid. Sir—

Man. Not one word, no insinuating argument more, or soothing persuasion; you'll have need of all your rhetoric with her : go strive to alter her, not me ; begone.
                [*Retires to the end of the stage, and exit.*

Fid. Should I discover to him now my sex,
And lay before him his strange cruelty,
'Twould but incense it more.—No, 'tis not time.
For his love must I then betray my own?
Were ever love or chance till now severe?
Or shifting woman posed with such a task?
Forced to beg that which kills her, if obtained,
And give away her lover not to lose him !   [*Exit.*

Enter Widow BLACKACRE, *in the middle of half-a-dozen* Lawyers, *whispered to by a fellow in black,* JERRY BLACKACRE *following the crowd.*

Wid. Offer me a reference, you saucy companion you ! d'ye know who you speak to? Art thou a solicitor in chancery, and offer a reference? A pretty fellow ! Mr. Serjeant Ploddon, here's a fellow has the impudence to offer me a reference !

Serj. Plod. Who's that has the impudence to offer a reference within these walls?

Wid. Nay, for a splitter of causes to do't !

Serj. Plod. No, madam; to a lady learned in the law, as you are, the offer of a reference were to impose upon you.

Wid. No, no, never fear me for a reference, Mr. Serjeant. But come, have you not forgot your brief? Are you sure you shan't make the mistake of—hark you —[*Whispers.*] Go then, go to your court of Common-pleas, and say one thing over and over again: you do it so naturally, you'll never be suspected for protracting time.

Serj. Plod. Come, I know the course of the court, and your business. [*Exit.*

Wid. Let's see, Jerry, where are my minutes? Come, Mr. Quaint, pray go talk a great deal for me in chancery, let your words be easy, and your sense hard; my cause requires it: branch it bravely, and deck my cause with flowers, that the snake may lie hidden. Go, go, and be sure you remember the decree of my Lord Chancellor, *Tricesimo quart'* of the queen.

Quaint. I will, as I see cause, extenuate or examplify matter of fact; baffle truth with impudence; answer exceptions with questions, though never so impertinent; for reasons give 'em words; for law and equity, tropes and figures; and so relax and enervate the sinews of their argument with the oil of my eloquence. But when my lungs can reason no longer, and not being able to say anything more for our cause, say everything of our adversary; whose reputation, though never so clear and evident in the eye of the world, yet with sharp invectives—

Wid. Alias, Billingsgate.

Quaint. With poignant and sour invectives, I say, I will deface, wipe out, and obliterate his fair reputation, even as a record with the juice of lemons; and tell such a story, (for the truth on't is, all that we can do for our client in chancery, is telling a story,) a fine story, a long story, such a story—

Wid. Go, save thy breath for the cause; talk at the bar, Mr. Quaint: you are so copiously fluent, you can weary any one's ears sooner than your own tongue. Go, weary our adversaries' counsel, and the court; go, thou art a fine-spoken person: adad, I shall make thy wife jealous of me, if you can but court the court into a decree for us. Go, get you gone, and remember — [*Whispers.*]—[*Exit* QUAINT.]—Come, Mr. Blunder, pray bawl soundly for me, at the King's-bench, bluster, sputter, question, cavil; but be sure your argument be intricate enough to confound the court; and then you do my business. Talk what you will, but be sure your tongue never stand still; for your own noise will secure your sense from censure: 'tis like coughing or hemming when one has got the belly-ache, which stifles the unmannerly noise. Go, dear rogue, and succeed; and I'll invite thee, ere it be long, to more soused venison.

Blund. I'll warrant you, after your verdict, your judgment shall not be arrested upon if's and and's. [*Exit.*

Wid. Come, Mr. Petulant, let me give you some new instructions for our cause in the Exchequer. Are the barons sat?

Pet. Yes, no; may be they are, may be they are not: what know I? what care I?

Wid. Heyday! I wish you would but snap up the counsel on t'other side anon at the bar as much; and have a little more patience with me, that I might instruct you a little better.

Pet. You instruct me! what is my brief for, mistress?

Wid. Ay, but you seldom read your brief but at the bar, if you do it then.

Pet. Perhaps I do, perhaps I don't, and perhaps 'tis time enough: pray hold yourself contented, mistress.

Wid. Nay, if you go there too, I will not be contented, sir; though you, I see, will lose my cause for want of speaking, I wo' not: you shall hear me, and shall be instructed. Let's see your brief.

Pet. Send your solicitor to me. Instructed by a woman ! I'd have you to know, I do not wear a bar-gown—

Wid. By a woman ! and I'd have you to know, I am no common woman ; but a woman conversant in the laws of the land, as well as yourself, though I have no bar-gown.

Pet. Go to, go to, mistress, you are impertinent, and there's your brief for you : instruct me !

[*Flings her breviate at her.*

Wid. Impertinent to me, you saucy Jack, you ! you return my breviate, but where's my fee ? you'll be sure to keep that, and scan that so well, that if there chance to be but a brass half-crown in't, one's sure to hear on't again : would you would but look on your breviate half so narrowly ! But pray give me my fee too, as well as my brief.

Pet. Mistress, that's without precedent. When did a counsel ever return his fee, pray ? and you are impertinent and ignorant to demand it.

Wid. Impertinent again, and ignorant, to me ! Gads-bodikins, you puny upstart in the law, to use me so ! you green-bag carrier, you murderer of unfortunate causes, the clerk's ink is scarce off of your fingers,—you that newly come from lamp-blacking the judges' shoes, and are not fit to wipe mine ; you call me impertinent and ignorant ! I would give thee a cuff on the ear, sitting the courts, if I were ignorant. Marry-gep, if it had not been for me, thou hadst been yet but a hearing counsel at the bar.

[*Exit* PETULANT.

Enter Mr. BUTTONGOWN, *crossing the stage in haste.*

Mr. Buttongown, Mr. Buttongown, whither so fast? what, won't you stay till we are heard ?

But. I cannot, Mrs. Blackacre, I must be at the council, my lord's cause stays there for me.

Wid. And mine suffers here.

But. I cannot help it.

Wid. I'm undone.

But. What's that to me?

Wid. Consider the five-pound fee, if not my cause : that was something to you.

But. Away, away ! pray be not so troublesome, mistress : I must be gone.

Wid. Nay, but consider a little : I am your old client, my lord but a new one ; or let him be what he will, he will hardly be a better client to you than myself : I hope you believe I shall be in law as long as I live ; therefore am no despicable client. Well, but go to your lord ; I know you expect he should make you a judge one day ; but I hope his promise to you will prove a true lord's promise. But that he might be sure to fail you, I wish you had his bond for't.

But. But what, will you yet be thus impertinent, mistress ?

Wid. Nay, I beseech you, sir, stay ; if it be but to tell me my lord's case ; come, in short—

But. Nay, then—   [*Exit.*

Wid. Well, Jerry, observe child, and lay it up for hereafter. These are those lawyers who, by being in all causes, are in none : therefore if you would have 'em for you, let your adversary fee 'em ; for he may chance to depend upon 'em ; and so, in being against thee, they'll be for thee.

Jer. Ay, mother ; they put me in mind of the unconscionable wooers of widows, who undertake briskly their matrimonial business for their money ; but when they have got it once, let who will drudge for them. Therefore have a care of 'em, forsooth. There's advice for your advice.

Wid. Well said, bóy.—Come, Mr. Splitcause, pray go see when my cause in Chancery comes on ; and go speak with Mr. Quillit in the King's-bench and Mr. Quirk in the Common-pleas, and see how matters go there.

Enter Major OLDFOX.

Old. Lady, a good and propitious morning to you ;

and may all your causes go as well as if I myself were judge of 'em !

Wid. Sir, excuse me ; I am busy, and cannot answer compliments in Westminster Hall.—Go, Mr. Splitcause, and come to me again to that bookseller's ; there I'll stay for you, that you may be sure to find me.

Old. No, sir, come to the other bookseller's.   I'll attend your ladyship thither.   [*Exit* SPLITCAUSE.

Wid. Why to the other ?

Old. Because he is my bookseller, lady.

Wid. What, to sell you lozenges for your catarrh ? or medicines for your corns ?   What else can a major deal with a bookseller for ?

Old. Lady, he prints for me.

Wid. Why, are you an author ?

Old. Of some few essays ; deign you, lady, to peruse 'em.—[*Aside.*] She is a woman of parts ; and I must win her by showing mine.

Bookseller's Boy. Will you see Culpepper, mistress ? "Aristotle's Problems ? "   " The Complete Midwife ? "

Wid. No ; let's see Dalton, Hughs, Shepherd, Wingate.

B. Boy. We have no law books.

Wid. No ! you are a pretty bookseller then.

Old. Come, have you e'er a one of my essays left ?

B. Boy. Yes, sir, we have enough, and shall always have 'em.

Old. How so ?

B. Boy. Why, they are good, steady, lasting ware.

Old. Nay, I hope they will live ; let's see.—Be pleased, madam, to peruse the poor endeavours of my pen : for I have a pen, though I say it, that—   [*Gives her a book.*

Jer. Pray let me see " St. George for Christendom," or, " The Seven Champions of England."

Wid. No, no ; give him " The Young Clerk's Guide." —What, we shall have you read yourself into a humour of rambling and fighting, and studying military discipline, and wearing red breeches.

Old. Nay, if you talk of military discipline, show him my " Treatise of the Art Military."

Wid. Hold ; I would as willingly he should read a play.

Jer. O, pray forsooth, mother, let me have a play.

Wid. No, sirrah ; there are young students of the law enough spoiled already by plays.   They would make you in love with your laundress, or, what's worse, some queen of the stage that was a laundress ; and so turn keeper before you are of age. [*Several cross the stage.*] But stay, Jerry, is not that Mr. What d'ye-call-him, that goes there, he that offered to sell me a suit in chancery for five hundred pounds, for a hundred down, and only paying the clerk's fees ?

Jer. Ay, forsooth, 'tis he.

Wid. Then stay here, and have a care of the bags, whilst I follow him.—Have a care of the bags, I say.

Jer. And do you have a care, forsooth, of the statute against champarty,[1] I say.   [*Exit* Widow BLACKACRE.

Re-enter FREEMAN.

Free. [*Aside.*] So, there's a limb of my widow, which was wont to be inseparable from her : she can't be far.— [*Aloud.*] How now, my pretty son-in-law that shall be, where's my widow ?

Jer. My mother, but not your widow, will be forthcoming presently.

Free. Your servant, major.   What, are you buying furniture for a little sleeping closet, which you miscall a study ? For you do only by your books, as by your wenches, bind 'em up neatly and make 'em fine, for other people to use 'em.   And your bookseller is properly your upholsterer, for he furnishes your room, rather than your head.

Old. Well, well, good sea-lieutenant, study you your

---

[1] A maintenance of any man in his suit, upon condition of having part of the thing if recovered.

compass; that's more than your head can deal with.—
[*Aside.*] I will go find out the widow, to keep her out of
his sight, or he'll board her, whilst I am treating a peace.
                                                [*Exit.*

Jer. Nay, prithee, friend, now let me have but " The
Seven Champions." You shall trust me no longer than
till my mother's Mr. Splitcause comes; for I hope he'll
lend me wherewithal to pay for't.

Free. Lend thee! here, I'll pay him. Do you want
money, squire? I'm sorry a man of your estate should
want money.

Jer. Nay, my mother will ne'er let me be at age: and
till then, she says—

Free. At age! why you are at age already to have
spent an estate, man. There are younger than you have
kept their women these three years, have had half a
dozen claps, and lost as many thousand pounds at play.

Jer. Ay, they are happy sparks! Nay, I know some
of my schoolfellows, who, when we were at school, were
two years younger than me; but now, I know not how,
are grown men before me, and go where they will, and
look to themselves. But my curmudgeonly mother won't
allow me wherewithal to be a man of myself with.

Free. Why, there 'tis; I knew your mother was in
fault. Ask but your schoolfellows what they did to be
men of themselves.

Jer. Why, I know they went to law with their mothers:
for they say, there's no good to be done upon a widow
mother, till one goes to law with her; but mine is as
plaguy a lawyer as any's of our inn. Then would she
marry too, and cut down my trees. Now, I should hate,
man, to have my father's wife kissed and slapped, and
t'other thing too, (you know what I mean,) by another
man: and our trees are the purest, tall, even, shady
twigs, by my fa—

Free. Come, squire, let your mother and your trees
fall as she pleases, rather than wear this gown and carry

green bags all thy life, and be pointed at for a Tony.[1]
But you shall be able to deal with her yet the common
way. Thou shalt make false love to some lawyer's
daughter, whose father, upon the hopes of thy marrying
her, shall lend thee money and law to preserve thy
estate and trees: and thy mother is so ugly nobody will
have her, if she cannot cut down thy trees.

Jer. Nay, if I had but anybody to stand by me, I am
as stomachful as another.

Free. That will I: I'll not see any hopeful young
gentleman abused.

B. Boy. By any but yourself.   [*Aside.*

Jer. The truth on't is, mine's as arrant a widow-mother
to her poor child as any's in England. She won't so
much as let one have sixpence in one's pocket to see a
motion,[2] or the dancing of the ropes, or—

Free. Come, you shan't want money; there's gold for
you.

Jer. O lord, sir, two guineas! D'ye lend me this? Is
there no trick in't? Well, sir, I'll give you my bond for
security.

Free. No, no; thou hast given me thy face for
security: anybody would swear thou dost not look like a
cheat. You shall have what you will of me; and if your
mother will not be kinder to you, come to me, who will.

Jer. [*Aside.*] By my fa—he's a curious fine gentleman!—[*Aloud.*] But will you stand by one?

Free. If you can be resolute.

Jer. Can be resolved! Gad, if she gives me but a
cross word, I'll leave her to-night, and come to you. But
now I have got money, I'll go to Jack-of-all-Trades, at
t'other end of the Hall, and buy the neatest purest
things—

Free. [*Aside.*] And I'll follow the great boy, and my
blow at his mother. Steal away the calf, and the cow
will follow you.   [*Exit* JERRY, *followed by* FREEMAN.

---

[1] Simpleton.   [2] A puppet-show.

Re-enter, on the other side, MANLY, Widow BLACKACRE, *and* Major OLDFOX.

Man. Damn your cause, can't you lose it without me? which you are like enough to do, if it be, as you say, an honest one : I will suffer no longer for't.

Wid. Nay, captain, I tell you, you are my prime witness ; and the cause is just now coming on, Mr. Splitcause tells me.   Lord, methinks you should take a pleasure in walking here, as half you see now do ; for they have no business here, I assure you.

Man. Yes ; but I'll assure you then, their business is to persecute me.   But d'ye think I'll stay any longer, to have a rogue, because he knows my name, pluck me aside and whisper a news-book secret to me with a stinking breath ? a second come piping angry from the court, and sputter in my face his tedious complaints against it ? a third law-coxcomb, because he saw me once at a reader's dinner, come and put me a long law case, to make a discovery of his indefatigable dulness and my wearied patience ? a fourth, a most barbarous civil rogue, who will keep a man half an hour in the crowd with a bowed body, and a hat off, acting the reformed sign of the Salutation tavern, to hear his bountiful professions of service and friendship, whilst he cares not if I were damned, and I am wishing him hanged out of my way ? —I'd as soon run the gauntlet, as walk t'other turn.

Re-enter JERRY BLACKACRE, *without his bags, but laden with trinkets,* (*which he endeavours to hide from his* Mother,) *and followed at a distance by* FREEMAN.

Wid. O, are you come, sir ? but where have you been, you ass ? and how came you thus laden ?

Jer. Look here, forsooth, mother ; now here's a duck, here's a boar-cat, and here's an owl.

> [*Making a noise with catcalls and other such like instruments.*

Wid. Yes, there is an owl, sir.

Old. He's an ungracious bird indeed.

Wid. But go, thou trangame,[1] and carry back those trangames, which thou hast stolen or purloined; for nobody would trust a minor in Westminster Hall, sure.

Jer. Hold yourself contented, forsooth: I have these commodities by a fair bargain and sale; and there stands my witness and creditor.

Wid. How's that? What sir, d'ye think to get the mother by giving the child a rattle?—But where are my bags, my writings, you rascal?

Jer. O, la! where are they, indeed!   [*Aside.*

Wid. How, sirrah? speak, come—

Man. You can tell her, Freeman, I suppose.

     [*Apart to him.*

Free. 'Tis true, I made one of your salt-water sharks steal 'em whilst he was eagerly choosing his commodities, as he calls 'em, in order to my design upon his mother.

     [*Apart to him.*

Wid. Won't you speak? Where were you, I say, you son of a—an unfortunate woman?—O, major, I'm undone! They are all that concern my estate, my jointure, my husband's deed of gift, my evidences for all my suits now depending! What will become of them?

Free. [*Aside.*] I'm glad to hear this.—[*Aloud.*] They'll be all safe, I warrant you, madam.

Wid. O where? where? Come, you villain, along with me, and show me where.

     [*Exeunt* Widow BLACKACRE, JERRY, *and* OLDFOX.

Man. Thou hast taken the right way to get a widow, by making her great boy rebel; for when nothing will make a widow marry, she'll do it to cross her children. But canst thou in earnest marry this harpy, this volume of shrivelled blurred parchments and law, this attorney's desk?

Free. Ay, ay; I'll marry and live honestly, that is,

---

[1] Trangame: a toy. *Wright.*

give my creditors, not her, due benevolence,—pay my debts.

Man. Thy creditors, you see, are not so barbarous as to put thee in prison; and wilt thou commit thyself to a noisome dungeon for thy life? which is the only satisfaction thou canst give thy creditors by this match.

Free. Why, is not she rich?

Man. Ay; but he that marries a widow for her money, will find himself as much mistaken as the widow that marries a young fellow for due benevolence, as you call it.

Free. Why, d'ye think I shan't deserve wages? I'll drudge faithfully.

Man. I tell thee again, he that is the slave in the mine has the least propriety in the ore. You may dig, and dig; but if thou wouldst have her money, rather get to be her trustee than her husband; for a true widow will make over her estate to anybody, and cheat herself rather than be cheated by her children or a second husband.

Re-enter JERRY, *running in a fright.*

Jer. O la, I'm undone! I'm undone! my mother will kill me :—you said you'd stand by one.

Free. So I will, my brave squire, I warrant thee.

Jer. Ay, but I dare not stay till she comes; for she's as furious, now she has lost her writings, as a bitch when she has lost her puppies.

Man. The comparison's handsome!

Jer. O, she's here!

Free. [*To the* Sailor.] Take him, Jack, and make haste with him to your master's lodging; and be sure you keep him up till I come.   [*Exeunt* JERRY *and* Sailor.

Re-enter Widow BLACKACRE *and* Major OLDFOX.

Wid. O my dear writings! Where's this heathen rogue, my minor?

Free. Gone to drown or hang himself.

Wid. No, I know him too well; he'll ne'er be *felo de se* that way: but he may go and choose a guardian of his own head, and so be *felo de ses biens ;* for he has not yet chosen one.

Free. Say you so? And he shan't want one. [*Aside.*

Wid. But, now I think on't, 'tis you, sir, have put this cheat upon me; for there is a saying, "Take hold of a maid by her smock, and a widow by her writings, and they cannot get from you." But I'll play fast and loose with you yet, if there be law, and my minor and writings are not forthcoming; I'll bring my action of detinue or trover. But first, I'll try to find out this guardianless, graceless villain.—Will you jog, major?

Man. If you have lost your evidence, I hope your causes cannot go on, and I may be gone?

Wid. O no; stay but a making-water while (as one may say) and I'll be with you again.

[*Exeunt* Widow BLACKACRE *and* Major OLDFOX.

Free. Well; sure I am the first man that ever began a love-intrigue in Westminster Hall.

Man. No, sure; for the love to a widow generally begins here: and as the widow's cause goes against the heir or executors, the jointure-rivals commence their suit to the widow.

Free. Well; but how, pray, have you passed your time here, since I was forced to leave you alone? You have had a great deal of patience.

Man. Is this a place to be alone, or have patience in? But I have had patience, indeed; for I have drawn upon me, since I came, but three quarrels and two lawsuits.

Free. Nay, faith, you are too curst to be let loose in the world: you should be tied up again in your sea-kennel, called a ship. But how could you quarrel here?

Man. How could I refrain? A lawyer talked peremptorily and saucily to me, and as good as gave me the lie.

Free. They do it so often to one another at the bar, that they make no bones on't elsewhere.

Man. However, I gave him a cuff on the ear; whereupon he jogs two men, whose backs were turned to us,

(for they were reading at a bookseller's,) to witness I
struck him, sitting the courts; which office they so readily
promised, that I called 'em rascals and knights of the
post.[1] One of 'em presently calls two other absent witnesses, who were coming towards us at a distance; whilst
the other, with a whisper, desires to know my name, that
he might have satisfaction by way of challenge, as t'other
by way of writ; but if it were not rather to direct his
brother's writ, than his own challenge.—There, you see,
is one of my quarrels, and two of my lawsuits.

Free. So!—and the other two?

Man. For advising a poet to leave off writing, and
turn lawyer, because he is dull and impudent, and says or
writes nothing now but by precedent.

Free. And the third quarrel?

Man. For giving more sincere advice to a handsome,
well-dressed young fellow, (who asked it too,) not to
marry a wench that he loved, and I had lain with.

Free. Nay, if you will be giving your sincere advice to
lovers and poets, you will not fail of quarrels.

Man. Or if I stay in this place; for I see more quarrels
crowding upon me.   Let's be gone, and avoid 'em.

Enter NOVEL *at a distance, coming towards them.*

A plague on him, that sneer is ominous to us; he is
coming upon us, and we shall not be rid of him.

Nov. Dear bully, don't look so grum upon me; you
told me just now, you had forgiven me a little harmless
raillery upon wooden legs last night.

Man. Yes, yes, pray begone, I am talking of business.

Nov. Can't I hear it?   I love thee, and will be faithful, and always—

Man. Impertinent.   'Tis business that concerns Freeman only.

Nov. Well, I love Freeman too, and would not divulge
his secret.—Prithee speak, prithee, I must—

Man. Prithee let me be rid of thee, I must be rid of thee.

---

[1] See note *ante*, p. 386.

Nov. Faith, thou canst hardly, I love thee so.   Come, I must know the business.

Man. [*Aside.*] So, I have it now.—[*Aloud.*]   Why, if you needs will know it, he has a quarrel, and his adversary bids him bring two friends with him : now, I am one, and we are thinking who we shall have for a third.

[*Several cross the stage.*

Nov. A pox, there goes a fellow owes me a hundred pounds, and goes out of town to-morrow : I'll speak with him, and come to you presently.   [*Exit.*

Man. No, but you won't.

Free. You are dexterously rid of him.

Re-enter Major OLDFOX.

Man. To what purpose, since here comes another as impertinent ?   I know by his grin he is bound hither.

Old. Your servant, worthy, noble captain.   Well, I have left the widow, because she carried me from your company : for, faith, captain, I must needs tell thee thou art the only officer in England, who was not an Edgehill officer, that I care for.

Man. I'm sorry for't.

Old. Why, wouldst thou have me love them?

Man. Anybody rather than me.

Old. What ! you are modest, I see ; therefore, too, I love thee.

Man. No, I am not modest ; but love to brag myself, and can't patiently hear you fight over the last civil war. Therefore, go look out the fellow I saw just now here, that walks with his sword and stockings out at heels, and let him tell you the history of that scar on his cheek, to give you occasion to show yours got in the field at Bloomsbury, not that of Edgehill.   Go to him, poor fellow ; he is fasting, and has not yet the happiness this morning to stink of brandy and tobacco : go, give him some to hear you ; I am busy.

Old. Well, egad, I love thee now, boy, for thy surliness.   Thou art no tame captain, I see, that will suffer—

Man. An old fox.

Old. All that shan't make me angry : I consider that thou art peevish, and fretting at some ill success at law. Prithee, tell me what ill luck you have met with here.

Man. You.

Old. Do I look like the picture of ill luck? gadsnouns, I love thee more and more. And shall I tell thee what made me love thee first ?

Man. Do ; that I may be rid of that damned quality and thee.

Old. 'Twas thy wearing that broad sword there.

Man. Here, Freeman, let's change : I'll never wear it more.

Old. How ! you won't, sure. Prithee, don't look like one of our holiday captains now-a-days, with a bodkin by your side, your martinet rogues.

Man. [*Aside.*] O, then, there's hopes.—[*Aloud.*] What, d'ye find fault with martinet ? Let me tell you, sir, 'tis the best exercise in the world ; the most ready, most easy, most graceful exercise that ever was used, and the most—

Old. Nay, nay, sir, no more ; sir, your servant : if you praise martinet once, I have done with you, sir.—Martinet ! martinet !— [*Exit.*

Free. Nay, you have made him leave you as willingly as ever he did an enemy ; for he was truly for the king and parliament : for the parliament in their list ; and for the king in cheating 'em of their pay, and never hurting the king's party in the field.

Enter a Lawyer *towards them.*

Man. A pox ! this way :—here's a lawyer I know threatening us with another greeting.

Law. Sir, sir, your very servant ; I was afraid you had forgotten me.

Man. I was not afraid you had forgotten me.

Law. No, sir ; we lawyers have pretty good memories.

Man. You ought to have by your wits.

Law. O, you are a merry gentleman, sir : I remember you were merry when I was last in your company.

Man. I was never merry in thy company, Mr. Lawyer, sure.

Law. Why, I'm sure you joked upon me, and shammed me all night long.

Man. Shammed! prithee what barbarous law-term is that?

Law. Shamming! why, don't you know that? 'tis all our way of wit, sir.

Man. I am glad I do not know it then. Shamming! what does he mean by't, Freeman!

Free. Shamming is telling you an insipid dull lie with a dull face, which the sly wag the author only laughs at himself ; and making himself believe 'tis a good jest, puts the sham only upon himself.

Man. So, your lawyer's jest, I find, like his practice, has more knavery than wit in't. I should make the worst shammer in England : I must always deal ingenuously, as I will with you, Mr. Lawyer, and advise you to be seen rather with attorneys and solicitors, than such fellows as I am : they will credit your practice more.

Law. No, sir, your company's an honour to me.

Man. No, faith; go this way, there goes an attorney; leave me for him; let it never be said a lawyer's civility did him hurt.

Law. No, worthy, honoured sir ; I'll not leave you for any attorney, sure.

Man. Unless he had a fee in his hand.

Law. Have you any business here, sir? Try me : I'd serve you sooner than any attorney breathing.

Man. Business—[*Aside.*] So, I have thought of a sure way.—[*Aloud.*] Yes, faith, I have a little business.

Law. Have you so, sir? in what court, sir? what is't, sir? Tell me but how I may serve you, and I'll do't, sir, and take it for as great an honour—

Man. Faith, 'tis for a poor orphan of a sea officer of

mine, that has no money.   But if it could be followed in
forma pauperis, and when the legacy's recovered—

Law. *Forma pauperis*, sir !

Man. Ay, sir.   [*Several crossing the stage.*

Law. Mr. Bumblecase, Mr. Bumblecase ! a word with
you.—Sir, I beg your pardon at present ; I have a little
business—

Man. Which is not in *forma pauperis.*   [*Exit* Lawyer.

Free. So, you have now found a way to be rid of people
without quarrelling ?

Enter Alderman.

Man. But here's a city-rogue will stick as hard upon
us, as if I owed him money.

Ald. Captain, noble sir, I am yours heartily, d'ye see ;
why should you avoid your old friends ?

Man. And why should you follow me ?   I owe you
nothing.

Ald. Out of my hearty respects to you : for there is
not a man in England—

Man. Thou wouldst save from hanging with the ex-
pense of a shilling only.

Ald. Nay, nay, but, captain, you are like enough to
tell me—

Man. Truth, which you won't care to hear ; therefore
you had better go talk with somebody else.

Ald. No, I know nobody can inform me better of some
young wit, or spendthrift, that has a good dipped [1] seat
and estate in Middlesex, Hertfordshire, Essex, or Kent ;
any of these would serve my turn : now, if you knew of
such a one, and would but help—

Man. You to finish his ruin.

Ald. I'faith, you should have a snip—

Man. Of your nose, you thirty-in-the-hundred rascal ;
would you make me your squire setter, your bawd for
manors ?   [*Takes him by the nose.*

[1] Mortgaged.

Ald. Oh !

Free. Hold, or here will be your third law-suit.

Ald. Gads-precious, you hectoring person you, are you wild? I meant you no hurt, sir : I begin to think, as things go, land-security best, and have for a convenient mortgage, some ten, fifteen or twenty thousand pound by me.

Man. Then go lay it out upon an hospital, and take a mortgage of Heaven, according to your city custom ; for you think by laying out a little money to hook in that too hereafter. Do, I say, and keep the poor you've made by taking forfeitures, that Heaven may not take yours.

Ald. No, to keep the cripples you make this war. This war spoils our trade.

Man. Damn your trade ! 'tis the better for't.

Ald. What, will you speak against our trade?

Man. And dare you speak against the war, our trade?

Ald. [*Aside.*] Well, he may be a convoy of ships I am concerned in.—[*Aloud.*] Come, captain, I will have a fair correspondence with you, say what you will.

Man. Then prithee be gone.

Ald. No, faith ; prithee, captain, let's go drink a dish of laced coffee,[1] and talk of the times. Come, I'll treat you : nay, you shall go, for I have no business here.

Man. But I have.

Ald. To pick up a man to give thee a dinner. Come, I'll do thy business for thee.

Man. Faith, now I think on't, so you may, as well as any man : for 'tis to pick up a man to be bound with me, to one who expects city security for—

Ald. Nay, then your servant, captain ; business must be done.

Man. Ay, if it can. But hark you, alderman, without you—

Ald. Business, sir, I say, must be done ; and there's

---

[1] Mixed with spirits.

an officer of the treasury [*Several cross the stage.*] I have an affair with—   [*Exit.*

Man. You see now what the mighty friendship of the world is ; what all ceremony, embraces, and plentiful professions come to ! You are no more to believe a professing friend than a threatening enemy ; and as no man hurts you, that tells you he'll do you a mischief, no man, you see, is your servant who says he is so. Why the devil, then, should a man be troubled with the flattery of knaves if he be not a fool or cully ; or with the fondness of fools, if he be not a knave or cheat ?

Free. Only for his pleasure : for there is some in laughing at fools, and disappointing knaves.

Man. That's a pleasure, I think, would cost you too dear, as well as marrying your widow to disappoint her. But, for my part, I have no pleasure by 'em but in despising 'em, wheresoe'er I meet 'em ; and then the pleasure of hoping so to be rid of 'em. But now my comfort is, I am not worth a shilling in the world, which all the world shall know ; and then I'm sure I shall have none of 'em come near me.

Free. A very pretty comfort, which I think you pay too dear for. —But is the twenty pound gone since the morning ?

Man. To my boat's crew.—Would you have the poor, honest, brave fellows want ?

Free. Rather than you or I.

Man. Why, art thou without money ? thou who art a friend to everybody ?

Free. I ventured my last stake upon the squire to nick him of his mother ; and cannot help you to a dinner, unless you will go dine with my lord—

Man. No, no ; the ordinary is too dear for me, where flattery must pay for my dinner : I am no herald or poet.

Free. We'll go then to the bishop's—

Man. There you must flatter the old philosophy : I cannot renounce my reason for a dinner.

Free. Why, then let's go to your alderman's.

Man. Hang him, rogue! that were not to dine; for he makes you drunk with lees of sack before dinner, to take away your stomach: and there you must call usury and extortion God's blessings, or the honest turning of the penny; hear him brag of the leather breeches in which he trotted first to town, and make a greater noise with his money in his parlour, than his cashiers do in his counting-house, without hopes of borrowing a shilling.

Free. Ay, a pox on't! 'tis like dining with the great gamesters; and when they fall to their common dessert, to see the heaps of gold drawn on all hands, without going to twelve. Let us go to my Lady Goodly's.

Man. There to flatter her looks. You must mistake her grandchildren for her own; praise her cook, that she may rail at him; and feed her dogs, not yourself.

Free. What d'ye think of eating with your lawyer, then?

Man. Eat with him! damn him! To hear him employ his barbarous eloquence in a reading upon the two-and-thirty good bits in a shoulder of veal, and be forced yourself to praise the cold bribe-pie that stinks, and drink law-French wine as rough and harsh as his law-French. A pox on him! I'd rather dine in the Temple-rounds or walks, with the knights without noses, or the knights of the post, who are honester fellows and better company. But let us home and try our fortune; for I'll stay no longer here for your damned widow.

Free. Well, let us go home then; for I must go for my damned widow, and look after my new damned charge. Three or four hundred years ago a man might have dined in this Hall.[1]

Man. But now the lawyer only here is fed;
And, bully-like, by quarrels gets his bread.

[*Exeunt.*

[1] Westminster Hall was anciently used as a banqueting-room to the old Palace of Westminster.

ACT THE FOURTH.

SCENE I.—MANLY'S *Lodging*.

Enter MANLY *and* FIDELIA.

*AN.* Well, there's success in thy face. Hast thou prevailed? say.

Fid. As I could wish, sir.

Man. So; I told thee what thou wert fit for, and thou wouldst not believe me. Come, thank me for bringing thee acquainted with thy genius. Well, thou hast mollified her heart for me?

Fid. No, sir, not so; but what's better.

Man. How, what's better?

Fid. I shall harden your heart against her.

Man. Have a care, sir; my heart is too much in earnest to be fooled with, and my desire at height, and needs no delay to incite it. What, you are too good a pimp already, and know how to endear pleasure by with-holding it? But leave off your page's bawdy-house tricks, sir, and tell me, will she be kind?

Fid. Kinder than you could wish, sir.

Man. So, then: well, prithee, what said she?

Fid. She said—

Man. What? thou'rt so tedious: speak comfort to me; what?

Fid. That of all things you are her aversion.

Man. How!

Fid. That she would sooner take a bedfellow out of an hospital, and diseases into her arms, than you.

Man. What?

Fid. That she would rather trust her honour with a dissolute debauched hector, nay worse, with a finical baffled coward, all over loathsome with affectation of the fine gentleman.

Man. What's all this you say?

Fid. Nay, that my offers of your love to her were more offensive, than when parents woo their virgin-daughters to the enjoyment of riches only; and that you were in all circumstances as nauseous to her as a husband on compulsion.

Man. Hold! I understand you not.

Fid. So, 'twill work, I see.　　　　　　　[*Aside.*

Man. Did you not tell me——

Fid. She called you ten thousand ruffians.

Man. Hold, I say.

Fid. Brutes——

Man. Hold.

Fid. Sea-monsters——

Man. Damn your intelligence! Hear me a little now

Fid. Nay, surly coward she called you too.

Man. Won't you hold yet? Hold, or——

Fid. Nay, sir, pardon me; I could not but tell you she had the baseness, the injustice, to call you coward, sir; coward, coward, sir.

Man. Not yet——

Fid. I've done :—coward, sir.

Man. Did not you say, she was kinder than I could wish her?

Fid. Yes, sir.

Man. How then?—O—I understand you now. At first she appeared in rage and disdain; the truest sign of a coming woman : but at last you prevailed, it seems; did you not?

Fid. Yes, sir.

Man. So then ; let's know that only : come, prithee, without delays. I'll kiss thee for that news beforehand.

Fid. So ; the kiss I'm sure is welcome to me, whatsoe'er the news will be to you.   [*Aside.*

Man. Come, speak, my dear volunteer.

Fid. How welcome were that kind word too, if it were not for another woman's sake !   [*Aside.*

Man. What, won't you speak ? You prevailed for me at last, you say ?

Fid. No, sir.

Man. No more of your fooling, sir : it will not agree with my impatience or temper.

Fid. Then not to fool you, sir, I spoke to her for you, but prevailed for myself; she would not hear me when I spoke in your behalf, but bid me say what I would in my own, though she gave me no occasion, she was so coming, and so was kinder, sir, than you could wish ; which I was only afraid to let you know, without some warning.

Man. How's this ? Young man, you are of a lying age ; but I must hear you out, and if—

Fid. I would not abuse you, and cannot wrong her by any report of her, she is so wicked.

Man. How, wicked ! had she the impudence, at the second sight of you only—

Fid. Impudence, sir ! oh, she has impudence enough to put a court out of countenance, and debauch a stews.

Man. Why, what said she ?

Fid. Her tongue, I confess, was silent ; but her speaking eyes gloated such things, more immodest and lascivious than ravishers can act, or women under a confinement think.

Man. I know there are those whose eyes reflect more obscenity than the glasses in alcoves ; but there are others too who use a little art with their looks, to make 'em seem more beautiful, not more loving ; which vain young fellows like you are apt to interpret in their own favour, and to the lady's wrong.

Fid. Seldom, sir. Pray, have you a care of gloating eyes ; for he that loves to gaze upon 'em, will find at last a thousand fools and cuckolds in 'em instead of cupids.

Man. Very well, sir.—But what, you had only eye-kindness from Olivia ?

Fid. I tell you again, sir, no woman sticks there ; eye-promises of love they only keep ; nay, they are contracts which make you sure of 'em. In short, sir, she seeing me, with shame and amazement dumb, unactive, and resistless, threw her twisting arms about my neck, and smothered me with a thousand tasteless kisses. Believe me, sir, they were so to me.

Man. Why did you not avoid 'em then ?

Fid. I fenced with her eager arms, as you did with the grapples of the enemy's fireship ; and nothing but cutting 'em off could have freed me.

Man. Damned, damned woman, that could be so false and infamous ! and damned, damned heart of mine, that cannot yet be false, though so infamous ! what easy, tame suffering trampled things does that little god of talking cowards make of us ! but—

Fid. So ; it works, I find, as I expected.   [*Aside.*

Man. But she was false to me before, she told me so herself, and yet I could not quite believe it ; but she was, so that her second falseness is a favour to me, not an injury, in revenging me upon the man that wronged me first of her love. Her love !—a whore's, a witch's love ! —But what, did she not kiss well, sir ?—I'm sure I thought her lips—but I must not think of 'em more— but yet they are such I could still kiss—grow to—and then tear off with my teeth, grind 'em into mammocks,[1] and spit 'em into her cuckold's face.

Fid. Poor man, how uneasy he is ! I have hardly the heart to give so much pain, though withal I give him a cure, and to myself new life.   [*Aside.*

Man. But what, her kisses sure could not but warm

---

[1] Fragments : scraps.

you into desire at last, or a compliance with hers at least?

Fid. Nay, more, I confess—

Man. What more? speak.

Fid. All you could fear had passed between us, if I could have been made to wrong you, sir, in that nature.

Man. Could have been made! you lie, you did.

Fid. Indeed, sir, 'twas impossible for me; besides, we were interrupted by a visit; but I confess, she would not let me stir, till I promised to return to her again within this hour, as soon as it should be dark; by which time she would dispose of her visit, and her servants, and herself, for my reception. Which I was fain to promise, to get from her.

Man. Ha!

Fid. But if ever I go near her again, may you, sir, think me as false to you, as she is; hate and renounce me, as you ought to do her, and, I hope, will do now.

Man. Well, but now I think on't, you shall keep your word with your lady. What, a young fellow, and fail the first, nay, so tempting an assignation!

Fid. How, sir?

Man. I say, you shall go to her when 'tis dark, and shall not disappoint her.

Fid. I, sir! I should disappoint her more by going.

Man. How so?

Fid. Her impudence and injustice to you will make me disappoint her love, loathe her.

Man. Come, you have my leave; and if you disgust [1] her, I'll go with you, and act love, whilst you shall talk it only.

Fid. You, sir! nay, then I'll never go near her. You act love, sir! You must but act it indeed, after all I have said to you. Think of your honour, sir: love!—

Man. Well, call it revenge, and that is honourable: I'll be revenged on her; and thou shalt be my second.

---

[1] Dislike.

Fid. Not in a base action, sir, when you are your own
enemy.　O go not near her, sir ; for Heaven's sake, for
your own, think not of it !

Man. How concerned you are ! I thought I should
catch you.　What, you are my rival at last, and are in
love with her yourself ; and have spoken ill of her out of
your love to her, not me : and therefore would not have
me go to her !

Fid. Heaven witness for me, 'tis because I love you
only, I would not have you go to her.

Man. Come, come, the more I think on't, the more
I'm satisfied you do love her.　Those kisses, young man,
I knew were irresistible ; 'tis certain.

Fid. There is nothing certain in the world, sir, but my
truth and your courage.

Man. Your servant, sir.　Besides, false and ungrateful
as she has been to me, and though I may believe her
hatred to me great as you report it, yet I cannot think
you are so soon and at that rate beloved by her, though
you may endeavour it.

Fid. Nay, if that be all, and you doubt it still, sir, I
will conduct you to her ; and, unseen, your ears shall
judge of her falseness, and my truth to you, if that will
satisfy you.

Man. Yes, there is some satisfaction in being quite
out of doubt ; because 'tis that alone withholds us from
the pleasure of revenge.

Fid. Revenge !　What revenge can you have, sir ?
Disdain is best revenged by scorn ; and faithless love, by
loving another, and making her happy with the other's
losings.　Which, if I might advise—

Enter FREEMAN.

Man. Not a word more.

Free. What, are you talking of love yet, captain ? I
thought you had done with't.

Man. Why, what did you hear me say ?

Free. Something imperfectly of love, I think.

Man. I was only wondering why fools, rascals, and desertless wretches, should still have the better of men of merit with all women, as much as with their own common mistress, Fortune.

Free. Because most women, like Fortune, are blind, seem to do all things in jest, and take pleasure in extravagant actions. Their love deserves neither thanks, nor blame, for they cannot help it: 'tis all sympathy; therefore, the noisy, the finical, the talkative, the cowardly, and effeminate, have the better of the brave, the reasonable, and man of honour; for they have no more reason in their love, or kindness, than Fortune herself.

Man Yes, they have their reason. First, honour in a man they fear too much to love; and sense in a lover upbraids their want of it; and they hate anything that disturbs their admiration of themselves; but they are of that vain number, who had rather show their false generosity, in giving away profusely to worthless flatterers, than in paying just debts. And, in short, all women, like fortune (as you say) and rewards, are lost by too much meriting.

Fid. All women, sir! sure there are some who have no other quarrel to a lover's merit, but that it begets their despair of him.

Man. Thou art young enough to be credulous; but we—

Enter Sailor.

Sail. Here are now below, the scolding daggled gentlewoman, and that Major Old—Old—Fop, I think you call him.

Free. Oldfox:—prithee bid 'em come up, with your leave, captain, for now I can talk with her upon the square, if I shall not disturb you.   [*Exit* Sailor.

Man. No; for I'll begone. Come, volunteer.

Free. Nay, pray stay; the scene between us will not
be so tedious to you as you think. Besides, you shall
see how I rigged my 'squire out, with the remains
of my shipwrecked wardrobe; he is under your sea
valet-de-chambre's hands, and by this time dressed,
and will be worth your seeing. Stay, and I'll fetch my
fool.

Man. No; you know I cannot easily laugh : besides,
my volunteer and I have business abroad.

[*Exeunt* MANLY *and* FIDELIA *on one side ;*
FREEMAN *on the other.*

Enter Major OLDFOX *and* Widow BLACKACRE.

Wid. What, nobody here ! did not the fellow say he
was within ?

Old. Yes, lady ; and he may be perhaps a little busy
at present ; but if you think the time long till he comes,
[*Unfolding papers*] I'll read you here some of the fruits of
my leisure, the overflowings of my fancy and pen.—
[*Aside.*] To value me right, she must know my parts.—
[*Aloud.*] Come—

Wid. No, no; I have reading work enough of my
own in my bag, I thank you.

Old. Ay, law, madam ; but here's a poem, in blank
verse, which I think a handsome declaration of one's
passion.

Wid. O, if you talk of declarations, I'll show you one
of the prettiest penned things, which I mended too myself, you must know.

Old. Nay, lady, if you have used yourself so much to
the reading harsh law, that you hate smooth poetry, here
is a character for you, of—

Wid. A character ! nay, then I'll show you my bill in
chancery here, that gives you such a character of my
adversary, makes him as black—

Old. Pshaw ! away, away, lady ! But if you think the
character too long, here is an epigram, not above twenty

lines, upon a cruel lady, who decreed her servant should
hang himself, to demonstrate his passion.

Wid. Decreed! if you talk of decreeing, I have such a
decree here, drawn by the finest clerk—

Old. O lady, lady, all interruption, and no sense
between us, as if we were lawyers at the bar! but I had
forgot, Apollo and Littleton never lodge in a head
together. If you hate verses, I'll give you a cast of my
politics in prose. 'Tis "a Letter to a Friend in the
Country;" which is now the way of all such sober solid
persons as myself, when they have a mind to publish
their disgust to the times; though perhaps, between you
and I, they have no friend in the country. And sure a
politic, serious person may as well have a feigned friend
in the country to write to, as an idle poet a feigned
mistress to write to. And so here's my letter to a friend,
or no friend, in the country, concerning the late con-
juncture of affairs, in relation to coffee-houses; or,
"The Coffee-man's Case."

Wid. Nay, if your letter have a case in't, 'tis something; but first I'll read you a letter of mine to a friend
in the country, called a letter of attorney.

Re-enter FREEMAN, *with* JERRY BLACKACRE *in an old
gaudy suit and red breeches of* FREEMAN'S.

Old. What, interruption still! O the plague of interruption! worse to an author than the plague of critics.

[Aside.

Wid. What's this I see? Jerry Blackacre, my minor,
in red breeches! What, hast thou left the modest
seemly garb of gown and cap for this? and have I
lost all my good inns-of-chancery breeding upon thee
then? and thou wilt go a-breeding thyself from our inn
of chancery and Westminster Hall, at coffee-houses,
and ordinaries, play-houses, tennis-courts, and bawdy-
houses?

Jer. Ay, ay, what then? perhaps I will; but what's

that to you? Here's my guardian and tutor now, forsooth, that I am out of your huckster's hands.

Wid. How! thou hast not chosen him for thy guardian yet?

Jer. No, but he has chosen me for his charge, and that's all one; and I'll do anything he'll have me, and go all the world over with him; to ordinaries, and bawdy-houses, or anywhere else.

Wid. To ordinaries and bawdy-houses! have a care, minor, thou wilt enfeeble there thy estate and body: do not go to ordinaries and bawdy-houses, good Jerry.

Jer. Why, how come you to know any ill by bawdy-houses? you never had any hurt by 'em, had you, forsooth? Pray hold yourself contented; if I do go where money and wenches are to be had, you may thank yourself; for you used me so unnaturally, you would never let me have a penny to go abroad with; nor so much as come near the garret where your maidens lay; nay, you would not so much as let me play at hotcockles with 'em, nor have any recreation with 'em though one should have kissed you behind, you were so unnatural a mother, so you were.

Free. Ay, a very unnatural mother, faith, squire.

Wid. But, Jerry, consider thou art yet but a minor; however, if thou wilt go home with me again, and be a good child, thou shalt see—

Free. Madam, I must have a better care of my heir under age, than so; I would sooner trust him alone with a stale waiting-woman and a parson, than with his widow-mother and her lover or lawyer.

Wid. Why, thou villain, part mother and minor! rob me of my child and my writings! but thou shalt find there's law; and as in the case of ravishment of guard—Westminster the Second.

Old. Young gentleman squire, pray be ruled by your mother and your friends.

Jer. Yes, I'll be ruled by my friends, therefore not by

my mother, so I won't : I'll choose him for my guardian
till I am of age ; nay, maybe, for as long as I live.

Wid. Wilt thou so, thou wretch ? and when thou'rt of
age, thou wilt sign, seal and deliver too, wilt thou ?

Jer. Yes, marry will I, if you go there too.

Wid. O do not squeeze wax, son ; rather go to ordinaries and bawdy-houses, than squeeze wax.   If thou
dost that, farewell the goodly manor of Blackacre, with
all its woods, underwoods, and appurtenances whatever !
Oh, oh !   [*Weeps.*

Free. Come, madam, in short, you see I am resolved
to have a share in the estate, yours or your son's ; if I
cannot get you, I'll keep him, who is less coy, you find ;
but if you would have your son again, you must take me
too.   Peace or war ? love or law ?   You see my hostage
is in my hand : I'm in possession.

Wid. Nay, if one of us must be ruined, e'en let it be
him.   By my body, a good one !   Did you ever know
yet a widow marry or not marry for the sake of her
child ?   I'd have you to know, sir, I shall be hard enough
for you both yet, without marrying you, if Jerry won't
be ruled by me.   What say you, booby, will you be
ruled ? speak.

Jer. Let one alone, can't you ?

Wid. Wilt thou choose him for guardian, whom I
refuse for husband ?

Jer. Ay, to choose, I thank you.

Wid. And are all my hopes frustrated ? Shall I never
hear thee put cases again to John the butler, or our
vicar ? never see thee amble the circuit with the judges ;
and hear thee, in our town-hall, louder than the crier ?

Jer. No, for I have taken my leave of lawyering and
pettifogging.

Wid. Pettifogging ! thou profane villain, hast thou so ?
Pettifogging !—then you shall take your leave of me, and
your estate too ; thou shalt be an alien to me and it
forever.   Pettifogging !

Jer. O, but if you go there too, mother, we have the deeds and settlements, I thank you. Would you cheat me of my estate, i'fac?

Wid. No, no, I will not cheat your little brother Bob ; for thou wert not born in wedlock.

Free. How's that?

Jer. How? what quirk has she got in her head now?

Wid. I say, thou canst not, shalt not inherit the Blackacres' estate.

Jer. Why? why, forsooth? What d'ye mean, if you go there too?

Wid. Thou art but my base child ; and according to the law, canst not inherit it. Nay, thou art not so much as bastard eigne.[1]

Jer. What, what, am I then the son of a whore, mother?

Wid. The law says—

Free. Madam, we know what the law says ; but have a care what you say. Do not let your passion, to ruin your son, ruin your reputation.

Wid. Hang reputation, sir! am not I a widow? have no husband, nor intend to have any? Nor would you, I suppose, now have me for a wife. So I think now I'm revenged on my son and you, without marrying, as I told you.

Free. But consider, madam.

Jer. What, have you no shame left in you, mother?

Wid. Wonder not at it, major. 'Tis often the poor pressed widow's case, to give up her honour to save her jointure ; and seem to be a light woman, rather than marry : as some young men, they say, pretend to have the filthy disease, and lose their credit with most women, to avoid the importunities of some. [*Aside to* OLDFOX.

Free. But one word with you, madam.

Wid. No, no, sir. Come, major, let us make haste now to the Prerogative-court.

Old. But, lady, if what you say be true, will you stig-

---

[1] Fr. *aîné:* first-born.

matise your reputation on record? and if it be not true, how will you prove it?

Wid. Pshaw! I can prove anything: and for my reputation, know, major, a wise woman will no more value her reputation, in disinheriting a rebellious son of a good estate, than she would in getting him, to inherit an estate.

　　　[*Exeunt* Widow BLACKACRE *and* Major OLDFOX.

Free. Madam.—We must not let her go so, squire.

Jer. Nay, the devil can't stop her though, if she has a mind to't. But come, bully-guardian, we'll go and advise with three attorneys, two proctors, two solicitors, and a shrewd man of Whitefriars, neither attorney, proctor, nor solicitor, but as pure a pimp to the law as any of 'em: and sure all they will be hard enough for her, for I fear bully-guardian, you are too good a joker to have any law in your head.

Free. Thou'rt in the right on't, squire, I understand no law; especially that against bastards, since I'm sure the custom is against that law, and more people get estates by being so, than lose 'em.　　　　　　　　　　[*Exeunt.*

SCENE II.—OLIVIA'S *Lodging.*

Enter Lord PLAUSIBLE *and* Boy *with a candle.*

L. Plau. Little gentleman, your most obedient, faithful, humble servant. Where, I beseech you, is that divine person, your noble lady?

Boy. Gone out, my lord; but commanded me to give you this letter.　　　　　　　　　　[*Gives him a letter.*

Enter NOVEL.

L. Plau. Which he must not observe.

　　　　　　　　　　[*Aside.　Puts letter up.*

Nov. Hey, boy, where is thy lady?

Boy. Gone out, sir ; but I must beg a word with you.
   [*Gives him a letter, and exit.*

Nov. For me? So.—[*Puts up the letter.*] Servant, servant, my lord ; you see the lady knew of your coming, for she is gone out.

L. Plau. Sir, I humbly beseech you not to censure the lady's good breeding : she has reason to use more liberty with me than with any other man.

Nov. How, viscount, how?

L. Plau. Nay, I humbly beseech you, be not in choler ; where there is most love, there may be most freedom.

Nov. Nay, then 'tis time to come to an eclaircissement with you, and to tell you, you must think no more of this lady's love.

L. Plau. Why, under correction, dear sir?

Nov. There are reasons, reasons, viscount.

L. Plau. What, I beseech you, noble sir?

Nov. Prithee, prithee, be not impertinent, my lord ; some of you lords are such conceited, well-assured, impertinent rogues.

L. Plau. And you noble wits are so full of shamming and drolling, one knows not where to have you seriously.

Nov. Well, you shall find me in bed with this lady one of these days.

L. Plau. Nay, I beseech you, spare the lady's honour ; for hers and mine will be all one shortly.

Nov. Prithee, my lord, be not an ass. Dost thou think to get her from me? I have had such encouragements—

L. Plau. I have not been thought unworthy of 'em.

Nov. What, not like mine! Come to an eclaircissement, as I said.

L. Plau. Why, seriously then, she has told me viscountess sounded prettily.

Nov. And me, that Novel was a name she would sooner change hers for than for any title in England.

L. Plau. She has commended the softness and respectfulness of my behaviour.

Nov. She has praised the briskness of my raillery, of all things, man.

L. Plau. The sleepiness of my eyes she liked.

Nov. Sleepiness! dulness, dulness. But the fierceness of mine she adored.

L. Plau. The brightness of my hair she liked.

Nov. The brightness! no, the greasiness, I warrant. But the blackness and lustre of mine she admires.

L. Plau. The gentleness of my smile.

Nov. The subtilty of my leer.

L. Plau. The clearness of my complexion.

Nov. The redness of my lips.

L. Plau. The whiteness of my teeth.

Nov. My jaunty way of picking them.

L. Plau. The sweetness of my breath.

Nov. Ha! ha! nay, then she abused you, 'tis plain; for you know what Manly said :—the sweetness of your pulvillio she might mean; but for your breath! ha! ha! ha! Your breath is such, man, that nothing but tobacco can perfume; and your complexion nothing could mend but the small-pox.

L. Plau. Well, sir, you may please to be merry; but, to put you out of all doubt, sir, she has received some jewels from me of value.

Nov. And presents from me; besides what I presented her jauntily, by way of ombre, of three or four hundred pounds value, which I'm sure are the earnest-pence for our love-bargain.

L. Plau. Nay, then, sir, with your favour, and to make an end of all your hopes, look you there, sir, she has writ to me—

Nov. How! how! well, well, and so she has to me; look you there— [*They deliver to each other their letters.*

L. Plau. What's here ?

Nov. How's this ?

[*Reads out.*]—" My dear lord,—You'll excuse me for breaking my word with you, since 'twas to oblige, not offend you ; for I am only gone abroad but to disappoint Novel, and meet you in the drawing-room ; where I expect you with as much impatience as when I used to suffer Novel's visits—the most impertinent fop that ever affected the name of a wit, therefore not capable, I hope, to give you jealousy ; for, for your sake alone, you saw I renounced an old lover, and will do all the world. Burn the letter, but lay up the kindness of it in your heart, with your—Olivia."

Very fine ! but pray let's see mine.

L. Plau. I understand it not ; but sure she cannot think so of me.

Nov. [*Reads the other letter.*] Hum ! ha !—" meet—for your sake "—hum—" quitted an old lover—world—burn—in your heart—with your—Olivia."

Just the same, the names only altered.

L. Plau. Surely there must be some mistake, or somebody has abused her and us.

Nov. Yes, you are abused, no doubt on't, my lord but I'll to Whitehall, and see.

L. Plau. And I, where I shall find you are abused.

Nov. Where, if it be so, for our comfort, we cannot fail of meeting with fellow-sufferers enough ; for, as Freeman said of another, she stands in the drawing-room, like the glass, ready for all comers, to set their gallantry by her : and, like the glass too, lets no man go from her unsatisfied with himself. [*Exeunt.*

Enter OLIVIA *and* Boy.

Oliv. Both here, and just gone ?

Boy. Yes, madam.

Oliv. But are you sure neither saw you deliver the other a letter.

Boy. Yes, yes, madam, I am very sure.

Oliv. Go then to the Old Exchange, to Westminster, Holborn, and all the other places I told you of; I shall not need you these two hours : begone, and take the candle with you, and be sure you leave word again below, I am gone out, to all that ask.

Boy. Yes, madam.   [*Exit.*

Oliv. And my new lover will not ask, I'm sure ; he has his lesson, and cannot miss me here, though in the dark : which I have purposely designed, as a remedy against my blushing gallant's modesty ; for young lovers, like game-cocks, are made bolder by being kept without light.

Enter VERNISH, *as from a journey.*

Ver. Where is she ?   Darkness everywhere ?   [*Softly.*

Oliv. What ! come before your time ?   My soul ! my life ! your haste has augmented your kindness ; and let me thank you for it thus, and thus—[*Embracing and kissing him.*]   And though, my soul, the little time since you left me has seemed an age to my impatience, sure it is yet but seven—

Ver. How ! who's that you expected after seven ?

Oliv. Ha ! my husband returned ! and have I been throwing away so many kind kisses on my husband, and wronged my lover already ?   [*Aside.*

Ver. Speak, I say, who was't you expected after seven?

Oliv. [*Aside.*] What shall I say ?—oh—[*Aloud.*] Why 'tis but seven days, is it, dearest, since you went out of town ? and I expected you not so soon.

Ver. No, sure, 'tis but five days since I left you.

Oliv. Pardon my impatience, dearest, I thought 'em seven at least.

Ver. Nay, then—

Oliv. But, my life, you shall never stay half so long from me again ; you shan't indeed, by this kiss you shan't.

Ver. No, no ; but why alone in the dark ?

Oliv. Blame not my melancholy in your absence.—
But, my soul, since you went, I have strange news to tell
you : Manly is returned.

Ver. Manly returned ! Fortune forbid !

Oliv. Met with the Dutch in the channel, fought, sunk
his ship, and all he carried with him. He was here with
me yesterday.

Ver. And did you own our marriage to him ?

Oliv. I told him I was married to put an end to his
love and my trouble ; but to whom, is yet a secret kept
from him and all the world. And I have used him so
scurvily, his great spirit will ne'er return to reason it
farther with me : I have sent him to sea again, I
warrant.

Ver. 'Twas bravely done. And sure he will now hate
the shore more than ever, after so great a disappointment. Be you sure only to keep a while our great
secret, till he be gone. In the mean time, I'll lead the
easy, honest fool by the nose, as I used to do ; and
whilst he stays, rail with him at thee ; and when he's
gone, laugh with thee at him. But have you his cabinet
of jewels safe ? part not with a seed-pearl to him, to keep
him from starving.

Oliv. Nor from hanging.

Ver. He cannot recover 'em ; and, I think, will scorn
to beg 'em again.

Oliv. But, my life, have you taken the thousand
guineas he left in my name out of the goldsmith's hands?

Ver. Ay, ay ; they are removed to another goldsmith's.

Oliv. Ay, but, my soul, you had best have a care he
find not where the money is ; for his present wants, as
I'm informed, are such as will make him inquisitive
enough.

Ver. You say true, and he knows the man too ; but
I'll remove it to-morrow.

Oliv. To-morrow! O do not stay till to-morrow; go to-night, immediately.

Ver. Now I think on't, you advise well, and I will go presently.

Oliv. Presently! instantly! I will not let you stay a jot.

Ver. I will then, though I return not home till twelve.

Oliv. Nay, though not till morning, with all my heart. Go, dearest; I am impatient till you are gone.—[*Thrusts him out.*] So, I have at once now brought about those two grateful businesses, which all prudent women do together, secured money and pleasure; and now all interruptions of the last are removed. Go, husband, and come up, friend; just the buckets in the well; the absence of one brings the other. But I hope, like them too, they will not meet in the way, jostle, and clash together.

Enter FIDELIA, *and* MANLY *treading softly and staying behind at some distance.*

So, are you come? (but not the husband-bucket, I hope, again.)—Who's there? my dearest?   [*Softly.*

Fid. My life—

Oliv. Right, right.—Where are thy lips? Here, take the dumb and best welcomes, kisses and embraces; 'tis not a time for idle words. In a duel of love, as in others, parleying shows basely. Come, we are alone; and now the word is only satisfaction, and defend not thyself.

Man. How's this? Why, she makes love like a devil in a play; and in this darkness, which conceals her angel's face, if I were apt to be afraid, I should think her a devil.

[*Aside.*

Oliv. What, you traverse ground, young gentleman!

[FIDELIA *avoiding her.*

Fid. I take breath only.

Man. Good Heavens! how was I deceived!   [*Aside.*

Oliv. Nay, you are a coward ; what, are you afraid of the fierceness of my love ?

Fid. Yes, madam, lest its violence might presage its change ; and I must needs be afraid you would leave me quickly, who could desert so brave a gentleman as Manly.

Oliv. O, name not his name ! for in a time of stolen joys, as this is, the filthy name of husband were not a more allaying sound.

Man. There's some comfort yet.   [*Aside.*

Fid. But did you not love him ?

Oliv. Never.   How could you think it

Fid. Because he thought it ; who is a man of that sense, nice discerning, and diffidency, that I should think it hard to deceive him.

Oliv. No ; he that distrusts most the world, trusts most to himself, and is but the more easily deceived, because he thinks he can't be deceived.   His cunning is like the coward's sword, by which he is oftener worsted than defended.

Fid. Yet, sure, you used no common art to deceive him.

Oliv. I knew he loved his own singular moroseness so well, as to dote upon any copy of it ; wherefore I feigned a hatred to the world too that he might love me in earnest : but, if it had been hard to deceive him, I'm sure 'twere much harder to love him.   A dogged, ill-mannered—

Fid. D'ye hear, sir ? pray, hear her. [*Aside to* MANLY.

Oliv. Surly, untractable, snarling brute ! He ! a mastiff dog were as fit a thing to make a gallant of.

Man. Ay, a goat, or monkey, were fitter for thee.

                                             [*Aside.*

Fid. I must confess, for my part, though my rival, I cannot but say he has a manly handsomeness in's face and mien.

Oliv. So has a Saracen in the sign.

Fid. Is proper, and well made.

Oliv. As a drayman.

Fid. Has wit.

Oliv. He rails at all mankind.

Fid. And undoubted courage.

Oliv. Like the hangman's; can murder a man when his hands are tied. He has cruelty indeed; which is no more courage, than his railing is wit.

Man. Thus women, and men like women, are too hard for us, when they think we do not hear 'em: and reputation, like other mistresses, is never true to a man in his absence.   [*Aside.*

Fid. He is—

Oliv. Prithee, no more of him: I thought I had satisfied you enough before, that he could never be a rival for you to apprehend. And you need not be more assured of my aversion to him, than by the last testimony of my love to you; which I am ready to give you. Come, my soul, this way.   [*Pulls* FIDELIA.

Fid. But, madam, what could make you dissemble love to him, when 'twas so hard a thing for you; and flatter his love to you?

Oliv. That which makes all the world flatter and dissemble, 'twas his money: I had a real passion for that. Yet I loved not that so well, as for it to take him; for as soon as I had his money I hastened his departure like a wife, who when she has made the most of a dying husband's breath, pulls away his pillow.

Man. Damned money! its master's potent rival still; and like a saucy pimp, corrupts itself the mistress it procures for us.   [*Aside.*

Oliv. But I did not think with you, my life, to pass my time in talking. Come hither, come; yet stay, till I have locked a door in the other room, that may chance to let us in some interruption; which reciting poets or losing gamesters fear not more than I at this time do.

        [*Exit.*

Fid. Well, I hope you are now satisfied, sir, and will be gone to think of your revenge?

Man. No, I am not satisfied, and must stay to be revenged.

Fid. How, sir? You'll use no violence to her, I hope, and forfeit your own life, to take away hers? that were no revenge.

Man. No, no, you need not fear: my revenge shall only be upon her honour, not her life.

Fid. How, sir? her honour? O Heavens! consider, sir, she has no honour. D'ye call that revenge? can you think of such a thing? But reflect, sir, how she hates and loathes you.

Man. Yes, so much she hates me, that it would be a revenge sufficient to make her accessary to my pleasure, and then let her know it.

Fid. No, sir, no; to be revenged on her now, were to disappoint her. Pray, sir, let us begone. [*Pulls* MANLY.

Man. Hold off! What, you are my rival then! and therefore you shall stay, and keep the door for me, whilst I go in for you; but when I'm gone, if you dare to stir off from this very board, or breathe the least murmuring accent, I'll cut her throat first; and if you love her, you will not venture her life.—Nay, then I'll cut your throat too; and I know you love your own life at least.

Fid. But, sir; good sir.

Man. Not a word more, lest I begin my revenge on her by killing you.

Fid. But are you sure 'tis revenge that makes you do this? how can it be?

Man. Whist!

Fid. 'Tis a strange revenge, indeed.

Man. If you make me stay, I shall keep my word, and begin with you. No more.

[*Exit at the same door* OLIVIA *went out by.*

Fid. O Heavens! is there not punishment enough
In loving well, if you will have't a crime

But you must add fresh torments daily to't,
And punish us like peevish rivals still,
Because we fain would find a heaven here?
But did there never any love like me,
That untried tortures you must find me out?
Others at worst, you force to kill themselves;
But I must be self-murdress of my love,
Yet will not grant me power to end my life,
My cruel life; for when a lover's hopes
Are dead and gone, life is unmerciful.

[Sits down and weeps.

Re-enter MANLY.

Man. I have thought better on't : I must not discover myself now I am without witnesses; for if I barely should publish it, she would deny it with as much impudence, as she would act it again with this young fellow here.— Where are you?

Fid. Here—oh—now I suppose we may be gone.

Man. I will; but not you. You must stay and act the second part of a lover, that is, talk kindness to her.

Fid. Not I, sir.

Man. No disputing, sir, you must; 'tis necessary to my design of coming again to-morrow night.

Fid. What, can you come again then hither?

Man. Yes; and you must make the appointment, and an apology for your leaving her so soon; for I have said not a word to her; but have kept your counsel, as I expect you should do mine. Do this faithfully, and I promise you here, you shall run my fortune still, and we will never part as long as we live; but if you do not do it, expect not to live.

Fid. 'Tis hard, sir; but such a consideration will make it easier. You won't forget your promise, sir?

Man. No, by Heavens! But I hear her coming.

[Exit.

Re-enter OLIVIA.

Oliv. Where is my life? Run from me already! You do not love me, dearest; nay, you are angry with me, for you would not so much as speak a kind word to me within: what was the reason?

Fid. I was transported too much.

Oliv. That's kind.—But come, my soul, what make you here? Let us go in again; we may be surprised in this room, 'tis so near the stairs.

Fid. No, we shall hear the better here, if anybody should come up.

Oliv. Nay, I assure you, we shall be secure enough within: come, come —

Fid. I am sick, and troubled with a sudden dizziness; and cannot stir yet.

Oliv. Come, I have spirits within.

Fid. O! don't you hear a noise, madam?

Oliv. No, no; there is none: come, come. [*Pulls her.*

Fid. Indeed there is; and I love you so much, I must have a care of your honour, if you won't, and go; but to come to you to-morrow night, if you please.

Oliv. With all my soul. But you must not go yet; come, prithee.

Fid. Oh!—I'm now sicker, and am afraid of one of my fits.

Oliv. What fits?

Fid. Of the falling sickness; and I lie generally an hour in a trance: therefore pray consider your honour for the sake of my love, and let me go, that I may return to you often.

Oliv. But will you be sure then to come to-morrow night?

Fid. Yes.

Oliv. Swear.

Fid. By our past kindness!

Oliv. Well, go your ways then, if you will, you naughty

creature you.—[*Exit* FIDELIA.] These young lovers, with their fears and modesty, make themselves as bad as old ones to us; and I apprehend their bashfulness more than their tattling.

Re-enter FIDELIA.

Fid. O madam, we're undone! There was a gentleman upon the stairs, coming up with a candle, which made me retire. Look you, here he comes!

Re-enter VERNISH, *and his* Servant *with a light.*

Oliv. How, my husband! Oh, undone indeed! This way. [*Exit.*

Ver. Ha! You shall not escape me so, sir.
[*Stops* FIDELIA.

Fid. O Heavens! more fears, plagues, and torments yet in store! [*Aside.*

Ver. Come, sir, I guess what your business was here, but this must be your business now. Draw. [*Draws.*

Fid. Sir—

Ver. No expostulations; I shall not care to hear of't. Draw.

Fid. Good sir!

Ver. How, you rascal! not courage to draw; yet durst do me the greatest injury in the world? Thy cowardice shall not save thy life. [*Offers to run at* FIDELIA.

Fid. O hold, sir, and send but your servant down, and I'll satisfy you, sir, I could not injure you as you imagine.

Ver. Leave the light and begone.—[*Exit* Servant.] Now, quickly, sir, what have you to say, or—

Fid. I am a woman, sir, a very unfortunate woman.

Ver. How! a very handsome woman, I'm sure then: here are witnesses of't too, I confess— [*Pulls off her peruke and feels her breasts; then aside,*] Well, I'm glad to find the tables turned; my wife is in more danger of cuckolding than I was.

Fid. Now, sir, I hope you are so much a man of honour, as to let me go, now I have satisfied you, sir.

Ver. When you have satisfied me, madam, I will.

Fid. I hope, sir, you are too much a gentleman to urge those secrets from a woman which concern her honour. You may guess my misfortune to be love by my disguise : but a pair of breeches could not wrong you, sir.

Ver. I may believe love has changed your outside, which could not wrong me ; but why did my wife run away ?

Fid. I know not, sir ; perhaps because she would not be forced to discover me to you, or to guide me from your suspicions, that you might not discover me yourself ; which ungentlemanlike curiosity I hope you will cease to have, and let me go.

Ver. Well, madam, if I must not know who you are, 'twill suffice for me only to know certainly what you are ; which you must not deny me. Come, there is a bed within, the proper rack for lovers ; and if you are a woman, there you can keep no secrets ; you'll tell me there all unasked. Come.   [*Pulls her.*

Fid. Oh ! what d'ye mean ?   Help ! oh !

Ver. I'll show you : but 'tis in vain to cry out : no one dares help you ; for I am lord here.

Fid. Tyrant here !—But if you are master of this house, which I have taken for a sanctuary, do not violate it yourself.

Ver. No, I'll preserve you here, and nothing shall hurt you, and will be as true to you as your disguise ; but you must trust me then. Come, come.   [*Pulls her.*

Fid. Oh ! oh ! rather than you should drag me to a deed so horrid and so shameful, I'll die here a thousand deaths.—But you do not look like a ravisher, sir.

Ver. Nor you like one would put me to't ; but if you will—

Fid. Oh ! oh ! help ! help !

Re-enter Servant.

Ver. You saucy rascal, how durst you come in?
When you heard a woman squeak, that should have been
your cue to shut the door.

Serv. I come, sir, to let you know, the alderman
coming home immediately after you were at his house,
has sent his cashier with the money, according to your
note.

Ver. Damn his money! Money never came to any,
sure, unseasonably till now. Bid him stay.

Serv. He says, he cannot a moment.

Ver. Receive it you then.

Serv. He says he must have your receipt for it :—he is
in haste, for I hear him coming up, sir.

Ver. Damn him! Help me in here then with this
dishonourer of my family.

Fid. Oh! oh!

Serv. You say she is a woman, sir.

Ver. No matter, sir : must you prate?

Fid. Oh Heavens! is there—

           [*They thrust her in, and lock the door.*

Ver. Stay there, my prisoner; you have a short reprieve.

    I'll fetch the gold, and that she can't resist,
    For with a full hand 'tis we ravish best.

                    [*Exeunt.*

ACT THE FIFTH.

SCENE I.—Eliza's *Lodgings*.

Enter Olivia *and* Eliza.

LIV. Ah, cousin! nothing troubles me but that I have given the malicious world its revenge, and reason now to talk as freely of me as I used to do of it.

Eliza. Faith, then, let not that trouble you; for, to be plain, cousin, the world cannot talk worse of you than it did before.

Oliv. How, cousin! I'd have you to know, before this *faux pas*, this trip of mine, the world could not talk of me.

Eliza. Only that you mind other people's actions so much that you take no care of your own, but to hide 'em; that, like a thief, because you know yourself most guilty, you impeach your fellow-criminals first, to clear yourself.

Oliv. O wicked world!

Eliza. That you pretend an aversion to all mankind in public, only that their wives and mistresses may not be jealous, and hinder you of their conversation in private.

Oliv. Base world!

Eliza. That abroad you fasten quarrels upon innocent men for talking of you, only to bring 'em to ask your pardon at home, and to become dear friends with them, who were hardly your acquaintance before.

Oliv. Abominable world!

Eliza. That you condemn the obscenity of modern plays, only that you may not be censured for never missing the most obscene of the old ones.

Oliv. Damned world!

Eliza. That you deface the nudities of pictures, and little statues, only because they are not real.[1]

Oliv. O, fy! fy! fy! hideous, hideous! Cousin, the obscenity of their censures makes me blush!

Eliza. The truth of 'em, the naughty world would say now.

Enter LETTICE *hastily.*

Let. O, madam! here is that gentleman coming up who now you say is my master.

Oliv. O, cousin! whither shall I run? protect me, or—
          [OLIVIA *runs away, and stands at a distance*

Enter VERNISH.

Ver. Nay, nay, come—

Oliv. O, sir, forgive me!

Ver. Yes, yes, I can forgive you being alone in the dark with a woman in man's clothes: but have a care of a man in woman's clothes.

Oliv. What does he mean? he dissembles only to get me into his power: or has my dear friend made him believe he was a woman? My husband may be deceived by him, but I'm sure I was not.   [*Aside.*

Ver. Come, come, you need not have lain out of your house for this; but perhaps you were afraid, when I was warm with suspicions, you must have discovered who she was.—And, prithee, may I not know it?

Oliv. She was!—[*Aside.*] I hope he has been deceived:

---

[1] Elle fait des tableaux couvrir les nudités ;
    Mais elle a de l'amour pour les réalités.
            —*Le Misanthrope*, act iii., scene v.

and since my lover has played the card, I must not renounce.

Ver. Come, what's the matter with thee? If I must not know who she is, I'm satisfied without. Come hither.

Oliv. Sure you do know her; she has told you herself, I suppose.

Ver. No, I might have known her better but that I was interrupted by the goldsmith, you know, and was forced to lock her into your chamber, to keep her from his sight; but, when I returned, I found she was got away by tying the window-curtains to the balcony, by which she slid down into the street. For, you must know, I jested with her, and made her believe I'd ravish her; which she apprehended, it seems, in earnest.

Oliv. And she got from you?

Ver. Yes.

Oliv. And is quite gone?

Ver. Yes.

Oliv. I'm glad on't—otherwise you had ravished her, sir? But how durst you go so far, as to make her believe you would ravish her? let me understand that, sir. What! there's guilt in your face, you blush too: nay, then you did ravish her, you did, you base fellow! What, ravish a woman in the first month of our marriage! 'tis a double injury to me, thou base, ungrateful man! wrong my bed already, villain! I could tear out those false eyes, barbarous, unworthy wretch!

Eliza. So, so!—

Ver. Prithee hear, my dear.

Oliv. I will never hear you, my plague, my torment!

Ver. I swear—prithee, hear me.

Oliv. I have heard already too many of your false oaths and vows, especially your last in the church. O wicked man! and wretched woman that I was! I wish I had then sunk down into a grave, rather than to have given you my hand, to be led to your loathsome bed. Oh—
oh--   [*Pretends to weep.*

Ver. So, very fine! just a marriage-quarrel! which though it generally begins by the wife's fault, yet, in the conclusion, it becomes the husband's; and whosoever offends at first, he only is sure to ask pardon at last. My dear—

Oliv. My devil!—

Ver. Come, prithee be appeased, and go home; I have bespoken our supper betimes: for I could not eat till I found you. Go, I'll give you all kind of satisfactions; and one, which uses to be a reconciling one, two hundred of those guineas I received last night, to do what you will with.

Oliv. What, would you pay me for being your bawd?

Ver. Nay, prithee no more; go, and I'll thoroughly satisfy you when I come home; and then, too, we will have a fit of laughter at Manly, whom I am going to find at the Cock in Bow-street, where I hear he dined. Go, dearest, go home.

Eliza. A very pretty turn, indeed, this!   [*Aside.*

Ver. Now, cousin, since by my wife I have that honour and privilege of calling you so, I have something to beg of you too; which is not to take notice of our marriage to any whatever yet a while, for some reasons very important to me. And, next, that you will do my wife the honour to go home with her; and me the favour, to use that power you have with her, in our reconcilement.

Eliza. That I dare promise, sir, will be no hard matter. Your servant.—[*Exit* VERNISH.]—Well, cousin, this, I confess, was reasonable hypocrisy; you were the better for't.

Oliv. What hypocrisy?

Eliza. Why, this last deceit of your husband was lawful, since in your own defence.

Oliv. What deceit? I'd have you to know I never deceived my husband.

Eliza. You do not understand me, sure: I say, this was an honest come-off, and a good one. But 'twas a sign your gallant had had enough of your conversation, since he could so dexterously cheat your husband in passing for a woman.

Oliv. What d'ye mean, once more, with my gallant and passing for a woman?

Eliza. What do you mean? you see your husband took him for a woman.

Oliv. Whom?

Eliza. Heyday! why, the man he found you with, for whom last night you were so much afraid; and who you told me—

Oliv. Lord, you rave sure!

Eliza. Why, did you not tell me last night—

Oliv. I know not what I might tell you last night, in a fright.

Eliza. Ay, what was that fright for? for a woman? besides, were you not afraid to see your husband just now? I warrant only for having been found with a woman! Nay, did you not just now, too, own your false step, or trip, as you called it? which was with a woman too! fy, this fooling is so insipid, 'tis offensive!

Oliv. And fooling with my honour will be more offensive. Did you not hear my husband say he found me with a woman in man's clothes? and d'ye think he does not know a man from a woman?

Eliza. Not so well, I'm sure, as you do; therefore I'd rather take your word.

Oliv. What, you grow scurrilous, and are, I find, more censorious than the world! I must have a care of you, I see.

Eliza. No, you need not fear yet, I'll keep your secret.

Oliv. My secret! I'd have you to know, I have no need of confidants, though you value yourself upon being a good one.

Eliza. O admirable confidence! you show more in denying your wickedness, than other people in glorying in't.

Oliv. Confidence, to me! to me such language! nay, then I'll never see your face again.—[*Aside.*] I'll quarrel with her, that people may never believe I was in her power; but take for malice all the truth she may speak against me.—[*Aloud.*] Lettice, where are you! Let us be gone from this censorious ill woman.

Eliza. [*Aside.*] Nay, thou shalt stay a little, to damn thyself quite.—[*Aloud.*] One word first, pray, madam; can you swear that whom your husband found you with—

Oliv. Swear! ay, that whosoever 'twas that stole up, unknown, into my room, when 'twas dark, I know not, whether man or woman, by Heavens! by all that's good; or, may I never more have joys here, or in the other world! Nay, may I eternally—

Eliza. Be damned. So, so, you are damned enough already by your oaths; and I enough confirmed, and now you may please to be gone. Yet take this advice with you, in this plain-dealing age, to leave off forswearing yourself; for when people hardly think the better of a woman for her real modesty, why should you put that great constraint upon yourself to feign it?

Oliv. O hideous, hideous advice! let us go out of the hearing of it. She will spoil us, Lettice.

[*Exeunt* OLIVIA *and* LETTICE *at one door,* ELIZA *at the other.*

SCENE II.—*The Cock in Bow Street. A table and bottles.*

Enter MANLY *and* FIDELIA.

Man. How! saved her honour by making her husband believe you were a woman! 'Twas well, but hard enough to do, sure.

Fid. We were interrupted before he could contradict me.

Man. But can't you tell me, d'ye say, what kind of man he was?

Fid. I was so frightened, I confess, I can give no other account of him, but that he was pretty tall, round-faced, and one, I'm sure, I ne'er had seen before.

Man. But she, you say, made you swear to return to-night?

Fid. But I have since sworn, never to go near her again; for the husband would murder me, or worse, if he caught me again.

Man. No, I will go with you, and defend you to-night, and then I'll swear, too, never to go near her again.

Fid. Nay, indeed, sir, I will not go, to be accessary to your death too. Besides, what should you go again, sir, for?

Man. No disputing, or advice, sir, you have reason to know I am unalterable. Go therefore presently, and write her a note, to inquire if her assignation with you holds; and if not to be at her own house, where else; and be importunate to gain admittance to her to-night. Let your messenger, ere he deliver your letter, inquire first if her husband be gone out. Go, 'tis now almost six of the clock; I expect you back here before seven, with leave to see her then. Go, do this dextrously, and expect the performance of my last night's promise, never to part with you.

Fid. Ay, sir; but will you be sure to remember that?

Man. Did I ever break my word? Go, no more re-plies, or doubts.　　　　　　　　　　　　　[*Exit* FIDELIA.

Enter FREEMAN.

Where hast thou been?

Free. In the next room with my Lord Plausible and Novel.

Man. Ay, we came hither, because 'twas a private house; but with thee indeed no house can be private, for thou hast that pretty quality of the familiar fops of the town, who, in an eating-house, always keep company with all people in't but those they came with.

Free. I went into their room, but to keep them, and my own fool the squire, out of your room; but you shall be peevish now, because you have no money. But why the devil won't you write to those we were speaking of? Since your modesty, or your spirit, will not suffer you to speak to 'em, to lend you money, why won't you try 'em at last that way?

Man. Because I know 'em already, and can bear want better than denials, nay, than obligations.

Free. Deny you! they cannot. All of 'em have been your intimate friends.

Man. No, they have been people only I have obliged particularly.

Free. Very well; therefore you ought to go to 'em the rather, sure.

Man. No, no. Those you have obliged most, most certainly avoid you, when you can oblige 'em no longer; and they take your visits like so many duns. Friends, like mistresses, are avoided for obligations past.

Free. Pshaw! but most of 'em are your relations; men of great fortune and honour.

Man. Yes; but relations have so much honour as to think poverty taints the blood, and disown their wanting kindred; believing, I suppose, that as riches at first make a gentleman, the want of 'em degrades him. But damn 'em! now I am poor, I'll anticipate their contempt, and disown them.

Free. But you have many a female acquaintance whom you have been liberal to, who may have a heart to refund to you a little, if you would ask it: they are not all Olivias.

Man. Damn thee! how couldst thou think of such a thing? I would as soon rob my footman of his wages. Besides, 'twere in vain too: for a wench is like a box in an ordinary, receives all people's money easily, but there is no getting, nay, shaking any out again ; and he that fills it is sure never to keep the key.

Free. Well, but noble captain, would you make me believe that you, who know half the town, have so many friends, and have obliged so many, can't borrow fifty or a hundred pounds ?

Man. Why, noble lieutenant, you who know all the town, and call all you know friends, methinks should not wonder at it ; since you find ingratitude too. For how many lords' families (though descended from blacksmiths or tinkers) hast thou called great and illustrious ? how many ill tables called good eating ? how many noisy cox-combs wits ? how many pert cocking[1] cowards stout ? how many tawdry affected rogues well-dressed ? how many perukes admired ? and how many ill verses applauded ? and yet canst not borrow a shilling. Dost thou expect I, who always spoke truth, should ?

Free. Nay, now you think you have paid me ; but hark you, captain, I have heard of a thing called grinning honour, but never of starving honour.

Man. Well, but it has been the fate of some brave men : and if they won't give me a ship again, I can go starve anywhere with a musket on my shoulder.

Free. Give you a ship ! why, you will not solicit it.

Man. If I have not solicited it by my services, I know no other way.

Free. Your servant, sir ; nay, then I'm satisfied, I must solicit my widow the closer, and run the desperate fortune of matrimony on shore.   [*Exit.*

Enter VERNISH.

Man. How !—Nay, here is a friend indeed ; and he that has him in his arms can know no wants.

[*Embraces* VERNISH.

Ver. Dear sir ! and he that is in your arms is secure from all fears whatever : nay, our nation is secure by

---

[1] Cock-fighting ; wantoning.—*Wright.*

your defeat at sea, and the Dutch that fought against you have proved enemies to themselves only in bringing you back to us.

Man. Fy! fy! this from a friend? and yet from any other 'twere insufferable: I thought I should never have taken anything ill from you.

Ver. A friend's privilege is to speak his mind, though it be taken ill.

Man. But your tongue need not tell me you think too well of me; I have found it from your heart, which spoke in actions, your unalterable heart. But Olivia is false, my friend, which I suppose is no news to you.

Ver. He's in the right on't.   [*Aside.*

Man. But couldst thou not keep her true to me?

Ver. Not for my heart, sir.

Man. But could you not perceive it at all before I went? Could she so deceive us both?

Ver. I must confess, the first time I knew it was three days after your departure, when she received the money you had left in Lombard-street in her name; and her tears did not hinder her, it seems, from counting that. You would trust her with all, like a true generous lover.

Man. And she like a mean jilting—

Ver. Traitorous—

Man. Base—

Ver. Damned—

Man. Covetous—

Ver. Mercenary whore.—[*Aside.*] I can hardly hold from laughing.

Man. Ay, a mercenary whore indeed; for she made me pay her before I lay with her.

Ver. How!—Why, have you lain with her?

Man. Ay, ay.

Ver. Nay, she deserves you should report it at least, though you have not.

Man. Report it! by Heaven, 'tis true!

Ver. How! sure not.

Man. I do not use to lie, nor you to doubt me.

Ver. When?

Man. Last night, about seven or eight of the clock.

Ver. Ha!—[*Aside.*] Now I remember, I thought she spake as if she expected some other rather than me. A confounded whore, indeed!

Man. But what, thou wonderest at it! nay, you seem to be angry too.

Ver. I cannot but be enraged against her, for her usage of you : damned infamous, common jade!

Man. Nay, her cuckold, who first cuckolded me in my money, shall not laugh all himself: we will do him reason, shan't we?

Ver. Ay, ay.

Man. But thou dost not, for so great a friend, take pleasure enough in your friend's revenge, methinks.

Ver. Yes, yes ; I'm glad to know it, since you have lain with her.

Man. Thou canst not tell who that rascal, her cuckold, is?

Ver. No.

Man. She would keep it from you, I suppose.

Ver. Yes, yes.

Man. Thou wouldst laugh, if thou knewest but all the circumstances of my having her. Come, I'll tell thee.

Ver. Damn her! I care not to hear any more of her.

Man. Faith, thou shalt. You must know—

Re-enter FREEMAN *backwards, endeavouring to keep out* NOVEL, Lord PLAUSIBLE, JERRY BLACKACRE, *and* Major OLDFOX, *who all press upon him.*

Free. I tell you he has a wench with him, and would be private.

Man. Damn 'em! a man can't open a bottle in these eating-houses, but presently you have these impudent, intruding, buzzing flies and insects in your glass.—Well,

I'll tell thee all anon. In the mean time prithee go to her, but not from me, and try if you can get her to lend me but a hundred pounds of my money, to supply my present wants; for I suppose there is no recovering any of it by law.

Ver. Not any : think not of it. Nor by this way neither.

Man. Go try, at least.

Ver. I'll go ; but I can satisfy you beforehand it will be to no purpose. You'll no more find a refunding wench—

Man. Than a refunding lawyer ; indeed their fees alike scarce ever return. However, try her ; put it to her.

Ver. Ay, ay, I'll try her ; put it to her home with a vengeance.   [*Exit.*

Nov. Nay, you shall be our judge, Manly—Come, major, I'll speak it to your teeth ; if people provoke me to say bitter things to their faces, they must take what follows ; though, like my lord Plausible, I'd rather do't civilly behind their backs.

Man. Nay, thou art a dangerous rogue, I've heard, behind a man's back.

L. Plau. You wrong him sure, noble captain ; he would do a man no more harm behind his back than to his face.

Free. I am of my lord's mind.

Man. Yes, a fool, like a coward, is the more to be, feared behind a man's back, more than a witty man ; for as a coward is more bloody than a brave man, a fool is more malicious than a man of wit.

Nov. A fool, tar,—a fool ! nay, thou art a brave sea-judge of wit ! a fool ! Prithee when did you ever find me want something to say, as you do often ?

Man. Nay, I confess thou art always talking, roaring, or making a noise ; that I'll say for thee.

Nov. Well, and is talking a sign of a fool?

Man. Yes, always talking, especially too if it be loud and fast, is the sign of a fool.

Nov. Pshaw! talking is like fencing, the quicker the better; run 'em down, run 'em down, no matter for parrying; push on still, sa, sa, sa! No matter whether you argue in form, push in guard or no.

Man. Or hit or no; I think thou always talkest without thinking, Novel.

Nov. Ay, ay; studied play's the worse, to follow the allegory, as the old pedant says.

Old. A young fop!

Man. I ever thought the man of most wit had been like him of most money, who has no vanity in showing it everywhere, whilst the beggarly pusher of his fortune has all he has about him still only to show.

Nov. Well, sir, and make a pretty show in the world, let me tell you; nay, a better than your close hunks. A pox, give me ready money in play! what care I for a man's reputation? what are we the better for your substantial thrifty curmudgeon in wit, sir?

Old. Thou art a profuse young rogue indeed.

Nov. So much for talking, which, I think, I have proved a mark of wit; and so is railing, roaring, and making a noise; for railing is satire, you know; and roaring and making a noise, humour.

Re-enter FIDELIA; *she takes* MANLY *aside, and shows him a paper.*

Fid. The hour is betwixt seven and eight exactly: 'tis now half an hour to six.

Man. Well, go then to the Piazza, and wait for me: as soon as it is quite dark, I'll be with you. I must stay here yet a while for my friend.—[*Exit* FIDELIA.] But is railing satire, Novel?

Free. And roaring and making a noise, humour?

Nov. What, won't you confess there's humour in roaring and making a noise?

Free. No.

Nov. Nor in cutting napkins and hangings ?

Man. No, sure.

Nov. Dull fops !

Old. O rogue, rogue, insipid rogue !—Nay, gentlemen, allow him those things for wit ; for his parts lie only that way.

Nov. Peace, old fool ! I wonder not at thee ; but that young fellows should be so dull, as to say there's no humour in making a noise, and breaking windows ! I tell you there's wit and humour too in both ; and a wit is as well known by his frolic as by his smile.

Old. Pure rogue ! there's your modern wit for you ! Wit and humour in breaking of windows : there's mischief, if you will, but no wit or humour.

Nov. Prithee, prithee, peace, old fool ! I tell you, where there's mischief, there's wit. Don't we esteem the monkey a wit amongst beasts, only because he's mischievous ? and, let me tell you, as good-nature is a sign of a fool, being mischievous is a sign of a wit.

Old. O rogue, rogue ! pretend to be a wit, by doing mischief and railing !

Nov. Why, thou, old fool, hast no other pretence to the name of a wit, but by railing at new plays !

Old. Thou, by railing at that facetious noble way of wit, quibbling !

Nov. Thou callest thy dulness gravity ; and thy dozing, thinking.

Old. You, sir, your dulness, spleen ; and you talk much and say nothing.

Nov. Thou readest much, and understandest nothing, sir.

Old. You laugh loud, and break no jest.

Nov. You rail, and nobody hangs himself ; and thou hast nothing of the satire but in thy face.

Old. And you have no jest, but your face, sir.

Nov. Thou art an illiterate pedant.

Old. Thou art a fool with a bad memory.

Man. Come, a pox on you both! you have done like wits now: for you wits, when you quarrel, never give over till ye prove one another fools.

Nov. And you fools have never any occasion of laughing at us wits but when we quarrel. Therefore let us be friends, Oldfox.

Man. They are such wits as thou art, who make the name of a wit as scandalous as that of bully: and signify a loud-laughing, talking, incorrigible, coxcomb, as bully a roaring hardened coward.

Free. And would have his noise and laughter pass for wit, as t'other his huffing and blustering for courage.

Re-enter VERNISH.

Man. Gentlemen, with your leave, here is one I would speak with; and I have nothing to say to you.

[*Puts all out of the room except* VERNISH.

Ver. I told you 'twas in vain to think of getting money out of her. She says, if a shilling would do't, she would not save you from starving or hanging, or what you would think worse, begging or flattering; and rails so at you, one would not think you had lain with her.

Man. O, friend, never trust for that matter a woman's railing; for she is no less a dissembler in her hatred than her love; and as her fondness of her husband is a sign he's a cuckold, her railing at another man is a sign she lies with him.

Ver. He's in the right on't: I know not what to trust to. [*Aside.*

Man. But you did not take any notice of it to her, I hope?

Ver. So!—Sure he is afraid I should have disproved him by an inquiry of her: all may be well yet. [*Aside.*

Man. What hast thou in thy head that makes thee seem so unquiet?

Ver. Only this base impudent woman's falseness; I cannot put her out of my head.

Wycherley.   S

Man. O, my dear friend, be not you too sensible of my wrongs ; for then I shall feel 'em too with more pain, and think 'em unsufferable. Damn her, her money, and that ill-natured whore too, Fortune herself! But if thou wouldst ease a little my present trouble, prithee go borrow me somewhere else some money. I can trouble thee.

Ver. You trouble me, indeed, most sensibly, when you command me anything I cannot do. I have lately lost a great deal of money at play, more than I can yet pay ; so that not only my money, but my credit too is gone, and know not where to borrow : but could rob a church for you.—[*Aside.*] Yet would rather end your wants by cutting your throat.

Man. Nay, then I doubly feel my poverty, since I'm incapable of supplying thee. [*Embraces him.*

Ver. But, methinks, she that granted you the last favour, (as they call it,) should not deny you anything.

Nov. [*Looking in.*] Hey, tarpaulin, have you done ?
[*Retires again.*

Ver. I understand not that point of kindness, I confess.

Man. No, thou dost not understand it, and I have not time to let you know all now ; for these fools, you see, will interrupt us : but anon, at supper, we'll laugh at leisure together at Olivia's cuckold, who took a young fellow, that goes between his wife and me, for a woman.

Ver. Ha !

Man. Senseless, easy rascal ! 'twas no wonder she chose him for a husband ; but she thought him, I thank her, fitter than me, for that blind bearing office.

Ver. I could not be deceived in that long woman's hair tied up behind, nor those infallible proofs, her pouting swelling breasts : I have handled too many sure not to know 'em. [*Aside.*

Man. What, you wonder the fellow could be such a blind coxcomb ?

Ver. Yes, yes—

Nov. [*Looking in again.*] Nay, prithee, come to us, Manly. Gad, all the fine things one says in their company, are lost without thee.

Man. Away, fop! I'm busy yet. [NOVEL *retires.*] You see we cannot talk here at our ease: besides, I must be gone immediately, in order to meeting with Olivia again to-night.

Ver. To-night! it cannot be, sure—

Man. I had an appointment just now from her.

Ver. For what time?

Man. At half an hour after seven precisely.

Ver. Don't you apprehend the husband?

Man. He! snivelling gull! he a thing to be feared! a husband! the tamest of creatures!

Ver. Very fine! [*Aside.*

Man. But, prithee, in the mean time, go try to get me some money. Though thou art too modest to borrow for thyself, thou canst do anything for me, I know. Go; for I must be gone to Olivia. Go, and meet me here, anon.—Freeman, where are you? [*Exit.*

Ver. Ay, I'll meet with you, I warrant; but it shall be at Olivia's. Sure, it cannot be: she denies it so calmly, and with that honest modest assurance, it cannot be true —and he does not use to lie—but belying a woman when she won't be kind, is the only lie a brave man will least scruple. But then the woman in man's clothes, whom he calls a man—well, but by her breasts I know her to be a woman—but then again, his appointment from her, to meet him again to-night! I am distracted more with doubt than jealousy. Well, I have no way to disabuse or revenge myself, but by going home immediately, putting on a riding-suit, and pretending to my wife the same business which carried me out of town last, requires me again to go post to Oxford to-night. Then, 'f the appointment he boasts of be true, it's sure to hold, and I shall have an opportunity either of clearing her, or revenging myself on both Perhaps she is his

wench, or an old date, and I am his cully, whilst I think
him mine; and he has seemed to make his wench rich,
only that I might take her off his hands. Or if he has
but lately lain with her, he must needs discover by her
my treachery to him; which I'm sure he will revenge
with my death, and which I must prevent with his, if it
were only but for fear of his too just reproaches; for I
must confess, I never had till now any excuse but that of
interest, for doing ill to him.   [*Exit.*

Re-enter MANLY *and* FREEMAN.

Man. Come hither; only, I say, be sure you mistake
not the time. You know the house exactly where Olivia
lodges, 'tis just hard by.

Free. Yes, yes.

Man. Well then, bring 'em all, I say, thither, and all
you know that may be then in the house; for the
more witnesses I have of her infamy, the greater will be
my revenge: and be sure you come straight up to her
chamber without more ado. Here, take the watch; you
see 'tis above a quarter past seven; be there in half an
hour exactly.

Free. You need not doubt my diligence or dexterity;
I am an old scourer, and can naturally beat up a
wench's quarters that won't be civil. Shan't we break
her windows too?

Man. No, no; be punctual only.   [*Exeunt.*

SCENE III.—*A Room in the same.*

Enter Widow BLACKACRE, *and two* Knights of the Post,[1]
a Waiter *following with wine.*

Wid. Sweetheart, are you sure the door was shut
close, that none of those roysters saw us come in?

---

[1] See note *ante*, p. 386.

Wait. Yes, mistress; and you shall have a privater room above, instantly. [*Exit.*

Wid. You are safe enough, gentlemen; for I have been private in this house ere now, upon other occasions, when I was something younger. Come, gentlemen; in short, I leave my business to your care and fidelity: and so here's to you.

1st Knight. We are ungrateful rogues if we should not be honest to you; for we have had a great deal of your money.

Wid. And you have done me many a good job for't; and so, here's to you again.

2nd Knight. Why, we have been perjured but six times for you.

1st Knight. Forged but four deeds, with your husband's last deed of gift.

2nd Knight. And but three wills.

1st Knight. And counterfeited hands and seals to some six bonds; I think that's all, brother?

Wid. Ay, that's all, gentlemen; and so, here's to you again.

2nd Knight. Nay, 'twould do one's heart good to be forsworn for you. You have a conscience in your ways, and pay us well.

1st Knight. You are in the right on't, brother; one would be damned for her with all one's heart.

2nd Knight. But there are rogues, who make us forsworn for 'em; and when we come to be paid, they'll be forsworn too, and not pay us our wages, which they promised with oaths sufficient.

1st Knight. Ay, a great lawyer that shall be nameless bilked me too.

Wid. That was hard, methinks, that a lawyer should use gentlemen witnesses no better.

2nd Knight. A lawyer! d'ye wonder a lawyer should do't? I was bilked by a reverend divine, that preaches twice on Sundays, and prays half an hour still before dinner.

Wid. How! a conscientious divine and not pay people for damning themselves! sure then, for all his talking, he does not believe damnation.   But, come, to our business. Pray be sure to imitate exactly the flourish at the end of this name.   [*Pulls out a deed or two.*

1st Knight. O, he's the best in England at untangling a flourish, madam.

Wid. And let not the seal be a jot bigger.   Observe well the dash too, at the end of this name.

2nd Knight. I warrant you, madam.

Wid. Well, these and many other shifts, poor widows are put to sometimes; for everybody would be riding a widow, as they say, and breaking into her jointure.   They think marrying a widow an easy business, like leaping the hedge where another has gone over before.   A widow is a mere gap, a gap with them.

Enter Major OLDFOX, *with two* Waiters.   *The* Knights of the Post *huddle up the writings.*

What, he here!   Go then, go my hearts, you have your instructions.   [*Exeunt* Knights of the Post.

Old. Come, madam, to be plain with you, I'll be fobbed off no longer.—[*Aside.*] I'll bind her and gag her but she shall hear me.—[*To the* Waiters.] Look you, friends, there's the money I promised you; and now do you what you promised me : here my garters, and here's a gag. — [*To the* Widow.] You shall be acquainted with my parts, lady, you shall.

Wid. Acquainted with your parts!   A rape! a rape! —what, will you ravish me?

[*The* Waiters *tie her to the chair, gag her, and exeunt.*

Old. Yes, lady, I will ravish you: but it shall be through the ear, lady, the ear only, with my well-penned acrostics.

Enter FREEMAN, JERRY BLACKACRE, *three* Bailiffs, *a*
   Constable, *and his* Assistants *with the two* Knights
   of the Post.

What, shall I never read my things undisturbed again?

Jer. O la! my mother bound hand and foot, and
gaping as if she rose before her time to-day!

Free. What means this, Oldfox? But I'll release you
from him; you shall be no man's prisoner but mine.
Bailiffs, execute your writ. [*Unties her.*

Old. Nay, then, I'll be gone, for fear of being bail,
and paying her debts without being her husband. [*Exit.*

1st Bail. We arrest you in the king's name, at the suit
of Mr. Freeman, guardian to Jeremiah Blackacre, esquire,
in an action of ten thousand pounds.

Wid. How, how, in a choke-bail action! What, and
the pen-and-ink gentlemen taken too!—Have you confessed, you rogues?

1st Knight. We needed not to confess; for the bailiffs
have dogged us hither to the very door, and overheard
all that you and we said.

Wid. Undone, undone then! no man was ever too
hard for me till now. O Jerry, child, wilt thou vex again
the womb that bore thee?

Jer. Ay, for bearing me before wedlock, as you say.
But I'll teach you call a Blackacre bastard, though you
were never so much my mother.

Wid. [*Aside.*] Well, I'm undone! not one trick left?
no law-mesh imaginable?—[*To* FREEMAN.] Cruel sir, a
word with you, I pray.

Free. In vain, madam; for you have no other way to
release yourself, but by the bonds of matrimony.

Wid. How, sir, how! that were but to sue out a
habeas-corpus, for a removal from one prison to another.—
Matrimony!

Free. Well, bailiffs, away with her.

Wid. O stay, sir! can you be so cruel as to bring me

under covert-baron[1] again, and put it out of my power to sue in my own name? Matrimony to a woman is worse than excommunication, in depriving her of the benefit of the law; and I would rather be deprived of life. But hark you, sir, I am contented you should hold and enjoy my person by lease or patent, but not by the spiritual patent called a licence; that is, to have the privileges of a husband, without the dominion; that is, *Durante beneplacito.* In consideration of which, I will out of my jointure secure you an annuity of three hundred pounds a year, and pay your debts; and that's all you younger brothers desire to marry a widow for, I'm sure.

Free. Well, widow, if—

Jer. What! I hope, bully-guardian, you are not making agreements without me?

Free. No, no. First, widow, you must say no more that he is a son of a whore; have a care of that. And, then, he must have a settled exhibition of forty pounds a year, and a nag of assizes, kept by you, but not upon the common; and have free ingress, egress, and regress, to and from your maids' garret.

Wid. Well, I can grant all that too.

Jer. Ay, ay, fair words butter no cabbage: but guardian, make her sign, sign and seal; for otherwise, if you knew her as well as I, you would not trust her word for a farthing.

Free. I warrant thee, squire.—Well, widow, since thou art so generous, I will be generous too; and if you'll secure me four hundred pounds a year, but during your life, and pay my debts, not above a thousand pounds, I'll bate you your person, to dispose of as you please.

Wid Have a care, sir, a settlement without a consideration is void in law; you must do something for't.

Free. Prithee, then let the settlement on me be called alimony; and the consideration, our separation. Come;

---

[1] See note *ante*, p. 425.

my lawyer, with writings ready drawn, is within, and in haste. Come.

Wid. But, what, no other kind of consideration, Mr. Freeman? Well, a widow, I see, is a kind of sinecure, by custom of which the unconscionable incumbent enjoys the profits, without any duty, but does that still elsewhere.   [*Exeunt.*

SCENE IV.—OLIVIA'S *Lodging.*

Enter OLIVIA *with a candle in her hand.*

Oliv. So, I am now prepared once more for my timorous young lover's reception. My husband is gone; and go thou out too, thou next interrupter of love.—[*Puts out the candle.*] Kind darkness, that frees us lovers from scandal and bashfulness, from the censure of our gallants and the world!—So, are you there?

Enter FIDELIA, *followed softly by* MANLY.

Come, my dear punctual lover, there is not such another in the world; thou hast beauty and youth to please a wife; address and wit, to amuse and fool a husband; nay, thou hast all things to be wished in a lover, but your fits. I hope, my dear, you won't have one to night; and that you may not, I'll lock the door, though there be no need of it, but to lock out your fits: for my husband is just gone out of town again. Come, where are you?
                                   [*Goes to the door and locks it.*

Man. Well, thou hast impudence enough to give me fits too, and make revenge itself impotent; hinder me from making thee yet more infamous, if it can be.
                                                                [*Aside.*

Oliv. Come, come, my soul, come.

Fid. Presently, my dear, we have time enough sure.

Oliv. How, time enough! True lovers can no more

think they ever have time enough, than love enough.
You shall stay with me all night ; but that is but a lover's
moment. Come.

Fid. But won't you let me give you and myself the
satisfaction of telling you how I abused your husband
last night ?

Oliv. Not when you can give me, and yourself too,
the satisfaction of abusing him again to-night. Come.

Fid. Let me but tell you how your husband—

Oliv. O name not his, or Manly's more loathsome
name, if you love me ! I forbid 'em last night : and you
know I mentioned my husband but once, and he came.
No talking, pray, 'twas ominous to us.—[*A noise at the
door.*] You make me fancy a noise at the door already,
but I'm resolved not to be interrupted.   Where are you ?
Come, for rather than lose my dear expectation now, though
my husband were at the door, and the bloody ruffian
Manly here in the room, with all his awful insolence, I
would give myself to this dear hand, to be led away to
heavens of joys, which none but thou canst give.—[*The
noise at the door increases.*] But what's this noise at the door ?
So, I told you what talking would come to. Ha !—O
Heavens, my husband's voice !—   [*Listens at the door.*

Man. [*Aside.*] Freeman is come too soon.

Oliv. O, 'tis he !—Then here's the happiest minute lost
that ever bashful boy or trifling woman fooled away ! I'm
undone ! my husband's reconcilement too was false, as
my joy all delusion.   But come this way, here's a back
door.—[*Exit, and returns.*]   The officious jade has locked
us in, instead of locking others out : but let us then escape
your way, by the balcony ; and whilst you pull down the
curtains, I'll fetch from my closet what next will best
secure our escape.   I have left my key in the door, and
'twill not suddenly be broken open.   [*Exit.*

[*A noise as if people were forcing the door.*

Man. Stir not, yet fear nothing.

Fid. Nothing but your life, sir.

Man. We shall know this happy man she calls husband.

Re-enter OLIVIA.

Oliv. Oh, where are you? What, idle with fear? Come, I'll tie the curtains, if you will hold. Here take this cabinet and purse, for it is thine, if we escape;—[MANLY *takes them from her*]—therefore let us make haste. [*Exit.*

Man. 'Tis mine indeed now again, and it shall never escape more from me, to you at least.

[*The door is broke open, enter* VERNISH *with a dark-lantern and a sword, running at* MANLY, *who draws, puts by the thrust, and defends himself, whilst* FIDELIA *runs at* VERNISH *behind.*

Ver. So, there I'm right, sure— [*In a low voice.*

Man. [*Softly.*] Sword and dark-lantern, villain, are some odds; but—

Ver. Odds! I'm sure I find more odds than I expected. What, has my insatiable two seconds at once? but—
[*In a low voice.*

[*Whilst they fight,* OLIVIA *re-enters, tying two curtains together.*

Oliv. Where are you now?—What, is he entered then, and are they fighting? O do not kill one that can make no defence!—[MANLY *throws* VERNISH *down and disarms him.*] How! but I think he has the better on't. Here's his scarf, 'tis he. So, keep him down still: I hope thou hast no hurt, my dearest? [*Embracing* MANLY.

Enter FREEMAN, Lord PLAUSIBLE, NOVEL, JERRY BLACKACRE, *and* Widow BLACKACRE, *lighted by the two* Sailors *with torches.*

Ha!—what!—Manly! and have I been thus concerned for him! embracing him! and has he his jewels again too! What means this? O, 'tis too sure, as well as my shame! which I'll go hide for ever.

[*Offers to go out,* MANLY *stops her.*

Man. No, my dearest ; after so much kindness as has passed between us, I cannot part with you yet.—Freeman, let nobody stir out of the room ; for notwithstanding your lights, we are yet in the dark, till this gentleman please to turn his face—[*Pulls* VERNISH *by the sleeve.*] How, Vernish ! art thou the happy man then ? thou ! thou ! speak, I say ; but thy guilty silence tells me all.—Well, I shall not upbraid thee ; for my wonder is striking me as dumb as thy shame has made thee.   But what ? my little volunteer hurt, and fainting !

Fid. My wound, sir, is but a slight one in my arm ; tis only my fear of your danger, sir, not yet well over.

Man. But what's here ? more strange things—[*Observing* FIDELIA'S *hair untied behind, and without a peruke, which she lost in the scuffle.*]   What means this long woman's hair, and face ! now all of it appears too beautiful for a man ; which I still thougnt womanish indeed ! What, you have not deceived me too, my little volunteer ?

Oliv. Me she has, I'm sure.   [*Aside.*

Man. Speak !

Enter ELIZA *and* LETTICE.

Eliza. What, cousin, I am brought hither by your woman, I suppose, to be a witness of the second vindication of your honour ?

Oliv. Insulting is not generous.   You might spare me, I have you.

Eliza. Have a care, cousin, you'll confess anon too much ; and I would not have your secrets.

Man. Come, your blushes answer me sufficiently, and you have been my volunteer in love.   [*To* FIDELIA.

Fid. I must confess I needed no compulsion to follow you all the world over ; which I attempted in this habit, partly out of shame to own my love to you, and fear of a greater shame, your refusal of it ; for I knew of your engagement to this lady, and the constancy of your nature ; which nothing could have altered but herself.

Man. Dear madam, I desired you to bring me out of confusion, and you have given me more. I know not what to speak to you, or how to look upon you; the sense of my rough, hard, and ill usage of you, (though chiefly your own fault,) gives me more pain now 'tis over, than you had when you suffered it: and if my heart, the refusal of such a woman—[*Pointing to* OLIVIA]—were not a sacrifice to profane your love, and a greater wrong to you than ever yet I did you, I would beg of you to receive it, though you used it as she had done; for though it deserved not from her the treatment she gave it, it does from you.

Fid. Then it has had punishment sufficient from her already, and needs no more from me; and, I must confess, I would not be the only cause of making you break your last night's oath to me, of never parting with me; if you do not forget or repent it.

Man. Then take for ever my heart, and this with it;— (*Gives her the cabinet*) for 'twas given to you before, and my heart was before your due: I only beg leave to dispose of these few.—Here, madam, I never yet left my wench unpaid.

> [*Takes some of the jewels, and offers them to*
> OLIVIA; *she strikes them down:* Lord
> PLAUSIBLE *and* NOVEL *take them up.*

Oliv. So it seems, by giving her the cabinet.

L. Plau. These pendants appertain to your most faithful humble servant.

Nov. And this locket is mine; my earnest for love, which she never paid: therefore my own again.

Wid. By what law, sir, pray?—Cousin Olivia, a word. What, do they make a seizure on your goods and chattels, *vi et armis?* Make your demand, I say, and bring your trover, bring your trover. I'll follow the law for you.

Oliv. And I my revenge.   [*Exit.*

Man. [*To* VERNISH.] But 'tis, my friend, in your consideration most, that I would have returned part of your wife's portion; for 'twere hard to take all from thee, since thou hast paid so dear for't, in being such a rascal. Yet thy wife is a fortune without a portion; and thou art a man of that extraordinary merit in villany, the world and fortune can never desert thee. though I do; therefore be not melancholy. Fare you well, sir.—[*Exit* VERNISH *doggedly.*] Now, madam, I beg your pardon [*Turning to* FIDELIA] for lessening the present I made you; but my heart can never be lessened. This, I confess, was too small for you before; for you deserve the Indian world; and I would now go thither, out of covetousness for your sake only.

Fid. Your heart, sir, is a present of that value, I can never make any return to't.—[*Pulling* MANLY *from the company.*] But I can give you back such a present as this, which I got by the loss of my father, a gentleman of the north, of no mean extraction, whose only child I was, therefore left me in the present possession of two thousand pounds a-year; which I left, with multitudes of pretenders, to follow you, sir; having in several public places seen you, and observed your actions thoroughly, with admiration, when you were too much in love to take notice of mine, which yet was but too visible. The name of my family is Grey, my other Fidelia. The rest of my story you shall know when I have fewer auditors.

Man. Nay, now, madam, you have taken from me all power of making you any compliment on my part; for I was going to tell you, that for your sake only I would quit the unknown pleasure of a retirement; and rather stay in this ill world of ours still, though odious to me, than give you more frights again at sea, and make again too great a venture there, in you alone. But if I should tell you now all this, and that your virtue (since greater than I thought any was in the world) had now reconciled me to't, my friend here would say, 'tis your estate that has made me friends with the world.

Free I must confess I should; for I think most of our

quarrels to the world are just such as we have to a handsome woman ; only because we cannot enjoy her as we would do.

Man. Nay, if thou art a plain dealer too, give me thy hand ; for now I'll say, I am thy friend indeed ; and for your two sakes, though I have been so lately deceived in friends of both sexes,—

> I will believe there are now in the world
> Good-natured friends, who are not prostitutes,
> And handsome women worthy to be friends ;
> Yet, for my sake, let no one e'er confide
> In tears, or oaths, in love, or friend untried.

[Exeunt.

EPILOGUE.

SPOKEN BY THE WIDOW BLACKACRE.

To you the judges learnèd in stage-laws,
Our poet now, by me, submits his cause ;
For with young judges, such as most of you,
The men by women best their business do :
And, truth on't is, if you did not sit here,
To keep for us a term throughout the year,
We could not live by'r tongues ; nay, but for you,
Our chamber-practice would be little too.
And 'tis not only the stage-practiser
Who by your meeting gets her living here :
For as in Hall of Westminster
Sleek sempstress vents amidst the courts her ware ;
So, while we bawl, and you in judgment sit,
The visor-mask sells linen too i' th' pit.

O, many of your friends, besides us here,
Do live by putting off their several ware.
Here's daily done the great affairs o' th' nation;
Let love and us then ne'er have long-vacation,
But hold; like other pleaders I have done
Not my poor client's business, but my own.
Spare me a word then now for him. First know,
Squires of the long robe, he does humbly show,
He has a just right in abusing you,
Because he is a Brother-Templar too:
For at the bar you rally one another;
Nay, fool and knave, is swallowed from a brother:
If not the poet here, the Templar spare,
And maul him when you catch him at the bar.
From you, our common modish censurers,
Your favour, not your judgment, 'tis he fears:
Of all love begs you then to rail, find fault;
For plays, like women, by the world are thought,
When you speak kindly of 'em, very naught.